Your Pilot's License

From the McGraw-Hill *PRACTICAL FLYING SERIES*

Your Pilot's License

Seventh Edition

Jerry A. Eichenberger

McGraw-Hill

New York   Chicago   San Francisco   Lisbon   London   Madrid
Mexico City   Milan   New Delhi   San Juan   Seoul
Singapore   Sydney   Toronto

Library of Congress Cataloging-in-Publication Data

Eichenberger, Jerry A.
    Your pilot's license / Jerry A. Eichenberger.—7th ed.
       p.   cm.
    Includes index.
    ISBN 0-07-140285-3
    1. Airplanes—Piloting.   2. Air pilots—United States—Licenses. I. Title.

  TL710.E4424   2003
  629.132'5217—dc21   2003054185

3 4 5 6 7 8 9 0 DOC/DOC 0 9 8 7 6 5 4

ISBN 0-07-140285-3

The sponsoring editor for this book was Larry S. Hager, the editing supervisor was Stephen M. Smith, and the production supervisor was Sherri Souffrance. It was set in Garamond by Joanne Morbit of McGraw-Hill Professional's Hightstown, N.J., composition unit. The art director for the cover was Anthony Landi.

Printed and bound by RR Donnelley.

McGraw-Hill books are available at special quantity discounts to use as premiums and sales promotions, or for use in corporate training programs. For more information, please write to the Director of Special Sales, McGraw-Hill Professional, Two Penn Plaza, New York, NY 10121-2298. Or contact your local bookstore.

Contents

Introduction

Your Pilot's License is now ending its fourth decade of publication. I remember reading the First Edition of this book, written by the late Joe Christy, when I was a student pilot. I've had the honor of carrying on the two most recent revisions of Joe's excellent work. The Sixth Edition was written in 1999, and a lot has changed since then that affects every fledgling pilot. These changes merit another revision to bring this book up to date.

This book is for both prospective and beginning pilots. It is not intended to be a formal text for, or to replace, ground school training. What this book will do is explain what a newcomer to the aviation world can expect to encounter, explore some licensing options, and cover some of the basics of aeronautical knowledge that will get far more complete treatment once you begin ground school. This book now covers not only the training steps to achieve a private pilot's license, but also discusses other options, such as the sport pilot and recreational pilot certificates and flying sailplanes, and the changes in the flight training industry that have occurred since 1999. The simple and straightforward approach of previous editions is retained, so that you are not confronted with overly complicated terms and subject areas. The theory of flight, navigation, control techniques, weather basics, air traffic rules, and aircraft instrumentation are all covered in easy-to-understand language that will not intimidate even the reader with no prior exposure to flying.

Virtually anyone can learn to fly and become a safe and competent aviator. With the coming of the newly created sport pilot license, this statement is truer than ever before. Yet all pilots need a good foundation in the basics and must have a willingness to expend the needed effort in order to enjoy this exciting new venture.

The world of the pilot and of personal aviation is boundless. Through these pages you can begin to understand why most pilots say, "The worst day flying is better than the best day doing anything else." Happy flying!

Jerry A. Eichenberger

1

The Most Frequently Asked Questions about Learning to Fly

Why Should I Learn to Fly?

Every pilot will probably have a different answer to this question. The important and correct answer depends upon you and your interests in life. Do you enjoy an exciting, yet safe challenge? If so, that can be reason enough to learn to fly without going any further. Some pilots, including me, like the idea of being able to do something that not everyone can do. Some people like watching other people do something, while others prefer to be doing it themselves. Most pilots value highly the fellowship that exists among pilots that transcends the barriers of income, job status, gender, and age that accompany so many other endeavors.

A lightplane can bring a freedom of travel that cannot be equaled by other means. Going to see relatives in a city 200 miles away can be an easy weekend in a general aviation airplane. A trip of 400 miles can be made in 3 to 4 hours, so that beach, mountain, or country getaway weekend ceases to be only a dream and becomes a reality. Smaller cities, towns, and remote destinations that can take all day to reach by car or commercial airline can be so close in a small airplane.

Most important, aviation is infectious. It changes your entire life, and your outlook on it. If you do give it a try, you'll soon have your own answer, and probably many answers, to this question.

How Long Does It Take?

In this book, we're going to discuss three levels of pilots' licenses—which are more correctly called *pilots' certificates,* but we'll use the terms interchangeably—and what it takes in terms of training to achieve them. The various qualifications are stated in flying hours and levels of experience. How long it will take you to meet those qualifications will depend on two primary factors.

The first of these is which personal-use pilot's license you want to get. A *sport pilot certificate,* as it is currently proposed by the Federal Aviation Administration (FAA), will require a minimum of 20 hours of flight time. A *recreational pilot license,* which is a license with greater operating privileges, will require a minimum of 30 hours of flight time. An applicant for a private pilot certificate must have 40 hours, but if you train at certain specially certified flying schools, this number is reduced to 35.

The second factor is how often you take your flying lessons. Like learning any new task, the more often you train, the less total time you will need to reach proficiency. Frequency and consistency will be the keys to learning more quickly how to fly. If you take one lesson every 2 weeks, your training will take more total hours to complete than if you fly twice each week. If you live in an area of the country with harsh winter weather, spring is the best time to begin flying lessons. That way, you'll have about 6 months of dependable weather ahead of you. Plus, for most people who work normal business hours, you'll also have the longer days, particularly evenings, in which to schedule your lessons. Flying in the last couple of hours of the day is generally very good for student pilots because the air is calmer and the winds are typically less than they are in the middle of the day.

Yet, if the flying bug has bitten you in September, you don't need to put training off for 6 months. Just realize that you may get some lessons cancelled due to poor weather, and unless you get your business day finished early, you won't be flying after work in the winter. Any number or frequency of lessons that you get in during the fall and winter are better than not flying at all.

When I learned to fly, I was a college freshman. I was able to go from my first solo to be licensed as a flight instructor in slightly over a year. There were fewer training requirements in those days, but nevertheless, today you can still learn a lot in a relatively short time if your determination and schedule allow.

What Will I Fly?

Even though the FAA is creating the new sport pilot level of certificate, most of the information in this book will be devoted to achieving a private pilot's license. If you are interested in getting a sport pilot's license, you'll be training in a newly created category of aircraft called a *light-sport aircraft*. Light-sport aircraft will encompass many different forms. They will run the gamut from what evolved from ultralight aircraft, through factory-built airplanes and home-built varieties, to powered parachutes and other machines that have not traditionally been considered conventional personal airplanes.

Assuming that you want to get licensed as a private pilot, what you'll fly today may be a bit different from the aircraft on which students learned to fly a decade or so ago. For about as long as airplanes have been around, students were typically trained in small airplanes with two seats. Back in the 1950s and 1960s, such popular types as the Piper Cub and Aeronca Champion were the trainers of choice at almost all flight training operations. These planes were developed in the 1930s, and they were fabric covered airplanes with 65-horsepower engines. They weren't even equipped with electrical systems, and they had to be started by hand propping, as you've seen in old movies. (See FIG. 1-1.)

As general aviation developed beyond the grass strip, these simple aircraft, the Cessna 150 and 152, Piper Tomahawk, and Piper Cherokee, became the trainers of the 1970s and 1980s, and they are still popular trainers in the twenty-first century. These are fully capable airplanes that carry radios and night flying lights, and they can be equipped for flying on instruments in poor weather. Many of them are still soldiering on in the flight training industry, and they are still producing good pilots. They are the least

1-1 *A classic airplane, the Piper Pacer.*

expensive of the modern trainers, and many pilots will continue to learn in them for the foreseeable future.

With the dawn of the twenty-first century, many flight schools began replacing the aging two-seat trainers with newer aircraft. The two major manufacturers of training airplanes in the United States are Cessna and New Piper, a company that arose out of the bankruptcy of Piper Aircraft in the 1990s. Neither Cessna nor New Piper make any two-seat airplanes anymore. So if you learn to fly at a flight school with newer equipment, you're likely to do your training in either a Cessna 172 or Piper Warrior. Both of these airplanes are manufactured in four-seat models with 160-horsepower engines. They are totally modern planes, and they are sold by their respective manufacturers with fully equipped and instrumented cockpits.

The older trainers, especially the Cessna 150 and Piper Tomahawk, are very good for teaching student pilots what we know as the basic skills of airmanship. About the only valid criticism of the newest airplanes used for training is that they can be too easy to fly and too forgiving of error. A good flight instructor will cure this deficit by her teaching methods and curriculum, so don't think that your training will be short-changed by flying in the most modern of aircraft. After you get your license, chances are that these are the types of aircraft that you'll be flying for a while before advancing to higher-performance airplanes. Many pilots fly the Cessna 172 and Piper Warrior performance class of airplanes for their entire flying careers.

What's the Cost of Learning to Fly?

We have to be realistic about a few things in life. One of them is that flying has never been inexpensive, but it isn't prohibitively expensive either for most folks. There are many recreational activities that match, and often exceed, the costs of flying personal airplanes. I've got friends, business associates, and clients who spend far more each year on their hobbies, such as golf, boating, skiing, and fishing than I spend owning and flying my own light airplane.

Most all student pilots learn to fly at flight training facilities where the student rents the airplane and then pays the flight instructor an instructional fee in addition to the airplane rental. As this edition of *Your Pilot's License* is being written in the summer of 2002, where I'm located in the Midwest, two-seat typical training airplanes rent for about $55 per hour, while the four-seat models go for about $20 more, making their rental rates around $75 per hour. Most flight instructors are presently charging around $20 to $25 per hour for their services.

Even though you can legally get a private pilot's license in 40 hours of flight time, few people are able to train as often and consistently as it takes to do it in that little time. To be on the conservative side, let's assume that you'll have about 60 hours of total flying time before you are ready to take the practical, in-flight examination to get your license. That'll give us a starting place to do a little arithmetic. Also assume, for our calculations, that you'll train at a modern flight school with the newest equipment. If you need 60 hours of airplane rental at $75 per hour, you'll have about $4,500 invested in aircraft rental. Of these 60 total flight hours, you will spend about half with an instructor onboard; you will spend the other half solo flying as you practice the various maneuvers that you have to learn and take the required solo cross-country trips. If you figure $25 per hour for the instructor, 30 hours of her services will cost $750.

In addition to the direct costs of flying the airplane, you'll very likely take a ground school to learn what you need to know to pass a test you will take by computer, called the *knowledge test*. Ground schools cost about $250, and for the school and your flying, you'll need to buy about $150 worth of books, aeronautical charts (a fancy term for maps), and miscellaneous supplies. Last, you'll take a simple physical exam from an FAA-designated doctor, most of whom charge around $75 for their services. When you add it all up, you can estimate about $5,725 for 60 hours of training, at a first-rate flight school, flying the newest of equipment. If you want to save a little money without sacrificing any of the quality of your training, you could fly one of the slightly older two-seat trainers for about $20 per hour less, shaving $1,200 off the previous total.

If you're able to follow our advice about flying consistently and frequently, your learning time will go down, and if you are like the average student, you may get the job done in about 50 hours of total flight time. If you're truly a quick learner, it's not impossible to get ready for the practical test in the minimum 40 hours of time required by the regulations. While these costs are certainly higher than an evening at the movies, in the long run, the cost of obtaining a private pilot's license need not be ruinous for most folks who really want to learn to fly.

Can the Cost Be Reduced Further?

The simple answer to this question is a resounding yes. There is almost always more than one way to accomplish any objective. You'll see in Chap. 2 that there are two levels of pilot's certificates below the private pilot. First, there is the sport pilot, with the most restrictions on one's operating privileges, and there is also a recreational pilot certificate, which allows a pilot a few more privileges but not nearly as many as a private pilot possesses. Another way to economize is to first learn to fly gliders, which we who fly them generally call *sailplanes*. They are much less expensive to fly than are powered airplanes. This option is also covered in Chap. 2.

The last way to really cut the cost of learning to fly may sound a little weird at first, but it does make sense if you read on. Buy your own airplane early in your flight training. Once you are sure that you really intend to get a pilot's license, and after you have passed the physical exam, and you are convinced that you want to fly after you get licensed, you can do as many aspiring aviators have done, including your author: You can purchase your first airplane early in your flying career. Once you've decided that this is something you are committed to doing, why continue to rent airplanes? Make some contacts with other pilots at the airport where you're learning to fly. You'll find no shortage of airplane owners who are willing to talk at length about their airplanes. Read the aviation magazines, especially the pilot reports on the different airplanes that appear in almost all of these publications. Discuss the thought of purchasing your own plane with your flight instructor. Get to know some of the maintenance technicians who can help you perform a good prepurchase inspection of an airplane when you find one you want to buy.

Give serious thought to buying the same type of airplane that you've been renting, assuming that you're comfortable with it. That way, you'll be stepping out of a rental plane into your own, and you will be able to go right on with your lessons without a hiccup. If a good deal comes along on, say, a Piper Warrior, and you've been renting a Cessna 172, the difference between the planes isn't a reason, in and of itself, to decline the Warrior.

The values of airplanes have increased dramatically over the past 2 or 3 decades. There has been a slight decline in the market since the terrorist attacks of September 11, 2001, but through the time of this writing, most all aviation professionals believe that this is only temporary. Assuming normality resumes its course, you can finish your training in your own airplane and then fly it for substantially less than the cost of renting. What counts is the hourly cost of owning versus the hourly cost of renting a plane. Many of the costs of owning an airplane are fixed annual amounts for things such as hangar rent or tie-down fees, insurance, and interest on your bank loan if you finance the purchase. If you fly enough per year to get the hourly cost below rental charges, think seriously about buying.

You'll fly a lot that first year, with your training time and the flying you'll enjoy on your own as a new pilot. Owning a trainer type of airplane can be satisfying because you're flying your own airplane, not some rental machine. You fly when you want to, not just when the rental airplane can be scheduled. You know how your airplane has been flown, babied, and maintained. With good advice from trusted advisors, the chances are very good that you can buy a trainer, fly it for a year or two, and probably get your money back out of it. It's even possible that you may enjoy some capital appreciation during the time that you own it.

One last bit of advice for students and new pilots about buying airplanes: Some new pilots have more money than common sense. Don't let yourself be fast-talked into more airplane than you are comfortable flying. Do some time in a simple airplane—that fire-breathing, 200-mph chariot can wait until you get a couple of hundred hours, or more, and the experience that goes with it, under your belt. I've seen new pilots buy elaborate planes a few times, and the eventual results aren't good. Either the new pilot gets overwhelmed by an airplane with performance and complexity far beyond his flying skills, or he fails to recognize that the plane is beyond his experience and comes to grief. Stay with a simple, trainer type of airplane in the beginning. Also remember that the costs of maintaining an airplane increase exponentially with increases in performance. There are many old sayings in aviation that are true, and one of them is that most pilots, like boat owners, will upgrade airplanes until they finally get the one that they can't afford. Don't let that happen to you either.

Where Should I Learn to Fly?

This question may have only one practical answer, or it may have multiple answers, depending primarily upon where you live. If you reside in a small town or in a rural setting, your options are fewer, and perhaps you have only one. In this situation, you'll learn at the local, or nearest airport. There probably will be only one or two airports close enough for you to consider. If you live in a larger metropolitan area, you'll be choosing from a larger number of airports and flight schools within a reasonable commuting distance from your home or office.

If you do have a choice of airports nearby, another question comes up. This question has been debated for decades, and it will probably continue to be debated forever. If you have a practical choice of whether to learn to fly at a large airport or at a smaller field, in which setting are you better off? Where will you learn what you need to know? Each has pluses and minuses, so let's take a moment and discuss a few of them.

Once you have a private pilot's license, you'll operate from time to time at a larger airport, likely one that also serves the commercial airlines and that will therefore have more traffic than will the local "country" airport. If you learn to fly from the outset of your training at a large airport, learning to fly will be akin to learning to drive in a large city. If you start out with a control tower, traffic consisting of a mix of airplanes of varying sizes from small trainers through business jets to airliners, you won't be intimidated by these factors later in your flying. We've all known the person who learned to drive 30 years ago in either a small town or in the country who to this day is still hesitant to drive in city traffic. Learning to fly at a large airport eliminates the fear of the big airport environment. But, like every other compromise, there are downsides to learning to fly at a larger airport.

Airplanes are typically rented by the hour. Almost all rental airplanes have an hour meter that begins running when the engine is started and doesn't quit clicking away until the engine is stopped at the end of the flight. At large airports, a considerable amount of time can be spent taxiing, sometimes more than a mile, to get to and from the parking area and runways. All this while the hour meter is charging you as if you were actually flying for that same amount of time. Also at large airports, you can expect to spend some time waiting on other airplanes ahead of you to land and take off. Depending on exactly how large the large airport is, you could easily spend at least 10 percent or more of each lesson taxiing around, or waiting to get into the air. Hence, your total cost of training can't help but be a little higher.

On the other hand, flying into small airports can be demanding, just as much so as going into large fields. There are many pilots who have learned to fly at large airports who aren't comfortable, and some aren't even competent, to safely handle the challenges posed by many small fields. If you've learned to fly on runways that are thousands of feet longer than a small, personal airplane needs, you may lack the comfort or even the ability to operate from runways that you will encounter at smaller airports.

When you learn at a huge airport with multiple runways, you won't often be faced with a wind howling directly across your runway. We call these *crosswinds,* and they can be the most daunting of all of the normal situations that pilots face. Large airports that have the space and money to build multiple runways do so for a good reason—to get airplanes more closely aligned with the wind during takeoffs and landings. One of the real advantages of personal flying is the convenience offered by smaller airports that serve smaller towns or that may be closer to your destination in a bigger city. But typically the smaller field will have only one runway. Every airplane has a maximum crosswind that it can safely handle. When you learn to fly at a single-runway airport, reasonable crosswinds will be the routine, and you'll learn from the beginning how to take off and land in them.

I liken this approach to learning to drive a car with a manual transmission. If you can drive a manual, you can drive an automatic transmission, but the reverse certainly isn't true. When my daughter was 16 and began driving, I insisted that she do so in a manual car. There was a little fussing, but a year later she asked me one day why anyone wants an automatic, given the fact that the driver has less control over the vehicle's operating parameters than does the person who can determine for herself what gear to drive in and can control the revolutions per minute of the engine. It all boils down to what you get used to.

Learning to fly at a smaller airport will generally be a little less expensive. Like most costs, smaller operations in the aviation industry tend to charge slightly less than do their counterparts in big cities. Besides a lesser rental charge for the airplane, you won't be taxiing all over the place to get from the flight school's ramp to the runway. Rural airports aren't as busy as the airline airport is in the big city, so you won't be sitting at the end of the runway waiting for a stream of jets to land before you can take off.

The FAA regulations require that an applicant for a private pilot's license perform a minimal number of takeoffs and landings at an airport with a control tower. So if you learn to fly at a smaller airport, your instructor will still take you to a large field to comply with the FAA requirements, which means that you will get some experience operating in that setting.

The negative aspect of learning at a small airport is analogous to that of the person who learned to drive in the country and then forever remained leery of driving in city traffic. If you fly an airplane, you'll have to face operating into large airports. Coping will be a challenge, and it will take some time to get comfortable there.

Nevertheless, in the final analysis, I prefer the small airport as a learning situation. The largest challenge of flying into large airports is dealing with the necessary radio communication skills. These can be learned at a smaller field by using the radios, and if you can dial numbers and talk on a telephone, you can dial up a frequency on a communications radio and speak into your headset. At the smaller field, you can learn to fly the airplane first, and then, after you aren't concentrating 100 percent on the physical acts of controlling this bird, you can easily learn to cope with increased amounts of airborne traffic. There are some other reasons for my feelings on this subject, which give rise to some more questions.

What Kinds of Flight Schools Are There?

In answering this question, we're again assuming that you are seeking a private pilot's license. When we talk about the sport pilot and recreational pilot certificates, along with the rating to fly gliders, we'll get more into how a person is trained for those unique operating privileges. Here we're going to cover what has been considered to be the more traditional route of training for a private license.

There are basically two general types of flight schools, with several permutations within each of the two categories. Let's deal with them separately.

The large approved schools

The flight training industry saw a good deal of growth in the 1990s. The airline industry was growing by leaps and bounds, and a professional pilot shortage was forecast by many segments of aviation. Airline pilots must retire at age 60, as the FAA long ago determined that the risk of physical incapacitation increases dramatically after that age. Many professionals in and out of health care will argue that point, but the federal regulation is what it is. The military services have served as the launching ground for many professional pilots' careers. After a few years of flying the biggest and best aircraft in the sky, it has been quite natural for the airlines to swallow up military pilots as they completed their service obligation. Historically, this supply of pilots, coupled with some who worked their way up through the general aviation ladder, have met the airlines' needs. Then things changed.

With the end of the cold war, the military services downsized dramatically, and the air services weren't immune from the budget cuts. This meant that the number of new pilots entering military flight training dropped significantly. At about the same time, age started taking its toll on the large number of pilots in the airline industry who came out of the Vietnam-era military buildup. While the supply of pilots was thus declining, the deregulation of the airline industry, together with the economic boom times of the 1990s, resulted in an increasing demand for pilots as the airlines' growth rates mushroomed. Enter the age of the civilian trained airline and corporate professional pilot.

The FAA regulates all flight training. That means that flight instructors have to be licensed specifically by the FAA to give instruction, and they must renew their licenses every 2 years. The feds long ago established a system whereby flight schools are "approved" by the FAA. This approval means that the school has submitted its curriculum to the FAA for review and acceptance. Once accepted, this curriculum becomes the training requirements that the school's students must meet. The approved school also must have a person on its staff who is qualified by special FAA review to administer the practical flight test for students to get their licenses. In essence, the school's final exams, both written and in flight, become the licensing tests.

Because of this extra scrutiny, the FAA allows graduates of approved schools to get their licenses in a minimum of 35 hours, rather than the 40 required otherwise. How practical is this difference is anyone's guess because so few students can master all of the necessary training in 40 hours, let alone only 35.

The large approved schools do a good job of training the future professional pilot. They also train private pilots to a professional standard, as every civilian trained pro first got a private license before advancing up the training and career ladders. Large schools tend to be more expensive, as you might imagine, than the other types of training operations. If you have the time to attend a full-time training facility for several months, and you treat your flying lessons like another go at college, the large approved school might be just the thing for you.

The "unapproved" schools

Most private pilots today have not attended the larger, approved flight schools. Rather, they took their instruction from a local instructor at a local airport. All flight instructors have to meet the same requirements, testing, and license renewal regardless of where they teach. However, the great majority of general aviation flight instructors do not work within the confines of a large, approved school. Nevertheless, learning to fly from the local instructor at your airport doesn't mean that the training will be any less complete, competent, or safe.

Becoming an approved school involves going through some regulatory hoops, which many smaller flight schools don't want to bother with. Nevertheless, their instructors have to be licensed just the same, and the airplanes that they use have to be maintained and inspected to the same standards as the approved school. There are approved schools and ones that haven't applied for approval at both large and small airports. In my experience as a flight instructor who first began teaching people to fly in 1966, the key to effective training is the flight instructor, not the school where he is employed.

There are some other issues in the aviation industry of which you should be aware, which may help you choose where to take your lessons. One of the first of these is the realization that no one ever got rich as a flight instructor. If the school charges you $25 an hour for instruction, the instructor probably gets no more than $20 of that hourly fee. In most flight training operations, a very hard working and busy instructor might get to teach 1,000 hours a year. The simple math shows us that, given full-time employment at a busy place, flight instructing might be a $20,000-a-year job, usually with no fringe benefits at all. That's not particularly enticing as one's lifetime career.

This is an unfortunate set of facts, but true. Therefore, most flight instructors are doing this work with an eye toward getting out of it as soon as they can move up to a corporate or airline flying job. What most instructors lack is enough pilot time to qualify for the next step, and flight instructing is a very efficient way for a person to log a good deal of flying time in a relatively short span of time. If you learn at a large approved school, don't be surprised if your instructor is quite young, maybe barely out of her teens, and is on the hunt for the next job from the day that she begins instructing. There's nothing wrong with that—I began instructing at age 19.

Don't be surprised too if your instructors are changed once or twice during your training. This turnover may be reduced or eliminated altogether by learning to fly at a smaller airport. The aviation industry is populated with businesses that we call *fixed-base operators,* or FBOs. An FBO is the operator at an airport that often sells fuel and maintenance services, has airplanes for rent, and offers flight training. FBOs exist at all airports, large and small. At the large airport, it's common to have more than one FBO, while at the small airport, there is usually business enough to support just one who operates the entire airport.

If you opt to do your flight training at a smaller field, you're likely to encounter one or more flight instructors who've been there awhile and who have no intentions of moving on.

Many instructors at small airports are freelance people who have other full-time careers and do flight instructing for the joy of it. I did most of my training at just such a place. My primary instructor was a retired gentleman who lived across the road from the airport and had a few students with whom he'd fly. He had been instructing for decades, and it seemed to this rookie that he could fly the box that an airplane came in. I couldn't have received a better introduction into the world of flying.

Later, I went to a different rural airport where the FBO was a one-person show. The owner was the mechanic and flight instructor. He had a helper in the shop who was learning to be an airplane mechanic and a receptionist at the front desk, and that was it. Since he sold the fuel, rented tie-down and hangar space, and did the maintenance for the airplanes based there, he wasn't depending on flight instruction as his sole source of income. This man really taught me what I know today. He taught his students how to fly, but he also taught them much more than that. A student gained an understanding about how the airplane worked, how to care for it, and which problems were minor and which weren't.

If you can find such an FBO, seriously consider learning to fly there. In all likelihood, you'll have a choice of at least one experienced instructor and probably more than one. These people aren't hunting for an airline job, and you likely won't be changing instructors unless you want to. The other big benefit is to remember that flight training at the smaller fields will probably cost less.

What Type of Trainer Should I Fly?

Earlier in this chapter we talked a little about the evolution from two-seat trainers to four-seat trainers at many flight schools. All of these airplanes that we discussed are equipped with what is known as *tricycle landing gear*. That means that there are two main wheels, either under the wings as in the case of low-wing airplanes like the Piper Warrior or attached to the sides of the fuselage as in the case of high-wing Cessnas. The third wheel is attached to the nose, just behind the engine and forward of the cockpit. The tricycle landing gear was developed just before and during World War II, and this configuration does make ground handling a bit more docile than it would be with *tailwheel* airplanes.

A tailwheel arrangement has the two main wheels placed similarly to a tricycle but they are a little farther forward on the airplane. This configuration results in the airplane's being tail heavy on the ground, and the tail rests upon a much smaller wheel at the very back of the plane. There was a time when tailwheel landing gear was called "conventional" gear, but today tailwheels certainly aren't conventional anymore. Most pilots who have trained since the 1960s will go through their entire flying lives without experiencing a tailwheel airplane. This is a shame.

Tailwheel and tricycle gear airplanes fly the same once they are in the air, but they have drastically different handling characteristics when on the ground. The tailwheel is more demanding, and it takes more attention from the pilot when taxiing, taking off, and landing, especially if there is a crosswind. If you learn to fly in a tailwheel, you'll have no problem at all transitioning later to a tricycle. But a pilot who has trained in a tricycle will have to undergo several hours of instruction in a tailwheel before being able to fly it competently and tame it on the ground.

To revisit one of my favorite comparisons, the difference is very similar to that between the car with a manual transmission and the car with an automatic transmission. If you know how to drive a manual car, handling an automatic is duck soup. But if you've never driven a manual, you'd better do a little reading and get some instruction first before you chug up the road, alternatively stalling the engine, slipping the clutch, and squealing the tires as you try to get the beast under control. There are many qualities about the handling of a tailwheel airplane that make the pilot more aware, by necessity, of what is going on with the wind, runway alignment, and control surface positions on the ground, that transfer very nicely to tricycle flying and make the pilot better in either type of landing gear. If you can find a flight school that trains in a tailwheel airplane (there aren't many that do), go for it. You'll be a better pilot in the long run.

What If I Get Airsick?

Very few people get airsick in small airplanes. When it does happen, it usually afflicts passengers rather than someone who is handling the controls. I sometimes get uncomfortable in the back seat of a car, especially on twisty roads and if I'm trying to read while riding. Yet I've never been airsick as the pilot of an aircraft, even when doing aerobatics.

You might encounter airsickness early in your training, and if you do, it's most likely the product of tension that you feel. For the few who do get sick, it's usually a passing thing that goes away after a few lessons as the person becomes more comfortable and familiar with the airborne environment. If you do get feeling queasy while taking a lesson, tell your instructor immediately and go back to the airport and land. There's no shame in feeling sick, and there's no reason to let an upset stomach degenerate into the ultimate result if you don't do something to remedy the problem.

In the next chapter, we're going to talk at some length about flying gliders, also known as *sailplanes*. You can solo a glider at age 14, but you have to be 16 to solo an airplane. Because of that distinction, I got into glider flying the summer that my daughter turned 14. She and I learned to fly gliders together at the same glider club. The normal practice at that club is for students to take three glider flights in a row if the atmospheric conditions aren't ripe for remaining aloft for a long time and if the glider simply descends, very slowly, from the point where it releases from the tow plane that towed it up.

Well, after a couple of those sessions, my daughter got sick. Gliders do tend to make more people sick than do airplanes because in gliders, there isn't a prolonged period of straight and level cruise flight as there is with airplanes. Glider pilots are always turning, sometimes steeply, hunting for and then staying in the updrafts that they need to find to stay up. We solved my daughter's discomfort by disregarding traditions of the club and having her fly only one, and sometimes two flights in a row, and then sitting out for an hour or so before she flew again. She hasn't ever gotten sick in an airplane.

What Safety Issues with Small Airplanes Should I Be Aware Of?

Airplanes are as safe as the pilot makes them. To be safe, you don't have to have superhuman physical skills or intelligence. During your flight training, you'll constantly be made aware of certain limitations inherent in every airplane, and you'll be taught to gain an understanding of your own limits too. Most accidents in aviation happen when a pilot tries to exceed either his own limitations or the airplane's. In my experience flying since 1965, there is only one type of person who shouldn't fly. That is the "macho" person who feels that he has no limitations and that caution and the rules were made for everyone but him. This is the guy who will come to grief, whether it's in an airplane, a boat, or a car. If you don't fit this mold, you can make flying a very safe endeavor.

In my profession as an aviation lawyer, I routinely defend companies and people who find themselves in lawsuits as a result of an airplane accident. Since I've been doing this since 1975, I've gained quite a bit of insight into what really causes accidents. The statistics are borne out by the simple facts— almost all accidents are caused by some failure of the pilot. Pilots cannot ignore common-sense rules, and common sense itself, without repercussions.

Modern airplanes are marvels of technology, and that statement isn't limited to large jets and military aircraft. Light airplanes are well designed in terms of safety, and many of today's products are refinements of airplanes that were first designed in the 1950s or early 1960s. Sure, mechanical failures do happen, but they are very rare compared to the human failures on the parts of pilots. Quite a bit of your training will focus on how the airplane functions, how to tell when something might be wrong with it, and how to deal with it. We don't try to make pilots into either engineers or mechanics, but with just a modicum of training, you'll be surprised at how much you'll learn about how this wonderful machine works.

A few decades ago, instructors used to tell students that a pilot's license was a license to learn. That's a truism that I wish were more emphasized today. I certainly don't know everything about anything—I'm constantly learning to fly, practice law, and everything else that I do. As your knowledge base grows, so will your limitations, and your ability to recognize them. There is another adage that is very wise: "There are old pilots and bold pilots, but there are no old, bold pilots." If you remember the essence of that one, you'll have a fun and safe experience in aviation.

Although you probably have other questions about the process of learning to fly, let's get into the rest of the book, and those queries will probably be answered as we go along in future chapters.

2

Sport Pilot, Recreational Pilot, and Glider Pilot Licenses

Every aspiring aviator should be somewhat conversant in the types of licenses that are governed by the FAA. The FAA grants different types of licenses that range from those that are more restrictive than private pilots' licenses to less restrictive. The best way to start is to see how the structure of the licensing system is organized.

The Jargon of Pilots' Licenses

Pilots' licenses are issued by the Federal Aviation Administration. These licenses, and the operating privileges that they bestow, are organized into two broad characterizations. The first is what we call a *pilot certificate,* and the second is what we know as *ratings*. There is an easy way to understand the difference between a certificate and a rating. A certificate defines the various levels of flying privileges the pilot has earned, while a rating, except for the instrument rating, defines the various categories and classes of aircraft in which the pilot may exercise the privileges of her certificate. The various certificates are the following:

- Student pilot
- Sport pilot (currently proposed by the FAA as this edition is being written)
- Recreational pilot
- Private pilot
- Commercial pilot
- Airline transport pilot
- Flight instructor

Sport pilots, if the certificate is created as currently proposed, will not have any ratings. Recreational pilots don't have many ratings because of the restrictive privileges that they can exercise, to be discussed later in this chapter. The ratings scheme applies mainly to private, commercial, and airline transport pilots and to flight instructors. Some of the common ratings that a private pilot can acquire are the following:

- Airplane, single-engine land (to fly typical single-engine airplanes with landing gear for operating off of land)
- Airplane, single-engine sea (for flying off of water)
- Airplane, multiengine land (again, for flying off of land)
- Instrument (to fly in poorer weather)
- Glider
- Rotorcraft or helicopter

The most basic and restrictive of the pilot certificates is that of the *student pilot.* This is the piece of paper that every pilot must have in order to solo any type of aircraft. It can be issued in one of two ways. If you are going for a private pilot's license, as is our assumption, you will get your student license when you pass your physical exam. Sport pilots are not required to pass any FAA physical, as long as they have a valid U.S. state driver's license, but private pilots have to have what's called a *third-class aviation medical certificate.*

Certain doctors have been authorized by the FAA to administer pilot physicals and to issue medical certificates. These physicians are called *aviation medical examiners,* or AMEs for short. When you go to the AME and pass the simple little physical required for a third-class medical certificate, the AME will give you one document that is both your medical and student pilot certificate.

That student pilot certificate is useless unless and until your flight instructor endorses it by signing in designated places on the reverse side. The first endorsements say that your instructor has deemed you competent to make solo flights in the specific type of aircraft as endorsed, and the later endorsement says your instructor considers you competent to make solo cross-country flights. At present, you don't need to have any kind of document from the FAA, student license, medical certificate, or other, to take flight instruction. There is some political rumbling to change that, because of concerns arising from the tragic events of September 11, 2001, and the later crash by the young, presolo student in Tampa, Florida, who took a Cessna 172 from under the nose of his flight instructor. We'll have to see if decades of a well-functioning licensing system are changed to require some sort of background check, or official OK, to take flight instruction.

The minimum age to solo a powered aircraft, such as an airplane or helicopter, is 16. A 14-year-old can get a student license from an FAA office or designated pilot examiner that will be valid only for flying gliders or balloons. Neither glider nor balloon flying require a medical certificate, so the 14-year-olds don't have to go see an AME.

After a student pilot passes the knowledge and flight tests, he becomes a private pilot, assuming that he was tested for a private pilot's license rather than a sport or recreational license. A private pilot is the full-blown certificate that we'll start talking about in earnest in the next chapter. For now, let's confine the discussion to the more restrictive licenses, after we talk a few moments about where personal aviation has been and how it got to where it is now.

A Bit of History

Aviation has always been a cyclical industry, particularly the general aviation segment. When World War I ended, the infant industry surged as military aviators came home and the market for airplanes was flooded with surplus craft being disposed of by the government. Unfortunately, the heydays of the 1920s, with the barnstormers and traveling air shows, were short lived; the tragedy of the Great Depression thwarted growth in almost all sectors of the economy, and aviation was no exception. Even though the period of the 1930s saw some dramatic increases in the capability and performance of the infant thing known as the "airplane," participation in aviation was only a dream for most people outside of the independently wealthy class.

Aviation got its real shot in the arm from another war. When World War II began in Europe in the fall of 1939, the United States started, quietly at first, to prepare for the inevitable day when we would be dragged into the conflict. Even before Pearl Harbor heralded our official entry into the war, the U.S. government had begun a program then known as the Civil Pilot Training Program (CPT). The CPT began training thousands of future military and naval pilots for the day when the United States would be at war. During this period a couple of years before the Pearl Harbor attack, the CPT used normal civilian airplanes and contracted with flight schools to carry out its mission. Airplane factories started humming, and flight training operations saw their first great influx of new students.

What happened to aviation after the United States' entry into the war itself is the stuff of many history books, novels, movies, and TV shows. World War II was the first war in which aviation had a material, if not deciding, influence. Although my Army buddies will always tell you that no war is ever won until a foot soldier occupies the conquered territory, most aviation-minded historians have championed the airplane as the deciding factor in that world conflict. In 1945, when that war finally ended, there were literally thousands of pilots and airplanes in the United States who were about to come out of the armed forces to reenter civilian life.

Aviation saw a terrific boom and then a horrible bust right after World War II. Mistakenly, most of the airplane manufacturers assumed that the host of trained military pilots would come home, buy airplanes, and go on flying. This apparently did come true for about 18 months after the Axis surrender, but then the joy of the industry turned to tears as the boom ended about as fast as it had begun. Why this happened has been the subject of historical analysis since, and is really beyond our purposes here. Just recognize that it did occur.

During the 1950s, the lightplane industry churned along, steadily if not mightily. Companies such as Cessna, Piper, Beechcraft, and Mooney continued to build airplanes at a steady pace. New student pilots came to FBOs and flight schools. General aviation, as the sector came to be known, was alive but not particularly growing. As the 1960s dawned, things got a little better, and general aviation started to grow slowly but steadily. As we moved into the 1970s, a lot was beginning to change.

Flight schools were busy, thanks to the inclusion of flight training in the educational benefits included in the GI bill for Vietnam-era veterans. But flying was not immune to the inflationary pressures that beset the rest of the economy. As airline traffic grew, and corporate flying really got into high gear, more complication and regulation followed. Yet lightplane production was at an all-time high. In 1978, about 19,000 airplanes left the factories of the general aviation manufacturers. But by the end of the decade, the peak of the curve had been hit, and things started to slow down. At that time, very few people foresaw how drastic the decline would soon be.

In the early 1980s, another depression hit general aviation, and it is one from which we haven't yet fully recovered 20 years later. We'll probably never see the airplane production levels of the late 1970s again, but things have improved since the dark days of the early 1990s. A few years ago, both the FAA and the private aviation sector took a hard look at where personal flying was going and what could be done to revitalize it. There were as many reasons given for the drastic decline in flying as there were reason givers. Some thought that product liability and other legal problems were hampering manufacturers to the point that they couldn't build affordable airplanes anymore. Others postulated that the training requirements for new pilots had grown so great that people weren't interested in flying and had turned their discretionary time and spending to luxury cars, boats, exotic vacations, and the like. There was some truth to all of the theories, but none of them could completely and exclusively explain the problems in aviation.

All pilots begin by getting an interest in aviation. Some never go beyond flying the simplest aircraft, while others become airline pilots. It isn't rocket science to realize that to get more pilots, more people have to want to go to flight school, earn their license, and start flying.

A new level of pilot certificate seemed to be the way to increase demand for instruction and licensing. The FAA thus created the recreational pilot license in an attempt to restore simplicity to personal aviation. Unfortunately, it didn't have the desired effect. People did not respond in droves to get this new license. So the FAA tried another approach, hoping to capitalize on the growing enthusiasm for sport flying.

Sport Pilot Licenses

In the 1970s, many people began flying what came to be known as *ultralight vehicles*. Ultralights evolved from hang gliders, as a few enterprising souls began hanging small engines on what had, until then, been only gliders. While the ultralight industry had its teething pains and had a fairly poor safety record early in its existence, ultralights came to be accepted as an alternative to flying certificated airplanes. The FAA took a hands-off approach to ultralights, and the industry matured on its own. Neither a license nor a medical certificate is required to fly them partly because these vehicles are required to be very light and slow and to have a limited range.

The sport aviation industry convinced the FAA that aircraft heavier than legal ultralights, yet lighter and of somewhat less performance than many certificated airplanes, could be safely flown by pilots who had less formal training than what is required of a recreational or private pilot. The industry also said that these pilots did not need to submit to a physical exam every 2 or 3 years (third-class medical certificates are valid for 3 years for pilots under age 40; 2 years for the rest of us).

In early February 2002, the FAA issued a Notice of Proposed Rule Making (NPRM), proposing the creation of both a sport pilot certificate and a class of aircraft to be called *light-sport aircraft* that sport pilots could fly. As this edition of this book is being written in the late spring and summer of 2002, the normal administrative process is far from complete. We won't know the exact details of the new sport pilot license until after this book goes to press. There may be some changes to the NPRM before the final rule is published by the feds, but we hope they won't be many or severe. In any event, check the current rule for any variance with what is discussed here.

As the proposal now stands, sport pilots will be limited to flying light-sport aircraft, which are a very few regular, certificated aircraft that meet the weight and performance limitations of light-sport aircraft. The highlights of these limitations, as applied to powered light-sport land airplanes are the following:

- A maximum gross takeoff weight of 1,232 pounds

- Capacity of no more than two occupants

- Maximum level flight speed with a maximum continuous power of 132 miles per hour (mph)

- Maximum stalling speed in landing configuration of 45 mph (51 mph if no flaps are provided)
- Single engine only, nonturbine
- Fixed landing gear
- Fixed pitch or ground adjustable propeller only

So it's easy to see that the sport pilot won't be flying any fire-breathing machinery. The idea is to allow a person to get a pilot's license that permits him to fly simple, sport aircraft, for pleasure flying. Many of us think that this is just the shot in the arm that personal aviation needs. The idea of flying simpler machinery in a less complicated environment is appealing to many aspiring pilots. Not everyone wants to fly for business or in a demanding regulatory and operating scheme. Let's see what the operating privileges for a sport pilot are envisioned to be and then discuss the NPRM as a total package.

To begin training to be a sport pilot, a person first needs to get a student pilot certificate for light-sport aircraft. This student license will be valid only for light-sport aircraft, and not for traditional airplanes. The minimum age will remain at 16, or 14 years for operating a glider or balloon. The biggest change in qualifications is the lack of any need for a medical certificate. All a student sport pilot or sport pilot will need is a valid driver's license issued by any state in the United States. If for some reason you don't have a driver's license, then you can get a medical certificate to fulfill this requirement.

You simply take your driver's license to an FAA office or to a designated pilot examiner, fill out an application form, and the student sport license is issued on the spot. To solo, the training won't be much different from what is required of a traditional student pilot, learning to fly a fully certificated airplane. Flying is flying, and you have to learn enough to fly the airplane before you can solo in it. A student sport pilot won't be able to solo any light-sport airplane that is capable of more than 100 mph in level flight at maximum power, which is less performance than he can enjoy once he has his sport pilot license.

To fly light-sport airplanes as a sport pilot, a total of 20 hours of flight time will be required: at least 15 hours of dual flight instruction from a sport pilot instructor (another new certificate in itself) and a minimum of 5 hours of solo flight. That's half of what is required for a private pilot applicant. In addition to the total time minimums, the sport pilot applicant will have to have 2 hours of dual instruction in cross-country flying, 1 hour of solo cross-country time, 10 takeoffs and landings to a full stop, and 3 hours of flight instruction in preparation for the practical flight test. She will also have to pass a knowledge test.

Sport pilot licenses won't have any ratings on them. The FAA has taken a different approach to how a sport pilot will qualify to fly different aircraft. He will have to take instruction and receive an instructor's endorsement in his pilot logbook for every different light-sport aircraft that he wants to fly, regardless of whether it's an airplane, glider, or anything else. The FAA has decided that since light-sport aircraft will run the gamut from airplanes that aren't much different from traditionally certificated ones, to gliders, powered parachutes, ultralight-like airplanes, gyroplanes, and weight-shift control aircraft, that they don't want a pilot to be able to have the latitude to train in one type and then jump into another. Conversely, many of the types are similar enough that it would be overly burdensome on everyone involved to make the sport pilot take another, formal flight test in each one. So, they've taken a common-sense approach of leaving it up to the sport pilot instructor to fly with the pilot and then endorse his logbook when he's competent to fly another type of light-sport airplane.

If a sport pilot wants to fly another category and class of light-sport aircraft, say, going from an airplane to a gyroplane, there will be an additional step. She'll need to take dual instruction in the gyroplane and get an endorsement. But before she'll be able to fly it solo or with a passenger, she'll have to demonstrate proficiency in the gyroplane to a different sport pilot instructor. That's a little bit like taking the flight check for an additional rating that is required of a private pilot, but not quite. When the second sport pilot instructor endorses her logbook that she's competent to fly the gyroplane, the sport pilot may then operate it with a passenger, or solo.

There won't be any instrument rating for sport pilots. They simply won't be allowed to fly in poor weather. Chapter 8 will talk a lot about aviation weather, and it will define some of the terms that we're going to use here. After you've read Chap. 8, you may want to take another look at these restrictions on a sport pilot certificate. In addition to not being allowed to fly by instruments, sport pilots won't be able to fly at night either. They won't be able to use their licenses outside of the United States without special permission from the country into which they want to go. Many anticipate that some sort of blanket approval will come from Canada, but it's far too early to call that one. Private pilots can fly internationally with no more than the typical international restrictions, such as clearing customs.

Sport pilots won't be able to fly higher than 10,000 feet above sea level, or 2,000 above the ground, whichever is higher. They will not be allowed to tow anything, like banners or gliders from their light-sport aircraft. Their weather minimums will be higher than private pilots have. Sport pilots will have to have visibility of at least 3 miles, and they won't be able to operate on top of clouds, which private pilots may do.

So why get a sport pilot certificate rather than a private pilot's license? There are several reasons that I can think of. Many people don't want to do any flying more complicated than that envisioned by the sport pilot NPRM. That's why the FAA came out with the proposal. They recognized that hordes of currently licensed private pilots are operating aircraft that are very similar to what will be light-sport airplanes. And those pilots are flying in ways that comport with the proposed limitations on a sport pilot. Over the last 50 years, the requirements to train and get licensed as a private pilot have increased quite a bit to keep up with the increasing complexity of newer airplanes as they have come along and to make sure that private pilots can fly at night and in higher-density traffic areas.

If your desire is to operate a simple airplane in a simple environment, there's no need to spend the time, effort, and money to legally be able to fly at night into Chicago's O'Hare or New York's Kennedy airports. The sport pilot training will be simpler but thorough for what a sport pilot will be flying.

The lack of the need for a medical certificate is important to some pilots. Medical certificates have never been required for glider and balloon pilots even if they have a commercial pilot or flight instructor certificate for those aircraft. The statistics over several decades have shown that the lack of a medical certificate has nothing at all to do with accidents. The percentage of all accidents caused by medical incapacitation of the pilot is virtually identical for airplane pilots, who need a medical, and glider and balloon pilots who don't. Couple that hard fact with the reality that the population is getting healthier all of the time, and it's plain to see that a medical isn't needed for flying simple aircraft in noncomplex operations.

Becoming a sport pilot will cost much less than training for a private pilot certificate. That is probably the biggest reason that the new NPRM is seen by most in the general aviation industry as just what we need. As we said in Chap. 1, flying isn't cheap, and anything that we can reasonably do to lower the cost has got to be a benefit.

Last on my list is the provision in the sport pilot NPRM that the pilot time that a sport pilot logs will count toward the total time required to obtain higher levels of certificates. By initially becoming a sport pilot, a person isn't fixing his future fate. He can use his sport pilot license for as long as he wants, while always having the option of taking the additional training to become a private, commercial, or airline transport pilot later.

Even though we're focusing this book on becoming a private pilot, don't overlook the sport pilot certificate if the aircraft in the light-sport category, and the operating limitations of a sport pilot, meet your needs. If you think that you'd like old-fashioned, low and slow flying in an uncomplicated setting, this might be just what the doc ordered for you.

Recreational Pilot Licenses

In 1987 the FAA created the recreational pilot certificate in an attempt to bolster personal aviation and to deal with some of the same issues having to do with the decline in the growth rate of personal aviation that we just talked about in our discussion of the sport pilot license. Unfortunately, this attempt to revitalize personal flying hasn't met with a lot of success. As of the writing of this edition, there are fewer than 1,000 active recreational licenses on the FAA's books. That's certainly not an outstanding success in almost 15 years.

Recreational pilots have significant limitations on their flying as compared with private pilots. Yet the training to achieve the recreational license is almost as much as that of a private pilot. Also, recreational pilots have to possess a third-class medical certificate, as do private pilots. Let's take a quick look at the differences between the privileges enjoyed by a recreational pilot and a private pilot.

First, a recreational pilot may not fly every type of aircraft that a private pilot may. A rec pilot can fly only single-engine airplanes and helicopters. If he's flying either an airplane or a helicopter, the engine may be rated at no more than 180 horsepower, and it may have no more than four seats. The four seats won't do a recreational pilot much good though because she is limited to carrying no more than one passenger at a time. Why is this?

The training for a recreational pilot is less than that for a private license. You'll see in your ground school, and it will be emphasized by your flight instructor, that very few general aviation airplanes can be filled with fuel, have all of their seats occupied by normal-size adults, and still be within their legal load limits. Most everything about an airplane's design involves many compromises by the engineers putting the machine together. When you know how to manage the loading of an airplane, you'll see that most small airplanes offer a choice. Fill the seats with adults and accept a fuel load less than full, with the resulting decrease in operating range. Or fill the gas tanks to the brim and then fly with a cabin load that is almost certainly less than an adult in each seat. The choice is left up to the wise pilot to determine which compromise best suits the mission of each flight.

Recreational pilots don't get this in-depth training. So to eliminate the problem, the FAA said that they may carry only one passenger. That way, the possibility of overloading the airplane becomes very remote. As a student seeking a private license, you'll learn the very simple calculations that are necessary to determine whether the airplane is within both its legal maximum weight, and whether its center of gravity is within the limit for any imaginable combination of fuel, people in the seats, and baggage. You'll also learn what happens when either of those two defining limits is exceeded.

Recreational pilots are not allowed to fly between sunset and sunrise. They don't receive any training in night flying in contrast to private pilots who will get that training. This limitation may not be very important from the practical viewpoint because a recreational pilot typically flies for fun, not for travel. Fun flying during the day is very different from purposeful flying at night, so the FAA eliminated an area of operations that can pose a hazard for someone not as well versed and trained as is a private pilot.

The greatest differences between the privileges of a recreational pilot and the holder of a private license come in two areas—cross-country flying and the classes of airspace in which they may fly. A recreational pilot may wander only 50 miles from an airport where he has received training. That isn't very far, but the limit exists for good reason.

Recreational pilots don't get the training in aviation weather and cross-country navigation that private pilots do. The rec pilot doesn't learn weather system recognition or the effects of en route weather changes, nor does he learn how to navigate over any meaningful distances. The 50-mile limit was seen by the FAA as the practical, outside limit in terms of distance whereby a pilot could look out of the window, decide that it's an OK day to go flying, and then not go far enough that the weather was very likely to be much different than it was at the departure airport. However, the 50-mile limit was so draconian that it limited the usefulness of the recreational license to such an extent that few people expressed much interest in becoming rec pilots.

Now the 50-mile limit can be removed from a recreational pilot's operating restrictions. The pilot is required to have an instructor and undergo training in cross-country navigation and aviation weather virtually to the same extent as a private pilot is required to do. When that training is complete, the flight instructor endorses the pilot's logbook to the effect that she is proficient in cross-country flying. As long as the recreational pilot then carries her endorsed logbook with her, she may make cross-country flights.

Even after getting the cross-country endorsement, a recreational pilot may not fly in any airspace where communication is required with air traffic control (ATC). That means that recreational pilots can't go into airports that have control towers, and they can't fly within specified distances of many busy airports where a pilot has to communicate with ATC, even though he isn't landing at the busy place. The entire concept behind the recreational certificate is to allow the flying of simple airplanes in uncomplicated airspace. So our rec pilot isn't trained in dealing with ATC or in operating from towered airports.

It's interesting to note that the sport pilot proposal contains no similar restriction upon sport pilots. They will be allowed to go to the busiest airports and to others that have control towers and radar services that require radio communication. Of course, private pilots may go anywhere because they're fully trained and tested on ATC procedures.

Recreational pilots can't fly internationally either. How severe this limit is depends mostly on where a rec pilot lives. Here in my home state of Ohio, private pilots frequently go into Canada since it's only across Lake Erie from the northern part of our state. In Florida, private pilots often jump the 60 miles over to the Bahamas. A recreational pilot can't do either. If you live in Iowa or Kansas, it's a long way to any international border, so the limitation may not bother you at all.

Recreational pilots have several other limitations. They can't tow anything from an aircraft. They cannot demonstrate an airplane to a prospective buyer, and they can't fly an airplane in a charitable airlift. Like sport pilots, rec pilots are limited to the higher of 10,000 feet above sea level or 2,000 feet above the ground. Both sport and recreational pilots have to fly in constant visual reference to the ground, which means that neither of them can fly over the top of a cloud layer. Also, recreational pilots can't fly in pursuit of business interests, which means that they can't take a business trip in an aircraft as pilot. Private pilots have no such limitation as long as they are not paid for their services as the pilot. That takes a commercial license.

Who knows whether the recreational certificate will survive long term. If forced to prognosticate, my guess is that it won't. If the sport pilot certificate is created in accordance with the new NPRM, it will be interesting to see. While the sport pilot can't fly four-seat airplanes and the airplanes that he can fly can't go more than 132 mph in level flight, that's not much, if any difference, from the airplanes that a recreational pilot can fly. The sport pilot will have many more avenues open to her than the rec pilot does now—flying internationally with permission of the country to visit and the ability to go into ATC-controlled airspace are huge differences to me.

The training time required to get a recreational license is 30 hours, which is more than the time required to get a sport pilot license. Perhaps those folks who already have recreational licenses will opt to exercise the "lower" privileges of a sport pilot, and fly on happily. All of the touted benefits of the recreational license, which are mainly lowered costs over what is expended to get a private certificate, are fulfilled by the sport pilot proposal. We may see the demise of new recreational licenses altogether as the sport pilot certificate takes over as the license for those pilots whose desire it is to fly for fun in simple, fun aircraft.

Glider Pilot Licenses

Flying gliders is a hoot. Before we talk about these wonderful machines and flying them, let's define a term or two. A *glider* is an aircraft that doesn't have an engine meant to sustain its flight. Some of these craft, called *motor gliders,* have engines strong enough to allow them to take off and climb like an airplane. However, when a motor glider gets to the altitude

2-1 *A Schweizer 2-33, a popular training glider.*

where the pilot wants to start soaring, the engine is shut off and then is typically stowed away, physically, into the body of the glider to get it completely out of the airflow. We're also not talking about hang gliders. See FIG. 2-1 for a picture of a popular training glider, the Schweizer 2-33. Gliders are frequently called *sailplanes* to emphasize their ability to "sail" air currents and stay aloft for lengthy periods of time, given the right atmospheric conditions. With the right mix of rising air currents, sailplane flights can go on for hours. We have one man in our glider club who has flown four separate flights that each went more than 1,000 kilometers. Many of my friends routinely fly cross-country trips of 100 to 200 miles in an afternoon in their higher-performance gliders.

The FAA uses the word *glider* throughout the Federal Aviation Regulations (FARs) to refer to these aircraft. Therefore, to avoid any confusion, just keep in mind that there isn't any difference between a sailplane and a glider; *sailplane* is only a term of art. We'll call them *gliders* from here on.

A person can get a student pilot certificate, limited to gliders, at age 14. Therefore, a youngster can learn to fly and solo a glider 2 years before she can qualify by age to solo a powered airplane. To get a private license with a glider rating, you have to be only 16, whereas you have to be 17 to be licensed for powered aircraft. Sport pilots will be able to fly gliders, but there is no rating allowed on a recreational license for gliders. The training to fly gliders is so simple that I can't see why anyone would want to limit his privileges to a sport pilot; you might as well be fully licensed as a private pilot with a glider rating. This is especially so because glider pilots at any level of certification—private, commercial, or flight instructor—are not required to have a medical certificate.

As we mentioned earlier, I got into glider flying in 1994 when my daughter was 14 years old. We joined the local glider club and flew together that first summer. As the next year came around, her interest waned, but I got hooked for good. As she turned 15 and became a teenage girl for real, she somehow managed to find things more exciting, in her mind, to do than hanging out with Dad and the old guys at the airport. She still enjoys flying with me in airplanes and gliders, and maybe someday, after college and getting her business truly off and running, she might regain her own interest in flying. Even without her company, most of my Saturdays in the summer are spent either flying in the tow plane or in the glider.

Glider flying has many advantages. The first and foremost is what you learn. Without an engine, you learn to manage the energy of a moving machine, and to conserve it when needed, and to take advantage of what the atmosphere offers when the conditions are right to stay up. You learn how the three-axis control systems of all airplanes (a glider is really nothing more than a powerless airplane) work, and you learn the control techniques to keep the thing going where you want it to go. Many military forces have seen the benefit of teaching future military aviators to fly gliders first, before they learn to fly powered airplanes. This includes our own U.S. Air Force Academy, which operates a very large glider flying operation for its cadets.

Glider flying is usually a club sport. There are many well-run commercial operators in the United States who have glider flight schools. Because of the atmospheric conditions that gliders thrive on, most of these schools are in the South, Southwest, and West. If you can find a glider club near where you live, you'll find that you can fly there at costs that airplane pilots can only dream about. The fee structure of our club is just one example of how affordable glider flying can be. Ours is a true club—we own everything, including our own hangars, gliders, tow planes, tools, trailers, and miscellaneous equipment. The club has been around for 50 years, and our only debt is last week's fuel bill for the tow planes.

We charge a one-time initiation fee of $300. After that, a member pays $12 per month in dues. Flying costs are billed in two segments: a charge for the tow plane to get you towed aloft, and a charge for using the glider. Training gliders cost $4 per flight, and a tow to 2,000 feet above the ground is $9. So a flight costs $13. Now that flight may last 15 minutes in the winter or on a day when the conditions are lousy, or it may go on for hours in the warmer weather. Where else can you fly for 2 or 3 hours for a total flying charge of $13? Nowhere.

For students learning to fly gliders at our club, our flight instructors charge the princely fee of $3 per flight. Couple that with the $13 it takes for the tow and glider, and a training flight runs $16. Still a bargain in anyone's book.

Glider flying is extremely safe; that's why 14-year-olds are allowed to solo gliders. Although no flying is idiot proof and all aviation requires competent instruction and good pilot judgment, flying a glider is far less complex than flying a powered airplane. When you look at the official FAA accident statistics, glider operations always come out at the very bottom of the numbers of accidents each year, when measured in the typical fashion of accidents per some number of flying hours.

As we've mentioned, glider pilots at all levels of certification don't have to have medical certificates. When you take your practical flight check for the rating, if you're already licensed for some other category of aircraft, or when you apply for a student license if you aren't already licensed, you sign a statement that you have no medical problems that would keep you from flying safely. That's called *self-certification,* and from then on, you're the judge of your medical fitness to fly a glider. Glider pilots save money by not having to spend about $75 every other year to take the physical for a third-class medical certificate, like private pilots do who fly airplanes.

Requirements for a private glider license

To be licensed to fly a glider, you first take instruction from a flight instructor, get ground training in certain areas of aeronautical knowledge, do some solo flying, pass a knowledge (written) test, and then take a flight test with a pilot examiner. These are the same basic steps you'd go through for a private license to fly airplanes, but you need to do much less at each point along the way for a glider pilot license. To get started, you need to find either a glider club or commercial glider operation that welcomes new students. A few clubs, but not many, restrict their membership to already licensed pilots. If you can't easily find a place to train, contact the Soaring Society of America, Post Office Box 2100, Hobbs, NM 88241, for a list of glider operations in your locale.

The progression that any student makes in learning to fly, regardless of the category of aircraft, is basically the same. First you take dual instruction from a flight instructor until you are ready to solo the aircraft. Then you fly some solo practice flights, interspersed with more dual instructional lessons. At some point along the way, you take what the FAA now calls a *knowledge test*, which is what we used to refer to as the *written test*. This change in nomenclature came about because the test is now administered via computer rather than the old-fashioned way of using a written, multiple-choice answer sheet. The knowledge test will cover the following:

- Aircraft performance
- Federal Aviation Regulations
- Weather
- Flight planning
- Aircraft weight and balance
- Aerodynamics and the principles of flight
- Navigation
- Safety of operations

You'll learn all of these subjects in one of two ways: either in a formal ground school or through self-study of materials that you purchase. Your flight instructor is an excellent reference source for deciding which of the two methods would be best for you.

After you pass the knowledge test, which almost everyone does on the first try, the last step in getting your license is to take a flight test with a person who is called a *designated pilot examiner* (DPE). The flight test is formally called a *practical test* because it tests your practical skills to fly the glider, or whatever other aircraft you've learned to fly. DPEs are very experienced flight instructors who have been specially designated by the FAA to administer practical flight tests and issue pilots' licenses to successful applicants. We'll talk a lot more about taking practical tests in Chap. 10.

To get a private pilot certificate with a glider rating, assuming that you have no previous logged pilot time in powered aircraft, you have to do the following:

- Log 10 hours of flight training, and 20 training flights
- Log at least 2 of the above hours in solo flight
- Have at least 10 solo launches and landings
- Fly at least 3 training flights in preparation for the practical test, performed within 60 days of taking the flight test

That's it for the regulatory minimum. As a practical matter, you'll probably fly more flights than the FARs require.

Most students who have no previous flight time will take anywhere from 30 to 50 dual instructional flights before they are ready for that all-important first solo flight. While this number of flights may seem high, it isn't because many flights in a glider are quite short compared to flights in a powered airplane. On days when the atmospheric conditions don't provide the lift that is needed for sustained flight, your glider flights won't last long. When you are towed to 2,000 feet above ground level (AGL), the flight will last only about 15 minutes, including the time you spend on the tow, if you don't find some rising air currents to prolong the trip.

As your skills build, you'll make several presolo flights releasing from the tow at much lower altitudes, usually around 1,000 feet AGL so that you can practice flying the landing approach. Because a glider has no ability to make a go-around under its own power, learning to judge the landing approach consumes a larger percentage of the presolo training than it does for airplane students. These tows to 1,000 feet, and the subsequent approaches and landings, often take 10 minutes or less per flight. So even though you might fly 50 flights before you solo in a glider, the cumulative number of flying hours will likely be less than you would spend as an airplane student before soloing.

At most glider fields, students get some number of repeated flights, one after another, to reduce training time and delays. At our club, students (including pilots who are already licensed for some other category of aircraft, and who are now learning to fly gliders) have first priority in the training gliders on Saturday mornings. They are allowed three flights in a row, or 45 minutes of cumulative time, whichever comes first. After that, they put their names on the waiting list, and when their turns come up, they just repeat the process. If a glider operation runs smoothly, as soon as you land, the tow plane pulls into position, the tow line is hooked up again, and off you go for the next flight. Lots of training can occur in a short period of time.

The obvious goal of glider flying is to stay aloft. Doing so is called *soaring*, and it is accomplished by finding thermals or other types of rising air. During your presolo training, you'll be taught the basic techniques of soaring in *thermals*, which are bubbles of heated, rising air. But the majority of your training flights won't concentrate on soaring; they'll be focused on learning how to control the aircraft and how to approach the field and land. It's interesting to me to see the high number of students at our club who manage to find some thermals and soar for quite a while on their first solo flight. When they return, approach the field and land, their smiles are so broad that their faces hurt.

After you solo the first few times, your instructor will get back in the glider with you and start honing your skills to enable you to pass the practical flight test. When you've passed the knowledge test and your instructor deems you ready to take the flight test, you'll make an appointment with the DPE to take the practical. Depending upon atmospheric conditions and whether there are any thermals that you can find, your flight test might take more than one short flight so that the examiner can see you demonstrate all of the maneuvers that are required to pass the test.

Flying skills unique to gliders

There is a lot more to flying a glider than simply being towed up to an altitude, releasing from the tow plane, flying around until you glide down to traffic pattern altitude, and then landing. You need to learn how to handle the controls of the glider and how to deal with a few rare emergency situations. FIGURE 2-2 shows a picture, taken from the cockpit of a glider, of what it looks like to be towed behind the tow plane. It is very important for the glider to be in the correct position relative to the tow plane ahead of it. As the tow plane flies through the air, it produces a wake beind it, which is an invisible torrent of turbulent air, produced by a mixture of the effects of the propeller blast and wing tip vortices that are shed by every wing in flight. This wake, as produced by small

2-2 *The view of the tow plane from the glider cockpit.*

airplanes, isn't so violent that you couldn't fly the glider in it, but you'd be very uncomfortable since you'd be bounced around a good bit. Glider pilots in the United States generally fly the tow position shown in FIG. 2-2, which is called high tow because the glider is above the tow plane's wake. In some countries, pilots use a position where the glider is below the wake of the tow plane, and this is quite naturally called *low tow.*

From the tow position shown in FIG. 2-2, you can imagine a training maneuver called *boxing the wake.* This maneuver involves flying in a square, around the tow plane's wake. First, you descend from the high tow position through and below the wake into the low tow. Then you move the glider to the left, staying in the low tow, to a position off of the tow plane's left wing. Then you climb the glider back up to the high tow, still while staying off of the left wing of the tow plane. From here, you "slide" the glider laterally to the right, until you get to a position off of the tow plane's right wing. After hesitating there for a second, you descend, staying off of the tow plane's right wing, back down into the low tow position. Again hesitate for a second, then fly left, stopping directly behind the tow plane, in low tow. The finish of the maneuver is accomplished by climbing the glider straight up, through the wake, into the stable high tow position.

Now you've boxed the wake, and the tow can continue to whatever altitude you want before release. Boxing the wake is not something that you normally do in getting towed aloft; rather, it's a training maneuver to teach you the art of controlling the glider's position behind the tow plane during the tow. As a side benefit, learning to box the wake teaches good control coordination between using the elevators, ailerons, and rudder that is applicable to flying all fixed-wing aircraft, be they gliders or powered airplanes.

When you learn to fly an airplane, you'll be taught what to do in the very rare event that the engine fails. Modern engines can quit, but the event is so rare today that almost all pilots go through their entire aviation careers with never a whimper of discontent from their engines. In glider flying, the emergency that is equivalent to an engine failure in a powered airplane is a break of the tow line. If the tow line breaks, the glider pilot has to know what to do, and react accordingly, especially if the break occurs at a low altitude, right after takeoff.

If the tow rope breaks when the glider is within 200 feet of the ground, the glider pilot flies straight ahead or makes gentle turns to find a landing site. Since training gliders land at speeds around 35 mph or sometimes even less, and then roll only about 150 to 200 feet after touchdown until they can be stopped cold, you can land a glider virtually anywhere. From 200 feet high, even a relatively poor performing training glider will travel about 5,000 feet forward, which is almost a mile, before it runs out of altitude and must land. These machines have glide ratios of around 25:1, and that means that they go forward 25 feet for every 1 foot of altitude loss, in still air. With slight turns, it's hard not to find the small space needed to land a glider within a mile of the spot where the rope breaks.

If the rope break occurs above 200 feet, glider pilots are taught to turn back to the runway from which we just departed and land on it. When we practice these rope breaks at 200 feet, it's amazing to see how far the glider glides along and above the runway, after it has been turned around, before it touches down. Above 200 feet, you're always in a position to get back to the runway if the rope breaks. When we train new tow plane pilots, one of the main things that we teach them is to keep in mind that they are "driving the train" and governing where the glider is going at all times during the tow. Tow pilots have to fly a tow pattern that keeps the glider within safe gliding range of the runway if the rope should break at any time while on tow, above 200 feet.

Tow ropes are traditionally 200 feet long. Breaks can happen for any number of reasons, but they aren't all that common. Breaks also happen because of human error. Before glider operations start each day, whether in a commercial operation or a club like ours, each tow rope is carefully examined over its entire length. We're looking for excessive fraying, or broken strands within the rope, either of which will compromise the rope's tensile strength. The ropes do eventually wear out, primarily from being dragged along the runway each time that the tow plane lands and rolls out, and they also get some dragging along the runway, for a short period of time, during each takeoff.

The other events that can break a rope happen in flight because the glider pilot allows the glider to get way out of position during the tow. The glider either gets too far to one side of the tow plane, or the glider pilot lets lots of slack develop in the rope. Then, after realizing the error of his ways, he'll jerk the controls too hard, trying to "snap" the glider around and get it back into a proper high tow position behind the tow plane. As it usually happens when a slack rope is snapped taut, the tow rope sometimes breaks. Glider pilot training covers the proper way to deal with slack in the tow rope, and the maneuver is covered on the practical flight test too. If you do a thorough check of the rope before flying and deal properly with any amount of slack that may develop during the tow, rope breaks will be only an academic subject that you'll practice every now and then for proficiency but will never experience unexpectedly.

Controls and control techniques unique to gliders

Gliders have the same basic flight controls that airplanes have; and they are explained in detail in Chap. 5. Obviously, gliders don't have engines, unless you're flying a motorglider, so traditional gliders don't have engine controls. A glider pilot can control the glider's angle and rate of descent just as, and often more precisely than can, the pilot of a powered airplane. This ability to vary how the glider is coming down is necessary for a glider pilot to be able to pick a spot to land and execute the plan exactly as she's conceived it. You'll see later that an airplane's glide path is controlled by adding or decreasing power and by using the wing flaps as needed. A glider must do this by different means since it has no power, and training gliders don't have flaps.

Gliders control their glide paths and the steepness of their descents by using devices called *spoilers* to vary the amount of lift that their wings produce. Spoilers come in a couple of different variants, but their effect is the same. As they are deployed from the wing's surface, they disrupt the otherwise smooth flow of air over a portion of the wing, thereby reducing the total quantum of lift being generated by the wing. When the total lift is reduced, the glider descends more rapidly. By extending the spoilers a little or a lot, the glider pilot can greatly alter the rate and angle of descent of the craft.

Glider students will spend a great deal of time in their presolo training learning to do what's needed to make a landing approach. You must learn to recognize when you need to either steepen or flatten your approach angle, so that you land where you want to touch down. The glide angle and rate of descent are modulated by having your hand constantly on the spoiler handle, and "milking" spoilers either on or off, as needed to make the glider go exactly where your want. With practice, you will be able to precisely land the glider, roll out, and stop within about 50 feet of a planned point. As you gain even more experience, you'll put the thing on a dime.

Soaring

A glider stays aloft when the atmospheric conditions permit the pilot to soar. The most common way that glider pilots prolong their flights in most parts of the country is by finding those rising bubbles of air called *thermals* and then staying in them. When you find a thermal and stay in it, you're using the free energy of the rising air to make the glider climb. Gliders can also stay aloft by flying in the rising air that occurs on the upwind side of a mountain ridge. As the wind blows against the ridge, it is forced upward and over the ridge. If you fly very close to the upwind surface of the ridge, you can fly for long distances. This type of rising air is called *ridge lift,* and using it to stay up is known as *ridge soaring.* Ridge soaring is not for the new or inexperienced glider pilot because you have to fly very close to the face of the ridge, sometimes only a wing's length or two away, to stay in the air mass that is being forced upward by the wind blowing against that ridge.

Another source of lift is found in a *mountain wave*. Mountain waves are generated when wind blows against a mountain and goes over the top of it, and downwind of the mountain a cyclical "up-and-down" wave develops. This wave happens because the air that was forced over the mountain continues to rise for some distance beyond the mountain's peak, and then descends again. This up-and-down wave of air can continue a long distance from the mountain, sometimes a hundred miles or more. The upward lift in a mountain wave can be awesome, and gliders have flown higher than 40,000 feet in mountain waves. As the name implies, mountain waves require the presence of mountains for their generation, so in the United States they are typically found in the western states.

For those of us in the flatlands, our only source of upward rising air is from thermal activity. Thermals begin when the sun's rays heat certain sections of the earth's surface more than another section nearby. Some terrain features are susceptible to being heated more than are neighboring areas. Large parking lots, dark fields, major highway interchanges, and large flat roofs on big buildings are great producers of thermals. These features rapidly absorb the sun's heat and create a bubble of hot air near their surfaces. Because hot air is lighter than cooler air, a thermal will form and start rising from these sorts of generators. Thermals can be strong, weak, large, or small. If it's a cool spring or early summer day, when the sun's rays are intense, while the basic air mass is cool, and when there is a good thermal generator on the ground, you've got the recipe for strong thermals.

When the differential of the temperatures between the warm thermal and the surrounding air mass is large, the thermal will be strong, creating what glider pilots call *boomers*. You can ride this thermal for thousands of feet above the ground. If you've flown in an airplane, particularly a lightplane, the turbulent air that you've encountered on a clear, sunny day was probably the result of the airplane's flying into and out of thermals. To an airplane pilot, this "rough air" can lessen the enjoyment of an otherwise smooth flight; to a glider pilot, it's the stuff of which a great flying day is made.

Because gliders are light weight and have huge wingspans compared to airplanes, they ride thermals much more smoothly than do powered airplanes, with their shorter wings. When a lightplane passes through a strong thermal, the occupants may feel a jolt. When a glider enters the same thermal, the pilot generally feels only a "push" upward from the rising mass of air.

It takes practice and some experience to dependably find thermals and then maneuver the glider to stay in them. Even though you might stumble into a good thermal by accident when on a presolo training flight and gain quite a bit of altitude, don't be fooled into thinking that it's always that easy. Finding lift is always a challenge, even for the most experienced glider pilot. It's this challenge that makes the sport so appealing to many. One day a couple of summers ago, my daughter came up to our glider club's field for a ride with me. When she arrived, I was flying because I had taken another person up, and that flight lasted 45 minutes. When I landed, that passenger got out of the glider, my daughter got in, we hooked up for the tow, and released at 2,000 feet above the ground. I couldn't find a single thermal just a few minutes after I had had a long ride. Our flight lasted only the 15 minutes that it took to tow up to release altitude and glide back down. So goes the ever-elusive thermal.

Landing out

Airplane pilots almost always land at an airport. Glider pilots have the same goal, but they accomplish it less often, once they begin flying cross country. When a pilot becomes proficient in soaring, the next big step in his development is to fly farther away from the glider field and eventually get beyond the range where he can glide back to it without finding some lift to sustain his flight. When you're out there, you've got to find some lift to stay aloft as you work your way either back home or toward another airport. If you don't find it, you have to accept an off-airport landing. In the jargon of glider flying, these off-airport landings are called *landing out*. Even though landing out is never the goal of a glider flight, this type of landing can become the outcome of a flight beyond the range at which the glider can make it back to the departure point without the pilot's finding some lift in the meantime.

Glider pilots don't fear landing out for a couple of reasons. First, they plan their cross-country flights to take them over hospitable terrain, where there are good fields in which to land if needed. Second, gliders land at very slow speeds, and usually the rollout after landing is no more than a couple of hundred feet if the pilot applies the wheel brake to stop within the minimum distance. If you really need to stop a glider, you can do it in a very short distance. The result of a landing out is that you make a call on your cell phone or from the farmer's house and arrange for your buddies to come with the glider's trailer and haul you home. While you're waiting for them to arrive, you take the wings off of the glider, which you can do since they're designed for simple and quick disassembly. Then, you have a cup of coffee with the farmer until your friends show up. You might owe the farmer $100 or so for a few bushels of whatever crop is growing in the field where you landed and was damaged by the landing and the retrieval of the glider from that field, but that's generally the extent of it. Out landings make for great conversation, over an adult beverage, at the end of a day of cross-country glider flying.

3

Instructors and Flight Schools

The rest of this book will concentrate on those pilots who are either fledgling student pilots, folks thinking about learning to fly, or students who have come some of the way along in their training. All of those people have the common goal of becoming a private pilot, rated to fly single-engine airplanes. Even if you think you want to become a sport or glider pilot, read on, as the topics to be covered will certainly have a good deal of application to your flying those aircraft as well.

Once someone has developed the urge to become a pilot, many questions will come to mind. Typical among them are: What's all of this going to cost, now and after I get my license? How tough is the physical exam? Can I try a few lessons and see if I really like flying, or do I have to sign up for an entire course? How do I get a good instructor and flight school? What if I don't get along with the instructor?

Most pilots hear these kinds of questions from their acquaintances who don't fly. Unfortunately, most pilots don't really have the information to accurately answer these queries because their direct knowledge is limited to their own experiences when they were student pilots. Their training regimen might have been good, bad, or indifferent, or it has become outdated with the passage of time. Although other pilots might tell you at great length how they did it, that might not be the right approach for you. It's unlikely that the average private pilot has kept abreast of the changes in flight training since he was trained, and more often than not, some friend who is already a pilot will not have a current and comprehensive view of the entire flight training scene and the options presently available.

The number of choices that you have are far more than might be apparent at first. Which one is best for you depends on many factors, including your age, goals, and the amounts of time, money, effort, and dedication that you are willing to invest in learning to fly.

The Physical Exam

In order to get a student pilot certificate that will be valid for your training toward a private pilot's certificate, you will have to pass a simple physical exam. As we said earlier, the student license is actually issued by a physician who has been designated by the FAA to administer airman physicals, and these doctors are referred to as *aviation medical examiners,* or AMEs for short.

Very few people have any problems with the exam that is required for a private pilot. The FAA has three classes of airman medical certificates, naturally called *first-, second-,* and *third-class certificates.* An airline captain has to have a first-class certificate, and commercial pilots, such as your flight instructor, are required to carry a second-class certificate. Private pilots need have only a third class, and it is valid for 2 years if they are over 40 years old and 3 years if they are youngsters under 40. Second-class certificates are good for a year, regardless of the pilot's age, and airline captains have to take their exams every 6 months, again regardless of age.

If you intend to become a sport pilot or to fly gliders only, you don't need a medical certificate of any class. You simply go to an FAA office or to a designated pilot examiner, and have a student pilot certificate issued. It will carry a notation that it is good only for gliders, balloons, or sport student privileges.

You can obtain a list of AMEs from your local FAA office, or from numerous Web sites, or generally your flight instructor can tell you who is an AME in your area. AMEs take special training at FAA seminars before they are designated as able to administer pilot physicals, and afterword AMEs must keep current on selected areas of aviation medicine. The physical that you'll take for a third-class certificate isn't at all as thorough as is a normal physical that your family doctor would give you. The FAA's medical standards are really designed to uncover conditions or diseases that would make it unsafe for you to be piloting an airplane or that could lead to sudden incapacitation.

Most instructors will recommend that you take your exam early in your training. In the slim chance that there is a problem, it can probably be cleared up with some time for the paperwork to go to and from the FAA. Even though you presently don't need a student license to take instruction and have to have it only to solo, don't wait until you're about ready to solo to take the physical. Get it over with early.

Eyesight is almost never a problem for applicants for a third-class certificate. You have to have visual acuity of at least 20/30, either uncorrected or corrected with glasses or contacts. There is no outside limit to your uncorrected vision for a third class, as long as you correct to 20/30 or better. If you've had one of the newer surgical procedures to correct your vision, such as laser surgery, that's OK too, as long as the correction results in 20/30 or better vision. Even if you are blind in one eye, you can still qualify through a waiver process.

One problem that does come up sometimes, especially in men, is color deficient vision. You need to be able to distinguish between aviation red, green, and white to be licensed to fly at night. The lights on aircraft, and on airport surfaces use these colors for certain purposes and positions. Most AMEs administer the color test using a little book with pages of pastel colors, from which a person with normal color vision can pick out certain geometric shapes like squares, circles, triangles, and such from the otherwise appearing maze of colored dots. If you flunk this test, all is not lost. You apply then to the FAA to take another test, for which you look at a light signal gun. If you can tell the bright red, green, and white from the light gun, you'll pass. If you fail this test, you won't be able to fly at night.

A private pilot must be able to hear normal conversational voice levels. If you wear any hearing aids, you can be approved on the condition that you wear them while flying. If a person cannot hear at all, she can still be certified, but she'll have a limitation on her certificate to the effect that she can't fly in airspace where she'd have to communicate with air traffic control.

Diabetes was a severe problem for pilots before 1997. Now, even insulin dependent diabetics can get a third-class medical certificate. There are certain requirements for testing the pilot's blood glucose levels before takeoff and while flying. People who are alcoholics can get certified if they've been alcohol free for 2 years and if they pass a special review of their treatment and history by the FAA. The same goes for those folks who have had a drug problem in their pasts.

If you have ever had a psychiatric or neurological problem in the past, you may well be certifiable, depending on the nature of the problem, its severity, and the length of time since you suffered it. But, generally, if you are taking any mood-altering drugs, such as those used often to treat depression, you cannot get a medical certificate under the current rules.

As you might imagine, the cardiovascular system, and any diseases or conditions of it, are of particular interest to the FAA. If you've had a heart attack in the past, there are special tests and procedures to see if you can get a waiver. I personally know of several pilots who fit into this category and who have been flying for a long time after they underwent treatment. Most folks who've undergone open-heart surgery can also get a waiver and a medical certificate. If either of these conditions has affected you in the past, call the AME before you appear for your exam, so you know what medical records to bring with you.

High blood pressure isn't a bar to certification if it's treatable and under control with medication. There once were fixed standards in the regulations that stated certain maximum levels of systolic and diastolic readings. Now, your blood pressure is subjectively evaluated by the AME, but you can assume that a reading of 155/95, or less, will qualify. If it's higher than that, you'll have to take some tests to prove the health of your cardiovascular and renal systems. If you're under treatment for high blood pressure, virtually all of the drugs now used are approved by the FAA. To be safe, call the AME first and tell him what drug(s) you take. If, by some slim chance, your drug isn't on the approved list, ask your treating doctor if your medication can be changed to an approved drug.

Other than these relatively uncommon situations, the physical exam is a breeze.

Choices in Flight Training

In Chap. 1 we touched briefly upon some of the options that are available to a person who wants to learn to fly. Now let's expand a bit on those thoughts. Depending mainly upon where you live, your choices may be fewer than all of the ones that we'll talk about. Regardless of how many options confront you, the important thing is that you make a choice, after some investigation, and start flying.

Training at the smaller airport

Many of the smaller airports are away from major metropolitan areas. Even so, now and then you'll find a small field tucked away in the corner of a larger city's densely populated areas. At these airports, you will probably learn to fly in much the same manner as it's been done since the 1950s. You just walk into the airport office and tell the operator that you'd like to start taking flying lessons. In this scenario, most students pay for each lesson as it is given and arrange an appointment for the next one immediately after the one they've just taken, or phone later to schedule a lesson as their time, money, and inclination permit. There has been some continuing debate among aviation professionals about whether this is the best way to learn to fly today. Some feel that modern training methods can be lacking in this less formal environment, whereas others opine that the old way has advantages not present at large schools located at major airports.

As the world has become so much more computerized in the last few years, some of the disadvantages of learning at smaller airports have disappeared. Today many small airport operators have computerized learning curriculums and training aids that were found only at the larger schools just a few years ago.

At the smaller, rural airports, not all that much has changed since I learned to fly at one of them in the 1960s. Our airport had a sod and gravel runway then, but before it closed to make way for a commercial development, that old strip had been lengthened and paved. The greatest changes that have occurred at the small fields have revolved around prices and additions to the training requirements that have been the products of the more expansive FAA regulations. I am one of those instructors who see merit in the older approach and in learning to fly in less complicated surroundings, as long as the philosophy of the place doesn't show disdain for the current and future requirements. However, there is no single, right place to learn to fly, and if you live in a major city, you need not fear flight instruction at a larger airport.

Flying lessons can be costly, and one of the primary benefits to beginning your flying at a smaller airport is that it's normally less expensive to train there, over what it costs at a large school located at an airport serving the major airlines. The overhead is typically quite a bit less at the rural field, and you don't spend the airplane time taxiing all over the place and waiting for other airplanes to take off and land. Flight instructor and airplane rental charges are universally priced by the hour when the airplane's engine is running. The savings are obvious when you consider that you won't be waiting for a string of airliners ahead of you to depart, or land.

Since everything is a compromise of some sort or another, you've got to be on guard for one thing about learning to fly at a small airport. You can't let yourself become reluctant to fly into major airports when the time comes. Today's regulations require that you fly into an airport with an operating control tower a few times before you get your license. But these few trips with your instructor won't ensure that you'll be comfortable flying into a place with airline traffic, corporate jets, and other aircraft all sharing the same airspace. Your instructor should expose you to high-density traffic areas if at all possible during your training days. If you don't get sufficient experience, then even after you get licensed, you should have an instructor fly with you into a large airport until you are at ease doing it alone. If you are hesitant about flying into large airports, you'll never realize the full utilization of an airplane or enjoy all of the transportation value provided by general aviation.

Learning at the large airport FBO

Fixed-base operators (FBOs) at large airports often offer flight training and frequently provide a private pilot course as a complete package. These FBOs may not be full-service operators in that they may not cater to the corporate jet customer; they may instead concentrate their efforts on flight training and the owner-pilot of piston engine aircraft.

These schools' package programs may include aircraft rental, instructors' fees, ground school, and your supplies all for a set price. These set prices will, of course, have a maximum number of aircraft and instructor hours that you get for that price, with time above the maximum charged at an additional rate. Some of these schools have time payment plans to allow a student to pay for a course in installments over the period of time estimated to complete the course.

Many of these flight schools at large airports, as well as a few at smaller fields, are officially known as *FAA-approved* flight schools. This means that they have sought and obtained a certificate from the FAA that approves their facilities and curriculum under Part 141 of the Federal Aviation Regulations. There can be several reasons why a school wants this approval, and most of them have to do with marketing their services.

We all know that many foreign nationals come to the United States for flight training. While the painful memories of September 11, 2001, may taint our impressions of foreign students, they shouldn't. Once you're in aviation, you'll realize that we in the United States and Canada fly far less expensively than do people almost anywhere else on earth. Foreign students can come here and get pilots' licenses at tremendous savings over what it would cost in their home countries. Many of these students are training to become professional pilots in their native countries, but they get all their training here, up through the airline transport pilot certificate, saving tens of thousands of dollars over what the cost would be at home, while at the same time injecting a great deal of positive impact into our economy. The foreign country or airline sponsoring them almost always requires that the flight school where they learn be an FAA-approved school.

There are other training programs sponsored by colleges and military ROTC courses, where flight students are taught in the civilian arena. Again, the sponsors of these programs typically require that the school be FAA-approved to qualify to teach their students.

FAA approval doesn't mean that the school will necessarily teach you better than an unapproved operation will. To get Part 141 approval, a school must have certain physical facilities, classrooms, and equipment that are not really essential in an informal setting. In both types of schools, the instructors have to have the same licenses, the airplanes have to be maintained to the same requirements, and the students have to pass the same tests to get licensed. Seeking FAA approval can be very expensive for the smaller operation. The flight instruction can be excellent or terrible at either type of school.

When you first go to the airport and inquire about flying lessons, whether at a small or larger FBO, don't be disappointed or put off if you don't get a hard sell and the red-carpet treatment. Sometimes newcomers to general aviation get the feeling that the FBO personnel think that they are doing the new student a favor by talking to her. One of my former law partners formed this opinion of a couple of operators, and she never did learn to fly because of it. That's too bad because no one should get discouraged or angry; aviators still often think of themselves as belonging to an exclusive club to which admission must be earned the hard way. This archaic philosophy is rapidly changing, but given the slight chance you run into it, don't give up. You'll soon be accepted, and you'll be glad for it.

Flight academies

In the last couple of decades we have seen the growth of training operations that devote themselves exclusively to flight training. They are not traditional FBOs because they offer almost none of the other services traditionally available from an FBO. They don't sell airplanes or perform maintenance for outside owners of aircraft, and they don't have charter departments. They teach people to fly, and they offer higher levels of training for pilots who are already licensed and little if anything else. Some of these large schools are even owned or controlled by airlines and exist to offer *ab initio* (literally, "from the beginning") training to students who dream of someday being a captain on a Boeing 747. Most of these aviation academies are located in the southern and southwestern parts of the country, where the weather is more dependably good for maintaining daily flight operations and keeping to rigorous training schedules.

They offer a good alternative for the person they are designed to serve—one who can get totally immersed in flying. These schools usually operate in a very formal, structured, full-time setting. For the average person who has a job, maybe children, and day-to-day living to contend with, this type of training is probably not feasible. If your interest is not in becoming a professional pilot, you might not enjoy the regimen. If you think that one of the academies might be for you, the training offered is generally excellent and professional. Most of the training academies advertise heavily in aviation magazines, so finding one should not be a problem.

Flying clubs

In addition to FBOs at small and large airports and the "super schools" at the flight academies, there are some other routes you can take to obtain a private pilot's license. One in particular is feasible for the average working person. Flying clubs exist almost everywhere. There are three distinctly different setups that call themselves *flying clubs*. The first of these is a an arrangement whereby many FBOs will rent their airplanes at a discounted rate to customers who pay a nominal initiation fee, and perhaps small monthly dues, to join what they call a "club." Really, this is no more than a way to offer a discount to regular customers who fly often at the FBO. During your training days, chances are that you may fly enough, per month, to more than make up the cost of the initiation fee and monthly dues in the discount that you'll receive from the normal rental fee for the training airplane. If you learn to fly at an FBO that offers this arrangement, do the arithmetic for yourself to see if you'll save some money by joining the "club."

The second type of club is one that is organized by an individual, or small group of people, who then either owns the airplanes or leases them to the entity that makes up the club. Sometimes the ownership person or group will lease the aircraft from third parties. Often this type of club exists as a source of business income for the person or group behind the club. Many times, the person who is the power behind the club will be a flight instructor who also gives the flight instruction to members of the club. There is nothing inherently wrong or bad with this type of operation, but there are a few things to watch for.

These clubs usually maintain their airplanes to the standards used by a first-class FBO. Although they are mechanically sound, theses airplanes' cosmetics may leave something to be desired. Rental and club airplanes take a beating in everyday use, and the seat upholstery, interior side panels, carpeting, and general appearance can suffer.

Although it's beyond the scope of this book to delve much into the subject of aviation insurance, once you get into flying, you'll need to be aware of the provisions of the insurance coverage that is in place on the airplanes that you rent. Quite often an FBO or club will have insurance to protect it from liability, but that insurance may well not protect the renter pilot. Sometimes these types of clubs can skimp on insurance coverage to keep overhead down. Be sure that you find out exactly what program of insurance any operator, be it FBO or club, has in place before you fly there.

The third type of club is a true club, usually a nonprofit corporation. The corporation owns the airplanes, or it may again lease them from third parties. The members of the club are members of the corporation, so they have a beneficial interest in the club's assets. Most of these "equity" clubs, as they are generally called, require a new member to pay an up-front fee that could represent the value of the new member's beneficial interest in the fleet of airplanes. Sometimes this fee is refundable when a member leaves the club, and sometimes it is not. There are, in my opinion, three real benefits to joining this type of club.

Because the club is not profit motivated, the hourly charges to fly the airplanes are usually less than renting airplanes at an FBO. Second, because the members of the club are also the owners of the airplanes, they usually take better care of the equipment and fly the airplanes with more respect for the piece of machinery than most people will treat something that they're only renting by the hour. Third, the club will typically have different airplanes at different points along the performance spectrum. When you get your license and become ready to fly more advanced and higher-performing airplanes, the club will likely have them in its fleet. Look for this advantage when considering a club to join.

Clubs of this type are very popular in larger metropolitan areas and can offer other advantages beyond those we've already mentioned. The hourly costs of flying the airplanes include such fixed expenses as insurance, hangar rent, and organizational overhead. Therefore, the more hours per year that the airplanes fly, the lower the cost per hour for those fixed items. So, in an active club, the costs of flying can reach very reasonable levels. Also, most of these clubs have an instructor or a few instructors on their membership rolls who can take care of the training needs of the members.

Many of these clubs have a social underpinning. One of the problems with aviation is that often the family of the aspiring aviator doesn't share the same level of dedication to flying. A club with an active social calendar of fly-ins, picnics, dinners, holiday gatherings, and the like can involve the pilot's family in the sport of personal flying, making it enjoyable for all.

College and the military

If you are still in high school, or haven't gone to college and have the desire to do so, there are many major universities and some smaller colleges that offer degree programs in aviation. Some of these are two-year institutions, but the majority are four-year, degree-granting colleges. Degrees in aviation are generally of two types. One stresses the business side of the aviation industry, preparing the student to work in aviation in a capacity other than as a professional pilot. The other type of degree focuses more on flight operations, and academic schooling is coupled with flight training, usually to certificate and rating levels that make for a student's career as a pilot.

Most major universities across the country have excellent aviation departments and programs. A few are publicly funded schools such as the University of North Dakota, Ohio State University, Purdue University, Auburn University, Ohio University, and University of Illinois.

Last to be discussed is military flight training. Those young people fortunate enough to meet the high standards for the U.S. Armed Forces flight training programs should consider themselves blessed indeed. There is no better flight training available anywhere than in military aviation. The requirements are tough: A four-year degree, often in the hard sciences or engineering, rigorous physical standards, and the ability to devote years of service are only the beginning. But the benefits are immeasurable. Military aviators fly the most fantastic aircraft available anywhere and are constantly on the cutting edge of developments in aviation. After one's service obligations are completed, a military background has historically been the surest way into the cockpit of an airliner.

Buying Your Own Airplane

Earlier we mentioned that buying your own airplane early in your training can have some benefits. These include potentially reducing your total costs to get your license, being able to fly your airplane when you want rather than put up with the uncertainties of scheduling rental airplanes when you want to fly, and the pride that comes with owning your own airplane. There are many good books and other publications devoted to the subject of aircraft ownership, and no effort will be made here to duplicate their depth of coverage.

When I learned to fly in 1965, I took my first lessons and soloed in an Aeronca Champ, which was still a somewhat standard trainer of the day, although its role was being overtaken by the Cessna 150 at many FBOs. After I had about 20 hours of flight time, even the 18-year-old kid figured that paying the FBO to rent the Champ wasn't a very wise deal because I knew by then that I wanted to fly for the rest of my life. So, I bought a little Taylorcraft BC-12D, which was a two-seat airplane of similar vintage to the Champ that I had been renting. I flew that Taylorcraft everywhere, building my flying time on cross-country flights from Ohio to Florida, out West, and everywhere else it would take me. I kept it only about a year, but in that year, I accumulated enough time to qualify for my commercial license.

Today, a simple training airplane such as a Cessna 150, 152, or Piper Tomahawk can be purchased for far less than most pilots spend for a car. As long as you buy wisely and don't get a dog, you could learn to fly in it, then build some time, and sell it, all the while flying for as little cost as possible. Used airplanes have gone up in value dramatically. My Taylorcraft, which I bought for $1,200 in 1965, goes for about 11 times that number in 2002. A Cessna 150 that I paid $5,700 for in 1976 is worth in the high teens now. Examples could go on for pages. If you fly a lot, and you should during your training, and buy a trainer type of airplane with the advance notion that you will sell it after you get a hundred hours of flight time, or thereabouts, that may be the least expensive way to learn to fly.

Like any other mechanical contraption, an airplane can bite your pocketbook. You must do your homework first and get advice from people you trust. Before any money changes hands, it's imperative that the airplane you're considering undergo a prepurchase inspection by a competent aviation mechanic who is familiar with the type. Some airplanes become holes in the sky into which their owners constantly pour money, and others reward their owners with years of economical flying. If you can afford around $22,000 in 2002 dollars and you tread carefully, buying an airplane after your first few hours of instruction can be a great experience.

Ground Study Options

The FAA requires that a candidate for a private pilot certificate, as well as for all of the other certificate levels beyond student pilot, complete two test regimens. The first is a *knowledge test,* which used to be called the *written test.* After you pass it, and when your instructor thinks you are ready, you have to pass a *practical test.* The practical test is a flight test, administered in an airplane, and it is given by either an FAA inspector or—and much more commonly—a designated pilot examiner. The flight test requires you to demonstrate to the examiner that you can fly the airplane at or above private pilot standards.

The knowledge test is administered electronically, with the student sitting at a computer, reading the test on the screen and selecting an answer to each question from a multiple-choice list of potential answers. This test used to be given from a test booklet, with the student putting the answers on a separate answer sheet. The answer sheet was then sent to the FAA headquarters for machine grading. Younger people take to the newer computer test very easily because their generation is computer literate in the first place. But even for us "old codgers," the computer format is very easy to use and not confusing at all. The beauty of the computer test is that you now get your grade instantly upon finishing the test, rather than waiting a couple of weeks for a letter from the FAA giving you your grade.

There are several ways to learn the material that you have to know to pass the knowledge test. The scope of knowledge that you have to garner in order to pass the knowledge test is more thoroughly covered in Chap. 10. Basically, it covers such subjects as the FARs as they pertain to private pilots, weather, navigation, theory of flight, flight planning, and other academic subjects. Some people do much better learning such things in a formal environment, where they have to prepare for class and study for a couple of practice tests or quizzes along the way. If you're such a person, get into a formal ground school training program. You cannot take the practical test until you pass the knowledge test; therefore, don't delay this step. The information that you'll learn in preparing for the knowledge test will make your flight training in the airplane more productive.

When I was gaining my certificates and ratings at a rapid pace in the 1960s, I did all of my ground study without ever attending any ground school or cram course. But I had several things working in my favor. I was 18, and then 19 years old during that span of time, in college, and very used to studying because I had little time for anything else. Picking up the aviation textbooks was a refreshing interlude between reading college texts. Also, other than the typical part-time jobs that any college kid has, I had few other demands on my time.

Now, with a career and family, I doubt that I could do it that way again. I cannot count the people I've known who have dropped out of flying because they never coped with juggling enough time into their schedules to learn what they needed to know to pass the knowledge test. That doesn't say that the test is difficult because it's not. If you are a high school graduate who can keep a checkbook balanced most of the time, and who can comprehend basic written matter, you've got nothing to fear about the knowledge test for a private pilot certificate. What you have to do, in some manner or another, however, is dedicate the time and a little effort to learn the subjects on the test. Let's see how to do just that.

Formal ground school

If you attend an FAA-approved (Part 141) flight school and participate in their approved curriculum, a formal, classroom-style ground school will be a part of it. Most of these ground schools are set up to meet for 10 or more sessions of 2 or 3 hours each. Quite often the lessons are given in the evenings to better fit into the off-work time of students who work normal hours. Naturally, if you attend one of the flight academies, ground school there will be very much like a high school or college class would be.

Even if you don't attend an approved school, most FBOs that offer flight training also offer some kind of similarly structured ground school. There is nothing magic about FAA approval for a ground school. Most FBOs that offer a formal ground school will teach the very same material, and usually from the same learning resources such as texts and videos provided by airplane manufacturers, as you'd see in the approved school.

There is certainly no requirement that you go to a formal ground school. A flight instructor or an FAA-licensed ground instructor must give you an endorsement to the effect that you are imbued with enough wisdom to pass before you can even take the knowledge test. But, as the old saying goes, "There is more than one way to do it."

Home study

Several companies sell very good videotape courses that you can put in your VCR and play at home. Typically it will take many hours to watch the tapes even one time through. Plan on seeing at least a few of them more than once. This approach to learning what you need to know has both a good and bad side to it.

If you are a disciplined individual who can set aside the time to truly study these tapes as you watch them, and then replay various parts as needed to totally absorb the material, this option can work well. If you opt for this method of home study, be sure that you have current tapes. Knowledge tests change frequently because the FAA wants to preserve their security. If you buy someone else's second-hand tapes, you may not get the up-to-date information that you need.

The bad side of home study of videotapes, and the same can be said of studying the books on the market that are designed to prepare you for the knowledge test, is that you must be disciplined enough to watch them and keep progressing. If you watch one tonight and then let 10 days pass until you see another, you won't succeed. Home study requires setting a schedule that you adhere to, whether the home study is of videotapes or textbooks.

Tutoring from your instructor

It is possible to purchase only the needed pilot supplies, like a copy of the FARs, a private pilot textbook, and an aeronautical chart, and then saddle up with your flight instructor for one-on-one tutoring. Trying to complete all of your ground study in this manner can be the least attractive option for a couple of reasons. First, two people's schedules have to coincide. If you're flying at a busy FBO, you might find that it gets a little tough, once in a while, to get your flying lessons coordinated between yours and your instructor's schedules. If you try the tutoring route, the problem persists. Second, the instructor is going to need to be paid for the time she spends with you. Like other professionals who charge by the hour, your instructor can't give time away. She'll probably want the same rate, or close to it, that she charges for flight instruction in the airplane; and why not? A good compromise of the various factors is to study at home, using either a video course or the textbooks, and then have a few tutoring sessions with your instructor, as you need them, to sharpen your knowledge.

Cram courses

There are a few companies that offer 2- or 3-day cram courses. These are usually held at a hotel someplace, and the idea is to get you away from the ordinary distractions of life and totally immerse you in the material at hand. You go at it for 8 to 10 hours a day, and then you take the knowledge test immediately, while everything is still fresh in your mind. Years ago, before the advent of home videoplayers, this was one of the most popular ways to get through the written test, and this approach can still be the best bet for the right person. If you're a busy professional or businessperson who has little free time, at home or elsewhere, to enroll in a multiweek ground school or to effectively study at home, this could be the right route for you to take.

Some study is helpful before you go to the cram course. It's best if the course can be used to wrap up the loose ends and prepare you for the test, rather than your going in cold and expecting to learn everything in a couple of days. Get the videos, or a good textbook that your instructor recommends, and come to the cram course prepared to make the best use of the limited amount of time.

The downside to these cram courses applies to similar ways of learning anything else. By their very nature, these courses are geared to preparing you to pass the knowledge test, and oftentimes the instructors don't have the time to get into various subjects as deeply as would be beneficial. Any educator will tell you that there can be a huge difference between truly learning a subject and learning just enough to pass a test. That's why it's wise to read the textbooks or watch the videos first. Learn the material first, and then use the cram course for what it does best, which is serve as a great review and putting it all together so that you can ace the knowledge test.

The Costs Involved

In Chap. 1 we touched upon the costs involved in learning to fly. Flight training has two distinct components: One is the physical and mechanical handling of the airplane, and the other is the academic study that we just discussed. For both of these components, there is a certainty: If you can start flying and studying and keep at both of them regularly, your total learning will proceed much faster than it will if you drag either of them out.

In my 35+ years as a flight instructor, I've seen people who learned to fly and got their licenses in a matter of months, and a few who took years. There is no question that you'll spend far less total money if you can keep at it. This isn't meant to discourage the person who can't fly several times a week, or even several times a month, for whatever reason, financial or otherwise. The person who does waste money is the one who flies for a lesson or two and then doesn't come back to the airport for weeks or months. With that kind of schedule, that student may never get a license.

If you can keep flying regularly, at least two or three times a month, you should be able to get a license in about 60 hours of flight time, give or take a little. For budgeting purposes, figure that about 30 of these will be dual instruction hours, and the other half will be solo flying hours. Add up 60 hours of airplane rental, and 30 hours' worth of instructor time. Then put in a number for your supplies and the method of ground training that you choose. The total won't be chicken feed, but it's affordable for a great number of folks who are motivated to do it. I suggest that you'll learn the most efficiently, and therefore at the lowest total cost, if you can arrange your finances to have that total sum available over about 6 months. That will enable you to keep flying at a reasonable pace.

Timing Your Lessons

We also touched on this aspect of learning to fly in Chap. 1. Depending upon where you live, you can keep training costs down by starting your lessons in the right time of the year. Here in Ohio, the flying weather is fairly dependable from April through November, and in some years, into December. Coincidentally, these are also the months when we go to daylight savings time, except for November and December. The time change allows more opportunity for most people to fly in the evening, after their normal workday ends. If you live in the parts of the country that have a winter season, and if you begin your flight training in the spring, and couple the timing with adequate financial reserves to keep going at a steady pace, you should be able to get a private pilot certificate that summer or by early autumn.

If you begin in the fall and don't live in the South or Southwest, you may have several days of lousy weather between lessons. It's also not possible to fly in the evening over the winter. If your schedule limits your flying to weekends, you might go 2 or 3 weeks between training flights. Although flying less often is certainly better than not flying at all, your total training time, in terms of flying hours, will probably get stretched out some. In our part of the country, it also tends to be windier more often in the winter, and windy days dampen flight training activity.

Instructors—Good and Bad

Flying and teaching are different skills. A good pilot is not always a good teacher. Almost all certificated flight instructors are good pilots—all of the training and testing required to advance to that level and obtain a flight instructor's certificate make it difficult for a bad pilot to get that far through the system. But not all pilots with a flight instructor's certificate are necessarily good teachers. Flight instructors have to pass a knowledge test on the fundamentals of instruction (unless they are college graduates who have majored in education), but the FAA can't really test anyone adequately for good communication and teaching ability.

A good flight instructor is somebody well worth searching for. He or she will be a knowledgeable, patient, and dedicated individual and will also be an experienced pilot. There is an unfortunate aspect to the profession of flight instructing. It is the primary method used by most aspiring career pilots, who haven't flown in the military, to build the flight time necessary to qualify for airline and corporate flying jobs. All too many flight instructors can't wait to quit teaching and get on to what they think are greater things. If you identify an instructor that your flight school has assigned to you as one of that kind, avoid him if at all possible.

A good instructor isn't defined by either his age or the number of flying hours in his logbook. I have flown with both young and older people who were good pilots or bad ones, great instructors or lousy ones. Aviation has always been a field of endeavor that is constantly developing and evolving, and the pace of the development of new rules, navigation systems, and aircraft isn't likely to slow down in the near future. Therefore, young instructors will often be on top of things and more up to date than a graybeard might be who hasn't bothered to stay current. Young people can be just as good in their teaching as older pilots may be, so don't be turned off by a young instructor just because she hasn't got any gray hair yet. Look first for the qualities of a good teacher, like personality, patience, perseverance, and communication skills. Then look for age and experience.

Many pilots drop out of flying, some before they get a license, some after. Although it's hard to pinpoint all of the reasons or excuses for dropping out, I suspect that poor quality instruction and rapid instructor turnover are two of the major causes. To avoid these situations, as mentioned before, consider the smaller field for your training, where you're more likely to get an instructor who is teaching flying as a career and not aiming for an airline or corporate flying job.

If you don't get first-rate instruction from the very beginning, you might never gain the confidence to feel in total control of the airplane at all times. Your time as a pilot could be plagued with a fear of situations in which you might find yourself in the future. It doesn't take a superhuman to fly an airplane and do it well and confidently. Flying is a skill that has to be learned, and to learn well you have to be taught well.

Some of the things that you have to do in pilot training can cause anxiety the first few times that they are performed. One example is learning to do stalls. When an airplanes stalls, it is put in a condition in which the wings lose their ability to continue to generate enough lift to overcome the forces acting against lift, which is explained in detail in Chap. 5. Stalling an airplane has nothing to do with whether the engine is running or a particular power setting. You can aerodynamically stall the wings at any power setting, from idle to full throttle. A stall is a normal training maneuver and it is not dangerous. In fact, an airplane should be stalled at the end of every flight, since a good landing in a lightplane is nothing more than a stall performed just a few inches above the runway. But some pilots go through their entire flying lives in fear of doing stalls because they were never properly taught to master them. If your instructor is afraid of something that ought to be a part of the normal training routine, change instructors.

The other extreme of instructor behavior can also be an indication of an instructor to avoid. Your flying lessons are not the opportunity for your instructor to demonstrate that he is the greatest pilot since Chuck Yeager or that he ought to be on the air show circuit. If he does anything that makes you truly uncomfortable, or that puts you in fear, he is not doing his job. Have a chat with the chief flight instructor at your school and switch instructors. If this person is the only instructor available, perhaps it's time to switch schools.

Some instructors teach private pilot candidates to perform certain maneuvers beyond those that are the minimum required to pass the flight test and get licensed. I am one of those instructors. Years ago, the 1960s, one of my students returned from a solo practice flight with his face as white as a sheet. After I got him calmed down a bit and we started to talk, we discovered what had happened. While he was practicing stalls, he had accidentally gotten himself into a spin. A spin occurs only when the pilot intentionally puts the airplane into one or mishandles the controls such that the airplane enters the spin itself. When the spin developed, my student had no idea what he had done wrong, and he was naturally terrified. He recovered because he was so scared that he actually let go of the controls. He was flying a Cessna 150, and it, like most airplanes, is designed to recover from a spin itself when the pilot removes the control inputs that were causing the spin. He did the right thing without even realizing it. From that day on, every student that I've taught to fly received a thorough discussion about spins: how they develop, how they are avoided, and how a pilot recovers from them. After that ground session, if the student is willing, and most are, we go up and do a spin entry and recovery together. Once a student experiences how benign a spin really is, and how easy it is to recover from one, the pilot is armed with the knowledge and experience that removes the fear that comes from ignorance.

Some instructors don't believe in actually spinning a student and prefer to concentrate on teaching spin avoidance. The debate over whether spin training is beneficial has been going on in the flight training profession since mandatory spin training was removed from the FAA's list of required maneuvers in the early 1950s. There's no right or wrong answer, just a difference of opinion among well-intentioned pros. I believe in spin training because I think that a pilot can never know too much about any aspect of flying an airplane.

Judging Your Instructor

It's not obvious to a new student pilot what makes a good or poor instructor. Equally competent instructors often differ in their perceptions of what their obligations are and how to best fulfill them to their students. Furthermore, your attitude toward learning is an equally important factor, and it will influence how a good instructor presents material to you. All that said, here are some indicators of a good flight instructor:

- It's not how much your instructor talks but what he says that counts. Good teachers have a knack for dispensing with the superfluous and presenting a concept clearly and simply, without being overly verbose.

- A good instructor will be keenly alert to your level of understanding. If you do not thoroughly understand what she tells you, she will sense that and rephrase it as many times as necessary. She knows that a statement that is perfectly lucid to one person can be confusing to another. We all have preconceived notions that tend to hinder our grasp of certain new subjects, so you, as a good student, will tell her if you aren't grasping her presentation.

- He will not overwhelm you with too many unfamiliar tasks or new concepts at one time.

- A good flight instructor will always explain, before each lesson, exactly what she wants you to do and how to do it. She'll talk no more than is necessary during the flight itself because the cockpit of an airplane is actually a poor classroom. Learning will happen far better and faster if there is no skimping on those all-important preflight briefings. She will also discuss the flight after landing, while your memory is fresh of what you've just done.

- A good instructor has a well-planned, proven syllabus and uses it. Yet, he'll be flexible enough to tailor it to your learning curve.

- A good instructor never pressures a student but relieves as much pressure as possible. He never hurries, shouts, or displays anger or impatience. When a student repeatedly makes the same mistake, the good instructor correctly concludes that the problem lies with the teaching.

- She knows that humor, correctly used, can be a pressure relief valve. That doesn't mean that she engages in horseplay or has a cavalier attitude toward the tasks at hand. A good teacher will have the proclivity to laugh, rather than curse, at minor frustrations.

- He is dependable and punctual. He won't cancel lessons at the last minute. If the weather looks doubtful for a lesson, he'll have the courtesy to call you and discuss whether you should come to the airport. He'll be on time, and he will expect the same from you.

Mutual Respect

Your instructor is a professional, and the relationship between the two of you must be rooted in mutual respect. In many ways, the importance of the relationship should be equal to the relationship you would have with a doctor or lawyer. Your life is in your instructor's hands, not only during your dual instructional lessons but also while you're flying solo, and after you get your license. What you learn, or don't learn, will follow you throughout the time that you fly. If a lack of respect develops from either of you toward the other, it's time to find a new instructor.

A good instructor is going to make you as good a pilot as you can be, and a part of this process will be demanding as much from you as you can deliver. Don't think that your instructor is an ogre for settling for no less than the best that you can deliver. When you are in an airplane alone, or with passengers, the helping hand of your instructor will be there only vicariously, through what you learned during your training days. You will do yourself an extreme disservice by looking for an instructor who will demand less of you than your best.

We have to remember that in the end, we humans aren't really taught much; we learn. Most of our learning happens when we are doing. No instructor can place a funnel in your ear and pour knowledge into your head. The most that your instructor can do is demonstrate, explain, and establish attainable goals. The rest is up to you.

Fewer Student Pilots and the Time Problem

You won't be in aviation for very long before you hear some other pilots lamenting that "back in the good old days" (which probably never were), aviation was a much more vibrant industry than it is today. There is some truth to that statement because flying activity has dropped substantially since the heydays of the 1970s. In 1978, the combined output of all of the general aviation airplane manufacturers was about 19,000 light aircraft units. In 1997, a low point was hit when only about 1,000 airplanes were built.

There are about as many explanations for this decline as there are pundits offering them. Some feel that flying has gotten too expensive. Without considering the new sport pilot certificate and light-sport aircraft regulations, which will lower the cost for those pilots who seek that kind of flying, I don't agree with that analysis of the decline in traditional students pursuing a private pilot's license. When I learned to fly in the summer of 1965, as a freshly minted high school graduate, I was earning $1.55 an hour at a local supermarket as a cashier and also pushing grocery carts out the door to cars waiting in the parking lot. Dual instruction, for both airplane rental and instructor fee, cost $14 per hour in the Champ in which I took my lessons. The multiple of my hourly wage that it took to buy an hour of dual was about 9. In 2002, in our part of the country, teenagers earn around $8 per hour for similar work. Apply the same multiple and you arrive at around $72—about what it costs to buy an hour of dual instruction in a much more capable airplane. Today's trainers have electrical starters (we had to hand prop the old Champ to awaken it), radios, electronic aids to navigation, and even heaters so you can fly in the colder times of the year without wearing a snowmobile suit. In a Champ in 1965, we had none of these amenities.

Some other writers have taken the position that flying has become so complicated now that the fun is gone. That is pure bunk. Sure, large airports have become busier, with more airline traffic than before. Yes, you have to have a bit more equipment in an airplane now to go to the busiest airports, and the rules of the air have expanded a little. But the basic art of flying hasn't changed since World War I, when airplanes became modern in terms of their basic design configurations and methods of aerodynamic control. In fact, it has become easier. Modern tricycle gear trainers are much easier to control on the ground than the older tailwheel airplanes. Training methods have improved dramatically from the days when grizzled old flight instructors yelled at students, and demonstrated that they knew very little about how to teach people anything, even though they might have been very good pilots themselves.

Don't let anyone tell you that flying is any less fun than it ever was. Being aloft is still being aloft. The sky hasn't changed, but the airplanes have, and for the better. They're now easier to fly, much more capable as transportation with modern equipment, much more comfortable, and much more mechanically reliable, and therefore safer. The changes in the regulations have been for good reason and aren't draconian. Thousands of people come into aviation every year, and you should be one of them. If you do want less complicated flying, get a sport pilot license and enjoy the freedom of flight in that environment.

The problem that I do think is real deals with time. I think it's true that middle- and upper-middle-income people do work more hours today for the same disposable income than did their parents' generation. This is simply a fact of the modern, faster-paced world in which we live. Parents have more demands on their leisure time because two-income households are the majority now, and kids' ballgames, school functions, and precious family time all take their toll on the time that people have for their own pursuits. Learning to fly does take some time.

If you are in this position, as many of us are or were, don't be disheartened. A couple of hours per week for a few months at the airport for your lessons isn't cheating your family, your business, or anyone else. Once you've become a private pilot, a whole new world opens up to you, as you'll see in the next chapter. This world of personal aviation involves family trips and business travel not available to those still bound to the ground.

Your family can get involved early in your flight training if they wish. After you've soloed, you will still take more instruction in cross-country trips, night flying, operating into larger airports (or smaller ones if you're learning at a large field), and other subjects. Although it's not wise to take a passenger along on flights when you're doing stalls, or the ground reference maneuvers that we discuss in Chap. 7, ask your instructor if he minds if a passenger or two accompanies you on the more benign training flights. When you fly your night cross-country with your instructor, use a four-seat airplane and take some of your family with you. They'll probably feel very comfortable going along with the experienced instructor, and it's a great opportunity to show them how much fun this is, how beautiful the world is from the cabin of an airplane, and how well you're being taught to be a safe pilot.

Almost everything we do is more enjoyable if it can be shared with good friends or family. Don't leave your loved ones out of the fun. Involve them in it, and everyone will appreciate your time at the airport, rather than possibly being jealous of it.

4

The Private Pilot Certificate

As we said previously, this book is geared to students who want to achieve a private pilot certificate. The reason is that the history of flight training has shown that the recreational pilot's license has not been very popular. We will have to wait a few years to see if the sport pilot certificate follows in the footsteps of the recreational license or if it becomes as popular as its proponents hope it will be. As you will soon see, the privileges of a private pilot are very broad and quickly eclipse those available to a recreational or sport pilot. However, do not forget the recreational and sport licenses. They can be all that some pilots ever need, or each can become a breaking point, with a pilot simply taking a breather from the training regimen and then going on to complete the requirements for a private pilot certificate. Let's take a look at what it takes to become first a student pilot and then to get the private license.

Student Pilot Requirements

As the regulations are currently written, you don't need a student pilot certificate until you are ready to fly solo. Presently, any person can take instruction, regardless of age or any other qualifying factor. But to solo, you've got to have a student pilot certificate. Since the tragic events of September 11, 2001, there is still some talk about background checks for anyone wishing to take instruction. Therefore, don't be surprised if you are queried some when you go to a flight school before your flight training actually begins.

FAR 61.83 lays out the requirements to obtain a student license. These requirements are very straightforward and simple. First, you have to be at least 16 years old unless you want student privileges that will be valid only in gliders or balloons, in which case the minimum age is 14. You have to be able to read, speak, write, and understand the English language. But if you can't meet those requirements for any medical reasons, the FAA can limit your certificate accordingly. Remember that we said that people who are totally hearing impaired can fly? That is an example of a person's failing the requirement to understand spoken English. The FAA will allow a deaf person to fly, but it will limit his flying to airspace where radio contact isn't required with air traffic controllers. Further, to solo in a powered aircraft that is not a sport-light aircraft, which includes helicopters and airplanes, you have to have a third-class medical certificate, which we discussed in the previous chapter. That's it; no more is required to obtain a student pilot's license.

Once a student pilot is trained, and once her logbook and student certificate are properly endorsed by a flight instructor, she may fly an airplane solo. Your instructor must give you a presolo knowledge test of his own making that covers specified areas of knowledge before you can solo. On your student license, which is combined in one document with your third-class medical certificate, there are places for the instructor to endorse it for local solo and solo cross-country flights. Your instructor may place any limitations that he wants in your endorsements, and they will be put in your pilot logbook. Your solo flight privileges can be restricted in any way that the instructor sees fit.

In addition to the limitations that your instructor may put in your logbook, the FARs also limit flights by student pilots. For instance, a student may not act as pilot in command of an airplane carrying a passenger. If you take any passengers along on any of your training flights, your instructor must be in the airplane and acting as the pilot in command. A student pilot cannot carry passengers in airplanes under any circumstances.

In addition, students can't make business flights if the student is acting as the pilot in command (PIC). You'll see that there are requirements for certain solo cross-country flight experience before you are eligible to take the flight test for your private pilot license. The regulations prohibit business flying by students, so while you are still a student pilot, you can't legally solo cross-country to attend a business meeting or to accomplish some other business purpose. But you can always make a business trip if your instructor is along and acting as the PIC. When we previously talked in the last chapter about the time problem that besets so many people who learn to fly, we didn't mention all the ways that the time problem can be alleviated. One way, for example, is asking your instructor to take you on dual instruction cross-country flights that fit in with your business travel needs. This is a great way to double up on the time effectiveness of your training. Don't be put off if your instructor is hesitant at some point in your training to accommodate these kinds of requests. You may be asking him to go too far, into an airport that is either too busy or too small to accomplish the real training that you need, or perhaps you would be trying to push things just a little too far, too soon for your level of experience and skill at the moment. But, at the right time, to the right places, dual instruction cross-country trips that fit into your other needs can be very productive, and you could even carry a passenger or two along.

Basic Private Pilot License Requirements

There are many requirements for getting a private pilot license that encompass training, knowledge, and experience standards. We'll deal with each of these in more detail and separately, but for now let's see what the basic requirements are. An applicant for a private pilot's license for airplanes must be at least 17 years old. A private glider and balloon pilot need be only 16. Just as those required of student pilots, the candidate must read, speak, write, and understand English. If you can't do one or more of these for a medical reason, you can still get a private pilot license that will be limited in such a manner that your physical deficit does not compromise flight safety.

Then you have to have undergone the required training for the knowledge test, get an endorsement from your instructor that you're ready to take it, and then pass it. You have to repeat those steps for the flight training—take the training, get an endorsement that you're ready to take the flight test, and then pass the flight test. Other than having a medical certificate, which must be at least third class, that's all you need to accomplish. Now let's break down the knowledge and flight portions of the requirements.

Aeronautical knowledge

FAR Section 61.105 outlines the areas of aeronautical knowledge that are required of a private pilot license applicant. We'll touch upon most of these subjects in later chapters in detail. Don't let this list be intimidating. It's a lot less complicated and severe than it looks at first sight. These are the basic subject matter areas covered on the knowledge test:

- Applicable FARs that relate to private pilot license privileges, limitations, and flight operations

- The accident reporting requirements of the National Transportation Safety Board (NTSB)

- Use of the *Aeronautical Information Manual* and *Advisory Circulars* as published by the FAA

- Use of aeronautical charts (maps) for navigation by various means

- Radio communication procedures

- Recognition of critical weather situations from the ground and in flight, windshear avoidance, and the procurement and use of aeronautical weather reports and forecasts

- Safe and efficient operation of aircraft, including collision avoidance and recognition and avoidance of wake turbulence

- Effects of density altitude on takeoff and climb performance

- Weight and balance computations

- Principles of aerodynamics, power plants, and aircraft systems

- Stall awareness, spin entry, spins and spin recovery techniques for ratings in airplanes and gliders

- Aeronautical decision making and judgment

- Preflight action that includes how to obtain information on runway lengths at airports of intended use, data on takeoff and landing distances, weather reports and forecasts, fuel requirements, and how to plan for alternatives if the planned flight cannot be completed or if delays are encountered

Even though this list can look foreboding to a beginning student, learning these things really isn't in practice. Your ground school training, supplemented by the preflight and postflight discussions with your flight instructor, will sail you through it. None of this is rocket science; if you're a person of normal intelligence, with a reasonable degree of dedication to the task at hand, you'll learn it all in time. We'll cover most of this material in the succeeding chapters, so just hang in there with us, and you'll see how easily it all comes together.

Flight proficiency

For the practical test, you will be required to demonstrate to the examiner that you can fly an airplane. What constitutes the ability to fly varies with the different levels of pilot certificates being sought and the ratings that you want to add to them. Again, remember that ratings apply to the kinds of aircraft that you seek to fly and in what kind of weather you want to fly in. As you can naturally expect, a private pilot isn't required to do the same things that a commercial pilot or higher is. But as you will see in a short while, when we discuss the privileges of a private pilot, private pilots have very broad operational privileges. So, the flight test is thorough, without being unduly daunting. Here's a list of what a candidate for a private pilot certificate must demonstrate during the flight check:

- Preflight preparation
- Preflight procedures
- Airport operations
- Takeoffs, landings, and go-arounds
- Performance maneuvers
- Ground reference maneuvers
- Navigation
- Slow flight and stalls
- Basic instrument maneuvers
- Emergency operations

- Night operations

- Postflight procedures

All of these procedures and the standards for them are detailed in an FAA publication called *The Practical Test Standards,* or PTS. There is a PTS put out for each level of certificate from private pilot through airline transport pilot, which is the highest pilot's license obtainable. There is also a PTS for each of the various ratings that can be attached to the levels of pilot certificates. Remember that a level of pilot certificate basically determines the privileges that a pilot has, and the rating describes, for the most part, either the various aircraft in which he may exercise those privileges or the weather conditions in which he may fly. Let's use my certificate and ratings as an example.

I hold a commercial pilot certificate. That means that I can fly for hire under certain conditions, but I cannot be the captain of a scheduled airliner; that job requires an airline transport pilot (ATP) certificate. On my commercial license, I have ratings for single- and multiengine land airplanes. That covers airplanes that have normal landing gear to operate from the ground. There are also ratings for single- and multiengine sea planes, which allow the pilot to fly from the water. I am also rated for helicopters and gliders, which means that I can exercise the privileges of a commercial pilot in those two vary dissimilar types of aircraft. I have an airplane instrument rating, which means that I can fly airplanes under *instrument meteorological conditions* (IMC) when *instrument flight rules* (IFR) are in effect. While you're doing your training, and until you get an instrument rating, you will be limited to flying under *visual flight rules* (VFR), which means that you must stay out of the clouds, maintain certain distances from them, and have forward flight visibility of certain distances.

In addition, I possess a flight instructor certificate, with ratings for single- and multiengine airplanes and instruments. This means that I can teach flying in those airplanes and also can instruct instrument flying.

There are many other ratings available. A pilot can be rated for balloons, airships, and a new class of aircraft called *powered lift.* The only civilian powered-lift aircraft that presently exists is still in the experimental form. Powered-lift aircraft have tilt rotors or tilt wings that enable the plane to take off vertically like a helicopter and then, with the tilting of either the wings or rotors to the horizontal position, fly like an airplane in cruise flight. Another type of powered-lift aircraft is the Marine Corps AV-8 Harrier, but this military attack aircraft has no civilian equivalent at present. When the FAA rewrote many of the pilot certificate regulations in 1997, it included powered lift as a new class of aircraft to provide a mechanism to rate pilots in them when these advanced aircraft do become available to the civilian market.

We're not quite finished yet with the requirements for a basic private pilot's license, with a rating for single-engine land airplanes, which is the typical first pilot's license that a person gets. Beyond the required areas of aeronautical knowledge in flight proficiency that we've just listed, the candidate must also have a minimum level of experience before she is allowed to take the flight test. At this point you should understand that very few students, if any these days, can accomplish all of the needed training and get up to the performance standard in these stated minimum amounts of time.

First, you must have a minimum of 40 hours of total flight time. That 40 hours must include at least 20 hours of instruction from your flight instructor and a minimum of 10 hours of solo flying time. Of these minimums, you must also have the following:

- At least 3 hours of cross-country dual instruction

- At least 3 hours of night instruction that includes a cross-country flight of no less than 100 miles, and 10 takeoffs and 10 landings, to a full stop, at an airport

- Three hours of instrument flight instruction

- Three hours of dual instruction in preparation for the practical test, with this training having been received within 60 days of the date that you actually take your flight test

- Five hours of solo cross-country flight

- One solo cross-country flight of at least 150 nautical miles total distance, with full-stop landings at a minimum of 3 points, with one segment of the flight consisting of a straight-line distance of at least 50 nautical miles between a takeoff and a landing

- Three takeoffs and landings to a full stop at an airport that has an operating control tower

That's the minimum experience required for a private pilot's license. Most people will take around 60 hours' or so total flying time to get the job done, even though the bare minimum is 40 hours. I've seen students take even far more hours than 60, and in the end they have become very safe and competent pilots. Don't ever be discouraged if you don't take the flight test at any given arbitrary number of total hours. What you learn, and retain, is far more vital than how long it takes you to do it. We are not running any sprints in flight training; rather, we are jogging in a lifelong marathon, and we will pace ourselves accordingly.

Privileges and Limitations

When you read the regulations, particularly FAR 61.113, you see that they speak more in the negative than they do in the positive concerning what a private pilot may or may not do. This is because a private pilot really has few limitations on the exercise of his certificate. The basic difference between what a private pilot can do compared to the higher commercial and airline transport licenses relates to operating an aircraft for compensation or hire. A private pilot may obtain virtually any of the ratings set out in the regulations for any category, class, or type of aircraft. Theoretically, a private pilot could be rated to fly an airliner type of aircraft. He simply can't do it for hire or in any common carriage of persons or property.

Many private pilots get instrument ratings, and, in fact, that should be the next training goal for any new pilot who wants to expand her knowledge and scope of operations. With an instrument rating, and in an airplane properly equipped, a private pilot may fly anywhere that any other pilot can go, and do it in IFR weather. Although airline pilots routinely get special authorization to operate in very low ceiling and visibility conditions, from a practical point of view, an instrument-rated private pilot is authorized to operate in almost all flight environments. It's not at all uncommon for private pilots to become rated in multiengine airplanes and fly light twin-engine airplanes. That rating, coupled with an instrument rating, means that the multiengine-rated private pilot can operate some very exotic machinery. Airplanes that weigh over 12,500 pounds for takeoff, and all jets regardless of weight, require what is known as a *type rating,* which means that the pilot must pass a flight test and get a special rating on her license for each such type of aircraft. I have a friend who is a private pilot and who is rated for a Cessna Citation, which is a twin-engine jet. He owns and flies this jet himself, not for hire but only in pursuit of his own business endeavors. The point is that a private pilot has the world of aviation open to him, except that he cannot fly for hire.

What constitutes "flying for hire" has been the subject of years of debate, litigation, and court decisions. In the 1997 amendments to the FARs, some of this confusion was eliminated.

When a private pilot wants to take some passengers along and asks them to share in the cost of the flight, how those costs were split used to be a subject of intense debate until the new regulations came out. Now it's pretty simple. If a private pilot owns the airplane, he may collect from each passenger only a pro rata share of fuel and oil consumed during the flight and incidental expenses attributable to that flight, like airport landing fees. If our private pilot rents an aircraft, he must pay a pro rata share of the rental costs, along with each passenger. Getting anything more from the passengers is illegal because that constitutes flying for hire.

In the past there was confusion about whether private pilots could fly tow airplanes, towing gliders, even though they weren't paid in the sense you and I think of paying for something. The FAA had taken the position that free flying time is compensation. Therefore, under the old regulations, a private pilot, flying in a glider club, towing gliders, was deemed to be receiving compensation because she was flying for nothing. Now the regulations clearly state that a private pilot who meets the other requirements for glider towing may fly an airplane that is towing gliders as long as she is not paid money to do it. Private pilots may also fly in the pursuit of their own or their employer's business as long as the flight is incidental to that business and no people or property are carried for hire. Let's say, for instance, that you are a regional salesperson who travels an area of a few states in the course of your job. You are paid by your employer for doing that job, regardless of how you choose to travel from one place to another. The reason that you may choose to fly an airplane, as a private pilot, on your travels has nothing to do with the flying as far as your job duties are concerned. You are just using an airplane instead of an automobile or an airliner or a bus to get you from one place to another. That is the definition of flying that is incidental to the business: The business is not the flying; it's the selling of whatever product or service it is that you peddle. It's perfectly legal to do that as a private pilot. I would venture a guess that close to a majority of the private pilots, if not more, fly at least some of their time for just such an incidental business purpose.

Private pilots can also fly if they are employed as an aircraft salesperson and demonstrate aircraft for sale to potential customers as long as they have a least 200 hours of total flight time logged. The rules also allow private pilots to fly in charity-sponsored airlifts for which the charity collects a donation for the airplane ride if the pilot has 200 hours logged and conducts the flight in day VFR conditions. There are some other hoops that the charity has to jump through to make it legal, but the idea here is that the pilot is not getting compensated. The FAA actually blesses this type of flight activity when conducted by private pilots.

As you can now begin to see, a private pilot has a world of operating privileges. The big "no-no" for private pilots is getting compensated for their services while flying an aircraft. As long as they stay within the boundary of not receiving direct compensation, once they get the proper ratings for aircraft and weather, there is little that a private pilot cannot do that pilots at higher levels can do.

Staying Current

Although a private pilot certificate never expires, you have to do a few things to remain current and able legally to exercise the privileges of that license. First, you must hold at least a third-class medical certificate. A third-class medical expires on the last day of the 24th month after it was issued. If you passed your physical exam on May 1, 2002, your third-class certificate is good through May 31, 2004. If you're fortunate enough to be less than 40 years old, a third-class medical is good for 36 calendar months instead of 24.

Private pilots must also complete a *biennial flight review* (BFR) with an instructor every 24 calendar months. This is an instructional session that must include a minimum of 1 hour of ground training and 1 hour of flight training. The FAA's idea behind this requirement is that every pilot needs recurrent training. To accomplish that, the FAA uses the BFR to ensure that a pilot meets with an instructor and discusses any changes in the regulations or operating practices that have arisen since the last BFR and flies with the instructor for at least an hour to ensure that there is no rust on that pilot's skills that needs to be cleaned off.

To carry any passengers or to fly at night, you also have to meet the *recent flight experience* requirements of FAR 61.57. In essence, to carry any passengers, you have to have made at least three takeoffs and landings in the past 90 days, in the same class of aircraft (which for most private pilots means a single-engine land airplane) as you will use to fly the passenger. If your flight is to be at night, you also have to have performed at least three takeoffs and landings at night within the last 90 days.

The Logbook

Pilots are also required to keep a logbook and enter into it all flight time that they intend to use to obtain any license or ratings. Pilots also have to log all of the time necessary to show that they meet the currency requirements that we just discussed. Other than that, there is no FAA requirement to log flying time. However, most insurance companies require that a pilot have a certain minimum amount of time in certain airplanes before they will insure that pilot in that airplane. Most pilots are very diligent in logging their time. In my flying, which began in 1965, I have had fewer than a dozen hours, at most, that aren't recorded in one of several logbooks. A pilot does himself no favor by failing to log time. All of your dual flight instruction must also be logged and endorsed by your flight instructor. Whenever a student pilot is flying solo cross-country, he must have his logbook with him because the FARs require that the instructor endorse, in the logbook, permission to make every solo cross-country flight. If you are spot-checked by an FAA inspector while on a solo cross-country flight, you will have to produce your logbook to show that you have the required endorsement.

Legal Documents

There are a few documents that have to be carried either in the airplane or on your person when you're flying. In the airplane itself, a certificate of registration and another piece of paper called the *airworthiness certificate* must be prominently displayed. The certificate of registration is a form from the FAA's Aircraft Registry that shows who is the registered owner of the airplane. The airworthiness certificate is also issued by the FAA, and it says that the airplane met all of the certification standards when manufactured and that as long as it is maintained in accordance with the regulations, the airplane is airworthy to fly.

Also, the FAA-approved flight manual must be carried in the airplane. This manual specifies certain operating and emergency procedures and parameters, and it also shows the weight and balance limits within which the airplane must be operated.

Whenever you fly as pilot in command, you must carry your medical and pilot certificates on your person. The FARs require that you must present either or both of these certificates for inspection upon the request of any FAA inspector, representative of the National Transportation Safety Board, or any federal, state, or local law enforcement officer.

You have to show the requested certificate to any of those people who ask to see it, but that's all you have to do. You do not have to surrender it to anyone without protracted legal proceedings aimed at you if you are charged with a violation of an FAR. Don't give up your certificate to any of those persons who are authorized to demand to see it—just show it to them. However, you may encounter a local police officer who might never have seen a pilot certificate before and doesn't realize that you aren't required to surrender it in the same way you might be required to surrender your driver's license. Use common sense, and don't get into a tussle with the locals over this fine point. You can always get a duplicate certificate from the FAA if that need arises.

5

The Airplane

Pilots have to have a working knowledge of enough aerodynamics and theory of flight to safely fly their airplanes. No one in the flight training industry is going to try to make you into an aeronautical engineer, and there are no fancy academics involved with what a private pilot must know. Most of us don't fully understand the inner workings of the computers on our desks, but we know enough about them to make them work and do what we need to perform on them. Look at this chapter the same way; learn what you need to know to understand how an airplane flies and how to get it do what you want it to do, but keep in mind that you certainly don't have to understand all of the inner details of its engineering to be able to safely and efficiently fly it.

An airplane flies on its wings. The wings produce *lift,* which is what we call the force that keeps us aloft. Lift must either overcome or equal the weight of the airplane, depending on what we want the airplane to do. Think of most of these concepts as involving two forces, each opposing the other. Lift opposes *gravity.* Wings produce lift, and they come in a variety of sizes and shapes. A jet fighter may have short wings, while a glider has long and narrow wings, and the Concorde has delta-shaped wings. Even a helicopter has wings—the main rotor blades do the same job as fixed wings do on airplanes. They all have one function: to produce enough lift to oppose gravity.

Wings produce lift as a product of the air that flows over them when the airplane is in forward motion. Most wings are designed to have *camber,* which is the term used to describe the curvature of the wing when viewed in cross section. The shape of the wing seen from looking at the wing tip is

5-1 *Typical lightplane airfoil: The shape of the wing produces the lift.*

shown in FIG. 5-1. The word *airfoil* is another term used to describe the lifting surface of an airplane, and, as you'll see a bit later, the propeller also produces lift. The curve on the upper surface of the wing is more pronounced than the curvature along the bottom of the wing.

The greater the difference between these two curvatures, the more lift the wing can produce at low speeds, where light airplanes operate. More lift is produced as the upper curvature becomes greater than the curve on the lower surface. Lift occurs because, as the airplane moves forward through the air, the stream of air is forced to separate at the *leading* (front) *edge* of the wing, after which the stream comes back together at the *trailing* (rear) *edge*. Because the upper surface has the more pronounced curvature, the molecules of air that flow over the top of the wing have to travel a greater distance than do the molecules that travel along the lower surface. The molecules then join up again as the stream of air reaches the trailing edge of the wing. For reasons determined by the laws of physics, the molecules that go over the top and those that go under the lower surface of the wing must remain opposite each other as they make their respective trips along both surfaces of the wing. To remain opposite each other, those molecules that go over the top have to go faster because they are going farther than do the ones going under the wing.

5-2 *Normal airflow pattern around a wing in flight.*

When the molecules of air that are going over the top of the wing gain speed, they thin out, and there is more space between them. When any gas (and air is a gas) thins out, the gas loses pressure, and a partial vacuum develops. This partial vacuum acts as a suction force on the top of the wing, constantly trying to pull the wing upward. FIGURE 5-2 shows this effect as it is seen in a wind tunnel.

The amount of lift that a wing produces can be increased in two ways. The first, and the least effective method, is to increase the absolute speed at which the wing is traveling through the air. As this absolute speed increases, so does the differential in the speed of the air going over the top and that which is moving along the underside of the wing. Because the partial vacuum that provides lift is a result of this differential, the greater the differential, the more lift that is produced. However, the range of the operating speeds of light airplanes is not very large. Most of the trainer types that you'll fly have minimum (stalling) speeds somewhere around 50 knots, and cruising speeds just slightly over 100 knots. It is plain to see that you can increase the absolute speed of this type of airplane only around 50 knots or so, which isn't very much. Jets, with minimum speeds around 120 knots and maximums over 500 knots, have a much wider operating range, so their differences in absolute speeds through the air are much greater.

The other method by which all airplanes can increase the amount of lift produced by the wings is to raise the leading edge upward, which can be thought of as tipping the wing so that the leading edge is higher than the trailing edge. This

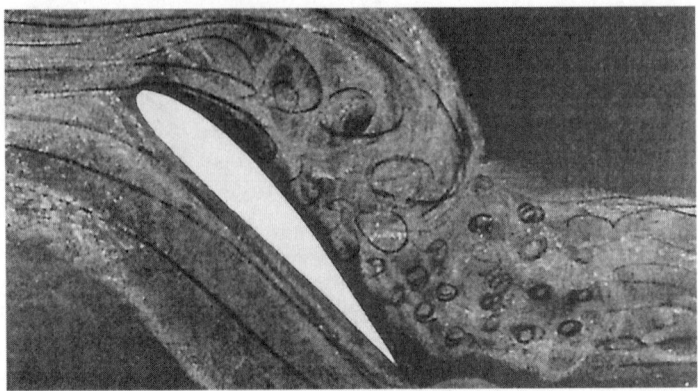

5-3 *A stalled wing. The flow of air over the upper surface is interrupted; therefore, the lift is destroyed.*

causes the oncoming stream of air, which we call the *relative wind,* to strike the lower surface of the wing, generating a deflection force from underneath, which also pushes the wing upward and supplements the lift that is produced by the partial vacuum on the wing's upper surface. The extent to which a wing can be tilted up is limited. If it's tilted too much, the airflow along the wing's upper surface is interrupted because it can no longer adhere to that upper surface. When the airflow over the top of the wing is interrupted, it loses its adherence to that surface, the partial vacuum is lost, and most of the wing's lift is lost with it. When this happens, the wing is *stalled,* and the airflow looks as it does in FIG. 5-3.

Angle of Attack and Stalls

Everything that an airplane does in flight depends on the angle at which the leading edge of the wing meets the oncoming stream of air. This angle is called the *angle of attack.* The angle of attack is the whole story of flight, as the relative wind meets the wing. A kite flies by the lift produced by the angle of attack alone. Kites don't have cambered lifting surfaces that aircraft wings have; they fly purely because of their attitude, which is in a nose-up position relative to the ground. This angle of attack causes the wind blowing across a kite to strike the underside of it and force it upward.

If you go too slowly in an airplane while pulling the nose higher to try to maintain flight, the wing will stall. A wing can be stalled at any speed, including the airplane's top speed. To accomplish a stall, all you have to do is simply increase the angle of attack past its critical point, which is normally between 16 and 18° in a light airplane. Doing so causes the relative wind to strike the wing below the leading edge, and, regardless of the speed, the air can no longer flow around the lifting surfaces in the smoothly adhered pattern that is necessary to produce lift. Then, the wing stalls. The wing can be stalled with the airplane in any attitude relative to the ground: in a turn, a climb, or a dive pull-out and with the wings either level or banked. Whether the wing is still producing lift, which we call "flying," or it is stalled has absolutely nothing to do with whether the engine is running or the power setting that the pilot has selected. Don't confuse stalling of the wing with the engine's output of power or lack thereof. Stalling is a product of only one thing: an excessive angle of attack.

Gliders have no engine, but they still fly. Their wings produce lift as a glider moves through the air just the same as do the wings of a powered airplane. In the rare instance that an engine fails in an airplane, the wings still produce lift, and the pilot glides down, selects a landing site, and lands. Airplanes don't fall out of the sky if the engine quits. Stalling the wing is what destroys lift, not shutting off the engine power.

The flying characteristics of modern light airplanes are such that you have to intentionally stall them or be totally unaware of what is happening, which would mean that you did not receive instruction in stalls. The airplane will give plenty of warning prior to stalling. The entire airplane will buffet, and you will feel the controls become very sloppy and ineffective before the stall actually develops. Only very poor piloting technique results in unintentional stalls in modern airplanes. During your flight training, stalls will be taught and practiced repeatedly. You need to know how to perform a stall in order to properly land the airplane because a good landing is nothing more than a stall performed just inches above the runway. The other reason that you learn stalls is so you can recognize the conditions that lead to them and thereby avoid unintentional stalls.

Recovery from a stall happens only one way, and that is by reducing the angle of attack so that the airflow can resume its normal smooth and adhered path across both the upper and lower surfaces of the wing. The angle of attack is normally reduced by lowering the nose attitude of the airplane; once that is done, the wing immediately starts producing lift again and the stall is ended.

Stall Warning Devices

All modern airplanes have some sort of device to warn the pilot of an impending stall. The first of these, which is built into the airplane by the design engineers, is the aerodynamic warning that occurs when the entire airplane buffets, possibly accompanied by the control wheel shaking in the pilot's hands. Without either of the other two types of stall warnings that we'll talk about in the next paragraphs, this first aerodynamic warning ought to tell any alert pilot that the airplane is about to stall. This warning will come in plenty of time to reduce the angle of attack to avoid an unintentional stall.

Almost all airplanes have an additional warning that is either visual or aural. There is a sensor on the leading edge of the wing, usually in the form of a little metal tab. This tab is mounted in such a way that it is forced upward, traveling about $1/2$ inch in its mounting hardware, when the relative wind begins striking the leading edge from too far below it to continue normal lift. The tab then moves and activates an electrical switch.

This switch then either sounds a horn in the cockpit or turns on a bright red light. The horn is usually mounted in the ceiling of the cockpit near the pilot's head. If you can't hear the horn, you've either been to too many rock concerts or your kid plays her CD player much too loudly at home. If your airplane is equipped with a light for the stall warning device, the light itself is placed on the instrument panel, right in front of your eyes. When the light comes on, it dominates all that you see. Regardless of which type of stall warning system is in your airplane, it is calibrated to activate before the stall is fully developed, so that you again have ample time to correct the angle of attack to prevent the unintentional stall.

These tabs on the leading edge of the wing can get out of adjustment. When you're practicing stalls or landing, if you don't hear the horn or see the light, have the maintenance people take a look. The tab could be misaligned, or there could be a fault in the electrical connections between the tab and cockpit horn or light, or there could be a blown fuse or popped circuit breaker in the system.

Thrust and Drag

The only purpose of the engine in an airplane is to propel it forward through the air. The propulsive force is called *thrust*. Propellers are airfoils, and they act upon the air in the same manner as does the wing. When you look at a propeller from the tip of its blade, sighting down the blade toward the hub, you can see that the propeller blade has increased curvature on the front side. This curvature produces lift. Because the propeller is mounted vertically, the lift that it produces is aligned to pull the airplane forward. The makeup of a propeller blade is shown in FIG. 5-4.

Propeller blades are also slightly twisted so that their undersides strike the stream of oncoming air at a positive angle of attack (see FIG. 5-4). This deflection of the air pushes the propeller forward just the same as the positive angle of attack of a wing pushes that wing upward. When you stand behind an airplane on the ground (at a safe distance from it) that has its engine running, you'll feel the "prop blast" as the air is deflected backward, away from the propeller.

As the airplane moves forward through the air, it has resistance to that motion. This resistance is called *drag*. Drag comes from many sources. The first source of drag is *induced drag*, which is the resistance created by the wing as it moves through

5-4 *The blade of a propeller.*

the air in the process of producing lift. When we raise the leading edge of the wing and increase the angle of attack, more of the wing's lower surface is presented to the relative wind. When you increase the amount of the surface area of the bottom of the wing that is struck by the oncoming air, the amount of drag goes up too. The pilot alters the amount of induced drag that is acting upon the airplane when the angle of attack is changed to climb, descend, or return to level flight.

To some extent, when the wing is tilted upward to increase the angle of attack, the increase in the induced drag is also caused by the body of the airplane, which is called the *fuselage,* as it naturally tilts up with the wing. Then, more of the lower surface of the fuselage is also struck by the oncoming airflow, and the fuselage offers resistance to it. This portion of the induced drag changes along with a change in induced drag from the pilot's varying the angle of attack of the wing throughout the flight.

The other source of drag is a *parasite drag.* Parasite drag is the resistance caused by all of the appendages and equipment on the airplane. Things like landing gear, wing struts, and radio antennas are the main contributors to parasite drag. That is why high-performance airplanes have retractable landing gear; they can be raised by the pilot once the airplane has taken off, and this gets the gear out of the airflow and eliminates the parasite drag that it would produce. Modern radio installations in higher-performance airplanes often incorporate the antennas in an internal mounting, either inside the wings or inside the fuselage.

Just as the lift produced by the wings must overcome, or in cruise flight must be equal to, the weight of the airplane, thrust must overcome, be equal to, or be less than total drag, depending on what the pilot wants the airplane to do. If he wants to increase speed while remaining at a level altitude, he will increase the thrust by increasing the power setting of the engine. If the goal is to go slower, he will decrease the power. In normal cruise flight, when a speed through the air is neither increasing nor decreasing, the thrust will be equal to all of the forces of the total drag.

Center of Gravity

In flight, an airplane is a balanced machine that can rotate three ways (on three axes) about its *center of gravity*. As shown in FIG. 5-5, these axes all converge at the center of gravity, which

5-5 *The three axes: An airplane "rolls" around the longitudinal axis Z, it "pitches" around the horizontal axis X, and it yaws about the vertical axis Y.*

is the balance point of the airplane. The exact location of the center of gravity will change and be at different points on the airplane according to how it is loaded with people, cargo, and fuel. The center of gravity will usually change a little throughout the flight as fuel is consumed. To prevent the airplane from becoming out of balance, there are specified limits on exactly where the center of gravity must be. This is necessary to have the airplane always be within its design center-of-gravity range. These limits are expressed as the *loading envelope.* The loading envelope is usually presented as a graph or series of graphs that depict where the center of gravity will be with alternative loading arrangements. The loading envelope also shows the pilot the maximum design weight of the airplane, which cannot be exceeded regardless of how the load is distributed.

You will be taught how to use the loading envelope during your training. It is extremely important to always know both where the center of gravity is and will be throughout the flight and also what the entire weight of the airplane is before you begin your takeoff. If you begin a flight within the total weight limit, you will be OK for that requirement throughout your flight because the airplane is consistently getting lighter as fuel is burned. But you cannot make the same assumption about the center of gravity. There are airplanes, particularly the

Beechcraft Bonanzas, in which you can be within the center-of-gravity range at takeoff but fall outside permissible limits before landing because the burning of fuel alters the location of the center of gravity.

The *center of lift* is a term that should not be confused with *center of gravity*. The center of lift is the center point of the low-pressure area on the top surface of the wing. The center of lift will change as the angle of attack changes. It also has a design range of limits, and exceeding the permissible range results in a stall if the center of lift is moved too far forward by too great an angle of attack.

The primary flight controls that the pilot uses to control the airplane are the *control wheel* or *stick* and the *rudder pedals*. These are connected to the movable surfaces on the wings and the tail by either steel cables or tubular mechanical linkages. The flight control system functions the same way on virtually all airplanes, whether they are light airplanes, jet fighters, or airliners (FIG. 5-6). By changing the camber of the wings and

5-6 *Flight control surfaces: A, ailerons; F, flaps; S, horizontal stabilizer; E, elevators; T, trim; V, vertical stabilizer or fin; R, rudder.*

the deflection of the tail surfaces, and their reaction to the changes in the relative wind that are produced as a result, the airplane will change its attitude.

Pitching the Nose Up or Down

Some airplanes have a control stick, but most modern ones use a control wheel. When the pilot pushes the wheel forward, the *elevators* (which are attached to the *horizontal stabilizer* on the tail) are deflected downward. The relative wind strikes the lowered elevators, which pushes the airplane's tail up and forces the nose down. When you pull back on the wheel, the elevators are raised, and this pushes the tail down and pulls the nose up. Because the airplane is balanced around its center of gravity, the motion of the tail, whether up or down, forces the nose in the opposite direction.

Another product of the control wheel's movement and effect is that forward and aft movement of the wheel control both the nose attitude of the airplane and the angle of attack of the wings. Forward motion decreases the angle of attack and lowers the nose at the same time; pulling the wheel back toward you simultaneously increases the angle of attack and raises the nose.

Trim

Trim is an adjustment of certain controls to eliminate the need for a pilot to constantly apply control pressure to hold the airplane in a desired attitude. All airplanes have trim for the forward and rear pressures that have to be applied to the control wheel to keep the nose at a desired attitude. Some higher-performance light airplanes also have a trim for the rudder, so that the pilot doesn't have to constantly push on one of the two pedals to keep the nose aligned where she wants it. Few, if any, trainers have any trim other than for the up and down pressures necessary to keep the nose attitude where the pilot wants it.

There are two mechanical ways in which nose trim is accomplished. The less common mechanism is to have a control in the cockpit that adjusts the entire horizontal stabilizer either up or down, thus changing its angle of attack so that the tail can be made to ride higher or lower in level flight. Changing the tail's angle of attack is used to compensate for varying loads in the airplane or for different speeds at which the airplane is flying. Older aircraft, such as the Piper J-3 Cub or the Piper TriPacer, are examples of airplanes that use this type of trim mechanism.

In more modern and typical training airplanes, elevator forces are trimmed by a device called a *trim tab,* which is attached to the trailing edge of one or both of the elevators. The trim tab on the Cessna 150 is shown as item T in FIG. 5-6. As the trim tab is moved up or down by means of a small wheel in the cockpit, the elevator rides higher or lower, with the same effect as adjusting the angle of the entire horizontal stabilizer.

Many popular trainers have a *stabilator* in place of the fixed horizontal stabilizer and hinged elevators. The stabilator is a one-piece system that moves in its entirety as the control wheel is pulled back or pushed forward. A stabilator is generally more aerodynamically efficient, for a given size, than is the more traditional combination of a fixed horizontal stabilizer and movable elevator. The use of a stabilator allows a design engineer to save weight by using a smaller control surface or a shorter fuselage. Regardless of how your airplane is equipped, both systems control the nose attitude and trim of the airplane through the control wheel and trim control in the cockpit. From the pilot's perspective as she flies the airplane, there isn't any difference between the two.

Once an airplane is properly trimmed, it will virtually fly itself without constant control input from the pilot. But any change in the power setting, such as that required to level off from a climb or to begin a descent, will call for a minor adjustment of trim. In 1997 there was an incident that gave us stark proof of just how stable a small airplane is. A pilot was hand propping (turning the propeller by hand) an Aeronca Champ to start it, which is the only way these old classic airplanes are started. Unfortunately, the throttle was not set at idle but had been pushed forward far enough for the engine to develop significant power once it caught and began running. The other unfortunate part of this story is that the airplane had no one in it when the engine started. It began to roll, gaining speed as it went. As it broke ground and began flying, it narrowly missed a hangar at the Urbana, Ohio, airport, where this misadventure began. It took off and flew for two hours, covering over 90 miles, climbing as high as 12,000 feet at one point, before it ran out of gas and came to rest in a bean field three counties away.

Throughout this flight, the airplane was being chased by a helicopter and an Ohio State Highway Patrol airplane and was monitored on radar by the FAA. In the end, this entire episode was comical because no one was hurt, and no property was damaged other than the airplane itself. Several of us wondered how the hapless owner was explaining this to his insurance company. I'm sure your instructor will be in your airplane before you start it.

Turning the Airplane

Turning the control wheel to the left or right causes the airplane to bank its wings in the same direction as the wheel is turned. Turn the wheel to the right and you raise the *aileron* on the right wing, while simultaneously lowering the one on the left wing. The stream of air over the wings hits these deflected ailerons and forces the right wing down and the left wing up.

Once the wings are banked, the airplane begins to turn. Now is the time to dispel some confusion. Airplanes also have a *rudder,* which is attached to the vertical stabilizer and is shown as item R in FIG. 5-6. Because most of us have had at least some passing acquaintance with boats, many people think that an airplane's rudder turns it as a boat's rudder turns a boat. This is not so. What turns an airplane is the force of lift. Lift always remains perpendicular to the wings, regardless of the attitude of the wings, level or banked. When we bank the airplane, the force of lift pulls the airplane around in the turn. You'll see in your training that the normal stalling speed of an airplane increases as the angle of bank increases. This is because some portion of the total lift being developed by the wings must now be diverted away from the task of overcoming gravity and directed toward the task of turning. Hence, to overcome gravity and keep the airplane flying, the total of all lift must increase in a turn because only a part of the total lift is being used to keep the airplane up. So the speed at which you will stall is higher in a bank because the total needed lift can't be produced at the same, slower speed that will suffice for level flight.

However, the rudder does have a function to perform in turning an airplane. To produce a balanced, coordinated turn, you have to use both ailerons and the rudder. If you bank an airplane using the ailerons alone, the entry into the bank is sloppy, and the nose actually slides, momentarily, to the opposite side. This is caused by a situation known as *adverse yaw.* If you are in normal straight and level flight and you press a rudder pedal, the nose will point in the direction in which you're pressing the pedal, but the airplane will turn only slightly, if at all. Rather, it will just *skid* through the air pointed sideways while still going almost straight ahead.

Properly executing a turn requires the coordinated use of both the wheel—to bank the wings through the action of the ailerons—and the rudder pedal to which you apply corresponding pressure in the same direction as you're turning the wheel. For a left turn, turn the wheel to the left and use the left rudder. When you've established the angle of bank needed to turn as steeply as you desire, neutralize both the wheel and the rudder, and the airplane continues turning until you begin the recovery from the turn.

When you've turned as far as you want, you stop the turn by applying wheel and rudder pressure opposite to those that you used to start the turn. If you've been turning to the left, just roll the wheel to the right and simultaneously apply some right rudder pressure. The airplane will roll out of the bank. When the wings are once again level, neutralize the controls and fly along in the new direction.

Most turns are normally done with a bank angle of around 30°. At this angle, the increase in stalling speed that is a by-product of every bank is very little. Also, a 30° bank is not uncomfortable for either pilot or passengers. Once in a turn, you'll find that you will have to apply a little back pressure to the control wheel to keep the nose attitude level and to keep from losing altitude. Remember that total lift must increase in a turn because some of that total is now devoted to turning the airplane rather than just keeping it aloft. To increase total lift, you increase the angle of attack, and you do that by pulling back a little on the control wheel.

If you bank very steeply, say, 60° or more, you will see that the needed back pressure to keep the nose level can increase quite a bit. In a 60° bank, most of the total lift is turning the airplane, and little remains to keep us flying. So the angle of attack has to be increased much more because much more total lift has to be generated. At some point, as the bank is increased even further, there just won't be enough lift to keep the airplane flying, and you will increase the angle of attack to the point of stalling the wing. In training, you'll do some steeply banked turns but probably not over 45° of bank. At 45°, everything is still quite controllable, and safe margins of stall speed compared to the speed at which you are flying can be maintained. But much beyond 60° of bank, you'll reach the design limit of the average light airplane, where you can't keep the nose level anymore without exceeding the critical angle of attack and stalling the wings. Once you reach that point, you'll have to either allow the nose to fall some in attitude or lessen the angle of bank.

Steep turns are practiced in training so that you can see these effects for yourself. But once you get your license, you will seldom, if ever, turn much more steeply than 45° of bank.

Wing Flaps

Wing flaps are hinged surfaces that are attached to the inboard trailing edges of the wings. Their primary purpose is to allow the pilot to change the shape of the wing as they are lowered. This increases the camber, or curvature, of the wing. When the flaps are extended, the new shape of the wing is more curved, and the wing is capable of producing more lift (FIG. 5-7). Because the wing is producing more lift as the flaps are extended, their use allows the airplane to fly at a slower speed than if the flaps are fully retracted. Flaps are most often used during a landing so that the airplane can fly at a slower speed during the approach. Because the wing is producing more lift as the flaps are extended, the stalling

5-7 *Extended flaps enable the wing to produce more lift, and they also add drag.*

speed of the airplane is also slower than if the flaps are up. Using flaps during the landing approach will enable the airplane to land more slowly because, as you now know, a good landing is nothing more than a stall performed only inches above the runway.

The wing flaps on small airplanes are always mounted on the trailing edges of the wings, primarily for simplicity of design and manufacture and ease of pilot operations. On large aircraft like jet airliners, flaps are frequently put on the leading and trailing edges of the wings. When all of these flaps are fully extended, the shape of the wing is dramatically altered. Because jets operate over such a wide spectrum of speeds, compared to light airplanes, the wing on a jet has to be capable of flying as slowly as 130 knots during takeoff and landing, yet also cruise in the neighborhood of 500 knots. Radically changing its shape by using a very complicated combination of both leading- and trailing-edge flaps is the only way that it can be accomplished on a conventionally designed wing.

The next time that you ride on an airliner, try to get a seat over or slightly behind the wings. You can watch the flaps work, especially during takeoff and landing. All of the airliner's flaps must be deployed for takeoff and landing because the wing would not be able to fly at such slow speeds otherwise. It would not create enough lift without the flap extension unless the speed were dramatically increased. In small airlines, we normally take off without using any flap extension, and we can also easily land without flaps if we want. Flaps in a light airplane enable us to approach and land at slower speeds than we could if we didn't use them, but the difference is not nearly as dramatic as it is in large airplanes.

When we discussed drag earlier in this chapter, we noted that induced drag is a by-product of lift. Therefore, when you deploy the flaps to increase the wing's lift, you also increase the wing's drag. Even though we don't normally use flaps for takeoff in light training airplanes, a Cessna 150, such as the one shown in FIG. 5-7 can use as much as 20° of flap extension for takeoff. If the flaps are extended any more than that, the increased drag associated with their extension will hinder the small airplanes' ability to accelerate down the runway and reach flying speed. Small deflections of the flaps, up to 20°, are used for soft runway conditions or sometimes for short runways, when you need to lift off of the ground as soon as possible at the slowest practical speed. However, when you use the flaps in this manner, you will learn that your climb-out, after you break ground, will suffer as a result of the flaps' deployment because the drag inherent in the use of the flaps compromises the rate at which the airplane can climb.

When there is a strong *crosswind,* which occurs when the wind is blowing across the runway rather than down it, flap extensions are kept at a lesser degree than when a crosswind isn't a factor. You'll see that using excessive amounts of flap extension in strong crosswinds increases the wind's reaction upon the airplane, making it more difficult to compensate for that crosswind.

When landing without heavy crosswinds, full flap deployment is generally used. A Cessna 150 has a maximum flap extension of 40°. When the maximum is used, the Cessna 150 descends at quite a slow forward speed and at a rather steep angle. This can be beneficial if you need to clear a power line, trees, or some other obstacle in the approach path, especially if the runway is a bit short. At times during your training, your instructor will have you make landings at all of the levels of flap extensions, from none to the maximum available in your airplane.

How the Propeller Works

We've already talked about how the propeller is shaped like a wing and produces thrust by actually creating lift in the forward direction. The angle of attack of the blades of the propeller relative to the oncoming airstream is referred to as the *pitch* of the propeller blades. When the pitch is low, the angle of attack of the blades is likewise low, and when the pitch is higher, so is the angle of attack. Changing the pitch changes the thrust characteristics of the propeller and the pull that it generates. If you can visualize a bolt that has fine threads, this would be one way to think of a propeller with low pitch. If you then think of a coarsely threaded bolt, that mental picture is analogous to a propeller with high pitch.

Most airplanes with engines of 150 horsepower or less have *fixed-pitch propellers* because of the smaller airplane's limited load capacity and narrow speed range (FIG. 5-8). This class of airplane includes most all of the popular two-seat trainers and almost all of the four-seat airplanes in which you might train. These limited-performance airplanes could not make enough use of the more expensive *constant-speed propellers* found in larger and faster airplanes. Constant-speed propellers are much more expensive to manufacture and require overhauls and

5-8 *This propeller is the fixed-pitch type. The landing light, engine air intake with air filter, and exhaust pipe are also visible.*

routine maintenance not requisite for fixed-pitch propellers. Therefore, small airplanes can't justify the cost of the constant-speed propeller.

The pitch of the blades of a constant-speed propeller can be changed by the pilot within certain limits. The internal mechanisms of the constant-speed propeller also change the pitch of the blades instantaneously, to maintain a constant revolutions per minute (rpm) of the engine as various aerodynamic loads are encountered during flight. Managing a constant-speed propeller demands more pilot technique than does operating an engine that has a fixed-pitch propeller. That's another reason that trainers don't normally have them; there's nothing to be gained during initial pilot training from overloading a student with needless tasks.

Almost all modern propellers are made of aluminum, but some of the newest types are constructed of composite materials. Composites are gaining fast as a material of which entire airplanes are made, and propellers are no exception. Composite materials can be stronger and lighter than metal. In the past, propellers were carved out of laminated wood stock. Wooden propellers are lighter than metal ones, but they require much more care and maintenance. Today you generally see wooden propellers only on classic and antique airplanes, and sometimes on home-built planes.

When the airplane is on the ground, a propeller is dangerous. It should be regarded as a potential killer. Never start an engine without *knowing for certain* that no one or no thing is in front of or approaching the airplane. You'll be taught to always open the cockpit window and yell "clear" before starting the engine. Be especially watchful for people who are unaccustomed to airplanes and who don't realize the danger of a spinning propeller. It can be very difficult to see a spinning propeller because it is virtually invisible. Of all the ways to have an accident, allowing a person to be struck by a rotating propeller is one of the most needless, and also it is always disfiguring at best and usually fatal.

Also, be on the lookout for animals. If you fly into rural airports where there might be dogs or other critters around the airport, they too can get caught by the propeller. Dogs seem to be attracted to spinning propellers and to have the "deer in the headlights" syndrome. If your airport has any animals around, don't start the airplane if they are anywhere close to you. If you do ever catch anything in the propeller, immediately shut the engine down and have a qualified maintenance technician look at it before any further engine operation. A propeller that is damaged to even the slightest degree might be out of balance and cause severe engine damage if ignored. Also, you'll be taught during your training to look for nicks in the propeller because nicks of any significant size, usually more than $1/_{16}$ inch deep, can cause the metal to fatigue and set up a crack in the propeller, which can then propogate and lead to in-flight separation of a portion of the affected blade.

Even when the engine is not running, a propeller has the potential to maim or kill. Airplane engines are normally shut down by using the *mixture* control to starve the engine of fuel. Then, after the engine quits running, the pilot turns off the ignition switch. On at least one occasion, most pilots will neglect the final step of turning off the ignition. Even if the pilot has turned the ignition switch off, trouble may still arise because the way the system is designed can allow an electrical short to develop. If this has happened, the pilot would not normally know it because the engine has already stopped running before the ignition switch is turned off. If the ignition is still in "hot," it is possible for the engine to start again if the propeller is rotated even slightly. Leaning on a propeller at rest has caused more than one engine to fire at least a stroke or two, if not actually start running. The one who was leaning on the propeller seldom knew what hit him.

In-Flight Effects of the Propeller

When the airplane is in flight, the propeller's rotation creates several forces that affect how the airplane flies. Most of these forces are manifested by the airplane's "wanting" to turn. Design engineers usually design the engine mounts and vertical tail offsets to greatly eliminate most of the effects of these propeller forces when in cruising flight.

As the propeller rotates, the airflow through it is twisted. Thus, there is a *spiraling slipstream* created by the normal operation of the propeller. This spiraling nature of the slipstream leaving the propeller, working its way aft, exerts a sideways force on the fuselage of the airplane and also upon the vertical tail surface.

American-made engines turn clockwise when viewed from inside the cockpit, and so, therefore, does the propeller attached to the end of the crankshaft. When anything rotates, it creates torque. *Torque* is a force that is generated in a direction opposite to the direction of rotation. Since American engines turn clockwise when viewed from the cockpit, the torque is counterclockwise as the pilot sees it. During operation of the airplane, the torque is seldom felt by the pilot because of the design and manufacturing countermeasures that we discussed above.

There is another force that causes a tendency for the airplane to turn, and this is called the *P-factor*. The P-factor is most apparent when the airplane is at a higher angle of attack, such as when it lifts off the ground at takeoff and during a climb. The P-factor will cause the nose to tend to go left because the propeller's descending blade (the blade on the right as viewed from inside the cockpit) has a greater angle of attack than does the opposite, ascending blade. This increased angle of attack of the descending blade gives it more effective thrust than the ascending blade produces. Therefore, the entire disc of the rotating propeller isn't producing equal thrust on both sides; rather, the right side has more pull than is created by the left half of the propeller disc. This unequal pull from the right side causes the nose of the airplane to be pulled to the left. This swinging of the nose is called *yaw*. To correct this tendency, which is inherent in all propeller-driven airplanes, the pilot holds a slight pressure on the right rudder pedal when the airplane is at higher angles of attack. When the airplane is in a nose-down attitude, such as when making a normal descent from cruise altitudes, the P-factor effect reverses because the ascending blade of the propeller now has the higher angle of attack and therefore creates more thrust. During descents, the pilot needs to apply some pressure to the left rudder pedal to correct for the P-factor and keep the airplane in coordinated flight.

European-made engines rotate backward compared to American powerplants. If you fly an airplane with a European engine, you apply left rudder pressure during takeoff and climb and right rudder pressure during a descent. When flying helicopters, pilots have to make similar corrections but for altogether different aerodynamic reasons. American helicopters need left pedal pressure as power is increased, and European choppers get right pedal. Because the chances are very high that you'll be flying American-built airplanes during your training and that you may never fly a European one at all, and you likely will not be a helicopter pilot, don't worry about the different techniques. Just remember, right pedal for takeoff and climb; left pedal for descents.

Using the Throttle

The throttle is the control that regulates the amount of fuel going into the cylinders of the engine just as does the gas pedal in a car. In modern small airplanes, the throttle is usually a large black knob mounted on the instrument panel. In some airplanes, particularly those made by Piper, the throttle can be a T-shaped handle mounted on a quadrant in front of and slightly below the panel. Either configuration works in the same way. When pushed all the way in, or forward, the throttle is wide open, and it allows the engine to run at maximum power. Pulled all the way back, or out, the engine is at idle power.

An airplane throttle is not moved constantly as though it were the gas pedal of a car. If you have any experience with farm or industrial machinery like tractors or bulldozers, note that the airplane's throttle is used more like the fuel control in these machines. Normally we use full throttle, or maximum power, for takeoff and climb.

Since you'll be training in an airplane that most likely has a fixed-pitch propeller, you will be taught to leave the power at maximum throughout the takeoff and climb after takeoff. When you reach your desired cruising altitude, you level the airplane from the climb and pull back the throttle to set the desired power for cruise flight. Most of the time, you will not touch the throttle again until it is time to begin a descent, at which time you will pull it back some, to a power setting less than cruise that allows the airplane to descend efficiently.

Because the throttle is the control that regulates the power output of the engine, it is also the control that primarily determines the altitude at which the aircraft is flying. Pulling back on the control wheel raises the nose of the airplane and increases the lift of the wings because raising the nose also increases the angle of attack of the wings. But remember, induced drag increases as lift does. So if you only pull the nose up without increasing power, you will see a momentary gain in altitude, which is what we call a *zoom climb*. As soon as the various aerodynamic forces stabilize, the increased drag that results from the increased angle of attack will slow the airplane and stop any further altitude gain. To climb consistently, the pilot must advance the throttle so that the engine is putting out more power. Such an increase in power then enables the airplane to continue climbing because the power is overcoming the increased induced drag that results from the higher angle of attack of the wings.

There are some airplanes, like jet fighters, that have such an excess of power that they can climb when the nose is raised without increasing the power setting. But in small airplanes, there isn't that much power available at the cruise setting, so we have to increase power in order to climb more than a few hundred feet at best.

Many modern airplanes are designed to use fuel injection systems rather than a carburetor to meter the fuel flow into the cylinders. Your trainer will probably have a carburetor induction system, but fuel injection is becoming more popular in newer airplanes. From the pilot's perspective, the difference between the two systems is almost negligible, and the throttle control in the cockpit is used the same way regardless of whether the airplane is fuel injected or is equipped with a carburetor. There are some minor differences in the techniques used in certain combinations of atmospheric conditions and power output, between flying a carbureted airplane or a fuel injected one. These differences are so slight as to be insignificant at this point.

The Engine

Airplanes have used many different types of powerplants over the history of aviation. Some have been equipped with diesel engines, and a few years ago, a very light airplane crossed the English Channel powered only by its pilot's muscle power as he pedaled like a bicycle rider. We all know that almost all airliners and military airplanes are powered by jet engines. As a private pilot, the powerplants that you're likely to encounter will be *air-cooled reciprocating gasoline engines,* which are identical in principle to automobile engines.

Airplanes generally use air-cooled engines for two reasons. First, they are lighter than liquid-cooled engines because they don't have radiators, water pumps, the associated plumbing, and the weight of the liquid coolant. Second, air-cooled engines are more reliable because there aren't any of the aforementioned components to fail. Those of us who have been driving for some years have probably encountered a problem, at one time or another, with cooling systems in our cars. A broken water hose or pump or a leaky radiator is an inconvenience on the highway. It's a more significant problem at 5,000 feet above the ground. Lately, we have seen a resurgence of liquid-cooled airplane engines, as the sciences of engine design and metallurgy have advanced. Therefore, you might have a liquid-cooled airplane engine in your future. Liquid-cooled engines are more efficient than air-cooled ones, and the price of fuel is driving aviation manufacturers to try to improve efficiency. These newer liquid-cooled engines are designed to run for an extended period of time even after all of the coolant has leaked out, which would match their safety to that of an air-cooled engine.

Most of the engines you will encounter are equipped with horizontally opposed cylinders, similar to the engines that powered the original Volkswagen Beetle and are still used in great number by Porsche. FIGURE 5-9 depicts a typical light-aircraft engine manufactured by Teledyne Continental.

The ignition system

One of the major differences between automobile and airplane engines is that in an airplane, the engine has two complete and separate ignition systems that supply power to the spark plugs in the cylinders. In an airplane engine, there are two spark plugs in each cylinder, and each one is powered by a different

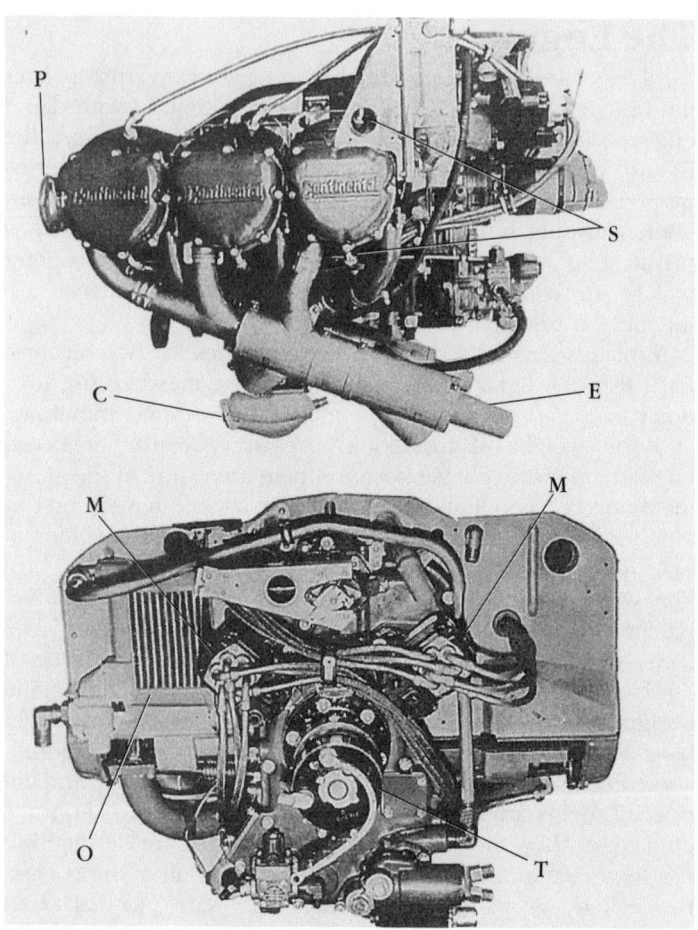

5-9 *This is a six-cylinder, opposed-type, air-cooled engine manufactured by Continental. Shown are: C, carburetor; E, exhaust; M, magnetos; O, oil cooler; P, propeller hub; S, spark plugs; and T, starter.*

ignition system. The electrical energy needed to provide power to the spark plugs is derived from two *magnetos,* each of which powers one of the separate systems. In this way, reliability and safety are enhanced in several ways.

We commonly refer to the magnetos as *mags,* and they are totally separate from the airplane's electrical system. The electrical system consists of a battery and either a generator or alternator. This electrical system supplies the power to start the engine and run the radios, night flying lights, and other electrical optional equipment. But this electrical system has nothing to do with keeping the engine running. An airplane can suffer a complete electrical failure; its battery can short out, its generator or alternator can cease to put out any electricity, or the voltage regulator can break. None of this will have even the slightest effect on whether the engine runs. Automobile engines have a different system that does rely on the car's electrical system to keep power going to the spark plugs. That's why, if your car's alternator fails, you can drive only a short distance because you are then using up the stored power in the battery to supply the electrical energy to the ignition. As soon as the car's battery runs dead, the automobile stops. Not so with an airplane, for the obvious safety reason.

The magnetos that power the airplane's ignition system are very old technology. Automobiles in the 1920s had magneto ignition. Also, your power lawn mower has a magneto to run its engine's ignition. There are some pundits who criticize aviation manufacturers for not employing the latest and greatest new advances in engine design. However, I prefer the older way of doing things, "If it ain't broke, don't fix it."

Because there are two magnetos in an airplane, and because each one powers a totally separate and unconnected ignition system, including one of the two spark plugs in each cylinder, one entire ignition system can fail, and the engine will continue to run on the other system. So any of the components in one system can fail, from the mag to a spark plug lead or the plug itself, and we can continue flying. When the engine is running on only one of the two ignition systems, it loses a tiny bit of efficiency and cannot produce quite all of its rated power output. But this decrease is so slight that it is barely noticeable even to experienced pilots. You will learn on your first flight that before takeoff there is a simple check that pilots perform to ensure that both ignition systems are working properly. If one is not, we certainly don't take off, even though we could, because if we did take off on only one of the systems, we'd be depriving ourselves of the significant safety margin that is inherent in having redundant ignition systems in the first place.

The ignition switch in the cockpit has five normal positions: OFF, LEFT, RIGHT, BOTH, and START. The START setting is just like that setting in a car; you turn the switch to that position to start the engine, and it's spring loaded—again as is your car switch—to return to the running position when you release the pressure on the key as the engine starts. The BOTH position is the normal position for flight; it allows both of the ignition systems to operate, again, totally separately and independently from each other. The LEFT and RIGHT positions, when selected, energize only the respective ignition system and disable the other one. The check that you perform before takeoff involves your advancing the throttle until the revolutions per minute of the engine is at a setting that the manufacturer specifies, which is usually around 1,700 rpm, and then your switching from the BOTH position to either LEFT or RIGHT.

When you perform this check, you will see that the engine keeps right on ticking using only the chosen ignition system while the other one is switched off. You'll also see that there is a minor decrease in revolutions per minute, usually around 75 to 100 rpm, because the engine does lose some efficiency running on only one of the two systems. The next step is to go back to the BOTH setting momentarily, and then switch to the other separate position. Again, the engine runs, and the revolutions per minute decrease a tiny bit. Go back to BOTH and your check of the ignition system is completed. When you switch to only one of the two systems, you can immediately tell if there is a problem with any aspect of that system. If the drop in the revolutions per minute exceeds the manufacturer's specification, or if the engine runs rough, taxi back to the hangar and have the maintenance folks take a look at it. It's that simple to have, and check, the safety factor that comes with two separate and completely independent ignition systems.

The primer

Unlike cars, airplanes with carburetors have a primer system that is activated with a push-pull knob on the instrument panel of the cockpit. The primer injects raw fuel into the intake manifold to help get the engine started. Some engines need lots of priming to start, especially in cold weather, whereas others need little or none. Your flight instructor will teach you the proper starting technique for the airplane in which you're training. Every modern airplane has a *pilot's operating handbook* (POH) published by the manufacturer. The POH describes virtually every technique and procedure the pilot needs to know or be able to find to properly operate the airplane. The procedures for priming your airplane will be covered in the POH, and these procedures will vary from one airplane to the other.

The POH is a vitally important document. There are some portions of it that you will have to commit to memory before you take the flight test for your license. If you are the kind of driver who has never opened the owner's manual for your car, your proclivity will change as you become a pilot. You can't ignore an airplane's POH.

The Flight Instruments

The basic flight instruments that are shown in FIG. 5-10 are the *airspeed indicator, altimeter,* and *turn coordinator* (or its predecessor, the *turn-and-slip* indicator). Most training planes that you will fly also have an *artificial horizon* (also called an *attitude indicator*), a *vertical speed indicator* (VSI)

5-10 *The Cessna 150 instrument panel: 1, turn coordinator; 2, airspeed indicator; 3, directional gyro; 4, attitude indicator or artificial horizon; 5, clock; 6, vertical speed indicator; 7, altimeter; 8, G-meter; 9, VOR course indicator; 10, communication transceiver and VOR navigation receiver; 11, automatic direction finder receiver; 12, tachometer; 13, fuel gauges; 14, ADF bearing indicator; 15, ammeter; 16, vacuum gauge; 17, oil pressure and oil temperature gauges; A, parking brake; B, engine primer; C, combination magneto and starter switch; D, electrical system master switch; E, toe brakes; F, rudder pedals; G, glove box; H, carburetor heat; J, fuel mixture; K, throttle; L, elevator trim; M, transceiver microphone.*

(which many pilots also call a *rate-of-climb indicator*), and a *directional gyroscope* (DG).

Airspeed indicator

The airspeed indicator is actually a pressure instrument that measures the velocity of the air moving past the airplane. To measure this impact pressure, a small tube is placed outside the cabin with its open end facing directly into the oncoming stream of air but outside of the propeller blast. This tube is called the *pitot tube,* pronounced "pea-toe" (FIG. 5-11). *Pitot* and many other aviation words and terms have French origins: fuselage, nacelle, chandelle, aileron, empennage, and the like. When aviation was in its infancy, and after the Wright Brothers had first flown a powered airplane, the French quickly took over as the leaders in aircraft development. Most of these terms had been solidified in the jargon of aviation before World War I.

We have to be careful not to confuse the airspeed indicator with an automobile's speedometer. The airspeed indicator is not a speedometer because the airspeed indicator merely shows the speed at which the airplane is moving through the air; it is actually measuring the speed of the air moving past the aircraft. The airspeed indicator cannot take into account

5-11 *Pitot tubes are usually heated to prevent ice blockage.*

the movement of the air mass supporting the airplane and through which it is flying. The movement of the air mass is the wind aloft, and the presence of wind aloft will always make the *ground speed* of the airplane different from its airspeed. The ground speed is the speed at which you're actually moving across the ground. We'll cover this distinction much more completely in Chap. 9.

Airspeed indicators cannot tell the whole story about airspeed because the type of indicator used in light airplanes is a pressure instrument that cannot compensate for the varying density of the air in which it is flying. As an airplane climbs higher, or as air becomes warmer or more humid, the air is less dense. When the airplane is moving at the same absolute speed through less dense air, the airspeed indicator shows a slower speed than if the air were denser. This occurs because the only thing that the airspeed indicator can measure is the impact of the oncoming stream of air into the open end of the pitot tube. Because less dense air has fewer molecules for a given volume than does denser air, the airspeed indicator is "fooled" into measuring a slower speed than the absolute speed when the airplane is flying in less dense air.

In your training, it is very unlikely that you'll fly very high, and almost always you will be below 10,000 feet in altitude. The inherent error in the airspeed indicator does not generally cause the pilot much concern at the lower altitudes. The error can be corrected when the need arises, through the use of a device that we call a "computer," but that is really nothing more than a circular slide rule or battery-powered calculator. You'll find many uses for an aviation computer, and many of them will be discussed in Chap. 9. When I learned to fly, we used the circular slide rule type, and it was marked off in miles per hour, knots, gallons per hour, and other aviation-related gradations. Today, many pilots prefer to use the electronic calculator version, which again is modified to display aviation information. I still use my circular slide rule type of computer because there aren't any batteries in it to die. Maybe it is truly hard to teach an old dog new tricks. You'll need to acquire one of the two types during your training because you can't do the navigational problems on the knowledge test or properly file a flight plan without one. My old circular slide rule type of computer is shown in FIG. 5-12.

Some airspeed indicators can correct for the varying density of the air and the resulting display right on the face of

5-12 *An electronic aviation calculator simplifies flight planning and provides accurate time, speed, and distance computations.*

the indicator. This is accomplished by using a rotateable ring around the outside of the dial on the indicator's display. The pilot rotates this ring to compensate for both the altitude at which she is flying and the temperature of the air outside of the airplane. When the ring is correctly rotated, the needle of the airspeed indicator then points to the *true airspeed* at which the plane is flying through the air. Without this correction, the indicator can only show the plane's *indicated airspeed*. You have to remember that when the indicated airspeed is corrected into true airspeed, either with a ring around the instrument or with a computer, you are still seeing only airspeed, not ground speed.

The altimeter

The altimeter is actually a barometer, with its dial calibrated in feet in the United States and in meters in some other areas of the world (FIG. 5-13). All barometers measure the density of the air, and the altimeter is no exception. It works on the principle that the density of the air, and therefore the pressure of the air, steadily decreases as you rise in altitude. The altimeter's readings need to be corrected for air temperature because the instrument can't adjust itself. This adjustment normally isn't critical at the lower altitudes where light airplanes

5-13 *The altimeter has two hands. The longest hand indicates hundreds of feet, and the shorter hand indicates thousands of feet. The altimeter is showing 1,010 feet above sea level.*

fly, but when it is necessary, your pocket computer can calculate this adjustment.

Air pressure, which is the result of the density of the air, constantly varies as a result of one or more of three variables. First, air pressure decreases as we rise in altitude. Second, as air becomes warmer, it gets less dense and therefore has less pressure. Last, the more humidity there is in the air, which means the more water vapor there is, the less dense that air is. These last two factors influence the pressure of an air mass at a constant altitude. Along with these three variables, the atmosphere contains air masses that are less dense than an arbitrary norm, and also, there are air masses with pressures above the norm. These air masses are called *highs* and *lows.*

As an airplane flies through the atmosphere, it encounters changing air mass pressures almost from the moment of takeoff to the point of landing. The air is seldom totally stable over a long distance. As the various weather systems and different air masses are traversed, the altimeter must be adjusted, or "set," to the barometric pressure of the air mass in which the airplane finds itself from time to time. The altimeter has a little rotatable knob to make that adjustment and a little window to display the barometric pressure to which it's been set.

For local flights to and from the same airport, you'll set the altimeter to correspond to the local barometric pressure, and it is done very easily. When an altimeter is set to the local barometric pressure, it will read altitude above *mean sea level* (MSL). If you know the local altimeter setting by receiving it from the control tower, you just rotate the knob until the stated pressure appears in the window. Then, while you're still on the ground, the altimeter should display the elevation of the airport above mean sea level.

Another way to set the altimeter for a local flight is simply to rotate the knob until the altimeter reads the mean sea level elevation of the airport. Then you should look at the setting in the barometric window and make sure that it is close to the barometric pressure at that time. In airplanes used in training, when you set the barometric pressure and then look at the indication of the altimeter, that indication should be within 75 feet of the actual elevation of the airport above mean sea level.

The elevation of every airport is shown on the *aeronautical chart* (that is, on the map). Of course, after the first couple of training flights, you'll memorize the elevation of your home airport.

When you fly away from your home base, you need to be able to set the altimeter from the time to time as your flight moves along so that you are reading your correct altitude. All altitudes below 18,000 feet are stated in MSL. If you look at your altimeter and see that you are at 5,500 MSL, you can look at the aeronautical chart and see the elevations of airports and obstacles such as radio towers and power plant stacks that are beneath you and quickly determine how high you are above them. If your altimeter hasn't been properly set, or the error between the barometric pressure and the true setting is more than about 75 feet, your display of altitude won't be accurate.

Every FAA control facility, such as control towers and flight service stations, with whom you will communicate will automatically give you the barometric pressure at its specific locale. That way, you can periodically set your altimeter and keep up with the inevitable changes in air pressure as you fly from one place to another.

The vertical speed indicator

The VSI is another barometric instrument. Its dial is calibrated to show whether the airplane is ascending or descending, and the display shows you this altitude change in hundreds of feet per minute (fpm). VSI readings are not instantaneous. Rather, the instrument lags several seconds behind what the airplane is actually doing. For that reason, a VSI cannot be used to maintain level flight, and if you try to use it for that purpose, your flight profile will look a like a roller coaster's. The VSI is used to establish a constant rate of climb or descent should that become necessary during a flight. As a private pilot, you won't need to do this very often. But once you progress to the training for an instrument rating, you will find that the VSI is very useful.

Turn coordinator or turn-and-slip indicator

The *turn-and-slip indicator* is one of the oldest instruments in your panel, and it dates back well into the infancy of flight instrument development. You may hear older pilots call it the "turn-and-bank indicator," but that term is a misnomer. This instrument is actually two separate instruments in the same case. One part of it looks like a carpenter's level, but it has a little ball suspended in fluid rather than an air bubble. When the ball is in the center of the tube, the airplane is in coordinated flight, which means that it is neither skidding nor slipping through the air. If the ball is off to one side, your flying isn't coordinated. There is an easy way to correct this situation. If the ball is off to the left, you need to add a little left rudder pedal pressure; and if it's off to the right, you need to press on the right rudder a little. There is an old saying to describe the corrective action, which is, "Step on the ball."

The other of the two separate instruments that make up the turn-and-slip indicator is a gyroscope that is connected to the needle on the face of the instrument. This gyroscope immediately senses any turning of the airplane and the needle deflects in the direction of the turn. When the airplane is on a steady path and not turning in either direction, the needle stays centered.

The newer type of instrument that gives you the same information is called the *turn coordinator*. It still has the glass tube filled with fluid and the little ball to tell you if you're in coordinated flight. But, instead of the needle to show turning, it has a little airplane symbol that banks in the direction of the turn. There are some inherent deficiencies in this newer turn coordinator's presentation of which every pilot must be aware.

First, the little airplane symbol shows only turning, and it does not give any information at all about whether the nose of the airplane is high, low, or level. Some inexperienced pilots can confuse the modern turn coordinator with the artificial horizon, which we'll discuss next. Second, the turn coordinator shows *only* turning. Although normal turns are made with the airplane banked, it is possible to cross-control an airplane, turning with just the rudder pedal and using the aileron to keep the wings nearly level. That isn't the correct way to turn, and its use is usually inadvertent, but it can be done. Just remember that when you see the little airplane symbol banked, it is telling you only one thing, and that is that the airplane is turning in the direction of the displayed bank. It is not telling you anything more.

The artificial horizon, or attitude indicator

The *artificial horizon,* which is now more commonly called the *attitude indicator,* is another gyroscopic instrument. Today, it is a primary and required instrument for instrument flying. It displays the attitude of the airplane by using a small airplane symbol superimposed upon a level line on the face of the instrument. The level line represents the horizon outside the cockpit.

Depending on the precise make and model of the instrument, either the airplane symbol moves up, down, or banks left and right, or the line does the moving while the airplane symbol remains stationary. In either type, the same information is displayed to the pilot. The instrument tells whether the wings are level or banked and, if banked, in which direction. The attitude indicator simultaneously shows whether the nose attitude is level, high, or low relative to the horizon. It will take you a short while to be able to interpret the attitude indicator's display. Once you master reading this instrument quickly, it is a very useful tool because it senses attitude changes and displays them almost instantly, with no perceptible lag.

Directional gyro

The *directional gyro* (DG) is yet another gyroscopic instrument. It does not have any ability to actually sense direction like the *magnetic compass* does. The DG has a display that is calibrated in the form of a circle, with the degrees of the compass direction inscribed on the dial of the instrument. The pilot must set the DG to correspond with the compass. This task is a part of the various pretakeoff checks that you'll learn. Setting the DG is very simple; you look at the compass and then grasp a rotatable knob on the DG and twist it until the DG's reading is the same as that shown by the magnetic compass. Once set, a properly functioning DG is extremely stable, and it changes its displayed direction, which is what we call the *heading* of the airplane, just as fast at the airplane is turning.

If you were in Scouts as a child, or if you have been a boater or a hiker, you've probably got some experience with and memories of using a magnetic compass. A magnetic compass is anything but stable, and it must be held still to give an accurate reading. If it is jostled about by a shaky hand, or in airplanes, by any air turbulence, its readings are approximate at best. In rough air, the compass in an airplane can swing around so much that it becomes virtually useless. The DG isn't affected at all by turbulence or the turning and pitching of the airplane. Therefore, in modern airplanes that are equipped with them, DGs are used by the pilot for primary indications of the airplane's heading.

There is a problem of which every pilot must be aware. All gyroscopes are subject to *precession,* which is their tendency to drift from a preset and stable setting. To make sure that the DG hasn't precessed too far, it is normally reset about every 20 minutes or so in flight. Pick a stable moment during your flight, when the airplane is established in straight and level cruise, and then use the setting knob to make sure that the DG's indication matches the magnetic compass. I've seen DGs that didn't drift off of a set heading more than a degree or so in as long as an hour. I've seen others that had to be reset every 10 to 15 minutes. Usually, when you find one that drifts a lot over a short period of time, it's because that instrument is about ready to be replaced. These gyroscopes spin at tremendous rates, as high as 30,000 rpm. The little bearings in them do wear out. When you see a DG start to precess at a rate that is faster than normal, that's a good sign that it is about at the end of its useful life. The instrument should then be removed from the panel and sent to a certified instrument repair shop for overhaul.

Both the attitude indicator and the DG are typically powered by vacuum in most small airplanes. The vacuum creates a stream of air that moves through each of them, and this jet of air spins rotors inside the instrument, which in turn spin the gyros themselves. The vacuum is created by a pump that is attached to the engine in most training airplanes. As soon as the engine starts, the vacuum pump starts producing the vacuum, which goes to the instrument through small plastic or rubber hoses. Air rushes in one side of the instrument's case, as it is sucked in by the vacuum. Then, the instrument may take a moment or two for the gyroscope to spin up to operational revolutions per minute and for the instrument's indications to be reliable. By the time you taxi to the runway and perform your pretakeoff checks, your gyroscope instruments are ready to go.

Some older airplanes don't have vacuum pumps. These airplanes may have funny looking little hornlike devices attached to the side of the fuselage. These are *venturi tubes,* which create a vacuum as the air moves through them. A venturi, or maybe two, can provide the vacuum needed to power the gyroscope instruments. But, because a venturi operates by air moving through it, the airplane must be flying for a sufficient amount of airflow to come through the venturi. The only problem with a venturi is that the gyroscope instruments won't get spun up to operational revolutions per minute and stabilized until a few moments after takeoff. A venturi also creates a small amount of drag because it protrudes into the air stream. The positive side of using venturis is that they are very reliable. Unless the opening is blocked by some obstacle, such as ice or bug nest, a venturi cannot fail. Vacuum pumps do break, and when they do, you have no gyroscope instruments until the faulty pump is replaced.

A very few of the most modern trainers have completely done away with vacuum systems and use gyroscopic instruments that are electrically powered. Vacuum pump failure completely denies the pilot the use of those instruments that are operated by vacuum. The benefit of using electrical gyroscopic instruments is that even if the alternator or generator fails, a properly maintained battery will have enough residual power to enable the pilot to fly for some time before the radios, lights, and electrically powered instruments begin to fail for lack of power. However, electrically operated gyroscopic instruments are much more expensive than those that are vacuum powered, and it is very likely that we will continue to see vacuum-operated flight instruments for quite some time in the future.

The Engine Instruments

There are three engine instruments that are common to all light airplanes; in fact, they are required to be installed by FAA regulation. In higher-performance airplanes, you will find some additional gauges to tell you about what and how the engine is doing. In trainers, you generally see only the three required engine instruments.

The *tachometer* indicates the rotational speed of the engine and expresses it in revolutions per minute. Tachometers are now standard equipment in most cars, so you should have seen one prior to flying an airplane. If you haven't, don't worry about it. The tachometer (often abbreviated as *tach*) is a simple instrument to read and use. Most of the tachs found in light airplanes are driven by a flexible cable that comes right off of the rear case of the engine. Some newer airplanes are equipped with electrically driven tachometers, but they are not very common yet in trainers. Because you'll almost certainly learn to fly in an airplane that has a fixed-pitch propeller, you'll be taught to rely on the tach as the indicator of the engine's power output. Because an engine equipped with a fixed-pitch propeller can have its power adjusted only when the pilot changes the revolutions per minute, you'll see that there are various revolutions-per-minute settings called for by the manufacturer that will, in turn, produce varying amounts of power from the engine. To increase power, increase the revolutions per minute by advancing the throttle; to decrease power, do the opposite, which will decrease the revolutions per minute.

The second of the three required engine instruments is the *oil pressure gauge*. This device tells us whether the engine's oil lubrication system is functioning properly. Every modern engine has an oil pump that pumps oil throughout the innards of the engine, under some pressure that the pump produces. Oil is the lifeblood of any engine; without constant lubrication, an engine will run only a few minutes at most before it tears itself apart internally and eventually seizes. Unless there is pressure circulating the oil throughout the engine, there won't be the needed lubrication.

The oil pressure gauge has a green-colored range of readings, which is the normal range of proper and acceptable oil pressure. Within a few seconds after the engine is started, you should see the oil pressure move up into the green range. In very cold weather, when the oil is very thick and somewhat congealed, it may take a minute or two for the oil pressure to come up to normal readings. Your airplane's POH will specify the maximum amount of time it should take for oil pressure to develop. If the pressure doesn't come up within this time, immediately shut down the engine to prevent any internal damage, and have a qualified maintenance technician take over. Running the engine without oil pressure will soon destroy it, and it will cost someone thousands of dollars.

You probably do not have an oil pressure gauge in your automobile. In an attempt to make instrument panels in cars less intimidating, most manufacturers have eliminated the oil pressure gauge and replaced it with a warning light. The warning light is activated only when the oil pressure drops below a certain minimum, and the light then illuminates to tell the driver that the oil pressure is too low to continue driving. Just as you would do in an airplane when the oil pressure doesn't come up after the engine is started, if the warning light comes on in your car, pull over to the side of the road as soon as you can and shut off the engine. Continuing to operate any internal combustion engine with insufficient oil pressure will quickly destroy it.

The last of the three engine instruments that we're discussing is the *oil temperature gauge.* This instrument does exactly what its name implies: It shows you the temperature of the oil inside the engine. Because the airplane's engine is air cooled, if the engine is cooling properly, and if it has enough oil in it, the oil temperature will remain within normal limits. The oil temperature gauge also has a green-colored range for normal operating temperatures. A rapid rise in oil temperature is a specter of a serious problem. The engine may be losing its oil supply, making the remaining oil increase in temperature. If you ever see the oil temperature rise suddenly, or rise above the normal operating range, discontinue the flight and land at the nearest airport, and have a maintenance technician find out what's happening.

Oil is also a coolant, and when the oil temperature rises rapidly, it usually indicates that the supply of oil has been depleted. If you ever develop an oil leak in either your airplane engine or in your automobile while you are either flying or driving, your first indication of a serious oil leak may be a rise in oil temperature. Immediately resolve the problem by landing (or parking) and seeking the advice of a qualified maintenance technician.

6

Flying the Airplane

Almost everyone has some sort of opinion about how safe or dangerous small airplanes are. The truth can be summed up in a few words: Airplanes are neither safe nor dangerous—pilots are. Like most other areas of human endeavor, flying is what you make of it. Remember that machines are inanimate objects that can't make mistakes—only people can. If you have common sense, a degree of self-confidence without foolish bravado, and normal physical coordination, you can learn to be a very safe pilot and enjoy an entire career in aviation. If you like taking risks, get a rush out of the dangerous, or if you think you are immortal, stop right now and find another pursuit for your leisure time; stick to the airlines for your flying.

If your desires are to be able to fly around the local area on nice days and maybe take a passenger along, the training for a sport pilot certificate is within the grasp of almost anyone. But if you want to go on and use an airplane for transportation, fly at night, go into large metropolitan and unfamiliar airports, and even fly in instrument weather conditions, you will spend a significant amount of time training for a private pilot certificate and follow that with the training for an instrument rating. Regardless of what level of certification, skill, and competence you want to eventually achieve, no good pilot ever really stops learning.

From the very beginning, the two most important things you can do in an airplane are to think and relax. Flying takes a good amount of planning and thought. No one can fly very well without being relaxed at the controls. "Relaxed" doesn't mean being inattentive; it means not being tense.

An airplane wants to fly and is, by its design and nature, a very forgiving machine. Remember the true story in the last chapter about the little Aeronca Champ that flew about 90 miles without the benefit of anyone in it. When an airplane is properly trimmed, it takes very little effort to fly it in cruise flight. There is another true story about a pilotless airplane: During World War II, a B-17 bomber was so badly damaged from combat that the entire crew, pilots as well as the other crew members, bailed out, thinking that their bomber was doomed. It then did the same thing as the Champ; it flew on, across the English Channel, and back over England. When it finally ran out of fuel, it glided down to a passable forced landing in a farm field, all without a soul on board.

Because airplanes are so inherently stable, pilots can get lazy and fall into sloppy flying habits. They forget the admonitions of their instructors to always think ahead of the airplane and have a plan ready. Laziness and thoughtlessness can and will eventually lead to trouble.

In aviation, you're not allowed the luxury of a great deal of time to defer a decision. When confronted with uncertain weather ahead or, perhaps, a dwindling fuel supply as darkness approaches and you're over unfamiliar territory, you can't procrastinate about what to do. In even the simplest of small airplanes, you're still moving along at around 100 mph, and you can't pull into a truck stop or rest area to ponder what to do next.

The solution is to have your options already identified and planned before you let things go that far. Pilots who tell of hair-raising adventures in airplanes are those who usually bring the situations upon themselves. They are poor planners, and they are not good thinkers. There is one personality trait needed by every pilot: the ability to think out options first, before crunch times comes, when events make your decisions for you. Then, a pilot has to evaluate those options, make a reasoned decision, and execute it properly. Your instructor will tell you to relax, and then remind you more than once. If your muscles are tensed, you won't be able to feel the multitude of sensations of flight in a way that they will be helpful or enhance your learning. Controlling an airplane in a coordinated fashion is a learned feel. You can't feel anything very well while you're tense.

Don't confuse alertness with tenseness. A pilot must always be alert. I have found that relaxation and alertness are perfect partners. Some of my most alert moments, whether flying or doing anything else, come at a time when I am otherwise relaxed. I can devote my attention to flying an airplane, staying alert, and letting my brain work at peak efficiency, unimpeded by tenseness.

When you actually put your hand on the control wheel and take control of the airplane, you'll quickly learn that it takes very little force on the controls to produce the desired input. Your instructor might do what I have often done during the years, which is to have you grasp the wheel with only two or three fingers at first, to prevent you from applying too much force to it. Airplanes are flown with fingertip pressures on the wheel, not with large movements of the hands and arms like the motions we sometimes use when making large turns in the average car. Pilots refer to this as *control pressure,* which is the term we'll use in this book. Don't think of the control wheel moving as you fly; just think of your applying pressure to it.

The same idea of pressure rather than control movement applies to the rudder pedals. It's best not to wear heavy-soled boots while flying because you won't have the sensitivity in your feet that you will if you wear thinner-soled shoes. I once knew a pilot who took his private pilot check ride in the early winter wearing heavy leather boots for the first time in an airplane. He nearly failed the test. His control coordination was very poor because he couldn't feel the pedals. This fellow went on to become my mentor in aviation. I could not imagine his control technique ever being poor; when you flew with him, it was very quickly apparent that the control surfaces of the airplane had become extensions of his fingers and feet.

Now let's go out to the flight line at a typical general aviation airport and become acquainted with a popular training airplane. In this book, we'll use the Cessna 150 as our trainer. Cessna made a new version of it, the Cessna 152, for a few years before production of two-seat Cessnas ceased in the mid-1980s. Basically, a 152 is the same as a 150 except that the 152 has a different engine, made by Textron Lycoming, in place of the Teledyne Continental engine used in the 150. The only other meaningful difference between the two is that the wing flaps on the 152 have a maximum extension of 30°, whereas the 150's flaps can go down to 40°. Properly handled, the 150 is a pure joy. Although not particularly difficult to fly, the Cessna 150 does demand enough of its pilot to teach good control technique. If your flight school uses Cessna 152s instead of

150s, don't worry. They fly virtually identically, but the newer 152 may rent for a few dollars more per hour than an older 150.

Piper and Beechcraft also made two-seat trainers. Piper manufactured an airplane called a *Tomahawk,* and it also made trainers out of their Cherokee line of airplanes. Piper Cherokees usually have four seats, but to make a trainer version, Piper put a smaller engine in one model of the series and restricted it to two seats. Beech made the Skipper, but it did not sell as well as the Piper trainers. All of the Piper and Beechcraft trainers are *low-wing airplanes,* which means that their wings are attached to the lower part of the fuselage, and the occupants sit above the wings. Cessnas are high-wing designs, in which the wings are mounted at the top of the fuselage, and the people inside sit below the wings.

Most pilots have an intense devotion to either high- or low-wing airplanes, and this feeling is usually rooted in whatever type they initially flew as a trainer. My preference is for high-wing airplanes, even though I've flown thousands of hours in both types. A high-wing airplane is usually easier to land, but it is harder to taxi, especially in much wind, than a low-wing plane. In flight, the cockpit visibility out of the high-wing airplane is excellent looking ahead and down but lousy in a turn when the banked wing blocks vision in the direction of the turn. The low-wing airplane has poor visibility downward, but in a turn, you can see very well into the turn because the banked wing is out of your line of sight. My preference for a high-wing plane started because I learned to fly in one and didn't fly a low-wing for quite a while after my additional training. Plus, have you ever seen a low-winged bird? It just seems natural to me to sit in the shade and have the wing on top.

Let's begin with some familiarization facts about the Cessna 150. This is a two-place airplane, meaning that it carries a maximum of two people. Its empty weight is about 1,000 pounds, depending on how each particular one is equipped, and it will carry about 600 pounds of people, baggage, and fuel. This weight of occupants, baggage, and fuel is called an airplane's *useful load.* Every airplane has a *maximum gross weight* that is the most that the entire airplane can legally weigh at takeoff, fully loaded. To find the useful load, you start with the gross weight, subtract from it the airplane's empty weight, and the result is the useful load. The useful load varies a bit from airplane to airplane of the same type because each one's empty weight is a little bit different, due mainly to optional equipment installed in one and not the other.

The Cessna 150 cruises between 110 and 117 mph, or between 95 and 100 knots. Today, we commonly express all speed in knots. I'm not sure why because to me, miles per hour registers better in my head. But when we get into navigation in Chap. 9, you'll see that using knots makes things a bit easier when computing the effects of wind on your flight. The Cessna 150 has a fuel capacity of 22.5 usable gallons out of a total of 26 gallons. Almost all airplanes carry some fuel in their tanks that cannot drain into the fuel lines that go to the engine. This is called *unusable fuel.* The 150 will burn about 5 gallons per hour at cruise power settings, and that gives the airplane a range of about 400 miles, with some reserve fuel for unexpected needs. That's not bad fuel efficiency, even in these times of fuel consciousness.

The Preflight Check

Take a look at the airplane as you first walk up to it. This is where and when the *preflight check* should begin. Some instructors refer to this phase as the *preflight inspection.* As you approach the airplane, see if it is resting in a level attitude. If it isn't, a landing gear strut may be damaged, a tire may be low or flat, or in a low-wing airplane, a landing gear strut may need air or oil. There could always be damage to the landing gear that could have occurred during a previous flight that wasn't reported by the pilot.

There is really no more important part of every flight than the preflight check. Only fools omit it, even if they own their own airplanes and no one has touched it since the last flight (FIG. 6-1). In your flight training, the odds are that you'll almost certainly be flying rental airplanes. Although flight schools do a very good job, on average, of maintaining their equipment, rental airplanes, because students and renter pilots are flying them, take more abuse than does the average airplane that is owner flown and is that owner's pride and joy.

For this reason, you should be taught, during your first few lessons, how to do a very thorough preflight inspection. If you arrive early enough for your next trip on an airliner, you will see the copilot (called the *first officer* in airline lingo) do a walk-around inspection of even the biggest airliner. No pilot is

6-1 *Preflight check. Look the airplane over carefully.*

ever too advanced, or too knowledgeable, to perform the pre-flight check.

The manufacturer of your airplane will provide a checklist for the preflight inspection in the POH. Some POHs refer to this as a *walk-around inspection.* Whatever you call it—preflight check, preflight inspection, or walk-around inspection—the process is the same and so is the goal: to ensure, the best a pilot can in an exterior visual look-see, that the airplane is airworthy and safe for flight. The best way to conduct a preflight inspection is to begin at the same point on the airplane each time. You can modify the POH's checklist to begin at a point most convenient for you as long as you check each item covered in the checklist.

I usually start a preflight inspection at the pilot's door for several reasons. First, I've approached the airplane with my headset, flight case full of charts (maps), and probably some other stuff in my hands. So, the first step for me in almost any flight is to unlock the pilot's door and put those things inside the airplane. While I'm doing that, I usually plug my headset into the jacks in or under the instrument panel and remove the *control lock.* The control lock is a device that most often fits through the shaft in the control wheel and has a metal sheet, usually about 2 by 4 inches, or thereabouts in size, that goes over the ignition switch and is designed to prevent a pilot from starting the engine while the control lock is still installed.

When an airplane sits on the ground, the control surfaces such as the ailerons and elevators can be blown up and down by the wind or the propeller blast of passing airplanes. If the controls are left unlocked, they can be severely damaged, and the control mechanisms and hinges of the control surfaces can suffer damage as well. The control lock immobilizes these control surfaces, eliminating this threat. Every year a few pilots still manage to start a takeoff with the control lock installed. I've never figured out how they do it, but a few people will always find a way to do some things that are unimaginable to the rest of us. So when you get the door open and get your briefcase and other carry-ons stowed inside the airplane, remove the control lock as the first step in your preflight inspection.

While your head is still in the cockpit, make sure that the ignition and electrical master switches are turned OFF. Then turn the master switch ON just long enough to do two things. First, take a look at the fuel gauges. In a Cessna 150 there are two fuel gauges, one for each tank. The tanks are mounted with one tank in each wing. After you check the fuel gauges, grasp the flap switch and run the flaps down to their full extension. Then turn the master switch back OFF. When the switch is ON, you are running the battery down, and there is no need to leave it on while you do the rest of the preflight check. Last, while still inside the cockpit, look at the floor area right ahead of and between the two seats. This is where you'll find the fuel selector handle. Make sure that it is in the ON position. In a Cessna 150, you cannot direct fuel to the engine from the two fuel tanks independently; they both feed the engine simultaneously. That is why the fuel selector has only two positions, ON and OFF.

Because the pilot's door is on the left side on all single-engine Cessnas, the next stop is to start walking toward the tail. While you're approaching the tail but before you get there, look at the side of the fuselage. The metal skin of the fuselage is an item to be inspected. If you see that the skin has any waves or wrinkles in it, immediately call a maintenance technician; this condition almost always means that there is some hidden structural damage inside the fuselage. Assuming that the fuselage is OK, go on back to the tail of the airplane.

Once there, squat down and untie the tie-down rope that is used to secure the tail. At the tail, you'll check three general areas. First, look at the elevators and check both their top and bottom surfaces. Look for bad or missing rivets and wrinkled skin. Inspect the hinges of the elevators very carefully where they attach to the fixed horizontal stabilizer and check the stabilizer, again top and bottom, for wrinkled skin or rivet problems.

Next, do the same inspections on the rudder, its hinges and the vertical stabilizer. While you're located directly behind the airplane, you can see and check the connections of the control cables to both the elevators and the rudder. Also check the trim tab, which is located on the trailing edge of the elevator, and especially examine its hinge and control cable attachment. Last, at the tail, while squatted down, look at the underside of the fuselage. Here you're looking for a couple of things. Check the skin for dents, wrinkles, or other obvious signs of damage. Also, look for any oil stains. If an airplane develops any but the most severe oil leaks in the engine, the oil will stream under the fuselage and be apparent if you look for it.

Continue around the tail and proceed up the right side of the fuselage, repeating the inspection that you have just made of the left side. The next step is to inspect the trailing edge of the right wing.

Your first point of interest in inspecting the wing will be the extended flap. Look at the flap itself and the roller tracks upon which it extends and retracts. Grab the flap's trailing edge and shake it a little. It will have a small amount of play in it. But with experience you'll be able to detect if the flap is loose or if there is excess wear in the rollers or tracks. Next, move outward along the trailing edge of the wing and look at the right aileron. Check its general condition, freedom of movement, hinges, and control cable attachments just as you did for the elevators and the rudder. Now walk around the tip of the wing and look at it. See if there is any damage to it or the small light, called the *navigation light,* that is mounted on the wing tip. Next, walk on around the tip to the leading edge of the wing. Disconnect the tie-down rope, and check the leading edge of the wing for dents or other damage. While at the leading edge, we need to inspect the fuel tank that is mounted in the right wing. Because the Cessna 150 is a high-wing airplane, and because the fuel tank filler opening and fuel cap are on top, you'll need a small step stool to get up there, unless you've recently played professional basketball. Most flight schools keep these stools or small step ladders in the baggage areas of their trainers. Get up on the stool where you can remove the fuel cap and look directly down into the filler opening. You should be able to see that the fuel is full. Then replace the cap and twist it until it's properly closed. This is one of the most important parts of the preflight check and should never be omitted.

Pilots never trust fuel gauges or ground service crews to make sure that they have full fuel in their airplanes. Remember when you looked at the fuel gauges in the cockpit; the reading you saw on them ought to match what you see when you physically look in the tanks. If not, get a maintenance technician to fix the fuel gauges. FIGURE 6-2 shows this part of the preflight properly performed. The ground service folks won't be along with you if you run out of gas. They will be sorry if it happens to one of their customers, but they won't suffer the physical consequences that you and your passengers will. No confident ground server will ever be insulted because you check the fuel and caps, even if it's right after the airplane was fueled and the gas truck driver is still there. The best of these folks, and the most caring, will offer you the opportunity to do so as they finish fueling your plane, even to the extent of leaving their ladder in place for you to use. Availing yourself of this offer will indicate to the FBO that they have a competent pilot renting their airplane.

6-2 *Always visually check the fuel tanks for quantity and correct type of fuel.*

While you're in this position at the leading edge of the wing, it's a good time to check the condition of the right landing gear. Look at the tire and check it for the appearance of proper inflation, and see if the tire's tread looks good. You are checking to see if there are any cuts in either the side walls or the tread, or if there is excess checking in the sidewall surface. Our Cessna will have either a spring leaf or a spring tube (in the later models) for the landing gear leg. Not much ever goes wrong with them, and if it does, it's immediately apparent. While you're checking the tire, also look at the brake on the wheel. There is a metal or flexible line running under the fuselage and down the gear leg that carries brake fluid to the brake. Look for any leaks or fractures in this brake line. Disc brakes are used on all modern trainers, and the disc and brake pads are exposed. Check for any cracking in the brake disc, which is sometimes called the *rotor*. Also look at the thickness of the brake pads. If you are not mechanically inclined and don't already recognize these parts, ask your instructor to point them out to you.

Now open the access door on the right side of the engine cowling. First, take a good look around inside the interior of the engine compartment, using a flashlight if necessary to illuminate it. See if there are any oil streaks inside the cowling because they are evidence of engine oil leaks. Look for any broken or loose wires inside the area and around the engine. Check the exhaust system pipes and muffler for holes and large exhaust stains. Stains indicate either an engine oil leak or an exhaust gas leak.

The next step in this area is to check the quantity of oil in the engine (FIG. 6-3). Nobody checks the oil in a car each time it's driven, but we do check the oil each time we fly an airplane. Air-cooled engines, by their nature, will consume some oil. Often flights last several hours, so we want to make sure that the oil is at the proper level before we begin a trip. You check the oil by pulling out the dipstick, just as you would for a car. Your POH will specify a minimum oil level for flight. If the oil is more than a quart or a quart and a half below the full mark, ask your instructor to look with you. Many airplanes burn so little oil that such a reading is just fine; others go through so much that you might want to add oil if you're going on a cross-country flight away from the local area. The FBOs often fill the rental airplane's oil to about a quart below the maximum reading because airplane engines often throw the first quart overboard quickly if they are filled to the maximum.

6-3 *Always check the oil before each flight.*

While you're still looking inside the engine compartment, you'll notice a small square pull knob that opens the fuel strainer. You'll want to use it to check for the presence of any water in the fuel. Because water is heavier than gasoline and doesn't mix into solution with gas, this is easy to check. Pull the knob out for about 4 seconds, and allow fuel to drain out into a transparent plastic cup. Then you can hold the cup up and visually examine the contents. The fuel sump that is opened by pulling out at the knob is at the very bottom of the fuel system, so that any water in the fuel will collect there and run out when you perform this fuel check. When you release the knob, be sure that the flow of fuel out of the strainer stops.

Now look carefully at the cup of gasoline. Any water should sink to the bottom, and it may form globules. Aviation fuel is colored on purpose so that its grade can be visually determined. The Cessna 150 was originally designed to run on grade 80, but 80 octane fuel has been relegated to the history of aviation. The Cessna 150 can also operate on 100 low-lead (100 LL) aviation gasoline, which is abbreviated as *avgas.* Grade 100 LL is light blue in color. Water is naturally clear, so water will show up in a fuel sample if it is present. In the past, when pilots were finished looking at a fuel sample, they just dumped it on the tarmac. In these environmentally conscious times, we have learned not to be so blasé. So be sure to dispose of your fuel sample properly. Many 150s also have a gas drain on the bottom of each wing tank, near the cockpit doors. If your airplane has them, check the quality of the fuel in each tank with the same plastic cup. In the winter, if the airplane has not been stored in a heated hangar, the water in the fuel, if there is any, may freeze into ice balls. Then, little or no flow comes out of one or more of the strainers. If you ever experience this condition, don't try to fly the airplane. Have a technician look at it because the flow of fuel is probably blocked by ice.

The most common ways that fuel gets contaminated by water are either ill-fitting gas caps that allow rain to leak into the fuel tanks, or through condensation. Overnight most of the year, water vapor condenses out of the atmosphere and forms water droplets, which are seen as dew on the grass, on the surface of the windshield of your car, and on any other solid surface. Unfortunately, this condensation also occurs on the inside walls of fuel tanks, and not just in airplanes. The best way to avoid water condensing on the inside of the fuel tanks is to fill them with fuel after each flight, and especially after the last flight of the day. This way, there is no room in the tank for water vapor to condense into liquid water. If the airplane is stored in a heated hangar, the chances of condensation are reduced somewhat, but the threat is still there.

It is possible for contaminated fuel to arrive at the airport in the tanker truck that delivers it, and some fuel farm systems at airports are more susceptible to contamination than are others. These are less common causes of water in fuel than are leaky caps and condensation. Regardless of the cause of its presence, engines don't run on water. So, always check the fuel for contamination from water or dirt.

After you've performed all of the inspections inside the engine compartment, close the cowling access door, and make sure that it's closed properly and tightly. These doors can come open in flight, rip off, and possibly bang into the windshield or the wings or tail if they're not closed properly.

The next item to check is the propeller. Stand directly in front of the nose and look at each blade of the prop. Run your fingers lightly down the leading edge of each of the blades. You're looking for nicks in the blades. If you find one, no matter how small, have a technician look at it before you fly. There are some allowable small nicks, but if one is too deep, it can set up a stress point in the metal of the propeller. Stress points are where cracks begin. If a crack starts in a propeller blade, it can very quickly propagate until a piece of the blade breaks off. During flight, the propeller absorbs tremendous forces and stresses in normal operation, so make sure that it is free of defects. Also look at the back and front sides of the propeller too, looking for any signs of damage. If the bolts that secure the propeller to the flange of the engine's crank shaft are visible (they often aren't), check them too. Look here to see if they are present, and look at the safety wire that connects all of the bolts together so that one cannot back off.

While still at the front of the airplane, the next item to check is the nose gear. The Cessna 150 has a nose strut that uses air and oil for shock absorption, and you should plainly see some of the chrome strut exposed. The POH will tell you the amount of strut that should be extended and visible. If the proper length of strut is not exposed, have a technician add the needed air or oil to it before you fly. Also, look at the nose tire, checking for apparent proper inflation and the absence of any physical damage to the tire. There is no brake on the nose gear, so we are going to inspect only the strut and the tire up here.

Proceed on around the nose to the pilot's side of the cowling area. Here there is a tiny hole in the side of the fuselage, just behind the cowling. This hole is the *static air vent*. The pressure instruments that we described in Chap. 5 depend on the functionality of this air vent, and they won't work if the vent is blocked. This hole is so small that it can get clogged with wax when the airplane is cleaned, and the hole also makes a very attractive home for nesting insects. If you find that it is blocked, maintenance people will have to clean it before you proceed, or your airspeed indicator, altimeter, and vertical speed indicator won't function properly and will give you erroneous readings.

From here, walk along the leading edge of the left wing. Near the point where the strut attaches to the underside of the wing, you'll see another vent tube, right behind the strut, which is the vent for the fuel system. It too must be clean and free of obstructions. If it is clogged, the fuel may not drain out of the tanks properly into the engine. Check this fuel vent very carefully.

Just outboard of the fuel vent is the pitot tube, which we talked about in Chap. 5. This is the tube where the ram air enters to operate the airspeed indicator. The airspeed won't work at all if the pitot is blocked. Like the static air hole, the pitot is very attractive to insects as a place to build a nest. Also check to see that the pitot tube is approximately parallel with the underside of the wing. They do not get damaged very often, but it is possible that a pitot tube can get bent. If it appears to be bent, have a maintenance technician look at it before you fly because a bent tube will cause erroneous airspeed indications.

From here, go down the leading edge of the left wing, around the wing tip, to the trailing edge, inspecting the leading edge and tip of the left wing as you did on the right wing. Inspect the aileron and flap on the left wing in the same way you did on the right side. When all of these tasks are done, so is your exterior preflight check of the airplane. And, you're standing right beside the pilot's door, where the entire process began a few moments ago.

Getting Started in the Cockpit

Now you know that the airplane is safe to fly because you checked everything during the preflight inspection. Now it's time to get in. You'll sit in the pilot's seat, on the left, starting with your very first instructional flight. The airplane has fully functioning dual controls at both seats, even down to having dual brakes. Therefore, your instructor will always sit on the right, where he can fly the airplane while you learn. The Cessna 150 is not the easiest or most graceful airplane to enter. The cockpit is a bit cramped but not overly so. The door is somewhat small, so you'll be tempted to look for something inside to grasp to assist your getting in. Don't grab the control wheel or instrument panel. Rather, there is an assist strap on the forward door post that is put there just for that purpose.

Both of the seats are adjustable fore and aft, just as they are in a car (FIG. 6-4). They slide on tracks, with a release lever located on the bottom front of the seat. Adjust the seat into a position so that you're comfortable and can reach all of the controls. Push on the rudder pedals, one at a time, throughout the full length of their travel to make sure that you can get full rudder deflection if you need it. The FARs require that the seatbelt and shoulder harness be worn by those in the pilots' seats during takeoff and landing. Get into the habit of adjusting and fastening both of them right now, before you even start the engine. It's such an ingrained habit in me that I "belt up" even

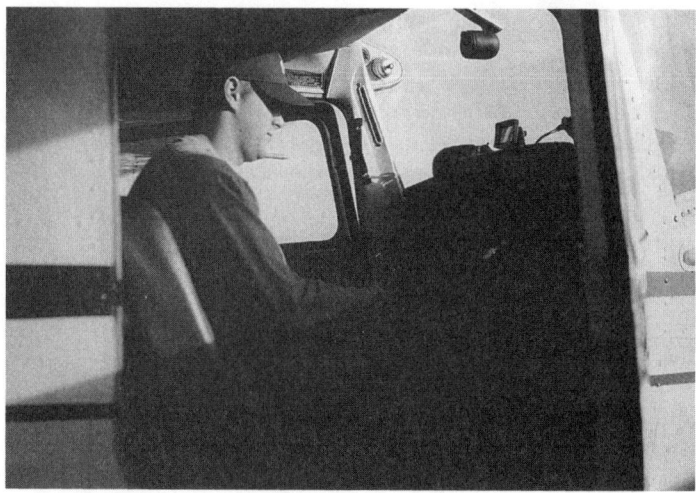

6-4 *Adjust the seat for comfort.*

if I'm only going to taxi an airplane from one spot on the airport to another, with absolutely no intention of flying it.

We still have a few more things to do before we start the
engine. Before engine start, it's smart to set the parking brake.
To do that, push down on both of the *toe brakes,* which are
the top halves of each rudder pedal. While you keep both
brakes depressed, pull out the parking brake knob to its
fullest extent of travel. Then, take the pressure off of the toe
brakes, and release your pull on the parking brake knob.
Cessnas have independent brakes on each main gear wheel,
activated by the toe brake on the respective rudder pedal. If
you've ever operated a tractor, or other such machinery, you
probably have experience with independent brakes. If you
haven't, the knack of using them comes very quickly. On the
ground, airplanes are steered by an interconnect between the
rudder pedals and the nose gear. Pushing a rudder pedal turns
the nose wheel in the same direction. The independent brakes
allow a pilot to turn in a tighter radius than could be done
using the nose wheel steering alone. It's a very bad habit to
turn by using the brakes, so it is something to avoid unless it
is absolutely necessary. If you lock a brake, you can turn the
airplane around in its own wingspan distance, but that is very
hard on the tire that isn't rotating. It is therefore a method that
should be used only when no other alternative is available.

Once you're in your seat, the instrument panel is directly in front of you. There are several electrical switches on a subpanel. Look at each of these, and make sure that they are all OFF. Then look at the floor, and check once more to see that the fuel selector is in the ON position. Even though you checked the fuel selector during the preflight, make sure that neither you nor the instructor kicked it to the OFF position as you got into the cockpit. If you start the engine with the fuel selector OFF, there is likely to be just enough fuel in the lines to allow you to taxi to the runway and commence the takeoff. As you lift off of the ground, things can get mighty quiet if the fuel selector isn't ON.

To the right of the subpanel where the electrical switches are, you'll find the three primary engine controls, the *carburetor heat, throttle,* and *mixture* knobs, in that order as you move from left to right. First, ensure that the carburetor heat (abbreviated as *carb heat*) is pushed all of the way into the panel, in the COLD position. We'll talk a lot more about its use in a little while. Move your hand to the right of the throttle, and you'll see the red mixture control knob. Make sure that it too is pushed all the way in, which will be in the RICH position.

Next, lay your right forefinger along the shaft of the throttle, with the knob of the throttle in the palm of your right hand. If you position your forefinger with the fingernail about $1/4$ of an inch from the stop, you can then push the throttle in about $1/4$ of an inch. That's about all the throttle opening you need for engine start. Never try to start an engine with the throttle opened much more than that for a couple of reasons. First, if the engine is cold, we want it to start running at a low revolutions-per-minute speed to allow it to warm up and to allow the oil to start circulating throughout the engine. It's very damaging to any engine to run it at high revolutions per minutes before it and the oil have warmed. Second, if the parking brake isn't set properly, or if there is any other problem with the brakes, we don't want the airplane to start moving rapidly across the ramp. If you start the engine with the throttle opening around $1/4$ of an inch, the airplane probably won't move at all even with the brakes off. If it does move, it will do so slowly, and you'll have time to shut the engine down before any trouble strikes.

Before starting the engine, most of the time you will need to prime it. If the weather is warm and the airplane has just returned from a previous flight, maybe you won't need to prime; your instructor will let you know. The primer is located on the subpanel, over to the left. To use it, you rotate it until it can be pulled out, and then you pull it out all of the way. Push it in slowly and repeat the process once. This will give the engine two shots of prime, which should be sufficient unless the weather is cold. It's always better to be conservative about priming because overdoing it will flood the engine. If the engine doesn't start readily with two shots of prime, you can always prime some more. But clearing a flooded engine is a nightmare of a job, and it sometimes runs the battery down if it's weak.

Now, turn the *master switch* to ON, which will energize the airplane's electrical system and enable you to use the starter. The master switch is a red button or rocker switch, depending upon the year of manufacture of your airplane, located near the throttle or near the primer (the exact location and type of switch changed from year to year during the production of the 150). Open the cockpit window and yell "Clear." Yell it loudly so that anyone near the airplane will hear you and know that you're about to start the engine. Wait a brief moment and look out the windshield and around the airplane to make sure that no one is nearby.

Once you've assured yourself that no one is near the airplane, turn the ignition switch to the START position, and as soon as the engine catches, release the key just as you do when you start your car. The ignition switch is spring-loaded to return to the BOTH position as soon as the starter is released. Some older 150s have a pull handle to engage the starter. If you're learning in one of those planes, turn the ignition switch to BOTH and then pull the T-handle out to engage the starter and release it as the engine starts.

After the engine starts, we want it to idle at about 1,000 rpm (FIG. 6-5). As soon as the engine gets going, look at the tachometer, and make whatever fine adjustment is needed with the throttle to achieve that idle speed. A speed of 1,000 rpm is enough to allow the alternator to kick in and start recharging the battery and powering the electrical system, yet it's slow enough not to unduly strain a cold engine. Take a look immediately at the oil pressure gauge. The needle should come up out of the red zone within 30 seconds in a Cessna 150, sooner if the weather is warm or if the airplane has been recently flown. If the pressure doesn't move up into the green range within that time frame, immediately shut the

6-5 *After you start the engine, adjust its idling speed with your forefinger along the throttle shaft.*

engine down to avoid any further damage from running it without oil pressure.

Assuming that the engine is running properly and that the oil pressure came up within limits, we're now ready to move out of our parking spot and begin taxiing. If you did not already raise the flaps from your preflight inspection, bring them up now. A tap of your toe on each toe brake, simultaneously, will release the parking brake. Keep your feet on the rudder pedals so that you can steer and be able to apply the brakes as needed. If the airport has a control tower, we'll have to contact ground control for permission to taxi from the parking ramp out onto a taxiway.

Applying a little power by pushing the throttle in a bit is all that it will take to start the airplane moving, assuming that it is parked on level ground. Keep the same hand position on the throttle that you did for starting, using your forefinger along the shaft, with the knob in the palm of your hand. That way you can make the kinds of fine adjustments in the throttle setting that will be needed during taxi. If we need to turn the airplane, pressure on the rudder pedal in the direction of the needed turn will usually get the job done. The connection between the rudder pedals and the steerable nose gear is designed to be a bit sloppy. It is not nearly as positive and precise as is the steering in a car. In Cessna airplanes, the steering linkage disconnects as soon as the airplane lifts off of the runway, and the shock strut in the nose gear extends. If you ever find that your 150 won't steer on the ground, check the extension of the strut in the nose. If it's got too much air in it, it is possible for it to be extended beyond the point where the steering disconnects. That's why the POH specifies a minimum and a maximum amount of strut extension when the airplane is on the ground, and it's what you should look for when you are doing your preflight check. If the extension is too little, there is not enough shock absorption; if it is extended too far, there is a likelihood that you will not have nose wheel steering.

The control wheel has no direct steering at all. During your first couple of flights, your instructor may ask you to taxi with your right hand on the throttle and your left hand in your lap. I have found that this is a very useful way to get a student accustomed to steering with rudder pedals and to eliminate the natural tendency, at first, to rotate the control wheel in an attempt to steer while taxiing. Later on, the instructor will show you that the wheel does play a part in taxiing if there is any appreciable wind (FIG. 6-6). If you have to taxi over any rough ground, unless you have a strong wind from behind you, pull the control wheel all the way back to take weight off of the nose wheel.

The tricycle landing gear is a wonderful invention. It has made ground handling of airplanes far easier than is the case with tailwheel airplanes. But the nose gear is inherently weak by the nature of its placement under the heaviest part of the airplane, right beneath the engine. When you taxi over sod, or other rough areas, pulling the wheel back will lighten the weight that the nose gear is carrying. If the sod is at all soft, the little nose tire can act like a knife and cut its way down into the mud to the point that you get stuck, or worse. Don't risk striking the propeller on the ground. Don't taxi on sod until your instructor and you talk about the techniques to use, she has demonstrated some of those techniques, and she has given you an okay to try it on your own.

At nontowered airports (we used to call them *noncontrolled airports*), it's up to each pilot to proceed on a see-and-be-seen basis. There is nothing inherently unsafe about operating at nontowered airports. If you drive on the Los Angeles freeway system, or in any other areas of congested auto traffic, you certainly don't have a control tower telling you what lane to be in or

TAXIING DIAGRAM

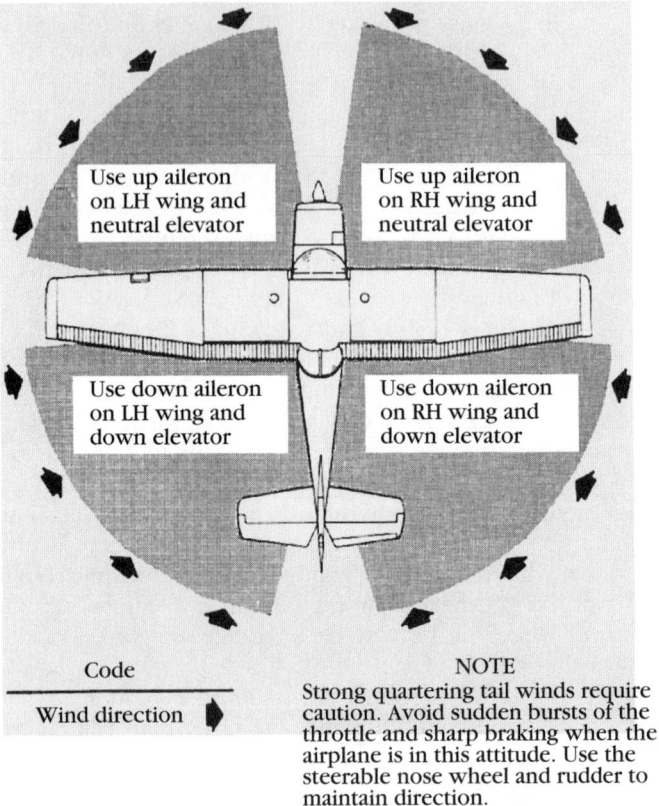

Use up aileron on LH wing and neutral elevator

Use up aileron on RH wing and neutral elevator

Use down aileron on LH wing and down elevator

Use down aileron on RH wing and down elevator

Code

Wind direction

NOTE
Strong quartering tail winds require caution. Avoid sudden bursts of the throttle and sharp braking when the airplane is in this attitude. Use the steerable nose wheel and rudder to maintain direction.

6-6 *Proper control inputs help compensate for wind during taxi operations.*

when to speed up or slow down, or making any of the other decisions for you that every driver makes every few seconds. For some reason, people not accustomed to aviation think at first that every airport needs a control tower. That just isn't so.

At nontowered airports, we still use the radio, which is discussed in more detail later. As you roll down the taxiway, keep your speed to that of a fast walk. If you creep along, it'll take forever to get to the runway, and you'll probably have difficulty steering the airplane because the response is a little sloppy. If you careen along, you may not have enough time to recognize and respond to hazardous situations. While taxiing, we have an opportunity to talk about the carburetor heat and how to use it.

The throat of the carburetor has a device called a *venturi,* which is shaped like an old-fashioned soda bottle. It's a tube that's narrower in the center of its length than it is at either end. Due to some laws of physics and fluid mechanics, a stream of fluid moving through a venturi undergoes a loss of both pressure and temperature as it leaves the narrow part of the tube where it was first compressed. As the stream of fluid (air and gasoline are both fluids) leaves the compression zone in the venturi, it rapidly expands as it is sucked into the intake manifold of the engine. This expansion results in the loss of pressure and, more importantly for this discussion, the loss of heat, so the temperature of the fuel-air mixture can decline dramatically. This decrease in temperature of the mixture of fuel and air flowing through the venturi in the carburetor can be as much as 40° Fahrenheit (F).

Air always has some water vapor in it, which we think of as humidity. Because of the temperature drop that occurs in the carburetor's venturi, this water vapor can freeze and ice can form in the carburetor throat when the outside air temperature is between 25° and 70°F. If this happens, the mixture of fuel and air going to the engine can be reduced or completely blocked by the accumulation of ice which may form in the carburetor's throat.

Carburetor ice usually occurs when the engine is running at relatively low revolutions per minute because the flow of the fuel-air mixture through the carburetor is going relatively slowly, allowing more time for it to freeze and become an ice block. If your car has a carburetor rather than the newer fuel injection, your engine may have stalled at stoplights in cool, rainy weather or at least have a hesitation in acceleration away from the stop. Now you know why: You may have had carburetor ice.

In normal cruising flight, carburetor ice isn't too much of a concern. With the engine running at or above the cruise power settings, the flow through the carburetor is sufficient to deter ice formation, unless atmospheric conditions are really favorable for icing. Carburetor ice at cruising speed usually occurs only when you are flying through air with really high humidity or when you're flying IFR through clouds or rain, where there is obviously lots of moisture in the air. The symptoms of carburetor icing are easy to recognize: The revolutions per minute will start to drop, sometimes very slowly, over a period of several minutes. If the pilot doesn't know what's happening, and he surely should if he's awake, the engine will start to run rough as more ice forms in the carburetor. If the pilot is really asleep, the engine will probably stop running.

Before the situation even gets to the point of rough running, you will have noticed that the revolutions per minute has fallen off a little, and you will have taken the curative measure, which is to pull out the carburetor heat knob. Almost instantly, the ice will melt. The carburetor heat system sends very hot air, which it takes from a muff around the exhaust pipes, and sends it directly into the carburetor. The induction of this hot air drives the temperatures in the carburetor throat up to a point where the ice melts very quickly. As the ice melts, the slug of water that results goes only one place, and that is through the engine. For that reason, the engine will run rough for a second or two as it ingests this water. Even if you delay taking remedial action until the engine is running rough from the presence of carburetor ice, the heat will still cure it. However, if you procrastinate until the ice blockage in the carburetor kills the engine, you will then be flying a glider. Without the engine running, there is no source of hot air to melt the ice.

We almost never apply carb heat for takeoff. The hot air is much less dense than cold air, and therefore, two things happen. The ratio of fuel to air in the normal mixture of the two gets very *rich*, which means that there is less air in the mix than there should be, because the hot air is so much less dense. Another product of running the engine with hot, less dense air going through it is that the engine can't produce its normal amount of power. Engines take loads of air to run properly, and when the air is less dense, the power production falls off. This also happens in higher altitudes, where the air is just less dense regardless of the temperature. Naturally, the hotter and higher you are, the less power the engine is producing. At takeoff we use full power in piston-powered airplanes that don't have turbochargers. We want to be able to get all of the power that we can for takeoff, and we don't want part of it robbed by using carb heat.

The red mixture control knob controls the ratio of fuel to air in the mix that is fed from the carburetor into the intake manifold and then into the cylinders of the engine. Any time that you leave the carburetor heat on for an extended period, such as when you are flying at very high altitudes or even at fairly low levels in very hot weather, you correct the overly rich mixture by using this control. The time-honored way to set a proper mixture is to *lean* the mixture by pulling out slowly on the control knob until you begin to note that the engine is just starting to run a little rough.

This roughness signals that the mixture is getting too lean; there is not enough fuel in the mix. Then, you push the mixture control knob back in, again slowly, until the engine resumes smooth running. Leave the mixture there until you either change the power setting or altitude, when you'll have to repeat the process to accommodate the new conditions.

We finally arrive near the runway after our taxi. Gently apply the brakes to stop the airplane on the *runup pad,* which is an area just short of the runway. This is where we will go through our final pretakeoff checks.

If we were flying at a towered field, the ground controller would have given us the barometric pressure so that we could set the altimeter. But because we're flying from a nontowered airport, we set the altimeter so that it reads the elevation of the airport in feet above mean sea level. Because this is our home base, your instructor knows the elevation and will tell it to you on your first instructional flight. When you go to another airport, you can get the information by looking for a sign, which is often posted near the ends of the runways. If there aren't any such signs, just pull out your aeronautical chart and look up the airport symbol, and you'll find the elevation in the printed block of data about that airport. Never fly without the chart that covers your area, even for local flights.

Turn the little setting knob at the bottom of the altimeter to move the indicator hands of the instrument until they read the field elevation. Here at our airport, the field elevation is 905 feet MSL. When you look in the window for the barometric pressure, you will see 30.00 in. Hg (30 inches of mercury). That's the barometric pressure right now. If we had a control tower here, the controller would have given us the pressure information, and we would have twisted the same setting knob until 30.00 showed in the window. Then the hands on the altimeter's face would have shown 905. Like other measuring devices, an altimeter can and will eventually get out of calibration, to the point that the correct elevation won't show when the right barometric pressure is dialed into the window. For VFR flying such as we're doing, an acceptable difference is about 75 feet. If there is more than that, the altimeter needs to be removed from the airplane and sent to an approved instrument repair shop for repair.

At most towered fields, the FAA provides a service known as *Automatic Terminal Information Service* (ATIS). This is a recorded broadcast that repeats itself over and over again, giving information about the airport and current conditions. It typically will tell us the weather at the airport, the local barometric pressure so that we can set our altimeter, and other information such as what runways are in use and any construction or other information important to pilots. Because we're operating from a nontowered field, we do not have ATIS at our home field.

Since we're flying in warm weather, we've taxied to the runway with the cockpit windows opened. Now there is an item on our pretakeoff checklist to latch them and also to give each door a little push to make sure that it is properly closed and latched. Check your door and the instructor's too. As the pilot, you'll be responsible to see that a passenger has a safe flight. A good instructor wants to be treated as a passenger to the extent possible so that you'll develop good habits right now, for the day after you get your license and fly with folks who don't know all of these things.

Your airplane's POH contains a checklist for every phase of flight, including the pretakeoff checks that we're now doing. *Always* use it. Most flight schools and FBOs copy the checklist and put them in laminated plastic sheets, often bound together with a ring at the top of the pages so that you can easily flip from one checklist to another depending on your phase of flight. If there isn't a bound group of checklists in the airplane that you're flying, take your copy of the POH, which you'll have to purchase for a nominal sum, and create this flip-page bound checklist for yourself.

The items on the checklists are too important to risk to memory. Later in your flying, as you advance to more complicated airplanes, the checklist will get more involved. If you fly more than one type of airplane, which many pilots do, you simply can never remember several different checklists. Now is the time that you will be forming the habits that will make you either a careful, safe pilot or a risky one, just as a child forms his or her personality early in life. Make the habits you develop now the kind that will bode well for you over the entire spectrum of your flying career. The rest of the steps that we'll describe now for the pretakeoff checks are normally performed on most airplanes. If your checklist differs either in

content or in the order in which the items are done, follow
your checklist.

We'll first check the flight controls for freedom of movement.
Many serious accidents have resulted from the pilot's error in not
removing the control lock or not checking the flight controls.
Any problems with the flight controls would have been easily
discernible had they been checked. On some airplanes, control
locks consist of blocks that are attached to the control surfaces
and clamp the rudder, elevator, and ailerons so that they can't
be moved. You don't have any indication inside the cockpit that
these clamps are in place until you try to move the controls
throughout their complete range of movement. Roaring down
the runway on takeoff is no time to discover that your controls
are still locked. You should have seen the external clamps when
you did the preflight inspection, but we're not going to leave
anything that important to chance.

Take the control wheel and rotate it fully from one side to
the other and then pull it all the way back. Next, push it all the
way forward. While you're doing this exercise, turn your head
and actually look at the control surfaces to ensure that they're
moving. Now do the same with the rudder pedals.

The elevator trim is controlled by a large black wheel that protrudes from the instrument panel below the throttle (FIG. 6-7). It
has a pointer that moves as the wheel is turned. There is a setting where the pointer will be opposite the word TAKEOFF

6-7 *Set the elevator trim prior to takeoff.*

printed beside the pointer. Rotate the trim wheel until the pointer lines up with TAKEOFF.

Next, we'll check the operational health of the engine. Hold the brakes firmly down all the way and advance the throttle until the tachometer reads 1,700 rpm. Look outside for a moment to make sure that the brakes are holding and that the airplane isn't moving. Because it's summer, we don't have to worry about the airplane sliding on snow or patches of ice that may be on the runup pad. Put that possibility away in your memory banks for winter flying. With the engine running at 1,700 rpm, grasp the key in the ignition and rotate the switch from the BOTH to the R position and watch how many revolutions per minute are lost now that the engine is running only on the right magneto and its associated separate ignition system.

The revolutions per minute should drop about 75 or so since the engine is slightly less efficient when running on only one of the ignition systems, when only one of the two spark plugs is firing in each cylinder. A larger drop than that should be checked by the maintenance folks before you fly. No drop could mean that the switch is faulty and might not be switching off the left magneto and its ignition system, which is another thing that needs to be fixed right now. A switch that doesn't turn off a magneto is very dangerous because the engine is "hot" at all times on the ground and could fire or even completely start if someone rotates the propeller, even slightly. After you've checked the right magneto, turn the switch back to BOTH for a few seconds.

When you have the engine running only one magneto, the spark plugs normally fired by the other one aren't firing and can slightly foul as carbon builds up on their electrodes. Turning the switch back to BOTH allows them to fire and clear up any of these deposits. Then, turn the switch to L and check the revolutions per minute when running only on the left magneto. Many POHs also have a specification for the maximum differential in the revolutions-per-minute drop between what you see from one magneto and the other. Our engine has thus far checked out OK, so let's go onto the next step.

Return the switch to BOTH; we're finished with the magneto checks. Now pull the carburetor heat knob all the way out. Again, there should be some drop in revolutions per minute because the hot air robs the engine of some of its power. If the engine runs more than a little bit rough, you should get it looked at. If there is no drop, then a trip to the maintenance shop is in order because when the carb heat is functioning normally, there is always some drop in the revolutions per minute, usually about 75 to 100. While you're doing this, glance over at the oil pressure and temperature gauges to make sure that their readings are both within the green, normal operating range. Then reduce the throttle to the 1,000 rpm idle setting. Next, pull the throttle all the way out to make sure that doing so doesn't reduce the setting so low that the engine quits. With the throttle all the way retarded, the engine should idle smoothly, usually at around 650 rpm. The alternator warning red light may come on, and that's all right at this very low engine speed as long as it goes off when you increase the power back to 1,000 rpm.

Now look at the vacuum gauge, which tells us if the engine-driven vacuum pump is providing the vacuum needed to run the attitude indicator and the directional gyro. It should read around 4 inches of vacuum. Although we don't actually need these instruments for VFR flying, if the pump isn't working, we will want to get it fixed. You may someday accidentally stray into IFR weather and have to avail yourself of the emergency instrument flying training that you'll receive as a part of your curriculum. You can't do that if the instruments aren't getting the vacuum that they need to operate.

Your instructor will show you how to position the airplane on the runup pad to perform these pretakeoff checks. If there is any appreciable wind blowing, the airplane should be heading into the wind for a couple of reasons. First, because we have an air-cooled engine, heading into the wind allows a flow of air into and over the engine to cool it. Sitting with the engine running, especially at the higher power settings that we used for the magneto and carb heat checks, can lead to higher-than-desired engine temperatures if we have the nose pointed away from the wind. Second, if the wind is blowing hard, it's much safer to have the nose pointed into that wind because that way the airplane is more easily controlled and far less likely to blow around or over.

After all of these checks are completed, the last thing to do before takeoff is to visually assure yourself that no one else is in the way. The FARs and common sense both provide that landing aircraft have the right of way over those that are waiting to take off. You don't want to be in the takeoff position on the runway until you're absolutely certain that nobody is landing on that runway, or even on a different runway at a nontowered field. If you have the physical room on the runup pad, turn the airplane completely around in a 360° circle, and look out of the windows to see the entire traffic pattern all the way around the airport. The *traffic pattern* is a planned and prescribed rectangular course around the airport that airplanes follow when landing or departing. We'll talk a lot more about traffic patterns later. At towered fields, the controllers are supposed to provide separation between airplanes under their jurisdiction. But all human beings make mistakes, and controllers are no exceptions. Even though you may be cleared by a control tower to get onto the runway, certainly look around yourself first, and taxi off of the runup pad, onto the runway, only when both you and the controller are satisfied that it's safe to do so.

Ready for Takeoff

Now we know that there isn't any other traffic, so we're ready to fly. Taxi the airplane onto the runway, and line up in the center of it. Almost all runways will have a white centerline painted down the length of the runway to aid pilots in remaining in the middle. Smoothly push the throttle all the way in to the full-power position. Maintain a straight course down the center by using the rudder pedals to steer the nosewheel. Be careful that your feet aren't planted up high on the pedals because you certainly don't want to be applying any pressure on the brakes at this point. As you roll down the runway, the airplane picks up speed rapidly.

After we've rolled down the runway about 800 feet, the airspeed indicator will have swept past 50 knots. You'll also realize that, in the meantime, the flight controls have "come alive," which means that enough air is flowing over them that they are now becoming effective. Now it's time to ease back on the control wheel so that the nose rises a bit to give the wings a positive angle of attack. Initially, you'll need to pull back a little more than you have because most people are a little tentative on the first takeoff. As soon as you have the nose tire off of the ground, the airplane will become airborne. Hold the nose right where it is, relative to the outside horizon, and we'll start climbing away from the runway.

The nose will want to start to swing a little to the left, due to the P-factor of the propeller, which we discussed earlier.

Apply a bit of pressure to the right rudder to keep the nose going straight, and use the control wheel to keep the wings level. You'll soon develop the habit of selecting a reference point beyond the end of the runway at which to aim the nose, and that will keep you going in a straight line during the climb-out. From your very first lesson, do not develop the poor practice of climbing out with the airplane slightly banked to the right to counteract the P-factor. Use the rudder for its intended purpose.

Airspeed Control

Now it's time for your first lesson in how to control airspeed. In light airplanes, pilots usually control the airspeed with a combination of nose attitude and power setting.

Whenever we have a fixed power setting, such as now while we're climbing at full power, the desired airspeed is maintained by adjusting the nose attitude either up or down, as the need arises. There are several different airspeeds at which we could climb. The POH sets out a certain climbing speed that would get us up over any obstacle in our path in the shortest horizontal distance over the ground. This is called the *best angle-of-climb speed*. Another climbing speed that the manufacturer has determined in testing will give us the most altitude gain in the shortest period of time, and that is known as the *best rate-of-climb speed*.

Here at our airport we do not have short runways, and we also do not have any obstacles in our path right after takeoff. Therefore, we don't need to climb at the best angle possible. We could climb at the best rate, which would get us up to altitude in less time than if we climbed at any other airspeed. But, even at the best rate-of-climb speed, the nose will be probably riding high on the horizon, somewhat blocking our view straight ahead. Develop a habit right now of thinking about where other airplanes might be and always keeping an eye out for any collision hazard. Few pilots have ever survived a midair collision. So, we'll use a compromise airspeed in our climb that gives us a decently good rate of climb and also allows the nose attitude on the horizon to be low enough that we can see if there are any other airplanes in our path. Experience with the Cessna 150 has determined that around 70 knots is a good climbing speed, and we call this the *cruise climb airspeed*. Using the cruise climb speed also allows more airflow through the engine compartment. On a hot summer day, this might be important because we don't want to see the engine temperatures get too high during our climb.

As we approach 400 to 500 feet above the ground, we'll make a 90° turn, usually to the left. At some airports, local rules call for a right turn if there are obstacles off to the left or if there are noise-sensitive areas over there. Once we make this 90° turn, we can climb out away from the airport. Most flight schools use a designated area somewhere near the airport but far enough away that training maneuvers don't present a threat to airplanes coming and going into the traffic pattern. This is called the *practice area*. We'll climb to our practice area, and we'll level off from the climb when we're about 2,000 feet above the ground. To level off from the climb, first put the nose in a level attitude by observing where the nose is on the horizon. To do this takes a little forward pressure on the control wheel. The first few times that you level off like this, look out at the wingtips on both sides of the airplane. When the undersides of the wings are roughly level with and parallel to the horizon, you'll be fairly close to a nose-level attitude. This technique will also help you to keep the wings level while you are transitioning to a level attitude. Once you have the undersides of the wings parallel to the horizon, it will take only minor adjustments to the attitude of the nose to achieve level flight. Then look at the altimeter to see whether you're continuing to gain altitude, losing it, or staying level. Don't chase the altimeter or become mesmerized by it; rather, use it only as a reference. If the airplane is still going up, lower the nose a little more, wait a few seconds, look at the wingtips, and see if that stops all of the climbing. If you have overcorrected and we start going down, raise the nose a little, wait, see what happens, and make whatever final adjustment in the nose attitude is needed to neither climb nor descend. Learn right now, early in your flight training, not to chase the indications of the instruments—you'll never fly level that way.

After we level off, and as the airspeed increases to around 90 knots, it's time to pull the throttle back to cruise power. If we were going on a cross-country flight, we'd run the engine somewhere between 2,350 and 2,500 rpm, depending on how high we were, how far we needed to go, and a few other factors. For most training flights, however, we aren't interested in flying as fast as practical, and there is no need to burn fuel at any higher rate than we need for flight training purposes. Additionally, even though we are wearing headsets and have a voice-activated intercom to enable us to talk to each other, we don't want any more cabin noise than is necessary. Headsets do a very good job of reducing the otherwise high cabin noise level, but any reduction in the ambient noise only makes it quieter and easier for us to talk to each other. And we're going to be talking constantly during most of these first few lessons. A good compromise power setting for most training in our Cessna 150 will be 2,350 rpm.

Your instructor will show you how to use a friction control knob on the throttle. Light airplanes have enough engine vibration during flight to cause the throttle to creep, sometimes in, sometimes out, during cruise flight. There is a knurled circular knob around the throttle shaft that can be tightened to prevent the throttle from unwanted movement. Tighten it down some to keep the power at 2,350 rpm, but don't tighten it so tightly that you can't move the throttle when you want to. Last, now that we're all leveled off, reach down to the elevator trim wheel and rotate it, usually forward, so that you don't have to keep constant pressure applied to the control wheel to keep the nose level. The goal is to trim the airplane for level flight so that it will stay level when you totally take your hands off of the wheel.

You'll quickly get the hang of the effects of each of the flight controls. It's best, now, to forget mechanical use of the controls. Don't think about moving them, but rather, sense the pressures that you need to apply to achieve a desired attitude. All performance from an airplane results from the combination of attitude and power that the pilot has selected. Just think of what you want to happen. Think in terms of left wing down, right wing down, nose up, nose down, and the like rather than trying to translate the desired attitude and the mechanically moving controls. Let the controls become extensions of your limbs and mind. If that sounds confusing, consider it this way. Your nervous system masters the techniques of physical movement quite easily. When you throw a baseball, you don't mechanically or mentally break down the action into the many muscle movements involved in the task. You just pick up the ball and throw it. When you teach a child to throw a ball for the first time, you don't analyze the action to any great extent. Rather, you teach the child to get the "touch" and "feel" of throwing.

Control handling is a technique that is difficult to verbalize precisely. You drive your car in the same manner by making constant small control inputs to do what you want without conscious thought about each tap on the brake, increase in pressure on the gas pedal, or small corrections with the steering wheel.

At first, you'll probably have a tendency to overcontrol the airplane by using too much movement of the controls. Don't worry about that. It's natural, and it is a habit derived from driving automobiles and operating other machines that are less sensitive to control inputs than airplanes are. Your technique will quickly improve as you get accustomed to the light control forces needed to fly an airplane. Most often only fingertip pressures will suffice, especially in making the small corrections necessary in straight and level flight.

Beginning a turn in an airplane differs from turning a car. In a car, you use the steering wheel; in an airplane you use the control wheel and rudder pedals. To begin a turn, simultaneously apply pressure on the wheel in the desired direction to begin banking. Also use your foot to apply pressure on the rudder pedal in the same direction. For a left turn, it's wheel to the left and left rudder at the same time. We refer to this simultaneous use of wheel and rudder as *coordinating the controls*. As soon as the angle of bank reaches what you want, release the pressure on the controls and return both the wheel and the rudder pedals to neutral. Remember that it is the lift of the wings, always acting perpendicular to them, that continues to pull the airplane around in a turn until you either recover from the turn or the airplane runs out of fuel.

If, instead of returning the controls to neutral after the turn reaches the desired bank angle, you continue to apply control pressure in the direction of the turn, the angle of bank and rate of turn will get steeper and steeper until the bank angle goes beyond 90° and the airplane makes an inverted roll. If you progress in your training beyond your private license to aerobatic flying, you'll see what we mean. But for now, we don't want to see the bank angle exceed 45° for most operations, or sometimes 60°, but no more than that. To recover from the turn and reestablish straight and level flight, just apply control wheel and rudder pressures opposite to the direction of turn. Wait a second or two while the airplane rolls out of the turn. When the wings are level again, return the controls to neutral and fly straight ahead. That's all there is to entering a turn, allowing the airplane to turn until it is headed where you want it, and recovering back to straight and level flight.

Because a part of the total lift that is generated by the wings is acting to pull the airplane around in the turn, we need to increase the total lift while we are turning. If the airplane weighs a certain amount, we will always need lift equal to the weight in order to stay at a level altitude. Whenever we turn, we have to add some back pressure to the wheel to keep from losing altitude during the turn. Pulling the wheel back a little increases the angle of attack of the wings, and that enables them to increase the total lift that they are generating. So, as you roll into a turn, your instructor will show you that you'll pull the wheel back at the same time as the wings are banking. The steeper the bank, the more you need to pull back. When you return the airplane to wings-level flight, you need to release the back pressure on the wheel as you roll the airplane out of the turn. If you do not, your nose will pop up as the airplane levels, resulting in a little climb. Coordinating all of these control pressures will become second nature after only a few hours of instruction.

Stalls and Stall Recovery

We've already talked some about stalls and how you know when the airplane is about to stall. Most modern airplanes are equipped with a stall warning indicator that either lights up, beeps, or whistles. Our Cessna 150 has a warning horn that sounds like a mournful cry when it is activated. In addition, there are also aerodynamic signs of an impending stall.

As the stall approaches, the controls in the cockpit get a mushy feeling to them. This is because they are losing effectiveness close to the stall, so the pilot has to use more control movement than is used at normal flying speeds to accomplish a particular result. When the airplane gets closer to the stall, the entire airplane will start buffeting or shaking. The buffet may come from the tail surfaces, the wings, or both; but in any event, it's hard to ignore. Last, there is an airspeed indicator right in front of you, and unless you've caused a very unusual stall called an *accelerated stall,* by overenthusiastic yanking of the control wheel back, or unless you're in a very steep bank, you'll see that the airspeed is getting very slow as you get closer to the stall.

The modern light airplane is designed to have a gentle stall that is easy to avoid and easy to manage if unintentionally entered. The days are gone when stalls developed without aerodynamic warning and quickly and violently degenerated into what is known as a *spin,* which laypeople incorrectly called a *tailspin.* Our Cessna 150 has good stall characteristics, especially for teaching stalls. It has excellent aerodynamic warnings, and the stalls are easy to manage. Yet, if the stall is ignored or if grossly incorrect recovery techniques are used, you'll quickly know it. Some other trainers have stall characteristics that are so benign that the student who trains in them barely learns anything about stalls. Heavier and faster airplanes have stall behavior that is a bit more sudden and quirky than does the Cessna 150. As you get your license and then check out in different airplanes, you should always practice a few stalls with an instructor onboard, in each type of airplane that is new to you. Now let's go through the process of performing a stall and seeing how we recover from it.

Practicing stalls takes attention to the task at hand. Therefore, the first thing that we want to do before performing any such maneuver that takes our attention away from constantly looking for other airplanes is to do a *clearing turn.* Enter a turn in either direction, and continue it for a 90° change of heading. Look around, above, and below your airplane. Then roll out of that turn, and do a turn in the opposite direction, continuing to scan all around for other traffic. After these two turns, you'll end up flying in the same direction as you were before the first turn. Now we're ready do to our first stall. Pull the throttle back to idle and raise the nose to the normal climbing attitude. It'll take several seconds for the airspeed to bleed off, during which you'll have to add continuing back pressure to hold the nose up. As you add the continuing back pressure, you will notice that the nose appears to get very "heavy." Soon you'll have the control wheel nearly all the way back in an attempt to keep the nose in the climbing attitude.

The nonevent is about to happen. The airspeed has fallen back to about 43 knots, and the needle on the airspeed indicator is bouncing a little and is hard to read precisely. The airspeed indicator isn't exact in this attitude anyway because the relative wind is coming from below the leading edge of the wing and is therefore entering the pitot tube at an angle instead of head on.

This inherent inaccuracy of the airspeed indicator at high angles of attack is called *position error.*

Soon the wings are stalled, the airplane is just mushing along, not doing anything remarkable or scary. The nose is bobbing up and down a little as the wings are doing what they are designed to do—trying to unstall themselves. A glance at the vertical speed indicator and altimeter will confirm that although we are keeping the wings level and the nose high, the airplane is actually descending and losing altitude. We are no longer truly flying; the wings' lift isn't overcoming gravity.

Modern airplanes are designed so that their wings don't stall, all at once, over the entire wingspan. What is now happening is that the inner portions of the wings are stalled, while the outboard sections are still producing lift. This design enables us to keep some control of the ailerons to a limited extent when the inner portions of the wings are stalled. If we suddenly jerk the wheel all the way back, we could probably get the angle of attack high enough to stall the outer sections of the wings too, but for now, we don't need to do that. All that we need to do to recover from the stall is to lower the angle of attack to restore airflow over the entire wing. To accomplish that, just lower the nose a little, and the wings are flying again. As soon as the nose is lowered, we add power, and the recovery comes a little more quickly.

The whole story to recovering from a stall centers on the concept of reducing the angle of attack to a point where airflow is restored over the wings. Power can hasten this process, but adding power does not end the stall until a positive control input is induced to lower the angle of attack of the wings. Some jet fighters and aerobatic aircraft have so much excess power that they can fly straight up. Their engines produce enough power to overcome the weight of the airplane. Our Cessna 150 isn't in their league.

If you learn to fly in a glider before transitioning to airplanes, you'll practice stalls in much the same way as we've just described. Because a glider has no engine, you learn from the beginning to lower the angle of attack to effectuate a stall recovery. Flying gliders teaches a lot to any pilot, and I highly recommend that every pilot take at least a few instructional flights in a glider. Even if you don't fall in love with the sport of powerless flight, your aviation education will be far more complete.

Other Stalls

We can also perform a stall with the flaps extended, instead of retracted where they are positioned for normal cruising flight. With the flaps hanging out, the stall speed is reduced some, and in the 150, the stall will occur at about 38 knots if the flaps are fully extended. The behavior of the airplane will be a little more dramatic at the point of stall, and the nose will "fall" more definitely than it does when the flaps are fully retracted. Also, when the flaps are extended all of the way, a stall is accompanied by more aerodynamic buffeting.

So far, we've been discussing stalls performed from a wings-level attitude. An airplane can stall in any attitude, and we will practice stalls done from turns. When an airplane is stalled in a turn, the stall will be more abrupt than when the wings are banked. In a 30° bank, which is about normal for most turns, there is more buffeting, and the break, which is the point of stall, will be more abrupt. The nose will fall into a nose-down attitude. Quite possibly, the airplane will "fall off," which is airplane jargon that means that the bank angle may increase as the stall occurs.

To recover from this type of stall, the first thing to do is to stop any yawing of the nose. First apply pressure to the rudder pedal opposite to the direction of the turning movement. The turning will stop almost immediately. Now, lower the nose and get the wings level. The wings will already have begun leveling from the rudder input that you used to stop the yawing of the nose. Also, apply power to hasten the recovery, and in less time than it took to read this paragraph, the airplane is flying again.

The big difference between a stall from turning flight and one from a wings-level attitude is that more altitude is lost in the maneuver and in the recovery during the turn. That's why unintentional stalls can be dangerous if the airplane is turning. You'll see that after a little practice, you can recover from a straight and level stall with almost no altitude loss. But not so for a turning stall. If you accidentally get into a stall while turning, especially at a very low altitude in the traffic pattern while approaching to land or just after takeoff, you may become a statistic. Low-altitude stalls, especially from turns, are one of the greatest causes of accidents in light airplanes. Now you know how to avoid an unintentional turning stall because you've practiced them at a safe altitude and know what they are like.

Stalls can also be performed with the engine producing any amount of power, all the way from idle to full throttle. During your training, you will do power-on stalls as well as the ones that we've just described when the power has been first reduced to idle. Power-on stalls tend to be more abrupt, and the breakaway of the airplane at the time of the stall becomes more exaggerated. That is why you will first learn to do stalls with the power reduced to idle before you begin doing them with the power above idle. Since the thrust of the engine tends to delay the onset of the stall, typically stalls performed with power on result in a more exaggerated nose-up attitude, before the wings actually stall.

There are more old sayings and clichés in aviation than the contents of the proverbial bottle of little liver pills. One of the time-honored concepts is that there are three things that never do a pilot any good: the altitude above him, the runway behind the airplane, and the fuel in the truck back at the airport. Practice stalls a lot; they are fun and provide great training. But remember that stalling is safe only when done at an altitude high enough to permit a recovery before any critical loss of altitude occurs. As a general rule, be about 2,500 feet above the ground before initiating any intentional stall. If your instructor wants you higher than that, all the better.

Approaching to Land

Approaches and landings in the Cessna 150 can be made with power on to some degree, with the power at idle, without any flaps extended, or with the flaps out at any angle of deflection up to the maximum of 40°. There isn't any "normal" approach configuration because the POH allows any of these variables to be used by the pilot. The determining factors that dictate the type of approach and landing to be made and the configuration of the airplane's flap settings are primarily the surface wind conditions, the turbulence of the air, and the size and kind of airport into which you are going.

When I learned to fly in the mid-1960s, we learned to make all of our approaches with power off, gliding the airplane all of the way around the traffic pattern and then landing in a fully stalled condition. Today there are fewer gliding approaches because airports are larger and generally have more traffic going into and departing from them. However, unless strong surface wings prohibit a full stall landing, that is still the only correct way to land a single-engine airplane, especially a trainer. Gliding approaches, made with the power at idle, are still a valuable skill for any pilot to master. Whenever there is no traffic ahead of you in the pattern, my advice is to make every approach with power at idle. If and when the day comes that you need this technique, such as when performing a forced landing after an engine failure, it'll be old hat. If you've always approached the runway with some power, you won't be well trained for the day when you don't have any power to use.

Another benefit of learning to fly a glider comes into play right here. Because a glider has no engine, every approach is made while purely gliding. There are controls in gliders that the pilot uses to vary the angle and rate of descent during the landing approach, such as spoilers, speed brakes, and flaps. Although no typical training airplane has anywhere near the glide performance of a glider, landing without power in an airplane is not much of an event for a glider pilot. A glider pilot learns to judge the approach while making it, and to vary the angle and rate of descent as needed to land at the intended spot. The pilot of a light airplane can and should be able to do the same, all without having to add power, once the throttle is retarded to idle while still in the traffic pattern.

Typically, we aim to touch down somewhere in the first third of the runway. Naturally, this rule of thumb varies to suit the conditions at hand. If we're landing in a large airline airport with 12,000-foot runways, and the turnoff to the area where we'll park is 8,000 feet down that runway, we don't need to land at the approach end and then taxi for well over a mile before leaving the runway. That would be very inefficient, and it would tie up the runway from use by other traffic until we vacated it.

Conversely, if we're going into a 2,000-foot strip, we don't want to let the first third of it (almost 700 feet) go needlessly underneath us and get ourselves into a position where we either have to use aggressive braking to stop or, worse, overrun the end of the runway. Judgment has to be developed and used. For our purposes, let's assume that we'll be landing at a typical general aviation airport, where the runway is adequate, without being either excessively long or short.

Take a look at FIG. 6-8 and learn the names and locations of the downwind and base legs of the pattern. After you roll out of a turn from the base leg, now aligned with the runway, you'll be on what's called *final approach,* or just *final* for short. At

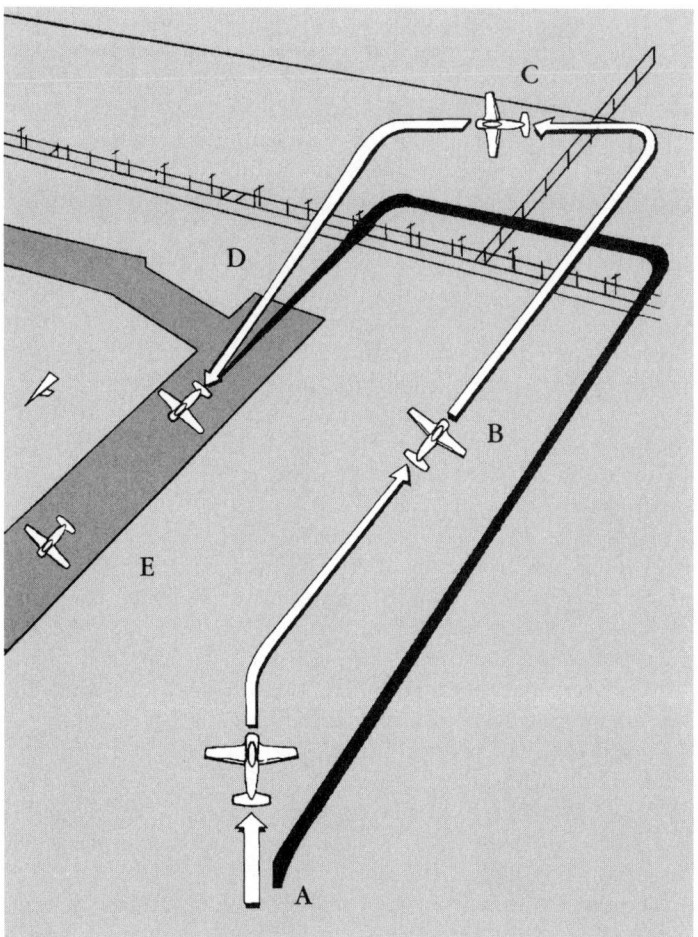

6-8 *Normal left-hand traffic pattern: Enter A at a 45° angle so that you can see other traffic. Lengths of the downwind leg B and the base leg C are determined by wind conditions and other traffic. Touch down at D, and roll out on the runway E.*

most small airports, plan to be at an altitude of 800 feet above the ground as you enter the downwind leg. Plan your approach to the pattern so that you can arrive at this altitude, called the *pattern altitude,* before you actually arrive on the downwind leg. Don't enter downwind high and then descend while flying this leg; you might descend right into another airplane below you who did it the right way. Realize now that the most difficult airplane to see is the one below you. It doesn't contrast very well with the terrain that is in your visual background. An airplane at the same altitude as yours is easier to see, and the one above you is easiest of all to pick out.

Aim for a point along the downwind leg that is at the halfway point along the runway as the place where you'll turn into, and become established on, the downwind leg. Plan to turn about 45° from your heading as you approach the airport onto the downwind leg. (See FIGS. 6-9 and 6-10.) Normally turns in the traffic pattern are made to the left, as is recommended in the *Aeronautical Information Manual.* But at some airports the traffic pattern uses right turns. *Right traffic,* as the pattern with right turns is called, is used at airports where tall buildings or other structures, noise-sensitive areas, or other justifications dictate flying on the other side of the runway, opposite where you would be if you were making left turns.

As soon as you become established on the downwind leg, keep your head on a swivel, looking around for any airplanes ahead of you in the pattern, taxiing toward takeoff, taking off from the runways below you, or entering the pattern behind you. Make sure that the mixture control is in the RICH position.

Now, pull the carburetor heat knob out all the way, and leave it in that position until just before we land. As you pass the approach end of the runway, pull the throttle all the way back to idle. Hold the nose up until the airspeed reads about 65 knots, and then lower the nose just enough to maintain that airspeed. Leave the flaps up for now, and the airplane will begin a gentle gliding descent.

The time to turn from the downwind leg onto the base leg is never the same on any two approaches, and this timing is something that you'll just have to learn to judge. Generally, the turn onto the base leg occurs when the intended landing spot is about 45° behind you, as you look at the runway over your left shoulder. If there is a strong wind blowing down the runway, you'll learn to turn sooner than you would if there were little or no wind. With a heavy wind in your face while on the final, you'll want to be in closer to the runway while on base leg, so that your time on the final isn't protracted by the slow speed that you'll have over the ground.

As soon as your turn to the base leg is completed, add about 20° of flap extension. Unless the wind is strong, we'll soon put the flaps all the way down, but not yet. Because the flaps are

6-9 *Here it is for real: entering the pattern at 800 to 1,000 feet above ground at a 45° angle to the downwind leg. The wind indicator is in the segmented circle in the foreground.*

6-10 *Flying downwind, parallel to the runway, at 800 or 1,000 feet above the ground, depending on the local requirements.*

now partially deployed, they are adding drag, and you'll need to lower the nose just a little bit more to maintain the gliding speed of 65 knots. Your instructor will harp about maintaining airspeed in many of your maneuvers, and none of them is more important than now. Remember that stalls are great to practice at altitude, and a stall is performed within a few inches of the ground as we land; but we don't want to risk a stall while in the traffic pattern.

Flaps should not normally be extended all at once even by an experienced pilot. While in the training stages of your career, periodic application of more flaps allows you to see how the airplane reacts and to maintain your airspeed and attitude in much better control. The flap switch on the newer 150s is an electric switch with a handle shaped like a paddle, just to the right of the mixture control on the panel. When flaps are extended, the angle of descent increases, and you have to lower the nose to keep the proper airspeed.

As we fly the base leg, we will want to time the turn to the final approach so that we roll out of the turn lined up with the runway. Don't worry if you overshoot this turn and aren't lined up for the first several times that you fly the pattern (FIG. 6-11). The timing of this turn is also a product of judgment that takes a little while to develop. Because we're making a power-off, gliding approach, we'll add the rest of the flaps as we fly down the final. We're also assuming that there aren't any adverse winds on this approach that would require our landing with only partial flap extension. As soon as the rest of the flaps are deployed, the nose attitude will have to be lowered significantly to maintain our 65-knot gliding airspeed. The angle of descent will steepen, and the visibility over the nose will enable you to easily see the entire runway environment right in front of you.

While in the glide during the final approach, it's time to pick out the spot on the runway where you think you'll touch down (FIG. 6-12). Watch this spot for a few seconds, and put it in relation to a fixed position on the windshield which we'll call our *windshield reference point*. If the spot on the ground starts moving up the windshield from the windshield reference point, we're not going to be able to get to that spot on the ground, in the present configuration, while gliding; we will touch down short of it. To cure that, add some power. By adding power, the angle of descent will flatten out, and the airplane will go farther along the ground before it reaches the landing spot. If your spot on the runway is moving down the windshield, away from the

6-11 *Turning from the base leg onto the final approach. The base leg is usually about a quarter mile from the end of the runway.*

6-12 *On the final approach. We're a little to the left of the runway centerline and correcting to get back in line with it.*

windshield reference point, we're not descending at a steep enough angle, and we'll touch down beyond the point on the ground that you picked out. Depending on the length of the runway, this may be okay, or we may be setting ourselves up for a trip into the weeds off of the end of the runway. If we're *overshooting* the runway, we have to descend at a steeper angle, which we do by either reducing power, adding flaps, or both. In an extreme circumstance, when we've done all that we can to steepen the angle of descent and it still looks like we'll overshoot, the only remedy is to add full power, begin a climb, retract the flaps, and fly the entire traffic pattern all over again. This is no sign of failure. All wise pilots have gone around in this situation more than once.

The use of the windshield reference point in relation to a fixed point on the runway is a time-honored way of learning to make precision spot landings. But for now, don't worry too much about touching down exactly on the desired spot on the runway. Greater precision will come with practice. During your training days in which you're now involved, use the windshield reference point simply to determine whether your approach is going to take you safely to the runway and not result in a serious over- or undershoot. For now, we'll be happy to use all of the runway that is safely available. A student pilot's major task at this point is to learn to fly the pattern and get the feel of the airplane and how to land it. Also, when using the windshield reference point, do not get mesmerized by staring at the runway. Continue to scan your instruments, and scan the ground and sky for other traffic.

Once the airplane is throttled back to idle power and established in the glide for the landing approach, the weather conditions and the laws of aerodynamics take control and dictate the maximum distance that the airplane can glide before it reaches the ground. With the engine idling, there is nothing that you can do with the wheel or rudder pedals to increase the gliding distance by even an inch. The only normal way to glide farther is to add power. Because we have flaps extended, we could increase the gliding distance somewhat by retracting them partially or all of the way. But this could be dangerous. The total lift being generated by the wings drops when the flaps are pulled up, and therefore, the stalling speed increases some. While we're fairly low on the final approach, usually between 400 feet and the ground, this isn't the place to put the airplane into a condition where the stalling speed goes up. If you've got flaps deployed on the final, which you normally will have, then add power when you need to go farther, and leave the flaps alone. You may encounter abnormal situations in which your instructor will alter this advice, and those procedures will be demonstrated further along in your training.

When a new student pilot sees that the glide is going to result in a touchdown short of the runway, his natural human tendency is to pull back on the wheel to try to stretch the glide. This won't ever work and will, in fact, actually have the opposite effect. When you raise the nose by pulling back on the wheel, you increase the angle of attack of the wings. As we've already discussed, a by-product of an increase in the angle of attack is an increase in induced drag as a result of the greater lift. Assuming that you don't add power, pulling the nose up only increases the total drag, and the angle of descent just steepens some more, and you end up reaching the ground at a point even shorter than you would have without pulling back on the wheel.

So, once you're on the final and decide that you need to glide farther, the only way to do it safely is by adding power. How much power to add is determined by how much farther you need to travel in the glide, how late you were in recognizing that your existing glide wasn't going to take you safely to the runway, and therefore how low you allowed the airplane to get before you took corrective action. This whole sequence is one of the best examples of the maxim that the control wheel controls pitch and therefore to a greater degree, also controls airspeed, whereas the power is the primary control of altitude.

When a landing approach goes sour, and many will in your career as a pilot, don't hesitate to shove the throttle in. Then safely establish your climb as though you've just taken off, retract the flaps smoothly and slowly, and go around the traffic pattern for another try. Early recognition of the need to abort a bad approach, coupled with an early decision to execute a go-around, is important to ensure a plentiful margin of speed and altitude. There is nothing embarrassing or amateurish about going around. Many accidents have occurred because pilots have either not recognized that the approach had gone south on them, or, for some silly reason motivated by ego instead of common sense, tried to "salvage" a landing out of a bad approach. Another wise saying in aviation is that a good landing is the product of a good approach. It's very difficult to make even a passable landing if the approach isn't nailed down early and properly. There is enough to do while performing a good, stable approach and subsequent landing. Don't overload your mental or physical limitations; just go around if anything about the approach is out of the ordinary, is uncomfortable, or becomes questionable.

Transitioning from a landing approach to a climb isn't difficult or dangerous in any airplane, but it's simpler in a Cessna 150 or similar trainer than it would be in a jet. Learn now to make the decision to go around when it first seems the prudent thing to do. A bad approach won't get any better, so solve the problem early. Most instructors will command a go-around when you aren't expecting it, even if the approach is going well. The day will come when another airplane, whose pilot isn't on the ball, will taxi out onto the runway as you're on a final approach to land, or maybe an animal will intrude into the runway area, or any one of a host of other such calamities will arise to prevent your safe landing. Most of the major airlines require their pilots, who are the most highly trained and competent anywhere, to go around if the approach isn't stable by the time they are 500 feet above the ground. It takes longer for the engines on a jet than it does for a Cessna 150 to spool up and reach climb power, but you might still want to adopt the same parameter for yourself. If the approach isn't suitable at 500 feet, abort and go around.

Landing the Airplane

Now, let's get back to our landing. As we come in over the end of the runway, and when we get down to an altitude of about 10 to 12 feet above the runway, we'll start a maneuver called the *flare,* or *roundout* (FIG. 6-13). This is done by applying some back pressure on the wheel to lessen the rate of descent. From here on down to touchdown, we'll continue to add more back pressure as the airplane continues to sink. We don't want to stop the descent entirely; what we want to do is gradually reach a point about 3 inches above the runway, when we have the wheel all the way back and the airplane stalls. This is done by constantly increasing back pressure during the flare and at the same time allowing the airplane to sink at an ever-decreasing rate until the stall occurs just barely above the pavement.

During your training, you'll spend a few hours in the traffic pattern doing many landings. Old-time pilots refer to this phase of learning to fly as "bounce drill." Don't get discouraged when you don't get the timing down after several tries. You will start by either stalling the airplane high, and sometime you will try to drive the airplane into the pavement without a proper flare. Your instructor is there, and she's been through this many times

6-13 *The last stage of the final approach, about ready to begin the landing flare.*

before, and she'll save the day with appropriate nudges on the wheel at the right time to avoid any damage, or she'll give you appropriate reminders of what to do yourself.

As the airplane nears the runway during the flare, you'll notice that the rate of sink lessens due to a condition called *ground effect.* Ground effect is a cushion of slightly compressed air that develops between the wings and the ground, and it usually extends up from the runway about half the distance of the wingspan of the airplane. We're flying a high-wing airplane, so the ground effect isn't as pronounced as it would be in a low-wing airplane because the wing on our Cessna sits higher above the ground even after we've landed. When you start flying low-wing airplanes, like the modern Pipers, Beechcrafts, and Mooneys, you'll see a more pronounced ground effect. Ground effect simply prolongs the flare a little bit because the cushion of compressed air delays the onset of the stall.

After we touch down on the runway, continue to hold the wheel back where you have it, and steer straight down the runway with the rudder pedals. Be careful that your feet aren't on the tops of the rudder pedals, where you'll be applying braking force. As the speed dissipates, the tail surfaces will lose aerodynamic effectiveness, and the elevator won't be able to keep the nose wheel off of the ground. The nose wheel will settle gently to the runway. Keep the wheel back, exactly where it was when you landed, until you've slowed completely and turned off of the runway.

A proper stall landing occurs with the main wheels touching down several seconds before the nose wheel settles. Don't allow the nose to come down early. Remember that it is an inherently weak structure, and premature "slamming" of the nose onto the runway can easily cause damage to the engine firewall or mounts to which the nose wheel is attached. When you land properly, you will hear the stall warning sound just before you make ground contact. This whole process involves many elements of feel, sight, and sound. But this experience is just the same as you had when you learned to ride a bicycle as a child. You thought that you'd never do it, but then, magically, it all came together one day, and it has been second nature ever since.

As we steer down the runway, leave everything alone. Don't raise the flaps until we've taxied off of the runway. We train this way for a very important reason. Some day you'll probably fly an airplane with a retractable landing gear. If you learn right now to leave well enough alone during the rollout after landing, and you do not start raising switches and fooling around with things in a hurry during the time that you should be occupied with controlling the rollout, you won't reach over, raise the wrong switch, and pull up the landing gear at a very inopportune moment.

Assuming that the runway is of normal length, allow the speed to drop as much as practical before applying the brakes (FIG. 6-14). Don't ride the brakes, and don't try to use them

6-14 *The landing roll. Allow the airspeed to dissipate. Use the brakes only as necessary to be able to turn off of the runway at a convenient intersection. Never "hog" the runway with excessive taxiing.*

until well after the nose wheel has settled onto the runway. Even though you're flying a rental airplane, treat it now as though it were your own. Every pilot dreams of the day when he owns his own airplane, and many do eventually own a airplane. If you are abusing airplanes when you start out flying, you won't ever know any better, and you'll abuse your own someday and increase your maintenance cost immeasurably.

Now that we've slowed to a comfortable taxiing speed, the next job is to get off of the runway at the next available intersection. Runways are for taking off and landing; taxiways are for taxiing. Don't tie up runway space with prolonged taxiing. Someone in the traffic pattern might have to do a needless go-around because you didn't exercise one of the common courtesies that all pilots extend to each other, that of getting off of the runway as soon as it is safe to do so. Courtesy has a partner in many aspects of life, and that is safety. Flying is no exception.

Weight and Balance Calculations

Flying an airplane safely and legally means more than just having undergone the proper training and having a pilot certificate. It also means putting that training and knowledge to work before and during every flight. A safe flight begins before you even get to the airport. In later chapters, we'll talk about weather information and cross-country flight planning. For now, let's chat about loading the airplane.

One of the most important tasks in planning a flight is to make sure that the airplane is properly loaded. Loading isn't much of a concern in two-seat trainers, assuming that the occupants are of normal weight, say, about 170 pounds or less. Airplanes like the Cessna 150 don't carry all that much fuel. On training flights, little if any baggage is routinely carried. Even with all of these levels of comfort in the type of flying you are doing now, you need to know how to figure your load and how it is distributed.

That's because the day will come, shortly, after you get your license, when you'll want to check out in a four-seat airplane so that you can carry more than one passenger with you. Four-seat airplanes generally carry lots more fuel, have a total of four seats, and have large baggage compartments. When you advance to these larger airplanes, weight and balance calculations become real concerns. There are very, very few airplanes that can legally, safely, and sometimes even physically fly with all of the seats full of adults, a full load of fuel, and baggage. You can do this with your car, but almost never with an airplane. Airplanes offer many options and compromises in loading. If you have to carry four adults, you may find that you have to take off with less than full fuel and accept that you may have to make a refueling stop along the way. If you need maximum range, you probably won't be able to carry four adults, let alone the kitchen sink too.

There are two concerns when you calculate the airplane's load. The first is called the *maximum gross weight,* and the second is the airplane's *center of gravity* (CG). The maximum gross weight is a figure that the manufacturer has established in the design and testing of the airplane, and it is the maximum amount that the airplane can weigh at takeoff. Larger airplanes often have a maximum ramp weight that is a little heavier than maximum takeoff weight. This accounts for the fuel that will be burned during engine start, taxi, and the pretakeoff checks. For the kinds of airplanes you'll fly as a private pilot, you will generally only see a maximum gross weight specified in the POH.

The center of gravity is the balance point of the airplane. If you could hypothetically suspend the airplane in the air from a string, the CG is the point where you would attach the string, suspend the airplane, and have it balanced in a level flight attitude. The manufacturer also specifies, in the POH, a range within which the actual CG must fall. It is very possible in many airplanes to have the total gross weight below the permissible maximum, yet at the same time, have the airplane loaded in such a fashion as to cause the CG to fall outside of the permissible range.

If the maximum gross weight is exceeded, several things happen, and they're all bad. The stalling speed increases, which also increases the landing speed. The aircraft's rate of climb suffers because the engine is trying to climb with more weight than it was designed to handle. When the plane is overweight, the struggle to climb results in increased fuel consumption and possible engine overheating. As can be expected, takeoff distances will increase dramatically, and if the gross weight is high enough, the airplane won't fly at all. Also, at weights higher than allowed, the structural strength of the airplane is compromised, and the airplane no longer has the safety margins that have been designed and built into it.

Excessive weight reduces the airplane's tolerance to gravity (G) forces. Assume, for the sake of discussion, that your airplane has the normally designed maximum load factor of 3.8 G. This means that at the maximum legal gross weight, the structure of the airframe, wings, and all can support 3.8 times the actual maximum gross weight. During accelerated flight, which is encountered during pull-ups, turns, and rough air, the actual load on the wings is greater than just the gross weight of the airplane. If the airplane's legal gross weight is 2,400 pounds, when 3 G is encountered, the wings are supporting 7,200 pounds, which they can still do. Keeping the same assumed 2,400-pound gross weight, the design factor of 3.8 means that the wings can support about 9,120 pounds before there is a risk of failure. If you overload the airplane by 600 pounds and get the actual gross weight up to 3,000 pounds, look what happens. The wings can still support only 9,120 pounds before you risk breaking something, so the maximum G factor is reduced from the normal 3.8 to 3.04. That's a reduction of 20 percent in what may keep you alive in very rough weather. I don't take those kinds of chances, and neither would any other competent pilot. Overloading can cause popped rivets, permanent distortion of the airframe, and even complete structural failure.

The allowable gross weight is composed of two elements: the airplane's *empty weight,* which together with the *useful load* equals the maximum gross weight. The empty weight is just that—what the airplane weighs empty, with only the unusable fuel added. Every airplane, even of the same type, has a slightly different empty weight, which is influenced not only by the design but by the various options installed and the slight variations in manufacture. There is always some small amount of fuel that is not usable but remains in the tanks after the useful supply is exhausted. Once an airplane first gets gas put in its tanks, this amount of unusable fuel is with it for life.

When you start with the maximum gross weight and subtract the empty weight, you then have the useful load. The useful load is the maximum weight of all usable fuel, occupants, oil, and baggage. This useful load must be distributed in such a manner that the CG falls within the allowable limits. Even if the airplane is loaded below maximum gross weight, if it is out of balance, its flying characteristics are adversely affected. Even a slightly out of balance condition will be unsatisfactory. If the CG is too far forward, you may not be able to pull the nose up enough to flare to land. If the CG is too far rearward (aft), the airplane can have very dangerous stall characteristics, and it will be difficult to keep the nose down in level flight. If the CG gets too far out of whack, an airplane can become impossible to fly.

Because baggage compartments are large, there is a tendency to overload them. Just because your baggage compartment is large enough to accept a certain item or items, don't assume that it's okay to put them there. Baggage compartments in typical single-engine airplanes are the most aft of the places that you can place any part of the useful load. Therefore, the loading of the baggage area has the most telling effect on where the CG is eventually located. The floor of the baggage area is a piece of the airplane's structure, and it also has a loading limit. It is often quite possible to load the airplane below the maximum gross weight, within the allowable CG range, but exceed the floor limit of the baggage area. You have to be cognizant of all of these factors.

A few airplanes have another loading scenario of which the pilot must be aware. As an airplane flies, it naturally loses weight (too bad we can't say the same for people as we travel through life). As fuel is consumed in flight, the weight of the airplane goes down. Due to the location of the fuel tanks in these airplanes, notably some models of the Beechcraft Bonanza, the CG shifts as the fuel is burned off in flight. It's possible to take off within all of the applicable limits and then have the CG go out of the allowable range before landing. Pilots of these airplanes then have to calculate their CG both at takeoff and at the end of the flight to keep everything safe.

Many POHs provide a shortcut method of calculating the location of the CG. You merely fill in some blanks on a form with the known load being taken aboard, figuring gasoline at 6 pounds per gallon, oil at 7.7 pounds per gallon (not per quart), and the actual weight of people and baggage. While we're on the subject of the weight of people, watch out to be sure that you use their actual weight. Most of us weigh ourselves on home scales when we're scantily attired. That's fine for our egos, but if we're flying in the winter and are loaded with heavy clothing and boots, you'd better add a good fudge factor to accommodate for everyone's dress. Also, make it clear to your passengers that you need to know their real weight, not what they wish they weighed or what their high school yearbook pictures would lead one to believe.

You also need to know how to mathematically calculate weight and balance without a shortcut form and to fully understand what is being determined. The math involved is not complicated; it's only arithmetic. When prospective pilots have asked me over the years about what level of education is required to be a pilot, my response is that all it takes is that you can read at a junior high school level and do basic arithmetic and a wee bit of geometry. Many of my military and airline pilot friends were history and English majors in college and aren't mathematicians.

The longhand calculation of weight and balance starts with adding up the empty weight and proposed useful load to see if

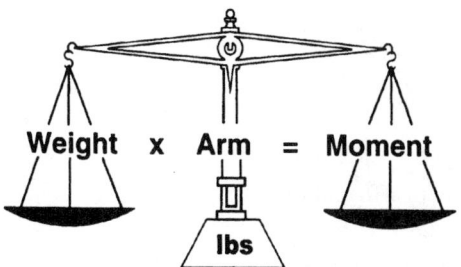

6-15 *The basic weight and balance formula.*

you're going to exceed the maximum gross weight. Assuming that you don't, now you only have to figure the location of the CG. Because the CG is going to fall someplace along the fuselage of the airplane, we need a reference point from which to measure it, and that is called the *datum point,* or just the *datum.* This datum point might be someplace on the airplane, or it can be an imaginary point out in front of the propeller. On many single-engine airplanes, the datum is the firewall at the rear of the engine compartment, but wherever it is, the location is clearly shown in the POH. What we want to find out is where the CG will fall with our proposed loading. The POH will show us the allowable range, usually measured in inches aft of the datum, and the CG must be located within that range. The placement of a given weight affects the CG; 20 pounds of weight right over the center of gravity affects it a little, but the same 20 pounds put back in the tail can move the CG dramatically. Think of it this way: Most adults can lift 40 pounds up over their head if they keep the weight in close to their body on the way up and then hold it straight above their heads. But there aren't many who can fully extend their arms, grab the same 40 pounds, and then hold their arms out in front of their face, holding that much weight. We're going to calculate the leverage exerted by a given amount of weight. The rule is: Weight × arm = moment (leverage) (FIG. 6-15). The arm is the position of the weight from the datum point.

Let's figure the CG for a six-place Cessna 310, which is a high-performance twin-engine business airplane. If you see how it's done for this class of aircraft, doing the same for a single-engine plan is duck soup. Assume that the allowable CG limits are given in the POH as 35 to 43.1 inches aft of the datum. This is the envelope, or range, in which the CG must fall for the airplane to be within its designed balance limits. Further assume that the empty weight is 3,450 pounds, and the maximum allowable gross weight is 5,100 pounds. A simple calculation would look like this:

Item	Weight, pounds
Aircraft empty weight	3,450
Pilot and front passenger, 155 + 165 pounds	320
Two passengers in middle seats, 160 + 200 pounds	360
One passenger, rear seat, 170 pounds	170
Baggage in nacelle lockers	200
Baggage in aft cabin compartments	160
Fuel, 130 gallons	780
Oil, 6 gallons	45
Total gross weight	5,485

First, we see that we're 385 pounds over the maximum gross weight. Something must be left behind—either fuel, passengers, baggage, or some of all of it. For the sake of example here, let's reduce the fuel load to 90 gallons, which lessens the load by 240 pounds, and eliminate 140 pounds of baggage from the lockers at the rear of the engine nacelles. This will bring us down to the maximum legal gross weight of 5,100 pounds.

Now we'll determine whether the load is distributed in such a manner that the CG limits are not exceeded. Using the information for the arms given in the weight and balance section of the airplane's POH, and the known weights as shown above, we obtain the following:

Item	Weight, pounds	× Arm, inches	= Moment, inch-pounds
Aircraft empty weight	3,450	36.5	125,925.0
Pilot and front passenger	320	37.0	11,840.0
Two middle passengers	360	71.7	25,840.0
One rear passenger	170	105.0	17,850.0
Baggage in nacelles	55	63.0	3,465.0
Baggage in aft cabin	160	124.0	19,840.0
Fuel (90 gallons)	540	35.0	18,900.0
Oil (6 gallons)	45	3.5	157.5
Total	5,100		223,789.5

The equation that we use to figure the center of gravity is: Center of gravity = total moment/total weight. When we do the arithmetic, 233,789.5 divided by 5,100 equals 43.88. In this example, the CG will be 43.88 inches aft of the datum, which is out of limits again. The CG as calculated is 0.78 inch behind the aft limit of this airplane, which is 43.1 inches. Some of the load will have to be moved forward. Let's shift 145 pounds of the baggage from the aft cabin compartment to the engine nacelle lockers.

Now the nacelle baggage will weigh 200 pounds, have an arm of 63.0 inches, and have a moment of 12,600.0 inch-pounds. The baggage in the aft cabin will weigh 15 pounds, have an arm of 124.0 inches, and have a moment of 1,860.0 inch-pounds. Substituting these new figures, the total moment has changed to 214,944.5 inch-pounds. Of course, our total gross weight of 5,100 pounds remains the same.

So, when we divide 214,944.5 by 5,100, we get a new CG location of 42.15 inches aft of the datum, which is within limits. Now we're ready to fly with this load in this airplane. We've intentionally done one of the more complex loading problems that a private pilot is likely to ever encounter. Few private pilots fly twin-engine airplanes with multiple baggage areas and six seats. When you're at the airport for your next lesson, ask your instructor to let you see the POH for a Cessna 172 or Piper PA-28 series airplane, which is probably what you'll fly immediately after you get your license. You'll see that the calculation for these airplanes is much simpler than the example that we have just used for a Cessna 310.

Doing the weight and balance calculation is one part of a pilot's preflight planning. In later chapters, you'll learn about weather decisions and navigational planning, which also must precede every flight outside of the airport's local area.

7

Control Techniques

There are two primary techniques that you need to master to control an airplane. First, you need to know, in terms of what controls to manipulate and in what manner, how to achieve the desired performance from your airplane. Second, you need to gain the skill to physically handle the controls in the desired way. Experienced instructors usually develop methods of teaching that contain useful explanations that students can understand and comprehend. Some student pilots learn best if everything is put into short, concise phrases, and others want and appreciate a long-winded explanation of everything.

If your instructor is the type who prefers short, simple explanations, and you want to know more, speak up. When I taught at a major university's flight department when I was in undergraduate school, one hour I would encounter a student pilot who had a doctorate in engineering or was otherwise highly educated, who wanted things explained in the greatest detail possible. The next hour I would be instructing a fellow undergraduate student, majoring in history, as was I, who didn't care about the advanced aerodynamic principles of things like boundary layer separation during stalls and exactly why you might get detonation within the cylinders of the engine if the mixture was grossly improperly adjusted for a given power setting at a given altitude.

I've always believed that a pilot can't know too much about the airplane and why it does what it does in all regimes of flight. I also understand why some people don't care about the advanced details. But the problem with not caring is that you have to be careful that you don't ignore something that really is important. There is a difference between learning the essential and casting aside what you may think at this stage does not matter, only to be ignorant of a fact or concept that is vital to safe flying. If your instructor can't, or won't, explain something in detail when you ask, change instructors. You may have been paired with someone who doesn't know and tries to mask that lack of knowledge with indifference.

Sometimes an explanation can be condensed into a cliché. But clichés should be accepted for what they are: reminders of the basics. Before you accept a cliché as a reminder, you need to know the whole story behind it. For instance, we said in Chapter 6 that the whole story of flight is the angle of attack. That's true, but it assumes that, for a powered airplane, the engine is running properly. When we talk about emergency procedures later in this chapter, we'll see the situations that arise when the engine fails and how we have to alter our control techniques to accomplish what we want the airplane to do.

Another training cliché is "Pitch plus power equals performance." This is totally accurate, again assuming that the engine is running. Yet, even this saying requires additional explanation and elaboration. Within limits, some performance values are interchangeable. It's possible to make some tradeoffs among altitude, airspeed, and vertical speed. Let's try a simple experiment in our Cessna 150 to demonstrate this idea. Assume you are flying along in normal cruising flight, with the power set at 65 percent of rated power and the airplane properly trimmed for hands-off flight. Now, without moving the control wheel or rudder pedals, push the throttle in to increase the power setting. What happens?

When you trim the airplane in cruise, you really have it trimmed to maintain an airspeed, which is whatever airspeed was generated at that 65 percent power setting. When you increase the power without doing anything else, the airplane still maintains the trimmed airspeed. The result is that, with the increased power, the nose pitches up slightly, and you begin to climb. Now we have excess power being produced by the engine, over that amount of thrust necessary to maintain the trimmed airspeed. Hence, the airplane climbs because the trim, attempting to maintain the trimmed airspeed, has pitched the nose up and has increased the angle of attack. This greater angle of attack has generated more total lift, and that lift is more than what is needed to remain level in cruise flight at a constant altitude; therefore, the airplane begins to climb.

Let's look at another easy example. Go back to a normal, stable cruising flight with the power set at 65 percent. Then pull back a little on the wheel, without adding any power. Initially, the airplane climbs some because raising the nose increases the angle of attack, which produces more lift and causes the airplane to climb. But remember, every time that you increase the angle of attack, you also increase the induced drag as a result. If more power is not added to overcome the greater drag inherent at an increased angle of attack, the climb won't last for very long. The forces acting upon the airplane soon reach equipoise again, and you are flying along with the nose higher, at a slower airspeed, and with a constant altitude. Everything eventually balances out, but before the balance occurs, there is a short climb. The cliché that you can "trade airspeed for altitude" applies to what we've just done. We gave up some airspeed from what it was before we pulled the nose up, and we gained some altitude in the short climb before all of the forces balanced out again.

The reverse can also be accomplished. While in stable cruising flight, if the pilot pushes forward a little on the wheel, several things happen. As the nose lowers, the angle of attack does also, which results in less total lift from the wings. Unless the power is reduced, the airspeed will start to increase because, with a lesser angle of attack, less power is needed to overcome the drag because there is less drag. When the power setting is unchanged, the airplane has an excess of power over what it needs to overcome drag, and consequently the speed goes up. This is what is known as "trading altitude for airspeed," which is a valuable technique. Assuming that you are high enough to give up some altitude and still be safe, this is a way that you can quickly increase airspeed if you ever find yourself in a situation in which the airspeed is too low or you need to maintain a gliding speed if the engine gives up its labors for the day.

These foregoing examples illustrate the notion of *limited interchangeability* of airspeed and altitude. In the real world of everyday flying, you will often make very minor altitude corrections with pitch—forward or back pressure on the control wheel—because the resultant airspeed changes will be very minor and insignificant.

When you advance to flying larger airplanes, those that have more excess power available, especially when lightly loaded, than does our Cessna 150 trainer, you'll be able to make greater trades of airspeed for altitude and control wider variations of altitude with the control wheel alone. All of this adds up to the fact that pitch and power are not separate in controlling the airplane but are, rather, interdependent. Until and unless you understand this interrelationship, aircraft control will be confusing.

Load and Air Density

To safely fly any airplane, every pilot must understand two critical factors that influence performance: the load that the airplane is carrying and the density of the air.

Aircraft load

Given the same amount of power, and therefore the same thrust being produced, a heavily loaded airplane must fly at a greater angle of attack than when it is lightly loaded. More weight must be supported by more lift, and the only way to get more lift out of the same wing is to fly that wing at an increased angle of attack.

Although an increase in power setting, if possible, will somewhat compensate for a heavier load by flying the wing at a faster airspeed and getting the needed lift in that manner, normally this excess power isn't available in light airplanes because the larger engines that it would take to produce that much thrust cost more to manufacture, buy, and maintain. They also burn more fuel, which means that the fuel tanks would have to be larger, and that fuel burn costs more too. The design of every airplane is a series of tradeoffs of many traits of performance, weight, and cost. In light airplanes, these compromises are many.

So smaller airplanes are simply trimmed to fly at an increased angle of attack when heavily loaded. Their pilots have to accept the tradeoff of reduced airspeed because the increased angle of attack that is needed to produce the lift necessary to carry that load means that the wings will be generating more induced drag. The more drag, with the same power setting, the slower the airspeed will be. Another by-product of heavier loads is that the airplane will stall at a slightly higher airspeed because it needs more lift to fly than it will when loaded with less weight. When the airplane is lighter, it can fly more slowly; when it is heavier, it must fly faster.

Effects of air density

Air density affects aircraft performance in two ways. As air density does down, the wings produce less lift and the engine produces less power. The density of the air lessens as altitude increases, as the ambient temperature goes up, and as the air becomes more humid. The effects of decreased air density multiply as two or three of these factors combine at a given time.

Effects on the engine of air density

An engine loses its ability to produce as much power as you climb to higher altitudes because the volume of the fuel-air mixture flowing through the carburetor and into the combustion chambers is steadily reduced. At somewhere around 7,500 feet MSL, normal light plane engines can produce only about 75 percent of their rated horsepower, which is the power they can produce at sea level when the throttle is pushed all the way in. As the airplane climbs higher than that, the output of power diminishes markedly. By the time a Cessna 150 has struggled up to about 14,000 feet MSL, it has reached its *service ceiling,* which by definition is the altitude at which its rate of climb has eroded to a meager and tentative 100 fpm. Shortly after we took off from our home airport, where the elevation is only 905 feet above sea level, the airplane was climbing at more than 600 fpm.

Some four-seat and larger light airplanes have engines that compensate for this inherent loss of power with increasing altitude by using a *turbocharger* to compress the air before it is fed into the carburetor, through the intake manifold and on into the cylinders. A turbocharged engine is capable of maintaining a much larger percentage of its maximum rated power output at much higher altitudes. Turbocharged airplanes can cruise at altitudes up to 25,000 feet, and occasionally higher. But turbocharging an airplane engine has some penalties. The engine runs hotter because compressing the intake air also heats it. This makes for more critical engine management techniques on the part of the pilot. The turbocharger itself adds cost to the airplane and increases the pilot's training needed to fly it. Turbocharged engines suffer greater internal stresses, which reduce their overhaul lives and which add increased maintenance costs in other ways. When flying up at the altitudes where its turbocharger gives some benefit, the airplane's occupants need supplemental oxygen, and a whole new host of weather and flight planning concerns present themselves. A turbocharger is a classic example of another old saying: "There's no free lunch."

Today, many popular automobiles also use turbocharging, but for different reasons. In cars, the object of using it is to extract more power from a smaller engine than would produce the same power if there were no turbocharger installed. The smaller engine allows the car to be smaller and weigh less and still have the horsepower output that, before the advent of turbochargers, was only obtainable from larger engines. Car engines have an entirely different set of design criteria than do airplane engines. First and foremost, airplane engines are designed for reliability and long service lives. Although we want our cars to last as long as possible, the result of the car's quitting on the freeway isn't the same as an airplane engine's quitting on takeoff at night.

Our Cessna 150 is not turbocharged. Its engine is *normally aspirated,* which means that the aspiration, the feeding of air into it, is normal and not augmented with the turbocharger. Hence, our little 100 horsepower engine will start running out of steam as the airplane climbs. Although it's not capable of producing its full rating of 100 horsepower at any altitude beyond sea level, the effect isn't very dramatic until we climb several thousand feet high.

Other effects of air density

Air density also decreases as the air becomes warmer. Warmth means that the air molecules are more active, with increased molecular motion. The molecules are more spread out, and a given volume of air contains fewer molecules when warm than it contains when cold. Hence, warm air is less dense than is cold air. At the same absolute altitude, the airplane will suffer more from the effects of lessened air density when the temperature is higher than when the air is cooler.

Next, humid air is less dense than dry air because some of the space in a given volume is taken up with water vapor, not air molecules. Because there are fewer air molecules in that given volume of humid air than would be present in the same volume when the air is dryer, that humid air is less dense. The performance of the airplane suffers accordingly. Fortunately, the adverse effect of higher humidity is not nearly as pronounced as are the problems associated with increased altitude and higher temperatures.

The atmosphere also varies in density from one day to the next or in times of rapidly changing weather conditions, even from one hour to the next. The sea of air that surrounds the earth is in a constant state of change, as high-pressure areas, lows, and fronts move across the world. The air density associated with weather changes is expressed as barometric pressure. There are times when, at a given geographical location, the barometric pressure won't change much for a day or so, but these conditions aren't encountered very often. Especially in the winter, any airplane in North America can see a wide variation in barometric pressure, and the air density that it is measuring in the course of a cross-country flight covering a few hundred miles.

To give us a means by which to calculate the effects of high altitudes and variations in temperatures, the aviation world has created the concept of *density altitude*. Density altitude results from a calculation that simultaneously takes into account the effects of absolute altitude, ambient temperature, and the atmospheric density of the air, the last of which is expressed as barometric pressure.

Figuring what the density altitude is at any given time and location is very easy because your pocket computer, whether of the electronic or circular slide rule type, will do it for you. To arrive at the current density altitude, you have to know the elevation of the airport above sea level. You can determine that by looking on the aeronautical chart for that area; the elevation of every airport is printed on the chart, right beside the airport symbol. Next you need to know the temperature. If there isn't a thermometer outside of the office building at the airport, you can either call the *Flight Service Station* (FSS) that has jurisdiction over the area, assuming that your airport reports its weather into the national network, or you can walk out to your airplane, which usually has an outside air temperature gauge built into the corner of the windshield, and determine the temperature by looking at the gauge. The last thing you will need to know is the current barometric pressure. Again, you can get this from the FSS if it is reported. If not, go to the airplane again, set the altimeter to read the field elevation, and read the barometric pressure from the little window in the altimeter.

Plug all of this data into your computer, and in a flash you will know the density altitude at that airport under those conditions. The airplane's POH has some graphs that are very easy to use that will show you what performance to expect out of the airplane at various density altitudes. Pilots who fly from high-elevation airports in the West are more keenly aware of density altitude than are pilots in other parts of the country. But even at lower elevations, air temperature makes a great deal of difference in the length of the ground run needed to take off and the ability of the airplane to climb once it has become airborne.

Because pilots from the flatlands aren't accustomed to density altitude making the difference between whether their airplane will fly or just run off the end of the runway, far too many of them come to grief when they fly in the mountainous areas or in the high desert regions. Pay attention to density altitude anywhere that you fly. Here in the Midwest, airport elevations usually run around 1,000 feet above sea level, give or take a little. On a hot July afternoon, with temperatures in the 90s, the density altitude can rise to several thousand feet.

At any given weight, an airplane will always require the same quantity of air molecules flowing across the wings to generate the lift necessary to support that weight. Airflow is the magic ingredient of lift. That means that when the air is thinner, more airspeed is required to produce the same airflow than would be needed in denser air. Therefore, more *true airspeed* is needed to fly in higher-density altitudes than in lower ones. Let's understand the difference between true airspeed and *indicated airspeed*. Indicated airspeed is what you actually see displayed on the airspeed indicator in front of you. The indicator works by sensing the amount of air being rammed into the opening in the pitot tube. When the air is thinner, containing fewer molecules in a given volume, the amount of air coming into the pitot tube is less; therefore, the indicator senses less airflow and displays a slower speed reading.

True airspeed is the actual speed of the airplane through the air. When you get into high-density altitude or high absolute altitude conditions, there is a difference between indicated and true airspeeds. This phenomenon works to our benefit. Because the wings need the same amount of air flowing over them at all times to support a constant weight, you can still rely on the airspeed indicator because it too will sense this diminished airflow in high-density altitude operations.

If the stalling speed of your airplane is 55 knots, assuming unaccelerated flight, it will always stall at 55 knots indicated airspeed. Even though you'll be going faster than 55 knots, in terms of true airspeed when the stall occurs at higher-density altitudes, the reading on the airspeed indicator will be 55 knots at any density altitude. The only thing that matters to your wings, engine, and propeller is the quantity of air molecules that is available for them to use to perform their respective tasks.

Takeoffs

To take off, the wings of the airplane obviously have to have enough air flowing over them to produce the necessary lift to overcome the airplane's weight. After the effects of density altitude are considered, the major determinate of the length of the ground run before flight is possible will be the surface wind at the airport. If you can take off into the wind, this headwind during the takeoff run allows the needed airflow around the wings to develop at a slower ground speed than in conditions when no wind is present. If you need 60 knots to take off and if the wind is blowing at 10 knots, and if you can take off directly into this wind, the airspeed indicator will show 60 knots when the airplane is only going 50 knots across the ground. This is because 10 knots of airflow is already present when the airplane is at a standstill.

We always do our best to avoid a takeoff with any tailwind component. If we try to take off with a 10-knot direct tailwind, the airplane would have to be running down the runway at 70 knots ground speed before there would be 60 knots of airflow around the wings. The difference involved in thundering down the runway to build that extra 20 knots of ground speed can result in a tremendous increase in the total length of the run. For this reason, we always take off into the wind. There are a few airports, but not many, where takeoffs and landings have to be made in a certain direction because of obstructions very near the end of one of the runways. However, this isn't encountered very often, and operations from these airports should never be attempted by a student or a newly licensed pilot.

If your airplane needs 50 knots of airflow over the wings to fly, which is very close to the requirement of our Cessna 150, a takeoff into a headwind of only 5 knots (which is 10 percent of the takeoff speed) will reduce the length of the takeoff run by approximately 19 percent over what would otherwise be required with no wind. A headwind of 25 knots (50 percent of the takeoff speed) will reduce the ground run by 75 percent. Conversely, a tailwind of only 5 knots will increase the run by about 21 percent over what would be required with no wind.

Many airports serving general aviation light airplanes have only one runway. Naturally, it is seldom possible to take off directly into the wind at these fields because the wind will be blowing across the runway at some angle or another most of the time. Even so, we take off in the direction that provides at least some headwind component from the existing wind. Your airplane's POH will contain tables and graphs that will enable you to fairly accurately determine the takeoff distance under most conditions.

The following factors influence the ground run's distance and are covered in the modern light airplane POH:

- Density altitude, figured by adjusting for airport elevation, atmospheric pressure, and temperature

- Actual gross weight of the airplane for this takeoff, which has a large effect on the length of the ground run

- Runway slope and direction, the effects of any incline in the runway, and the retarding effects of snow, high grass, loose dirt, or similar runway conditions

- Wind speed and direction, which will have a major impact on takeoff distance

As you can see, the most adverse takeoff conditions are present when you are faced with a combination of a heavily loaded airplane taking off from an airport at a high elevation above sea level, with a runway of sod or similar retarding configuration, on a hot day, with an unfavorable wind. In the western United States and Canada, these factors operate together during many months of the year. There are situations when a normally aspirated (not turbocharged) light airplane just cannot take off from some airports. But even at lower elevations, unfavorable conditions of weight, wind, and temperature can be deadly if you try a takeoff that your airplane just cannot perform. Use your POH and believe what it says about all aspects of airplane performance, including its ability to make a given takeoff.

Climbs

Quite early in your training, you'll be exposed to the various manners in which your airplane will climb. In light airplanes equipped with fixed-pitch propellers, as is our Cessna 150, climbs are always made at full throttle, with the desired climb airspeed being obtained by controlling the pitch of the airplane with the control wheel. Remember that pitch controls the angle of attack. There are two angles of attack that produce the two different climbs typically used in flying light airplanes. *Best rate of climb* is a climb that results in the most altitude gain in a given amount of time. *Best angle of climb* is the climb that gives us the most altitude gain in a given distance over the ground. Best-angle climbs are seldom used in the real world of everyday flying. The airspeed for a best-angle climb is slower than for a best-rate climb, which means that when climbing at the best angle, the nose attitude is quite high. Your visibility over the nose is compromised, and the high attitude combined with the slower forward speed can also overheat the engine. Best-angle climbs will be practiced in training, but you probably won't use them unless there is an obstacle near the end of the runway that you need to clear right after takeoff.

The best rate of climb will be flown at an airspeed faster than the best-angle speed, and the nose attitude will be more comfortable, and the engine will have more air flowing through it from the increased speed, and it will therefore cool better. If you do need to get over an obstacle after takeoff, limit your climbing at the best-angle speed. As soon as the obstacle is cleared, allow the airspeed to build to the best-rate value. Don't abuse the engine or sacrifice forward visibility any more than you have to.

Military fighters and airliners have angle-of-attack indicators in their cockpits that enable the pilots of these sophisticated airplanes to very precisely control the angle of attack in all situations. But, due to cost and complexity, virtually no light airplanes have such indicators, so we are left to determine our angle of attack by using airspeed. The airspeed indicator is not as precise a display of angle of attack, but it is certainly good enough for flying light airplanes. So we learn what the speeds are, as called out in the POH, for best rate and best angle of climb and use them accordingly to derive the needed performance from our smaller airplanes.

At full throttle and at the same indicated airspeed, no two airplanes of the same type ever produce exactly the same rates or angles of climb. This is due to the inherent, minor variations in manufacture and rigging from one airplane to the next. Similarly, even the very same airplane won't duplicate its performance from one flight to the next because there will always be at least some small variation in load and density altitude. So even though the POH quotes the values for best rate and best angle of climb, and the expected rates and climb angles derived from using them, be aware that there is inherent and inescapable variation in performance. If the POH figures show you that a certain takeoff will be critical in any given situation, amend that situation. Lighten the load if you can, or do something else to get into a favorable condition. Many times, especially flying in the western United States in the summer, you can't take off from certain airports in the heat of the day. You either do it in the early morning or later in the evening, after the temperature has cooled some.

As with other maneuvers, climbs should be made using both instrument and outside visual references to control the airplane. The POH often gives a *cruise climb* speed, which is the manufacturer's determination of the best climbing airspeed that will produce a reasonable rate of climb and at the same time be faster than the best rate-of-climb airspeed. When you use the cruise climb speed, your visibility over the nose will be better still, and the engine will cool adequately during protracted climbs because there is much better airflow through the engine compartment.

When climbing, you will notice the effects of the P-factor. Remember that at higher angles of attack, the airplane has a tendency to turn to the left because of the asymmetrical thrust being produced by the propeller. To correct for this, add a little right rudder pressure. When you have the wings level, not banked, sneak a look at the ball in the turn-and-slip indicator. To keep the ball centered, you'll need that little constant pressure on the right rudder pedal. You will occasionally see a sloppy pilot who climbs with the right wing banked down a little. That pilot either doesn't know better or is too lazy to do it right by holding a little right rudder pressure during climbs. In larger airplanes, you'll probably encounter a trim control for the rudder. If you're climbing several thousand feet, you can move the rudder trim over to the right a small amount and give your right leg a rest. To reduce the plane's complexity and cost, and also because this airplane's little 100-horsepower engine and small propeller don't produce that much P-factor, we don't have a rudder trim in the Cessna 150.

Elevator trim is also important during climbs. When the power and airspeed have been established to produce the desired climb, trim away the pressure that would otherwise have to be held on the control wheel to keep the nose attitude where you want it to be. A part of relaxing and enjoying the flying experience comes with learning to use the trim to remove the necessity of holding control pressures, needlessly, for extended periods of time. Also, your climb will be more efficient when the airplane is properly trimmed because you won't have the variations in nose attitude that will result from trying to hold pressure constantly to attempt to keep the attitude at a given point.

In summary, you establish a climb by adding full power, then applying back pressure on the wheel to raise the nose, and adjusting the airspeed to the value that will produce the desired climb. As this is done, add right rudder pressure to compensate for the P-factor, and then trim away the pressure on the control wheel once the climb is stable. Like all of the other training maneuvers, in a short time you'll do all of this without really thinking about the steps involved, and it will become a smooth and coordinated transition from level flight to climbing.

When the time comes to level off from the climb at the desired altitude, that process actually begins about 50 feet before reaching the desired height. Lower the nose gradually, and while the airplane is coming down to a level flight attitude, the airplane will climb that last little bit. Keep the power up at full throttle until the airspeed builds to cruising speed, and then reduce the revolutions per minute to cruise power. As the nose comes down, and the airspeed increases, remove the pressure on the right rudder that you applied during the climb to overcome the P-factor. Again, when you're stable and in cruising flight, finish the job by rotating the trim control wheel forward a little to remove the forward pressure that it takes to hold the nose level. That's all there is to it.

If your climb has taken you high enough, after you're stable and in cruise, it's time to start leaning the mixture for engine efficiency. In the past, we used to ignore leaning of the mixture in normally aspirated engines, below 5,000 feet. In those good old days (that maybe never were), avgas cost far less than $1 per gallon. As fuel prices rose in the 1970s, much of the conventional wisdom about powerplant management underwent some critical reexamination. Today, most engine manufacturers approve leaning the mixture of normally aspirated engines at any altitude as long as the power setting is below 75 percent, and the engine doesn't run rough when leaned. Read what your POH has to say about leaning practices, and consult your instructor.

Leaning the mixture has several benefits. First, fuel consumption is reduced. The engine runs best at a proper mixture, and when you climb high and don't lean, the mixture becomes too rich because of the thin air at high altitude. Running the mixture too rich can foul the spark plugs. Also, when the mixture is too rich, the engine can't produce the power that it will at the right mixture setting. When you're cruising much above 5,000 feet, you need to have the engine producing the proper amount of power to give good, efficient cruise performance and airspeed.

Descents

Descents can be made in a power-off glide or more commonly by reducing the power from the cruise setting, but not all the way back to idle. Glides with the power at idle need to be learned, but they are seldom used outside of the traffic pattern, during your landing approach. Power-off glides are not an efficient way to come down from cruising altitudes because glides are done at a relatively slow airspeed, and therefore, you don't cover much ground while gliding.

A long power-off glide from higher altitudes can damage the engine. While cruising, you've probably run the engine somewhere between 65 and 75 percent of its rated power output. At those settings, the engine is producing quite a bit of heat, which is being dissipated through the normal airflow through the engine compartment. When the power is suddenly reduced to idle and left there for an extended period of time, the engine can cool too fast because at idle power it won't produce anywhere near the amount of heat that it did at cruise. This phenomenon is called *shock cooling*. The name implies what happens. The engine cools at such a fast rate that it is shocked, and the shock can result in warped or cracked cylinder barrels or cylinder heads. *Shock cooling* refers to the rate at which the engine cools down, not the absolute temperature difference between cruise and idle power. To avoid shock cooling, if you must do a power-off glide, as you will in the traffic pattern, the key to avoiding damage to the engine is to reduce power in a few steps to allow the engine to cool more slowly rather than all at once. A good pilot always learns how to take care of an airplane, regardless of who owns it.

Power-off glides are the first phase of learning how to descend. After you learn how to glide, your instructor will teach you how to descend with the power reduced but not all the way back to idle. Many aspects of learning to fly involve the building-block approach to teaching, and this is only one of those examples.

To perform a power-off glide, first look in the POH and find the manufacturer's recommended gliding speed. Usually it is an airspeed very close to that used to obtain the best rate of climb. There are two gliding speeds that you should learn, and unfortunately, only one of them is usually shown in the POH. The POH gliding speed is known as the *maximum lift-over-drag speed,* which is abbreviated as the *best L/D.* This is the speed, when gliding, at which the wings are producing the maximum amount of lift and the minimum amount of drag. Gliding at the best L/D results in the most distance covered over the ground during the glide.

The other glide speed, not usually disclosed in the POH, is the *minimum sink* speed. This glide speed allows the airplane to sink at the minimum possible rate, expressed in feet per minute. The minimum sink speed is very important to glider pilots because it is the speed at which they can remain aloft for the longest time, while searching for thermals that will allow the glider to climb. But there is a potential danger to airplane pilots in using the minimum sink speed because a minimum sink speed is very close to the stalling speed, often only 5 to 10 percent above stall. Gliding at an airspeed this slow demands excellent pilot technique, especially in maintaining a constant airspeed and being aware of how the stall speed automatically increases any time that the wings are banked, or when other acceleration is put on the wings.

The minimum sink speed does not provide much coverage over the ground while gliding because the airplane is moving so slowly. Using the best L/D results in traveling the farthest distance during a glide. There are a few times when it would be valuable to glide at the minimum sink speed, and we'll talk about those situations later. For now, when we speak of the *gliding speed,* assume that we'll use the best L/D speed as shown in the POH. Let's get back to how to enter a glide.

When in cruising flight, gradually pull the throttle all the way back to idle. You need to apply back pressure on the control wheel to hold the nose level, or very slightly below level, until the airspeed bleeds off and reaches the gliding speed. Also, in our Cessna 150, you want to pull the carburetor heat control out as you reduce the power to idle.

Then, just release a little of the back pressure on the wheel, and allow the nose to fall a little bit. You will then need to either raise or lower the nose to establish the glide speed. If you're gliding at too fast a speed, raise the nose some; if you're below the target glide speed, lower it a little. Then, when the airspeed is stable and you've nailed down the nose attitude to keep the speed where you want it, use the trim control to trim away the control pressure. You're now gliding.

The recovery from a glide—to resume a normal cruise configuration and speed—is also a fairly simple transition. About 100 to 150 feet before you reach the target altitude, remove the carburetor heat, smoothly add power all the way to full throttle, and raise the nose to the level flight attitude. Let the airspeed build to the cruising speed, and then pull the throttle back to cruise. Then make whatever minor adjustments are necessary in both nose attitude and revolutions per minute to establish stable cruising flight. Retrim to relieve the control pressure that it takes to hold the nose level, and you're back in cruise from the glide.

Turns

To review what we've previously mentioned, turns are accomplished by banking the wings down in the direction of the desired turn and simultaneously applying rudder pedal pressure in the same direction. The banking action causes the airplane to turn because the force of lift, generated by the wings, always remains perpendicular to the wings and consequently pulls the airplane around in the turn. The correct amount of rudder pressure keeps the turn coordinated so that the airplane is not skidding toward the outside of the turn nor slipping into it. Some instructors tell their students to think of the rudder as the control that trims the turn, and that is not a bad way to view its use. Just remember that, unlike a boat, an airplane doesn't turn by rudder action; it turns by banking. The rudder is not needed to cause the turn, just to keep it coordinated.

The rudder is also used, as we enter the turn, to counter *adverse yaw*. Adverse yaw is the natural tendency of the airplane's nose to swing in the direction opposite to that of the turn. This occurs primarily because of the way that the ailerons create forces upon the airplane as the wings are banked. If we turn the control wheel to the left, the left aileron goes up, which forces the left wing down. At the same time, the right aileron deflects down, and the relative wind acting upon it forces the right wing up. The amount of drag that each moving aileron creates is not the same; the aileron going down, which is the right one in our example of a left bank, creates more drag than does the one on the inside of the turn, here the left one. This excess drag on the outside wing tends to pull that wing and causes the nose to swing to the outside of the turn.

Another factor in the creation of adverse yaw is that the outside wing has to move farther in the arc of the circle of the turn and therefore is moving faster through the air than is the wing on the inside of the turn. When the wing goes faster, it naturally creates more drag, which also has a pulling effect on that outside wing, which in turn pulls the nose to the outside of the turn as well. If we use rudder pressure in the proper amount as the airplane is banked with the control wheel, the nose isn't allowed to swing in the opposite direction. It remains right there on the straight and level heading for a split second, and then the nose starts to move in the direction of the turn, as the banking of the wings actually starts the turning movement of the entire airplane.

Turns are normally divided into three classes, all related to the angle of bank: *shallow, medium,* and *steep.* Shallow turns are those in which the bank angle is less than about 20°. They require some control wheel pressure actually to be held into the turn to counter the airplane's inherent design stability that wants to keep the wings level. This stability is achieved by what is known as *dihedral.* When you stand in front of the airplane, looking right at the hub of the propeller, about 20 feet or more in front of the nose, you'll notice that the wings are attached to the fuselage in such a manner that they each appear to be bent upward toward the tips. They aren't really bent but are built so that the wing tip is slightly higher than the root of the wing, which is the fuselage end. By the use of dihedral, the design engineers have created a natural tendency of the airplane to level itself from minor excursions from wings-level flight. When one wing does go down a little, it creates more lift than its counterpart on the other side because the wing that has gone down ever so slightly is now level. More lift means that the lowered wing wants to rise. In this way, the force of lift produced by each wing is always working to remain in concert with the lift generated by the opposite wing and fly in a wings-level attitude.

Medium turns are those resulting from bank angles of approximately 20 to 45°. At these angles of bank, the aerodynamic forces designed into the airplane are such that there is, in smooth air, little or no requirement to hold pressure on the control wheel to keep the airplane banked. For that reason, medium turns are the easiest to perform correctly, which is why flight instructors introduce them first. You'll see that about 30° of bank results in an easy, relaxed turn.

Steep turns are those in which the angle of bank exceeds 45°. At these steep bank angles, the airplane will have a tendency to *overbank*, which means that the bank angle will tend to increase unless opposite aileron pressure is used to overcome it and prevent the airplane from rolling on over. Steep turns also require more of the total lift of the wings to be used to turn the airplane, and therefore, less of it is available to overcome gravity. Hence, during a steep turn, the angle of attack has to be increased substantially to add the lift needed to maintain a constant altitude; and that requires a hefty pull-back on the control wheel.

As the steepness of the turn increases, so must the back pressure on the wheel. If the turn is very steep, much over 45° of bank angle, you'll need to add some power to maintain a constant altitude. As the bank increases from wings level, so does the airplane's stalling speed. The increase in stalling speed is not in a linear relationship to the bank increase, but rather, the stalling speed starts going up dramatically after about 45° of bank. If you perform a turn at 60° of bank, you have little margin between the cruising airspeed in that turn and the stalling speed at that bank angle.

When you're in a steep turn, it's very easy to not apply enough back pressure to keep the nose level, and thereby allow the nose to fall. Once this happens, the airspeed can build rapidly, depending, of course, on just how far you've let the nose fall below the level attitude. Then, the airplane is in what is known as a *spiral dive,* with a high bank angle, nose low, losing altitude, and the airspeed increasing. This condition can get dangerous if it is not recognized early and if corrective action isn't taken. Your natural tendency will be to pull back on the wheel because you see the airspeed getting into the danger zone, but that's the exact wrong thing to do. At very steep bank angles, pulling back on the wheel, while the wings are still rolled over in a steep bank, just tightens the turn and exacerbates your problem.

To recover from a spiral dive, you must first lessen the bank angle by using the control wheel to apply the opposite aileron, and roll out some of the bank. Then, as the bank is shallowing, you should reduce the power (which will help keep the airspeed from increasing even more) and then use back pressure on the wheel to gradually pull out of the resulting dive. If you don't lessen the bank first, excessive back pressure on the wheel, in an ill-fated attempt to reduce airspeed, can cause a stall. A stall while in a steep turn, with high power and high airspeed, can be a very violent maneuver and should be done only in airplanes that are certified by the FAA for aerobatics and only by a competent aerobatic pilot. Although it seldom happens, there is a worse risk yet.

If things have really gone to pot on you, and the airspeed is screaming, the bank is very steep, and you haul back on the control wheel, it is possible to so overload the structure of the airplane with high G loads that the structure fails and something breaks, usually the tail first, followed quickly by wing separation. Don't be scared by this recitation of the possibilities; your instructor will never let things get dangerous, and you won't either, once you're trained.

The Typical Medium Turn

Now let's get back to reality and examine the typical medium banked turn in detail. Before starting any turn, always look carefully in the direction of turn, and be sure that there isn't any other traffic conflicting with where you are going to turn. Then start the turn by gradually and simultaneously applying both aileron pressure with the control wheel and rudder pressure in the direction of the desired turn. The rate at which the airplane rolls into the turn is governed by both the rapidity and amount of control pressure added, so be smooth and gradual.

As the airplane rolls into the turn, you'll add a little back pressure on the wheel. In all turns, some of the total lift is devoted to the task of turning the airplane, instead of all of it being singularly working to overcome gravity. You need to increase the angle of attack a little to increase the total lift so that you remain at a constant altitude. In a medium turn, the amount of needed back pressure isn't very much, so be smooth and gradual here too.

As soon as the airplane rolls from the level attitude into the bank, the nose should start to move along the horizon in the direction of the desired turn. The rate at which the nose moves will increase as the bank increases. Any variation in the coupled action of the nose movement with the angle of bank indicates that a control is not being used properly and that the turn is not coordinated, as follows:

- If the nose starts to move before the turn begins, the rudder pressure is being applied too soon.

- If the bank starts before the nose starts turning, or if the nose swings in the opposite direction, due to adverse yaw, the rudder pressure is either being applied too late or an insufficient amount of rudder is being applied.

- If the nose moves up or down when entering the bank, excessive or insufficient back pressure is being applied to the control wheel.

When the desired angle of bank is reached, relax the pressure on the ailerons and rudder, taking out the rolling movement of the control wheel and the pressure on the rudder pedal. This allows the ailerons and rudder to streamline themselves in their neutral positions. The back pressure on the wheel should not be released but rather, should be held constant, with minor adjustments in the nose attitude applied to maintain a constant altitude.

Throughout the turn, check your visual references on the horizon, and occasionally glance at the altimeter to determine whether your pitch (nose) attitude is correct. Learn now that a pilot never gets all of the information needed from only one source, which we call a *reference*. In this case, the view outside of the windshield is the primary reference because it tells you how steep the bank is, how fast you're turning, and where the nose attitude is. Flying is an art of absorbing the information from more than one reference, primary and secondary, and then using this information to decide how to manipulate the controls to achieve a desired result. The altimeter is the secondary reference for determining if the nose attitude is correct.

You should also determine what you need to know about the bank angle from looking outside; but it will be a while in your flying career before you can tell if a turn is coordinated without looking at the turn coordinator. Glance at it; don't stare at it. Don't become mesmerized by any flight instrument. Using the instruments properly involves learning to scan them, see what they're saying to you, and doing what is needed to get back to the flight condition that you want. Scanning ability takes a while to develop, but start the process now. Scanning also means that your primary references are outside the airplane's windshield and windows, not inside the cockpit.

When you look at the turn coordinator, you want to see where the ball is inside of the fluid-filled tube. It should be in the center. If it's not, which side is it on? The old adage "Step on the ball" will get your turn coordinated. If the ball is on the inside of the turn, the airplane is slipping around and needs a little more rudder pressure in the direction of the turn. If the ball is on the outside of the tube, relax some of your rudder pressure in the direction of the turn, and the ball will slide back into the center. When the ball is on the high side of the turn, the airplane is skidding, and that needs to be corrected also. Now you've got a coordinated turn going for you.

Turn coordination will eventually become automatic, and you'll rarely need to look much at the ball to see how you're doing in this regard as long as you have visual reference outside the cockpit. But when you advance into instrument flying, you'll find that your senses will play tricks on you when you're deprived of the ability to see outside the airplane. In instrument flying, the ball is an important reference. The human senses of balance and eyesight work together. When we are deprived of our ability to see whether we're upright, the sensory organs in our inner ears can send confusing signals to the brain. We think we're turning when flying straight and level or vice versa.

Viewing the airplane's nose attitude through the windshield is the primary reference for correct attitude, but it doesn't necessary tell you the whole story. That nose attitude that you see may not be the correct one for maintaining a constant altitude. Steal a glance, as part of your instrument scan, at the altimeter and the vertical speed indicator. In combination, these two instruments tell you the altitude and any associated trends in whether you're climbing or descending, and how quickly any change is occurring.

Remember that the VSI has a significant lag (several seconds) in its response to changes in altitude and the indications that it gives. So don't chase the VSI in an attempt to hold altitude. When you see that you are high or low or are climbing or descending, make a small correction with elevator pressure, pulling back or pushing forward slightly on the wheel to put the nose on a new reference point on the horizon. Wait a few seconds for the dynamics of the situation to settle down, and look again at the instruments to see if more or a different correction is needed. Don't stare at any one spot on either the instrument panel or outside of the airplane. Scan the instruments and scan your eyes around the outside world. Then you can assimilate the information available from all your references to make whatever control adjustments are necessary. The sooner you develop the habit of adequately scanning both the panel and outside, the sooner your control of the airplane will improve and become second nature.

During all of the turn, use both ailerons and rudder to correct minor variations, just as you do in straight and level flight. Soon your turns will be stable, and your corrections will be so smooth and slight that they will be almost imperceptible.

The recovery from a turn is begun a few degrees before you reach the desired new heading, usually about 10° or so. Scan the DG while you are in the turn, and check its progress to know when to start the recovery to straight and level flight. The DG has no lag, and you can depend on it to let you know just how far a turn has progressed. Also, you should know from looking outside how the turn is going and when you're near to the new direction in which you want to fly. Apply aileron and rudder pressures together in the direction opposite to that of the turn. As the angle of bank decreases, smoothly release the back elevator pressure that you've been holding throughout the turn; the back pressure isn't needed now that the wings are becoming level again.

It's important to coordinate and combine the release of the back pressure with the rollout of the bank; otherwise, the nose will pop up at the end of the turn, and you'll gain some unwanted altitude. When the turn is completed, scan all of the outside and instrument references as you return to straight and level flight. Check the nose and wing tip positions on the outside horizon, and then quickly look at the turn coordinator to make sure that you're not still unwittingly holding some aileron or rudder pressure. Finally, scan the altimeter and VSI to see if you need any correction to the nose attitude to hold a constant altitude.

Climbing Turns

Climbing turns have more factors at play than do turns while maintaining a given altitude. First, a turn while climbing results in some loss of rate of climb. Because some of the total lift from wings must be diverted toward the task of turning the airplane, there is less lift available to climb. All climbs in our Cessna 150 are made at full power, so you can't increase the power any more to offset the loss of climb rate inherent in performing a climbing turn. You have to settle for a minor degradation in climb rate during the turn.

If you turn at a bank angle that is either too shallow or too steep while climbing, that results in decreased efficiency too. Too steep a bank results in too little lift remaining available to keep climbing, and in an airplane like our 150, which doesn't have a plethora of excess power, the climb rate will suffer dramatically. If you bank at too shallow an angle, the turn is difficult to control and maintain because of the airplane's dihedral, which wants to keep the wings level.

We want to strive for a medium bank turn as the best compromise and keep a constant angle of bank and rate of turn. It takes practice to do this well. Diverting your attention and dividing it from looking just at the airplane's nose into using all of your visual and instrument references available give you a total picture of the maneuver.

There are three ways to begin a climbing turn. You can first enter a climb and then turn, first enter the turn and then pitch up and add power to start the climb, or do the climb and turn entries together. The thing that makes climbing turns difficult initially is that you are using and coordinating all of the flight controls together. You're pitching, rolling, and yawing (turning) all at the same time. The easiest of the three ways to enter a climbing turn is to start the climb first and then when you've got a stable climb under control, begin turning. As your skills rapidly develop, which they will, you will progress to doing it all together and simultaneously entering both the turn and the climb.

Climbing turns have one important difference from turns conducted in straight and level flight, and that relates to the use of rudder pressure. During a straight-ahead climb, without turning, we have to hold the right rudder to compensate for the P-factor, which wants to turn the airplane to the left. So, when making a climbing turn to the left, you'll find that, to enter the turn, you'll actually release right rudder pressure more than you'll feel that you add left rudder. When making a climbing turn to the right, you'll need to add far more right rudder pressure than you would to turn to the right in level flight because it takes some right rudder in a climb just to prevent the airplane from turning to the left. Don't be concerned because it takes you longer to learn to naturally coordinate climbing turns. Use the turn coordinator—that's why it's in the airplane.

Descending Turns

When you start learning to make descending turns, you will see that the rate of descent goes up while you are turning, especially if you are making your descent by using a power-off glide. The laws of physics don't change; whenever a turn is performed, some of the total lift is channeled into turning the airplane, and that portion of the lift is no longer available to overcome gravity. To maintain a proper gliding airspeed while turning, you will need to drop the nose attitude a little below what it would be for a straight-ahead glide. When you drop the nose attitude, the rate of descent will increase.

Maintaining good control coordination is important in all maneuvers, but it is vital in a gliding turn. During every flight, you'll be using gliding turns while approaching the airport in the traffic pattern. That phase of flight is, by necessity, conducted close to the ground, where you don't have the comfort and safety net of altitude to negate errors. During a glide, you will already have some left rudder pressure applied because of the P-factor. Just as the P-factor wants to turn the airplane to the left during a climb, as we have already said, it has the opposite effect during a glide. Therefore, the natural tendency of the airplane is to turn right when gliding. So, a left gliding turn takes more left rudder pressure than does a gliding turn in straight and level flight, and a right gliding turn involves releasing the left rudder pressure that is already there, to a greater degree than it does actually applying the right rudder.

Most of the accidents that happen as a result of control mishandling occur in the traffic pattern, close to the ground. The majority of these involve a stall, followed very shortly by a spin. The turn from the base leg to the final approach is a particularly vulnerable place and time for this misfortune to occur. Often the turn is not timed properly, and the pilot senses a need to hurry the rate of turn, to avoid having the final approach off to the side of the center line of the runway. Then this hapless pilot shoves in the rudder to speed up the turn and yanks back on the control wheel at the same time. Presto, the yank causes an accelerated stall, and the heavy amount of rudder pressure, which caused a very uncoordinated turn, results in the nose snapping over into a spin. At this point, things unravel so fast that the pilot does not know what just happened. When you're only a few hundred feet above the ground when a spin starts, it's all over.

There are two fast and rigid rules to live by to keep this accident from happening to you: First of all, never make steep turns in the traffic pattern, and keep your medium turns coordinated. Second, any time that an approach, or any other part of the traffic pattern goes south, push the throttle in, get out of there, go around, and try again. If you obey these rules, you can't become the victim of a stall-spin accident.

Your instructor will teach you what are known as *cross-controlled stalls,* whereby the airplane is purposefully put in an uncoordinated turn and then stalled. This maneuver is taught up high, and it will be part of your flight test when you get a license. At a high altitude, the maneuver is totally safe and should make you aware of the risks involved in violating the two above-mentioned rules about flying in the traffic pattern.

Ground Reference Maneuvers

The descriptive term *ground reference maneuvers* is applied to certain training maneuvers that are performed to teach you to control what the airplane is doing by paying attention to the relationship between the airplane's flight path and a particular track on the ground. These maneuvers consist of the *rectangular course, S-turns across a road,* and *turns about a point.*

These exercises teach the effect that the wind has on the airplane's course over the ground. You will learn how to recognize and anticipate what the wind will do. The maneuvers show you how to control an airplane so that it goes where you want it to go and it is where you want it to be in relation to either a specific point on the ground or a path over the ground. About the only place that one of these training maneuvers is used in everyday flying is in the traffic pattern, which is nothing more than a rectangular course. Turns about a point may be used if you are trying to get a good look at some point on the ground. S-turns across a road are almost never a practical part of a flight, but all three of these maneuvers reinforce talents that you need to develop and that you will show to the examiner during your flight test.

An airplane flies through and is supported by the air mass in which it finds itself. Except on rare occasions, that air mass will be moving, and we call that movement of the air *wind*. In flight, the wind doesn't blow against or in relation to the airplane; the airplane is moving straight through the air mass that is supporting it. If you're a boater, you're already familiar with this concept, except that you've known it as current in the water instead of wind in the air. Visualize a simple example of what we mean. Picture yourself in a large room, like a ballroom, walking in a straight line across the floor, except that you're walking on a huge throw rug that covers most of the floor. You have a friend at one side of the room holding onto the edge of the throw rug, who begins to pull the rug toward the edge of the room, at a right angle (90°) to your line of walking.

The result is that your path over the floor, below the rug, will be at an angle across the room. Even though you're walking in a straight line across the rug, the rug is moving, causing your direction of travel across the floor of the room to be different than your direction across the rug. You'll end up toward one side or another of the room depending on the side toward which your friend is pulling the rug. That's exactly how wind affects the path of an airplane over the ground.

An airplane in flight cannot "feel" the wind because that airplane is contained within the moving mass of air, just as you were contained on the moving rug. Some student pilots grasp this concept quickly, and others have trouble understanding it. Ground reference maneuvers are a tremendous aid in seeing, firsthand, how the effects of wind operate in flight.

Rectangular Course

The rectangular course (FIG. 7-1) is a practice maneuver in which the ground track of the airplane is directly over all four sides of a selected rectangle on the ground. The central United States was originally surveyed, in the days of the pioneers, into mile-long sections, and the fences and tree lines that define these sections still exist in almost all of the rural areas. Country roads also generally follow these section lines. Pilots flying in other parts of the country may not have these convenient section lines, but they can easily find large farms, parallel roads, or other surface features that will work just as well.

One objective of these exercises is to develop your ability to pay attention to your flight path, and the ground references, while at the same time making a periodic instrument scan, while you are controlling the airplane and watching out

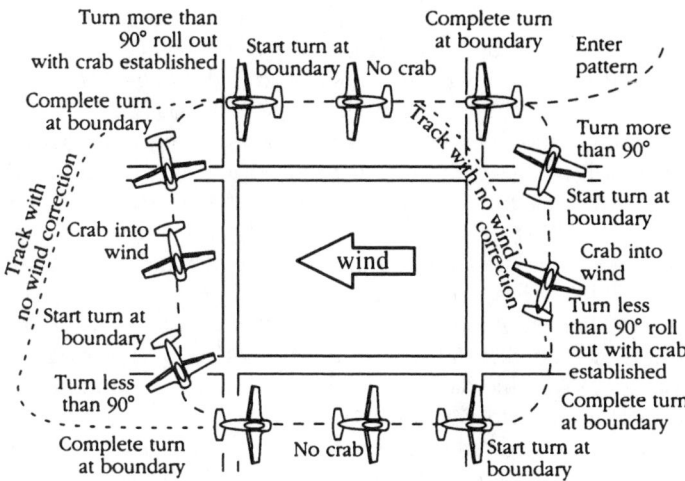

7-1 *The rectangular course maneuver teaches proper compensation for wind in a traffic pattern.*

for other traffic in your vicinity. Another objective is for you to learn how to recognize the drift of your flight path, caused by the wind, toward or away from your intended track over the ground.

To perform the rectangular course maneuver, first select a square or rectangular field, with sides approximately 1 mile in length. This maneuver is flown at a constant airspeed and altitude; about 600 to 1,000 feet above the ground will work best. If your field has sides of about a mile, you'll fly the course somewhere from one-fourth to one-half mile outside of the box. If your field has longer sides, where you can keep a good view of the boundaries under your nose, without the nose obscuring that view, you can fly right over the sides. Most of the time you'll be paralleling the sides, and your distance from each side should be the same and remain constant throughout the maneuver.

All of the turns in the rectangular course should be made when the airplane is abeam the corners of the course, and the bank angle should normally not exceed 45°. On a very windy day, steeper banks may be needed, but as a student pilot you won't be flying on days when the winds are high. As your training and skills progress, your instructor will expose you to stronger winds, but not for a while.

Take a look at FIG. 7-1. Let's begin the rectangular course where shown, at the upper right corner of the figure, which is at the start of the downwind leg. We call this leg *downwind* because the wind is at your back, in line with your desired track over the ground. While you're flying down this leg, your ground speed will be the sum of your airspeed and the speed of the wind. The first turn occurs at the end of the downwind leg. Notice two things. First, you're going fairly fast over the ground, and there is a consequence of that high speed, which is that your turn will have to be made at a fairly steep bank angle. You need a steep bank to produce a rate of turn that is fast enough to get your turned parallel to the next leg and not get blown out away from it. Look at the dashed line that depicts a ground track that would be obtained if you didn't turn steeply. You want to stay within the desired distance from the next leg and not wander all over the place. Second, to be able to parallel the next road or fence line, you'll have to actually point the nose of the airplane into the wind so that the wind doesn't cause you to be blown farther away from the road or fence line than you want to be.

So you'll have to make this first turn more than just 90° to end up pointed into the wind. Start the turn with coordinated control pressures to result in a fairly steep bank, maybe as much as 45°. Roll out of the turn smoothly but smartly, after the turn has gone beyond 90° of directional change. Just how much directional change you'll need beyond 90° is a function of how strong the wind is. It's a matter of judgment, which is why you're learning this maneuver—to gain the experience that you need to develop that judgment.

Once you've completed the first turn, you're flying along one of the two *crosswind legs* of the rectangular course. The term *crosswind* implies that the wind is blowing across your track over the ground and not either from behind you or into your face. The feat to be performed along this leg is to have the airplane pointed into the wind just enough to parallel the desired course over the ground without flying in over the road or getting blown out away from it. This angle between the heading of the airplane, which is the direction in which the nose is pointed, and the direction of your path over the ground is called the *crab angle*. As you fly down this first crosswind leg, you undoubtedly will need to adjust the heading of the airplane to maintain the desired track over the ground. Do so with small coordinated turns so that you don't overcorrect and head off into the opposite direction.

At the end of the first crosswind leg, you'll next make a turn onto the upwind leg. The upwind leg is parallel to the wind, flying directly into it. During the time that you're flying the upwind leg, your ground speed will be less than the airspeed, by whatever value the speed of the wind happens to be.

Note in FIG. 7-1 that when you are going down the first crosswind leg, the crab angle resulted in the airplane's already being pointed somewhat toward the direction of the upwind leg. Therefore, the turn from this first crosswind leg to the upwind leg requires that the airplane be turned less than 90° of directional change. The angle of bank necessary to accomplish this turn and end up at the correct position is about the normal angle for a medium turn, probably about 30° of bank. If the wind is really strong, you'll need less bank and less change of direction, the opposite of the steeper bank that you needed at the end of the downwind leg on a blustery day. Flying the upwind leg requires no crab angle because the wind is not trying to blow you from your desired ground track. The only effect that the wind has upon the airplane during the upwind portion of the rectangular course is a reduction in the ground speed.

Now we're ready to turn from the upwind leg into the second of the two crosswind legs. Look again at FIG. 7-1 and you'll see that this turn also needs to be less than a full 90° change of direction because you want to end up on the second crosswind leg with the necessary crab angle already built into your heading. This will keep you from being blown in, over the road or fence line. Plan this turn ahead of time, just as you did when you turned from the first crosswind leg onto the upwind leg. Make this turn onto the second crosswind leg a little shallower, in terms of the bank angle, than the previous turn, and roll out of it before you've changed direction a full 90°. Then carefully observe your track over the ground and make whatever adjustments are needed to fly parallel to the road or fence line, again by making small, coordinated turns to finely tune your heading.

The last turn, which will complete your first circuit of the rectangular course, comes at the end of this second crosswind leg, and it is a turn onto the downwind leg. This turn needs to be more than a 90° change of direction, just like the first turn you made from the downwind onto the first crosswind leg. At the same time that you're turning from the second crosswind leg back onto the downwind leg, realize that the wind will be blowing you into the downwind, and your ground speed will begin to increase as you go around the turn.

This last turn is made with a fairly steep bank because you need to turn more than a 90° directional change, and you need to do it fairly quickly. If you bank only slightly, the ensuing slow rate of turn will cause the turn to take too long to complete, and your ground track will suffer because you'll be blown into the rectangle. After going around the course once, your instructor will probably have you do a few more laps. Nothing that is this complicated can be learned, let alone mastered, on the first attempt. Also keep in mind that an illustration in a book can assume a perfect world, where a rectangular course has wind blowing perfectly parallel to two of the sides. In practice, this seldom happens. In real-world flying, chances are that your course over the ground will require some degree of crab angle on all four sides of the rectangle.

Two rules of thumb will help, whatever the wind is:

- When the wind is behind you, the turn must be steeper and faster.

- When the wind is head on, the turn must be shallower and slower.

The rectangular course can be understood sooner if you can pick out a course that has longer legs. I've had students find a course that has had legs as long as 2 miles each. Then, you get a good chance to relax for a bit between turns and adjust the needed crab angle because each leg takes 1 to $1^1/_2$ minutes to fly. If you pick out a short-legged course, you'll be whipping around it so fast that you won't have time to either think about what to do next or contemplate and absorb what just happened on the leg or turn that you've just completed.

The turns are the keys to this maneuver, and they require most of your effort, planning, and judgment. The rectangular course prepares you to fly the traffic pattern at the airport, and everything you need to learn about turns and crab angles is applicable in both a rectangular course and the traffic pattern. Remember what we said earlier about the turns from downwind onto crosswind and the turn from crosswind onto the final approach in the traffic pattern. These turns are performed at lower altitude, and the turn from downwind onto crosswind is steeper and faster than a normal medium turn. It's not difficult to get either of these turns uncoordinated, especially if you try to hurry them along with excessive rudder application. The result is that if you stall the airplane, the stall can be accompanied by yawing, which can cause the airplane to snap into a spin.

The solution is to learn the rectangular course maneuver, but first and foremost, never allow yourself to be so devoted to maintaining any track over the ground that you fail to fly the airplane properly. If you're in the traffic pattern, you can always abandon the approach, add full power, and climb out to try the whole operation again. The same thing goes if you're doing a rectangular course and feel uncomfortable about any phase of it, including a safe outcome. Every wise pilot executes a safe go-around more than a few times in his flying career. Only the unwise and unsafe pilot remains so determined to make every approach conclude in a landing that she never executes a go-around. Flying airplanes is not an activity in which to engage with blind determination, except for the determination to always be safe.

S-Turns across a Road

S-turns across a road are a series of 180° turns that cross a road between each semicircular turn. Imagine a dollar sign ($) in your mind. The vertical line through the dollar sign is the road, and the S is the depiction of the 180° turns. The ground track that is flown won't stop with just two turns, one each in the opposite direction, but the maneuver should continue for several turns so that the path over the ground looks like two or three dollar signs stacked on top of each other. Each S is equal in size and uniformly proportioned when the maneuver is done correctly. This maneuver promotes your ability to compensate for the effects of the wind and also enhances the habit of employing a scan that divides your attention between references inside and outside of the cockpit.

Choose a straight stretch of road, at least $1\frac{1}{2}$ miles long, preferably longer, with the wind blowing directly across it at a 90° angle. For our explanation here, we'll assume that the wind is blowing from the right toward the left in relation to the desired dollar sign pattern. We'll begin the exercise by flying at an altitude of between 600 and 1,000 feet above the ground and by flying directly toward the road, at the top of the S with the wind directly behind the airplane's heading. When you are exactly over the road, start the first turn, to the left, immediately. Because the airplane began by being headed downwind, the ground speed is the greatest at this point, and the rate at which we're leaving the road is rapid. Therefore, roll into a steep bank so that the rate of turn is fast to minimize the drift away from the road. As you near the halfway point in this first 180° turn to the left, the airplane's heading is changing from downwind to crosswind, so the ground speed decreases. Begin to shallow out the bank, noting that your crab angle is toward the road and is the greatest at this point due to the effect of the crosswind's trying to blow you away from the road.

After completing the first half of the first turn, your heading becomes more and more an upwind heading as the turn progresses and your ground speed slows even more. Continue to gradually reduce the bank through the second half of the first turn. By doing this, your crab angle is completely gone, and the wings are once again level as you cross the road at the conclusion of the first 180° turn. When an S-turn is done correctly, the wings become level just as the road passes beneath the cockpit. But there is no time to waste. As you cross the road, start a right turn. You are now flying directly into the headwind, so the turn needs to be made with a shallow bank and results in a slow rate of turn, at first. After this turn is halfway completed, it progressively takes you from a crosswind to a downwind heading. Then the bank angle and rate of turn both need to be increased to keep the turn properly proportioned. The bank angle increase will be steady, and not all at once, because the crosswind component is being removed gradually as you complete the second half of the right turn. The goal is to once again roll the wings level just as you cross over the road at a right angle to it.

You should maintain a given altitude throughout this maneuver, just as you did when you were flying the rectangular course. The bank angles and rates of turn will be constantly changing to achieve a truly symmetrical semicircle over the ground on each side of the road. The bank angles and turn rates are changing because the objective in these ground reference maneuvers is to fly a precise, predetermined track over the ground. When you are flying in normal cruising flight and you turn the airplane to a new heading, you aren't worried about the actual track over the ground. The minor variations that the wind makes in the ground track is of no concern up high, while you are in cruise. But down in the traffic pattern, a precise ground track is the goal.

Turns about a Point

Turns about a point involve flying a perfectly circular path over the ground, circling around a reference point that is in the center of the circle. The point of this maneuver is to have the radius of your circle around the point remain constant at all times.

Flying a turn around a point is very similar to flying an S-turn across a road. First, find a good reference point, such as a large tree in the middle of an otherwise empty field, a large silo, or a prominent intersection of two roads. Begin the maneuver in the same way as you did the S-turn, by flying exactly downwind with the wind directly behind you. Students tend to prefer to do turns around a point with a reference point off to their left because they can see it more easily out of the left cabin window as they sit in the pilot's seat. But after you've learned to do it to the left, you need to also practice turns around a point to the right because the examiner can ask you to do it either way, or both ways, during your flight test.

As you come abeam the reference point, start your turn with the coordinated application of aileron and rudder pressures. As the turn progresses around the first quarter of the circle, you're coming to the place where you'll be flying into a direct crosswind. The combination of your increased ground speed because the wind has been behind you and the fact that you'll be flying into a direct crosswind means that you have to roll into the turn using a fairly steep bank, continuing to steepen it, and thereby obtain a faster rate of turn during this first quarter of the way around the circle. When you get a quarter of the way around, you need to be crabbed into the wind, which means that the nose of the airplane has to be pointed slightly toward the reference point on the ground.

During the next quarter of the turn, two things are happening. Your ground speed is lessening as you fly into the wind and end up flying directly into it as the halfway point in the circle is reached. Also, the crosswind component is decreasing as you turn into the wind. Therefore, during the second quarter of the turn, your bank angle needs to be shallowed some from the steep bank that you had during the first quarter.

For the third quarter of the turn, your bank will constantly be shallowed because the wind has slowed your ground speed and it will be trying to blow you into toward the reference point as soon as you turn away from the heading that was directly into the wind. From this point until past the three-quarter position, your bank will be the shallowest of the entire maneuver. During this third quarter, you won't make a turn of 90° directional change because the airplane needs to be crabbed into the crosswind that you're now encountering again.

When you get to the three-quarter point in the entire turn, the effects of the wind change again. Now the crosswind starts lessening because you're turning away from the wind, toward the downwind portion of the turn. Your ground speed starts to pick up due to the tailwind. So, leaving the three-quarter point, you need to begin to steepen the bank once more to compensate for the increased ground speed and the elimination of the crosswind.

Turns about a point end when you're once more abeam of the reference point, flying downwind, where you began. These turns, combined with S-turns across a road, teach you how to control your airplane's ground track in all wind conditions. S-turns are almost never an end in themselves, but turns around a point can be. There will probably come a time in your flying career when you will want to have a look at something on the ground (from a safe altitude). We fly turns around a point at the same 600 to 1,000 feet above the ground as we do most of the ground reference maneuvers. After you get a license, always obey the FARs and use common sense; don't fly around an object of interest any lower than that. The only way to examine an object on the ground is by flying circles around it. Good pilots fly circles; poor ones will end up flying in ovals because they don't know how to compensate for the effects of the wind.

There are other ground reference maneuvers that include figure eights on pylons and around pylons, figure eights across a road, and power-off descending spirals around a point. All of them accomplish the same goal—honing your ability to fly the airplane in constantly changing wind conditions and paying attention to the ground reference point(s), the track over the ground, the instruments in the cockpit, watching for other traffic, and flying the airplane with good control coordination. The pilot who masters these maneuvers is also a master of the airplane.

Not-So-Normal Landings

At the end of your first few lessons, you will make a normal landing with either calm wind or a wind right down the runway, in relatively smooth air, and on a nice, long paved runway that has no serious obstacles to the approach. If you face more challenging circumstances early on in your training, your instructor will probably make the first few landings so as not to overload you with more than you can handle.

In reality, particularly in cross-country flying, such landings are not the norm. As a pilot, you have to be able to deal with uncooperative winds, turbulent air, soggy sod runways, and short fields that are surrounded by factories, power lines, and broadcast antenna towers. Let's discuss a few of these situations and the techniques for dealing within the real world in which pilots fly.

Crosswind landings

Crosswind landings are actually more normal than are landings when the wind is blowing directly down a runway. If you fly from a single-runway airport, as most general aviation airports are, you have only two directions in which to put the airplane on the ground. Seldom will the wind be blowing right down the runway from either direction. You'll be making most of your landings with at least some amount of crosswind. Even if you fly from an airport with multiple runways, you can't always avoid crosswinds. The chances of having to battle a 90° crosswind may be less, but you'll still often have some crosswind component. During World War II, when most airport runways were still sod, the British had the right idea. Airports in the United Kingdom were large circular fields, with no "runways" per se. Rather, pilots just observed the wind and took off and landed across the circular field, directly into the wind. With the advent of paved runways, we lost that advantage and now have to cope with crosswinds.

There are two methods of doing a crosswind approach and landing: the *crab method* and the *wing-low method*. Your instructor will teach you one or the other as a primary way of approaching and landing in a crosswind, depending upon her preference. Regardless of which way becomes primary for you, you should also learn the other.

The wing-low method

The wing-low method is the easier of the two to perform because, when you're set up for the approach, the dynamics of the crosswind correction don't change much throughout the remainder of the approach and landing. To do a crosswind landing using the wing-low method, you fly a normal traffic pattern (correcting for the wind on the various legs as you did the rectangular course) and roll out of the turn from base to the final, aligned with the center line of the runway if possible. Then you immediately lower the wing that is on the upwind side (the side from which the wind is blowing). Next you apply as much *opposite* rudder pedal as is needed to keep the airplane's nose from turning. You make only minor adjustments in the bank angle and opposite rudder pressure as needed, all the way down the final, to keep the airplane lined up with the runway. You hold the wing down and opposite rudder control condition all of the way to touchdown.

During the final approach, and just before the wheels touch the ground, the airplane is *slipping* into the wind. The wing-down condition pulls the airplane into the wind, and the rudder pressure keeps it aligned with the center line of the runway. The opposite rudder keeps the nose, and hence the entire airplane, from turning. The ball in the turn coordinator is near the end of the tube on the upwind, wing-low, side. Slipping is a bad technique when making normal turns in cruise flight, when you want the ball in the center. But here, the slip is intentional.

Be aware that the rate and angle of descent increase when slipping because some of the wings' lift is devoted to pulling the airplane into the wind, just as some of the lift is not used to overcome gravity any time that the wings are banked. Slipping is a very good technique to correct for a crosswind, and it has other uses as well. Additionally, during a slip, some of the side of the fuselage is more exposed to the oncoming relative wind, and hence the entire airplane presents more drag. Because we are gliding during the final approach, this increased drag also increases our angle and rate of descent.

In airplanes that don't have wing flaps, like many of the older classic ships, slipping is the only way to increase the angle of descent during final approach, once the airplane is already in a power-off glide. More modern airplanes, equipped with wing flaps, allow us to use those flaps to modulate our descent. Some airplanes are placarded against slips when the wing flaps are extended. If yours is, extend the flaps only to the limit permitted when slipping; otherwise, you can't use the wing-low method in making a crosswind approach and landing. Most of the time you won't be using full flaps in crosswinds anyhow because full flap deployment makes the airplane a bit more difficult to control in the crosswind; their full extension provides more surface area for the wind to act upon, and the increased drag associated with full flaps can make it take longer for a power application to take effect if you need power to shallow the glide or to execute a go-around.

It is probable that most pilots do not like to use the wing-low method of crosswind correction because of the necessarily long period of slipping all of the way down the final approach. A slip can feel awkward until you really get used to it. Passengers are sometimes uncomfortable with the airplane in this attitude, particularly if the crosswind is strong and the resultant bank angle in the slip is steep to stay in line with the runway.

When the wind is so strong that the bank angle needs to be so steep that even full opposite rudder will no longer keep the airplane from turning, you have exceeded the *maximum crosswind component* for your airplane. You've reached the limits of controllability, and you just can't land on this runway with this wind. This rarely happens, but if it does, recognize that you can't change the laws of physics nor the design of the airplane. You've got to either use another runway at that airport, or go to another airport that has a runway more favorably aligned with the prevailing wind.

Low-wing airplanes and those that have long wings have another problem with the wing-low method. They can get into a situation in which the bank angle would result in the wing tip's striking the ground before the landing gear touches down. For this reason, you'll seldom see an airliner, with its long wings, perform a wing-low crosswind approach and landing.

Crab method

The other method of coping with a crosswind is called the *crab method* because the airplane is crabbed into the wind, with the wings level, during the final approach (FIG. 7-2). The airplane is crabbed into the wind to keep the final approach path aligned with the center of the runway. Again, you now see the relevance of learning the ground reference maneuvers discussed earlier, especially the rectangular course

This crab angle is held, and adjusted as necessary with slight coordinated turns, until just before the moment of touchdown, when the upwind wing is lowered and the nose must be kept aligned with the center line of the runway by applying opposite rudder pressure. You absolutely must not allow the airplane

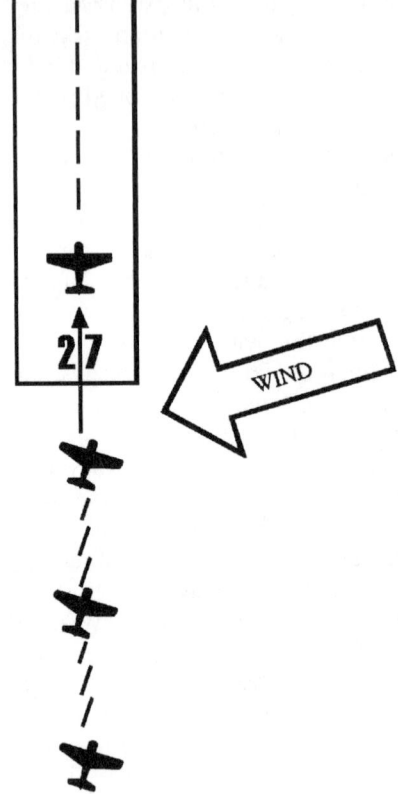

7-2 *The crab method of crosswind correction. Be sure to straighten the airplane in line with the runway before flare and landing.*

to contact the ground while still crabbed because the landing gear is not designed to absorb the strong sideload that would result. The gear legs will break if the crab angle and resulting sideloads are great enough. At best, if you touch down while still in a crab, you'll skip the airplane on the runway, risk what is known as a *ground loop,* and quickly explore the weeds off to the side of the runway.

The crab method is more difficult to learn and use with consistently good results because at the last minute significant control inputs have to occur and equally significant attitude changes have to be made to get the wing down, align the nose with the runway center line, and complete the landing. Everything is happening all at once.

Perhaps the best method of crosswind approaches is a compromise between the two methods just described. You can crab the airplane most of the way down the final approach, shifting to the wing-low configuration several moments before landing. This way, you can make everyone comfortable for most of the approach, rather than having a protracted period of slipping, yet you eliminate all of the gyrations with the controls at the last instant. This is the way that I fly most crosswind approaches. Being "born and bred" in lighter airplanes, and having learned to fly in my youth in a classic tailwheel airplane that had no flaps, I learned to slip early on and still fly all the way down the final in a slip when the crosswind is strong. To me, slipping is fun, and I'll often use a slip to modulate my angle of descent on the final, even if I'm landing into a direct headwind or on a day when the wind is calm.

Crosswind landings (continued)

The *flare,* or *roundout* as it is sometimes called, still has to be made before you touch down. Only naval aviators land without flaring because that's the way carrier landings are done. Their airplanes are designed and built with landing gear that is as strong as a bridge girder, and it can take that pounding. Your airplane isn't and can't. When we flare for a crosswind landing, we still have to carry the crosswind correction (now wing-low regardless of how you flew the final approach; FIG. 7-3). As you flare, two things happen. First, your airspeed decreases so that the control surfaces lose some effectiveness, and you may have to increase the control pressures on the ailerons and rudder to keep the airplane straight and aligned with the runway. Second, the velocity of the wind often lessens very near to the ground, so maybe some of the correction for

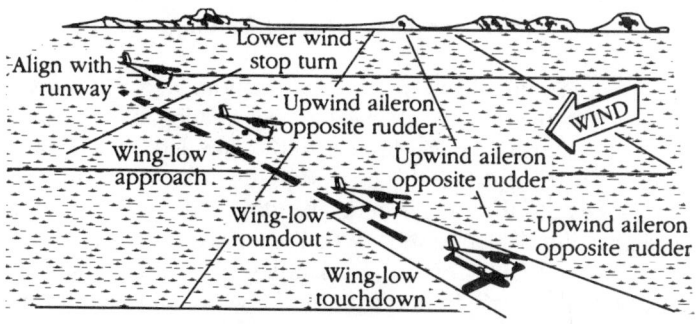

7-3 *The wing-low method of crosswind approach and landing.*

the crosswind that you experienced while on the final will now need to be lessened. Wind speeds usually are less within the last 50 to 100 feet of the approach due to *surface friction,* which is the friction that the moving air encounters as it blows across the actual surface of the earth. Friction tends to slow the movement of the air across the ground, and hence the wind speed lessens.

During the flare for a crosswind landing, do not level the wings; keep the upwind wing down all the way throughout the flare and contact with the runway. You'll intentionally touch down on one main landing gear, which is the one on the upwind side, and the nose wheel should still be off of the ground when that main gear touches down. Don't try to lower the other main gear, but continue to use the ailerons to keep the upwind wing down, and the other main wheel up, off of the ground. As your forwarded momentum decreases, and as the wings lose their last vestige of lift, the downwind main wheel will settle to the runway even though you've been trying to keep it up with aileron and you may well have the ailerons fully deflected before the downwind gear touches the ground.

When we make a landing in an appreciable crosswind, we vary one other aspect of normal landings. If the wind is very strong, you don't need to worry about holding the airplane off of the runway until it stalls. Rather, allow it to contact the ground just a few knots above stall but still in a good flared attitude with the nose wheel off of the ground (FIG. 7-4). When the wings stall, we cannot control the airplane with ailerons as well as we can while the wing is still flying. During crosswind landings, we want to preserve control authority so that we can keep the upwind wing down and the nose aligned with the center line of the runway by using the rudder. But don't forget to maintain a pronounced flare; the last thing that you would ever want to have happen is for an airplane to contact the runway, during any conceivable type of landing, on the nose wheel first.

Now comes another important distinction. Recall the comment earlier that the Cessna's nose wheel steering is deactivated in flight, when the nose strut is fully extended as weight is removed from it? When the nose strut fully extends as the airplane takes off, the rudder pedal steering to the nose wheel is mechanically disconnected. When the nose wheel of the Cessna does touch down upon landing, it is already streamlined straight ahead, in line with the longitudinal access of the

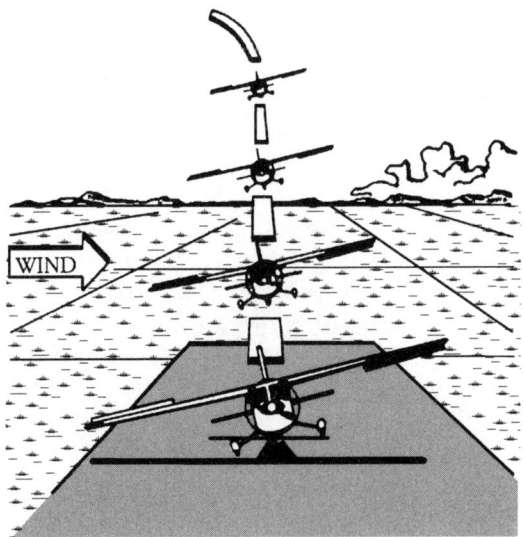

7-4 *Crosswind flare and touchdown.*

airplane. Our Cessna 150 will roll straight ahead, even if you're a little behind the eight ball in straightening the rudder pedals to neutral after touchdown. Obviously, if you do touch down with the opposite rudder input still applied, as the nose strut depresses and the weight of the nose comes to bear on it, and if you continue to hold that rudder pressure, the nose wheel will start to steer and off you go into the weeds again.

In most Pipers, and some other makes, nose wheel steering is never deactivated. The nose wheel turns in flight every time that a rudder pedal is moved. You need to know which system your airplane has because if yours doesn't disconnect the ground steering as soon as the nose wheel lifts off, it is imperative that you kick the rudder pedals to neutral, during landing, the split second before the nose gear touches. If you don't, it'll be cocked over to one side, and the sideloads that you put upon it will probably bend or break the nose wheel structure.

During the landing rollout, you need to keep the aileron correction applied, and increase the amount of control wheel pressure and aileron deflection as you slow down because the control surfaces become less effective as the speed drops. By the time your rollout is finished, you should have the control wheel fully deflected toward the wind, if you haven't done so already.

As you slow down during the landing rollout, the effects of the crosswind can become more pronounced. All airplanes have more vertical surface area behind the main gear than in front of it. The sides of the fuselage, vertical stabilizer, and rudder contain a lot of square footage. When the crosswind blows against them on the ground, it pushes against them and tries to turn the airplane into the wind. This effect is called *weathervaning,* and it is familiar to any boater who has tried to dock a boat in a crosswind. You have to keep the upwind wing "down" by turning the control wheel toward the direction from which the wind is coming and use the rudder pedals to steer as you roll out and taxi. Weathervaning is an even more pronounced problem for tailwheel airplanes because their main gear is farther forward along the fuselage than is a tricycle gear arrangement. Therefore, more of the fuselage is exposed to the turning effect of the crosswind because more of the fuselage is aft of the main landing gear.

Also remember FIG. 6-6, the taxiing diagram. Wind is always affecting an airplane that is still in contact with the ground, and you have to compensate for its effects by proper control surface position.

Landing in turbulent air

When the air is rough or it's windy, it's best to use power-on approaches and leave power-off glides for calmer days. When the airplane is being bounced around by rough air, which usually accompanies stronger winds, we will also want to fly the final approach with some extra airspeed. We'll need the extra speed to keep the effectiveness of the flight controls up where they can compensate for the rocking and rolling induced by the rough air. Remember that control surfaces lose effectiveness as airspeed decreases, and their effectiveness, which is called *control authority,* is better at high airspeeds.

If the wind is gusting, which it usually is when the air is rough, we need to determine how much to increase the airspeed while on the final approach. We do this by finding out what the gust factor is. The *gust factor* is the strength of the wind, during the gusts, over what the speed of the steady-state wind happens to be. For instance, if the control tower reports that the wind is 15 knots, gusting to 25, the gust factor is 10. Then figure on adding $\frac{1}{2}$ of the gust factor to the normal approach speed. In this case, we should add 5 knots. If the POH for your airplane recommends anything different, by all means follow the dictates of the POH, as you should do in all circumstances.

Because you are carrying that extra airspeed on the final approach, you could make very minor attitude adjustments with the control wheel, varying pitch. But don't get carried away; make sure that you don't pitch the nose up enough to bleed off your extra speed. Such tradeoffs are limited, and a coordinated combination of pitch change and power corrections is preferred.

Partial flap deployment may be helpful, but full flap extension would be detrimental because of the large amount of drag created when the flaps are fully extended. In rough air, you want to be able to add power if needed, to either arrest a sink rate that develops or to recover lost airspeed. If you have the flaps hanging all of the way out, you compromise your ability to do that quickly. When you are using partial flaps during the final approach, the nose attitude will be higher and flatter than it would be with full flaps, especially if you're carrying very much power during the approach. Therefore, the flare will not be as pronounced as usual because the nose is already somewhat higher, and less pitch change has to occur to get into the landing attitude. Just as we did in the crosswind landing, let the airplane land just a few knots above stalling speed to preserve control authority. Of all things, don't let the nose wheel touch first. Touching down on the nose wheel will probably result in a condition euphemistically called *wheelbarrowing,* which is what happens when the airplane is rolling on its nose wheel alone. To extricate yourself from this predicament without seriously bending the airplane will require some artful control handling, together with a larger measure of luck.

In moderate to severe turbulence, landings should be made from power-on approaches with the airplane as nearly level as possible with the nose up at touchdown and avoiding all possibility of wheelbarrowing. When the wind is howling, and the air is like a washboard, you need good, positive control authority all of the way down to the touchdown. The throttle is not fully retarded until the airplane is firmly planted on the runway and rolling on all three wheels. This extra power is used to provide an extra margin of control; if things start looking haywire, or if the airplane starts bouncing or feeling like it's going to wheelbarrow, the only out is to immediately apply full takeoff power and get the airplane airborne again. Then you can go around for another try.

As a student, you won't be flying solo in this kind of weather. Unfortunately some pilots encounter real turbulence and wind only after they've left the instructor's nest and are on their own. Sometime late in your training, your instructor should take you out on a rough, windy day so you can see what it's like before you experience these conditions by yourself for the very first time. If you don't get a chance to fly in winds or rough air before you get your license, grab an instructor and fly afterward when the opportunity presents itself. Once you get your license, you aren't finished taking instruction when you need it to further your flying skills.

Landing on soft fields

Originally all airports were sod fields. Today, few actually are, but you need to know how to operate from them because you'll deprive yourself of some of the utility of a personal airplane if you always shy away from grass fields. If the surface is firm and smooth, there is no practical difference between using a sod or a paved runway except that even neatly mowed grass is not as friction free as is pavement, so your takeoff runs will be a little longer, and your landing rolls will be shorter. If the grass hasn't been mowed lately, these effects can become marked, so watch out when trying to take off from a sod runway where the grass is long and the runway is short.

The most common difference between grass and pavement occurs when the field is soggy or soft. In the spring, a grass field is often soft before the winter moisture has thoroughly dried out from the ground and from the spring rains. During the winter, in many parts of the country we see rain rather than snow, which can keep a grass runway soft for months on end. Many of the same effects on airplanes result from a snow-covered runway, regardless of whether the surface underneath of the snow is pavement or sod.

When you land on a soft field, you have to judge before you attempt the landing just how soft the field is. Airplanes with tricycle landing gear, which are certainly the norm today, can easily get stuck. Nose tires are usually smaller than the main gear tires, and they support a lot of weight, with the engine and propeller right above the nose gear. Those small nose tires can act like a knife, slicing down through the soft surface deeply enough that the airplane is quickly rendered immobile.

Remember that the nose gear structure is the weakest of the three landing gear components, and if it digs into the surface, it'll probably bend or break if you keep trying to blast the power in an attempt to get the airplane moving again.

One of the ways to operate in soft ground conditions is to keep moving and not let the airplane stop before you want it to. If you keep moving, while holding the control wheel all the way back, you can generally, but not always, lighten the nose gear's load enough to prevent it from digging into the mud or snow. You'll need a lot more power to taxi because the soft surface is hindering the progress of the main gear too. This extra propeller blast acts on the elevators, and if you've got the wheel all the way back, the tail will tend to ride lower, keeping the nose wheel light.

If the nose wheel does start sinking into the soft surface, be careful. The last thing that you want to have happen is to dig the propeller into the ground. Any propeller strike, no matter how slight, requires an immediate shutdown of the engine and a thorough inspection by a qualified maintenance technician before it is started again. If the propeller strike results in stoppage of the engine, most engine manufacturers require that the engine be disassembled and inspected for internal damage. For all of these reasons, tailwheel airplanes operate much better from soft fields.

If all of your landings are full-stall landings, as they should be unless the wind conditions dictate otherwise, there isn't much difference between the actual landing on a soft field and your normal landing. When performing a soft field landing, the secret is to keep the wings supporting the airplane's weight as long as possible and to touch down at the slowest possible speed. The approach to a soft field is the same as for a hard one except that after the flare has begun, you don't want to let the airplane touch down early. Keep the flare going, and hold the main gear off of the ground for as long as you can. It's absolutely imperative that the nose gear be off of the runway when the main gear touches down.

Be ready to need to apply power to keep the airplane moving. If the field is truly soft, you won't have much roll after landing, and you can be bogged down very quickly. Keep the control wheel all the way back after touchdown, which you should be doing anyhow, and stay off of the brakes. Be prepared to push the throttle in so that you don't get stuck. If you do get stuck in the mud or snow, accept it and don't blast the power to try to get moving again. If you're stuck, you probably haven't damaged anything yet; but if you try to get unstuck by using engine power, you probably will. Shut the engine down, get out, walk to the FBO and get a tow bar and tug to move the airplane. Then the only damaged part will be your pride.

Landing on short fields

On occasion, you'll be faced with the need to land on runways that aren't much longer than the minimum distance required to stop your airplane. Short-field landings are achieved by making a precise approach, where the final is usually flown at 1.3 times the airplane's power-off stalling speed when it is in landing configuration. In our Cessna 150, *landing configuration* means having the flaps fully extended. Our landing gear is firmly welded in place, so we don't worry about having it retracted or extended. In airplanes with retractable gear, landing configuration implies that the gear will be down. On the flight test for your license, you will be asked to demonstrate a short-field landing, assuming that there is an obstacle, 50 feet high, right at the approach end of the runway. In real-world flying, most short fields have fairly clear approaches; otherwise, flying into and out of them might be impossible for many airplanes during many months of the year (remember density altitude). But you do need to know how to get over an obstacle and then get the airplane down and stopped in the minimum distance.

The techniques used to accomplish this short-field landing are quit different from those used to make a normal arrival. Remember what we said earlier about a good landing requiring a good approach? It could not be any more true than when making a short-field landing. A stable, slow approach is imperative; you want to concentrate on getting the airplane down as soon as possible and then stopped before running out of runway. With this concern, you can't still be trying to stabilize the approach only moments from touchdown. If the approach isn't as perfect as it needs to be, make the decision early to go around and set up for another try.

While flying down the final approach, adjust the angle of descent as necessary to clear the obstacle without any excess altitude, yet be safe. You don't want to be 100 feet over the obstacle when you pass it, but you don't want to scrape the tires on it either. As you clear the obstacle, smoothly reduce the power to idle if you've carried any power on the final. Don't chop it all at once because at this slow approach speed, a high sink rate may well result from a sudden reduction of power, and you might not have enough airspeed to arrest that sink rate during the flare.

When you flare, be ready for the airplane to land sooner than it does with a faster approach speed. Because you've got less airspeed to bleed off in the flare, the landing happens more quickly. Let the airplane touch down on the main gear, as always. Achieving minimum landing roll will require heavy braking. On an ordinary rollout after a normal landing, you let the aerodynamic drag of the airplane do the slowing and use brakes sparingly, if at all. In tricycle gear airplanes like our 150, the aerodynamic drag really declines once we're rolling at a speed below about 60 to 70 percent of the touchdown speed, so it won't help much when you've got to get stopped now.

We want to get the airplane on the ground as soon as possible. Land with the nose wheel off of the ground, but then let it settle sooner than you normally would because we can't safely apply the brakes until the nose wheel is down. The minute that the nose wheel touches, get on the brakes, and start retracting the flaps, which were fully extended for the landing. Raising the flaps robs you of some of their aerodynamic drag, but getting them up helps much more by getting rid of whatever lift is still left in the wings. This transfer of the weight of the airplane from the wings to the landing gear as soon as possible will dramatically increase the effectiveness of the brakes. While braking, make sure that you're holding the control wheel all the way back to transfer as much of the weight as possible to the main gear; as you know, there is no brake on the nose wheel.

Applying heavy braking while the wings are still supporting an appreciable amount of the airplane's weight can result in locking the brakes and skidding the tires. Skidding actually increases the stopping distance and also compromises your ability to steer, causing a loss of directional control. That's why antilock brakes have become so popular on cars. It is interesting to note that they were first invented for large airplanes as were the disc brakes that we have now come to expect on our automobiles.

Many general aviation accidents happen during the landing roll because pilots get complacent and end up losing directional control. The same thing is even more likely to occur during heavy braking because airplanes are not designed to be ground vehicles—they are flying machines. The ground-handling characteristics of all airplanes are terrible compared to the driving stability of a car. The landing gear is a weak structure, the brakes aren't nearly as effective as are modern automobile brakes, and the tricycle gear arrangement is much less stable than the four or more wheels of a ground vehicle. Always remember that you're flying an airplane until it is parked and the engine is shut down.

Emergency landings

Chances are very great that you will never be faced with the prospect of making an emergency landing away from an airport. Modern airplanes and their engines, when properly maintained, are probably about the most reliable machines of their complexity that have ever been developed. However, you need to learn about three general categories of emergency landings, two of which are precautionary and one of which has to be made immediately.

The one that requires an immediate landing occurs when the engine fails completely. Most total engine failures occur because the pilot has mismanaged the fuel supply. You might forget to change tanks (more than one airplane has landed in a farmer's field with an entire tank full of gas), might not have properly preflighted the airplane and therefore didn't discover water or some other contaminate in the fuel supply, or more inexcusably, just plain run it out of gas. Sudden engine failures due to actual mechanical failure are very rare if you take care of your airplane and perform the scheduled maintenance.

Two types of precautionary landings away from airports aren't the result of sudden and total power loss. If some sort of mechanical failure occurs in the engine, as has happened to me, seldom does the engine quit without warning. In one of my cases, a cylinder fractured, and the revolutions per minute dropped to around 2000. But I was able to fly the airplane, albeit at a slower speed, for the few minutes that it took to get back from the practice area to our airport. If the airport hadn't been so close, I would have selected a good field and made a precautionary, off-airport landing.

The second type of precautionary emergency landing doesn't imply a current engine failure. This type of off-airport landing can occur because the pilot has the good sense to land while the engine is still running but the fuel supply is critically low. It is better to accept the inevitable and land in a nice field, under full control while you still have the services of the engine than to blindly fly on until fuel exhaustion occurs. Other reasons for precautionary landings can be approaching bad weather (many accidents also happen because VFR pilots bore on into IFR weather without the training or airplane equipment to handle it), approaching darkness in an airplane not equipped for night flight, or becoming totally lost, in inhospitable terrain. In the last situation, the pilot needs to land as soon as a decent place can be found.

If you do a precautionary landing, you'll probably have some explaining to do to the FAA, your insurance company, and maybe to the airplane owner. I would much rather compose such letters or have such conversations from the comfort of my office chair than from a hospital bed, which is where I might be if I were to blunder ahead and have a serious accident.

The National Transportation Safety Board (NTSB) investigates all fatal aviation accidents and many nonfatal ones as well. The NTSB has found that several factors operate to interfere with a pilot's ability to act promptly and properly when faced with an emergency. Many of the aviation safety organizations have come to similar conclusions, which are, in no particular order:

- *Reluctance to accept an emergency situation as it develops.* A pilot who allows her mind to become paralyzed at the thought that the airplane will shortly be on the ground, regardless of what is done, is severely handicapped in the handling of the situation. An unconscious desire to delay this dreaded moment might lead to such errors as failure to maintain flying speed and unintentionally stalling the airplane, delay in the selection of a suitable landing area within gliding distance, and general indecision.

- *Desire to save the airplane.* In an off-airport landing, some damage to the aircraft is likely. The other truth is that if a light airplane comes to earth, under control, and with the wings level at touchdown, serious injury to the occupants is very unlikely, unless, of course, the airplane hits a building or something similar while still traveling very fast. The landing speeds of light airplanes are slow in the first place, and if they are landed in a field where even some braking can occur before they hit something, the impact speed will be very slow indeed. But metal is never as important as flesh and bones. The moral is: Don't worry about the airplane; protect yourself. There are even situations in which sacrificing the airplane will protect those who are inside of it.

- *Undue concern about getting injured.* Fear is a vital part of a person's natural self-preservation instinct. But panic is one of our biggest enemies. No one can handle pressure if panic sets in. One of my airline captain friends said it best: "If emergency procedures are practiced to the point that they just become additional procedures, they cease to be emergencies." Don't panic and you'll come through about anything that an airplane can dish out to you.

Another friend who is a corporate pilot and flies as captain on large intercontinental corporate flights has another great saying. It goes like this: "An airplane might disappoint you, but it will never surprise a properly trained pilot."

When you are flying cross country, don't get too complacent, and develop good habits. Watch along the way for suitable landing fields in which to land if the engine quits or starts to fail, or any other emergency arises that would justify a precautionary landing. It's a very good idea to always know the wind direction on the surface. It can easily be determined from smoke stacks, trees, ripples on ponds or lakes, or myriad other sources. If the time comes that you do have to set up for a forced landing, you'll be way ahead of the game if you don't sacrifice precious time and altitude in the glide, trying to figure out the wind conditions before you can even begin to plan a landing approach.

The best emergency landing spot is an airport. Don't laugh; in most parts of the country an airport of some kind is seldom more than a few minutes flying time away from your present position. The keys are good navigational skills, knowing where you are at all times, and reading your chart (map) often enough to know what's around you. Even if you don't fly into sod fields often, or maybe you never have, practice locating them. Go out and make a flight with the objective being to locate small sod fields that you have never seen before. This isn't very easy the first few times that you try it, but being able to find a farmer's private landing strip may be just the ticket someday to an uneventful landing when you need to get down in a hurry.

Next to an airport, the best site for landing is a good, long, hard, smooth field without obstacles. Be alert for power lines; they can be invisible until it's too late to avoid them. Major transmission lines are marked on your chart, so know where they are as your flight progresses. Assume that any road has normal electrical and phone wires running along it, so if you have to cross a road on the final approach to your landing site, plan to be at least 100 feet high as you cross it, to avoid the wires that are almost certainly there.

If you have any agricultural background and can pick out a field of wheat, oats, rye, or other grass crops, great. It's likely to be relatively smooth, and the crop won't hurt the airplane as you land. But don't shy away from a plowed field if it otherwise is the best field in which to land. If possible, and if the wind conditions allow, land parallel to the furrows.

Landing downwind will result in your contacting the ground with more forward speed than if you land upwind. But if the wind isn't strong, a downwind landing might be acceptable if it results in an approach with few obstacles or with less maneuvering at low altitude (FIG. 7-5). It's much more likely that if anything goes wrong, and a serious accident ensues, it

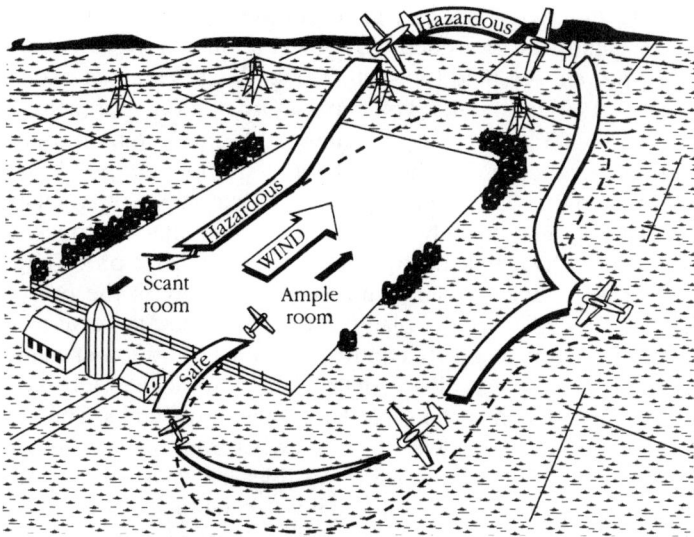

7-5 *In an emergency, a downwind landing might be safer. Notice the obstacles in the path of a normal upwind landing.*

will be a result of the pilot's forgetting to always fly the airplane first and keep it under control with adequate airspeed. Maneuvering at low altitude, with the stress of a forced landing already playing on the pilot's mind, has led to many a loss of control and low-altitude stall, when the result should have been an acceptable landing and a walk to the farmer's house to ask to use the phone to get a ride home.

Another of aviation's time-honored clichés is that the sky above you is of no use. This applies to practicing stalls and other maneuvers at a safely high altitude, but it also has something to say about cross-country flying. The more altitude you have if an emergency develops, the more flexibility and options that you have in dealing with it. I'm not suggesting that every flight has to be made at 10,000 feet above the ground, but why fly cross-country so low that your options are seriously compromised?

Excess altitude can always be shed, but if the engine quits, you can't climb. If you pick a good field while still quite high and circle above it as you glide down, you can give it an even closer look for wires, ditches, livestock, and other hazards to a safe landing. If you're high enough, you might just be able to find a better site. But again, use common sense. Except in the most dire of circumstances, don't change fields at the last minute. You're now flying a glider for the first time, and a good landing must be preceded by a good approach. If you abandon your chosen field for another one, don't make that choice when you're so low that you can't set up a good approach for the landing. Your chances of making a decent landing from an approach concocted at the last minute are not very good.

If the engine does ever stop, or you notice signs of an incipient failure, immediately go through the engine-out checklist and drill, which will be found in the emergency procedures section of your POH. First and foremost, establish the proper gliding speed for your airplane, and maintain it. Above all else, keep the airplane under control and don't allow other attentions to cause you to lose control. Then check the fuel selector, and if possible in your airplane, switch fuel tanks. The rest of the checklist items will vary somewhat from one airplane to another, but look at FIG. 7-6 for an idea of what is contained in most engine-out drills. Although you can't totally commit the engine-out section of your airplane's POH to memory, you should be familiar with it. Know where the checklist is, be able to find it quickly, and then use it.

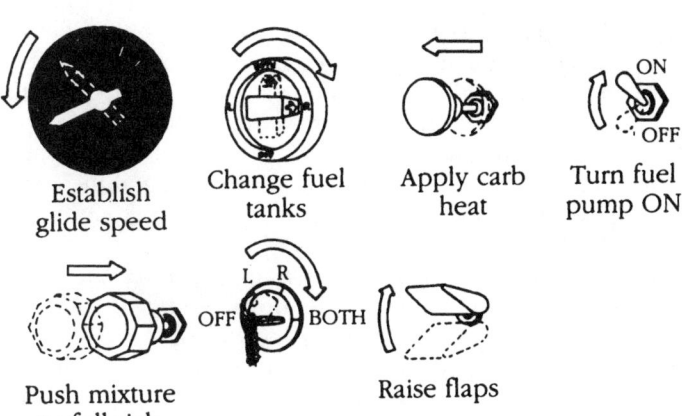

Establish
glide speed

Change fuel
tanks

Apply carb
heat

Turn fuel
pump ON

Push mixture
to full rich

Raise flaps

7-6 *Typical engine failure checklist.*

The most critical time for a total engine failure is within the first 100 to 1,000 feet after takeoff. The natural urge is turn back to the runway from which you just departed. As a student or newly minted private pilot, *don't* even think about it. When an engine fails during the departure climb, the first thing to do is to quickly get the nose down to the gliding attitude. The high nose attitude that is normal in a full-power climb will result in a very fast depletion of airspeed if the engine quits producing power. You're climbing in an airspeed that is fairly close to the glide speed, and if you don't lower the nose immediately when an engine failure happens, you suffer a very high risk of stalling. Get the nose down right now.

Before you even think about turning back to the runway, take some time now, in the quiet time of reading this book, to consider several of the factors that dictate that you should not try to get back to the runway. First, you would need to make a steep turn, and you have to actually turn more than 180° just to get aimed at the runway. During that steep turn, you would have a very high rate of descent, and you would be losing lots of altitude, as is always the case in a steeply banked gliding turn. Next, remember that you have already flown some distance from the runway and that same ground must be traversed again if you are going to make it back to the pavement. The chances are very slim that you would make it, after the altitude loss that is inevitable from the steeply banked gliding turn. Then you wouldn't actually be lined up with the runway's center line, and therefore some low-altitude maneuvering would be required to get lined up, and that's always potentially lethal. Even if you make it through the turn and still have enough altitude left to maneuver and get lined up with the runway, you're then facing a downwind landing. If you don't have sufficient altitude and you land short, your ground speed will be fast (because you're going downwind), and the risk of injury goes up exponentially with an increase in ground speed at touchdown.

So the only real choice if faced with an engine failure right after takeoff is to put the nose down and land relatively straight ahead. Of course, some maneuvering to find the best landing site is okay. The acceptable amount of turning depends on how high you are when the total engine failure occurs. Maybe as much as a 90° turn would be allowable, unless you're already fairly low.

Glider pilots get different training. Since a glider has no engine, its pilot doesn't worry about engine failure. But there is an analogy. In the United States, most gliders are launched by being towed aloft by a powered airplane. In Europe, many more glider launches occur by using a winch, with a long cable that pulls the glider up and launches it. Glider pilots are trained to deal with a break in the tow rope or an engine failure of the tow plane. Gliders perform so much better than airplanes do during a glide that a glider pilot can turn back to the runway if the tow rope breaks on takeoff. Conventionally in the United States, glider pilots are taught how to turn back at or above 200 feet above the ground if the tow rope breaks or if the tow plane has a problem.

As an airplane pilot, you can't do that. As you gain experience and develop the judgment that it will bring, you can decide when a turnback may work. If you're at 2,000 feet after departing from a 2-mile-long runway at a major airport, you might have enough height and room to turn around and land. But if a total engine failure happens right after taking off from a typical general aviation airport, it's suicidal to attempt to go back to the runway. A wise pilot thinks about every flight and plans necessary alternative courses of action. When you are on the runway for takeoff, glance around and see what's off of the end of it. Know where the obstacles are that a minor amount of turning would avoid. At your home airport, where most of your takeoffs will occur, you should know the environs of every runway as well as you know the layout of your home. If the rare engine failure does occur, you know where to go almost without thinking about it. Just as is the case for dealing with most of life's anomalies, preparedness and a cool head will get you through almost any emergency.

Before we leave this subject for more enjoyable discussions, take a moment again to emphasize in your own mind that the most important thing to do in any emergency, including but not limited to engine failure, is to keep the airplane under positive control, and that means maintaining adequate airspeed. Pilots have landed in woods, forests, on hillsides, and even in the water and walked or swam away completely uninjured. If you land almost anywhere, under control, with the wings level and perform a stall landing before you let the airplane touchdown, the most likely outcome will be a hike to the nearest house to use the phone or to the nearest road to bum a ride.

Flight Plans

A *flight plan* is a form that you'll fill out prior to takeoff for any cross-country flight (FIG. 7-7). Most of the time, you'll telephone the nearest FAA FSS and give the data to the briefer there. The form lists your aircraft identification, route of flight, destination, fuel onboard, number of people onboard, estimated time en route, and other pertinent information about the flight that you are about to undertake.

7-7 *The FAA flight plan form.*

Flight plans aren't required by the FARs for VFR flights. While you're still a student pilot, your instructor will insist upon your filing one for every dual instructional and solo cross-country flight. After you gain your private pilot certificate, you should still use them. If you are taking a cross-country flight very far from your local area, or at night, or if the trip will take you over sparsely populated areas, water, rough terrain, deserts, or swamps, a flight plan should always be filed.

If you are ever forced down and have filed a flight plan, the Civil Air Patrol (CAP) search-and-rescue procedures begin automatically 30 minutes after your scheduled arrival time at your destination if the flight plan hasn't been closed by the pilot of the flight. So when you arrive at your destination, be sure to always close your flight plan with the nearest FSS. If you encounter any delays en route, call the nearest FSS either by radio or by phone and modify your flight plan to show a new arrival time. I've served in the CAP since the 1960s, as a search and rescue pilot and squadron and group commander. It's no fun to be awakened at 3:00 A.M. to get your troops out to start a search mission, only to be looking for somebody whose airplane is safely in a hangar and who, himself, is snuggly in bed at home and who didn't close his flight plan.

Emergency Locator Transmitters

The FARs require that airplanes used for cross-country flying be equipped with a device called an *emergency locator transmitter* (ELT). The ELT is a radio transmitter that is mounted in the airplane. It is battery operated and is automatically activated by the G forces that occur during a crash. When it is subjected to these forces, it emits a distinctive "whoop-whoop" audio signal tone on both of the international emergency frequencies, 121.5 and 243.0 MHz. ELTs are designed to continuously transmit for at least 48 hours over a wide spectrum of temperature ranges.

Both the United States and Russia have earth satellites in orbit that continually listen for ELT signals. Again, from my own CAP experience, I can tell you that very few ELT signals go unheard by at least one of these satellites. Both countries cooperate, and they immediately share the location of any signal that one of the satellites hears within the boundaries of the other nation, as well as anywhere else on earth. As a further safety measure, the FAA encourages pilots, while flying cross-county, to tune their communication radios to 121.5 MHz and listen for an ELT signal. You won't be able to monitor 243.0 MHz; that is the military emergency frequency, and your civilian radios don't tune for it.

If you hear an ELT, there won't be any doubt as to what it is. Take out your chart and mark the position of your airplane when you first heard it and where you were when the signal faded away. In the meantime, immediately contact the nearest FAA ATC facility, and let them know what you're hearing, your location, and route of flight. Knowing these details will enable the CAP search planes to better "box" a search area. CAP planes are equipped with a direction finder that enables them to home in on an ELT signal and fly to the aircraft in distress. Your alertness might save some lives.

Emergency Instrument Procedures

While it should never happen to any pilot who has had proper flight planning, it is always possible, since we all make mistakes, that sometime you might find yourself smack in the middle of instrument weather conditions. Weather forecasting is far from an exact science, but human nature is the greatest cause of inadvertent IFR encounters. Let's go through a typical example of how this misfortune has unfolded countless times (FIG. 7-8).

7-8 *Never allow "get-there-itis" to rule your decision making. About 40 percent of all lightplane accidents are related to poor weather judgment.*

A private pilot has a critical sales presentation to make in a city 300 miles away from her home, and the meeting is scheduled for 2:00 P.M. At 7:00 A.M. that morning, our aviator calls the FSS for her weather briefing, starting the process of planning her flight. She learns that the weather is excellent VFR at both the departure and destination airports. However, there is a warm front lying between the two cities that contains a 50-mile-wide area of low clouds and freezing rain. But the conditions are expected to improve as the day goes on, according to the weather mavens.

So our pilot drives to the airport, gets some coffee, and kills a little time chatting with the folks at the FBO. At 9:00 A.M., she checks with the FSS again and learns that the area of poor weather has improved a little, but that it's strictly IFR. So back she goes to the coffee machine.

Now at 10:00 A.M. she's getting antsy. It's only 4 hours until the time that she's got to see the customer who will make her sales quota for the year. She checks the weather again, and the FSS briefer is still dispensing doubt about whether this flight can be made under VFR. After hanging up the phone and now realizing that there isn't enough time to catch an airline flight or to drive, she makes her decision. The bad weather is lifting, just like the forecast said it would, but not quite as quickly as forecast. It's got to be at least minimal VFR by the time she gets to the frontal area, and it's only 50 miles wide anyhow, so there won't be much of a problem. Sure, she's not instrument rated, but she has been flying for 2 years now and has almost 300 hours of flying time. Plus, what will the sophisticated, quota-busting customer think of doing business with someone who can't travel only 300 miles to make an appointment that has been on the calendar for over a month?

But that sales quota never got met or exceeded, our pilot never even got there. CAP search crews, who themselves waited until evening to start searching so that the bad weather could go by, found the wreckage just before dark. The hometown newspaper carried the story the next day, and a depressing story it was. Remember this scenario because without a doubt it will happen more than a dozen times each year. Those who are ignorant of general aviation will reinforce their feelings that little airplanes are dangerous—just look what happened to their smart, ambitious, and career-climbing friend.

Acting on the proven theory that people are human and will, on occasion, make dumb decisions in the face of their better judgment, the FAA has attempted to cut the accident rate of non-instrument-rated pilots "pushing the weather" by requiring that, as a part of the private pilot flight test, each applicant must demonstrate an ability to control the airplane by reference to flight instruments alone. Also, the pilot must be able to show the examiner that she can fly well enough on instruments to save her life by turning around, climbing, or descending if necessary and flying back to the good weather that she left behind her.

This doesn't mean that you have to have an instrument rating or that such advanced skills are necessary, desirable, or even practical for everyone. But a few hours of dual instruction on instrument flying could keep you alive on a day that your judgment falters. It is therefore required by the FARs that you have some instrument training before you take the private pilot practical exam, which we often call the *flight test*. While this elementary training is a far cry from that needed to qualify for an instrument rating, it is intended only to provide you with the minimum skills needed to get you out of trouble if you stumble into IFR weather. Think of it as a lifeboat.

In most cases when a pilot is accidentally caught in instrument conditions, there is VFR weather behind him, from where he just came. Therefore, by being able to keep the airplane under control, execute a turnaround, and fly on a constant heading for a few minutes, most hapless pilots can extricate themselves and return to VFR weather. It's not particularly hard to do, but it's not as easy as it sounds.

Flying the Instruments

When you lose visual contact with the ground, your senses of balance and direction go haywire. Nonflyers find this hard to believe, but it is absolutely true. Your sense of equilibrium is gone. Although the brain gets a part of its balance information from the inner ear, the data are incomplete and must be supplemented with visual cues. You will find yourself leaning to one side, straining against a bank that isn't there. If you're turning in a coordinated turn, it might feel like you aren't turning at all.

The flight instruments know better and don't lie. But it takes a while for most of us to place our trust, and our lives, in the hands of little gyroscopes, needles, and gauges. There is one important rule about instrument flying:

Believe the instruments.

If the turn needle says that you're turning, disregard whatever you feel is happening and *believe the turn needle.*

This is the central theme to learn about controlling your airplane without visual reference to the ground. Your body and its senses will definitely lie to you. Don't ever forget that unfortunate but infallible fact. Believe only the inhuman instruments.

Most non-instrument-rated pilots will get into serious trouble within a minute or two after flying into the clouds. A wing drops slightly, the airplane starts a general turn, and next, the nose drops a little to increase airspeed in order to make up for the loss of lift resulting from the bank. Then the bank continues to increase, and the nose keeps slowly falling, trying to compensate for less and less lift.

Finally, the pilot notices—and probably hears—the wind noise generated by the increased airspeed that was caused by the falling of the nose. Doing what he thinks is right, he pulls back on the wheel, which begins the now-fatal sequence of events. Pulling back on the wheel while the airplane is in a steep bank accomplishes only one thing: The bank steepens some more. The pilot will never realize that he is in a spiral and that he cannot pull the nose up until he first levels the wings.

Then one of two things happens next: Either he continues spiraling and pulling back on the wheel until he has overloaded the structure of the airplane with G forces and the airframe fails, or he just spirals, ever faster in airspeed and turn rate, until he hits the ground. Either way, the rest of us read about him in the accident statistics. To avoid this scenario and to save your neck, you have to realize the importance of the turn needle (turn coordinator) any time you stumble into a condition in which you lose visual reference with the surface.

While we're on the subject of the loss of visual reference with the outside world, be aware that clouds aren't the only cause of that loss. At night, without moonlight, it can be very difficult to keep visual reference if the area over which you're flying is sparsely populated. With no city lights or extensive road systems to provide visual cues, you're an island in a sea of air, totally without visual reference points to keep your senses working properly.

Two other ordinary conditions can also lead to a loss of visual reference. One is dense haze, such as the kind that besets the eastern part of the United States in the summer, and its cousin, smog. With the visibility at the 1-mile minimum for VFR flight in certain areas of airspace, or even at 3 miles as is required in other airspace, especially if flying into the sun, ground contact can easily be lost, even if there is not a cloud in the sky. If you have to fly in marginal visibility, keep your altitude as low as reasonable, considering the terrain and what obstacles may be lurking. The disabling effects of haze on visual reference increase with altitude.

The other situation is present when flying over water. Unless the visibility is very good and there is a distinct horizon, it's very easy to become disoriented and lose visual reference over large bodies of water, especially when you're at some considerable distance from the shoreline. This can happen to any pilot who flies along the seacoast or the Great Lakes. Night flying over water should be attempted only by an instrument-rated pilot. It's virtually impossible to keep adequate visual references to control an airplane over water after dark, regardless of how good the weather is. The Caribbean nations don't even allow VFR flights at night for this very reason.

If you keep the turn wheel centered, you won't be turning, and without a turn, the *graveyard spiral* can't develop. Under instrument conditions, you can pretty much ignore the ball in the tube, unless it gets ridiculously out of center. The best way to fly the needle or the turn coordinator under emergency instrument circumstances is to use your feet to keep the needle centered. If you see the needle showing a left turn, apply a little right rudder pressure. Don't cross-control with the wheel and prevent the airplane from banking. Just initiate the correction with your feet and allow the bank to follow. You're not interested in precisely coordinated flight; you're interested in keeping the airplane upright and not turning, and in the process keeping yourself alive.

Your airplane will also almost certainly be equipped with an attitude indicator, commonly called an *artificial horizon*. You have to learn to use it as a reference also. It cannot tell you if the airplane is turning, but it does let you know if the wings are level or banked, and what the nose attitude is. So use the turn coordinator and attitude indicator together to keep out of a turn and keep the wings and nose basically level. Now you've learned rule number 2, which is:

Stay out of turns. Keep the wings level.

That takes care of directional control; now let's work on keeping the nose level. The attitude indicator is the primary instrument to use for this task. We use the attitude indicator as the primary reference because it has no lag between airplane attitude changes and its indications, and it is one of the easiest instruments in the panel to interpret. The secondary information about the nose attitude will come from the airspeed indicator. Unless you alter the power setting, which you should not do in this emergency situation unless things get really out of whack, the airspeed will change as the nose attitude does.

Don't chase minor deviations in either the airspeed or the attitude indicator. Overcontrolling is something you definitely want to avoid. Relax and look for turns that need to be altered, and don't try to eliminate every little blurb in attitude deviation. Using the airspeed indicator alone to control the nose attitude is more difficult because it requires far more interpretation than does the attitude indicator. Also, there is some lag in time between a change in nose attitude and the resultant change in airspeed. Therefore, it is very easy to overcontrol if you try to chase the airspeed indications. What we're looking for is a trend that needs to be corrected.

If you notice, for instance, that the airspeed is lower than cruise speed, look for a moment to see if it's continuing to decrease or if it's stable. If the airspeed is continuing to go down, the nose attitude is probably quite high and needs to be lowered. The faster the trend is developing, the greater the deviation in the nose attitude from level. Likewise, if the airspeed is increasing, the nose is below level. If the buildup in speed is occurring rapidly, you're in a dive; if the speed is slowly increasing, the nose is only slightly below level.

The altimeter can also be used to cross-check the nose attitude. Remember the discussion of the interchangeability of altitude and airspeed? When the nose goes up or down, some altitude change will also occur, assuming a constant power setting. This information is not as reliable an indication of nose attitude as is the information gleaned from the attitude indicator and airspeed because eventually the effects of a *zoom climb* or *dive* will play themselves out. But the altimeter is useful as a cross-check.

As long as the attitude indicator shows the little airplane symbol as being close to level, and if the airspeed is relatively constant, the airplane's nose is level enough.

Whenever you're flying, you know to use light, relaxed control pressures on the wheel and rudder pedals. This is even more important in instrument flying. Overcontrolling will get you into trouble a lot faster than will too little pressure, as long as you're doing something to correct for attitude deviations.

Back to Better Weather

Now that you have stabilized the airplane and have it under positive control, the next goal is to get turned around and fly out of the bad weather, toward the good conditions that are probably close behind. You'll need to turn only about 180° to solve your predicament. We're going to turn a little bit differently than we do under VFR conditions because the goal here is to keep the airplane under control and not lose it; we're not concerned about the best coordination of rudder and aileron pressures.

Using the Turn Indicator

We need to talk a little more about the turn indicator. In some airplanes, the indicator is made so that it is very easy to establish a controllable rate of turn. This indicator has two little marks at the top, one mark on either side of the center. These marks are commonly referred to as the *doghouses,* after their distinctive shape. When the turn needle is deflected so that the top of the needle lies directly under a doghouse, the airplane is turning in the direction of the needle deflection at a rate of 3° per second, which is known as a *standard rate turn*. There is also a type of turn indicator that does not have the doghouses. If your airplane is equipped with this type, a standard rate of turn (3° per second) is achieved by deflecting the turn needle just outside of the center mark, without covering any of it. This is called a *one-needle-width turn*. These indicators are not typically installed in modern airplanes or in an airplane that has had its instrument panel updated to a more modern configuration.

The more common instrument, which you're far more likely to encounter, is the turn coordinator with a little airplane symbol in place of the outdated vertical turn needle. The turn coordinator is also calibrated to allow a pilot to make a standard rate turn. Look at FIG. 7-9, which shows a turn coordinator in the panel of this airplane instead of a turn needle. See the little marks with L and R directly below them? When the little airplane symbol is deflected so that the wings of the symbol line up with these marks, you're in a standard rate turn.

7-9 *Read the turn coordinator as you would the needle in the older-style turn-and-slip indicator. Remember that the turn coordinator does not indicate pitch.*

The third rule is this:

A standard rate turn continued for 1 minute will result in a 180° change in direction.

Now, before starting the turnaround to get out of the IFR weather, you need to know what direction to fly to accomplish that. You need to know the *reciprocal heading* of the heading that you are flying when the conditions deteriorated. The best rule of thumb to quickly figure reciprocals is to add or subtract 200 from the present heading and do the reverse with a number 20. Here's how it works: If you're flying along on a heading of 120° (southeast), add 200 in your head, which gives you 320, and then quickly subtract 20, which results in the reciprocal of 120, which is 300°. Some folks can directly add or subtract 180 with mental math, but most of us can't, especially when under stress.

If your original heading is 290°, you can't accomplish anything by adding 200, because there are only 360° in a circle. So subtract 200, resulting in 90, then add 20, resulting in 110°, which is the reciprocal of 290. Practice these mental gymnastics a few times while flying in normal conditions, and they will become very easy.

Look again at FIG. 7-9. In this picture, you'll see a DG immediately to the right of the turn coordinator. This is the newer type of DG, which you'll probably see in your trainer. If you have this newer type, notice how it shows the full 360° circle of headings. With this type of DG, it's possible to read a reciprocal right from the face of the instrument. If your airplane has the older drum-styled DG, you have to resort to the mental math to determine your reciprocal heading.

To begin the turn, use only the rudder. You are flying the turn coordinator, and it is crucial that you establish and maintain the standard turn rate of 3° per second. Do it with your feet because you can be much more precise that way. Allow the airplane to bank during the turn, and keep the bank under control with ailerons. Don't fight the airplane's tendency to bank, but don't let the bank get steep, say, beyond about 30° at the most. You are turning in an unconventional way, which results in flight that is somewhat uncoordinated, but it is done this way because it's easier to keep things upright and to keep the turn at a standard rate.

As you start the turn, notice the time. Almost every airplane has a clock in the instrument panel, but many of them don't last very long in the high-vibration environment of an airplane instrument panel. I usually fly with a wristwatch that has a sweep second hand, and sometimes I wear my digital athletic watch. Either will do as long as you can time 1 minute on something. Continue the standard rate turn for 1 minute; then using pressure on the opposite rudder pedal, which is a bit abrupt, roll out of the turn. Don't overdo the rollout pressure—you're not stomping grapes into wine. You want to roll out quickly but without overcontrolling. Look at the DG and check your heading, and cross-check it against what the magnetic compass is saying. If you need some minor corrections to get onto that reciprocal heading, do them easily and gently with the rudder pedals.

Don't get lazy and depend on the DG—time the turn. DGs can fail too, and you shouldn't depend on them for everything you need to know. During the turn, it's okay to monitor the progress by glancing at the DG, but don't get transfixed on it and forget to maintain control of the nose attitude. Remember that during a turn, you're vulnerable to losing control much more so than during straight and level flight.

Then, when you're established on the reciprocal heading, you have only two things to do: First, prevent turning by keeping the turn coordinator centered; second, keep the nose level by using the attitude indicator and the airspeed indicator. Repeat these two things over and over again in your mind to maintain the reciprocal heading until you are in VFR conditions again. Time

will seem to creep by, so don't get excited if it seems to take forever to fly out of the weather. As long as you're going forward
toward the good weather that you were in before this entire
problem occurred, you will get there eventually.

The chief value of this method lies in its simplicity. Don't
change the trim because doing so will cause the non-instrument-
rated pilot far more trouble than benefit. Anything that diverts
your attention from the turn coordinator or needle, attitude indicator, and airspeed indicator must be regarded as extraneous
and ignored until you are out of the soup. Nor should it be necessary to adjust the throttle any more than once, unless you lose
control and end up either in a stall or in a high-speed spiral.

As soon as you find yourself in instrument conditions, it may
be helpful to set the power to about 10 percent below normal
cruise, especially if you're flying an airplane that is faster than our
Cessna 150. This slowdown will ease the loadings on wings if
there is turbulence. Also, less power will help slow any airspeed
changes that result from getting the nose too low and will help
prevent the graveyard spiral. It also helps ease any tendency that
you might otherwise have to overcontrol the nose attitude.

One way to make this power change is to pull out the carb
heat, without touching the throttle; then you don't have to
monitor the tachometer while reducing the throttle, which
would divert your attention from the flight instruments. If the
outside air temperature is below approximately 75°, there is a
good possibility of carburetor ice forming when flying in visible moisture or in clouds. Applying carb heat as soon as you
are in those conditions can act to remove that possibility from
the list of your potential problems.

As long as you keep the airplane under positive control,
chances are extremely good that this adventure will be something that you'll talk about, and help others learn from, for
years to come. Just remember that your goal is control, not
finesse. For a non-instrument-rated pilot to try to be extremely precise in the clouds will almost undoubtedly lead to serious overcontrolling and eventual loss of control. Keep your
wits about you, don't let panic set in, and you'll do fine.

But because you're a careful person to start with, you're
learning to fly from a competent instructor, and you have the
desire to learn as much as you can, which is evidenced by
your reading material like this book, you won't wander into
IFR weather in the first place, will you?

8

Weather

Airplanes fly in the sea of air that supports them. The condition of the atmosphere at the low altitudes where we fly is constantly changing, and we use the word weather when we talk about the state in which we find the lower levels of the earth's blanket of gases. Weather can be the most decisive factor in making for an extremely pleasant flight, and it can also be a demon at times, tossing an airplane about, restricting a pilot's visibility outside of the cockpit to nil, and occasionally making it nigh impossible for us to fly. Next to knowing how to physically manipulate the controls of an airplane, every pilot needs a working knowledge of the elementary principles of meteorology and its terms and jargon.

From a mechanical point of view, airplanes became reliable machines long before World War II. Since then, pilots have been able to depend, with ever-increasing confidence, on the aircraft itself to maintain flight. But humans will never control the weather. It is the one variable with which we must deal as impotent bystanders. Although we can equip larger airplanes with radar sets to see precipitation associated with thunderstorms, deicing gear to enable them to fly in conditions that generate inflight icing, and similar modern electronic aids, we still can't change the basic fact that the weather will be what it will be.

Weather is the cause of most accidents in small airplanes. To put that statement more correctly, the cause of these accidents is pilots' inability to handle certain types of weather conditions, their ignorance of them, or both. Machines don't make mistakes; people do. Rarely, a maintenance technician might err, or a design engineer might let something get past all of the design processes and reviews. The greatest number of mistakes that influence aviation safety are made by pilots. We need to know which weather conditions present hazards to flight in small airplanes, how to discern where those conditions are, how to avoid them, and what to do if we inadvertently encounter them.

To enable us to know what the weather is around the country and beyond its borders in many instances, the FAA maintains a network of regional automated FSSs to serve the weather and flight planning needs of pilots. These stations are relatively new, having replaced a nationwide system of smaller FSSs that were far more numerous and in the past linked to each other by teletype. The newer stations still have human personnel working in them 24 hours a day, and you may personally go to the FSS for a weather briefing if you live near one. However, pilots visit in person less frequently now because the number of FSSs has been drastically reduced, and thus pilots live farther away from the stations. But the newer stations are far larger and more capable in their primary role of disseminating weather and other flight safety information.

A few years ago, in-person weather briefings were quite common, and there was an unmatched comfort in being able to see all of the weather maps yourself, instead of just hearing a description of the conditions affecting your planned flight from a briefer, over the telephone. But the price of progress in keeping these government services free to pilots has been the closing of most of the smaller FSSs and the consolidating of them into regional operations. The FAA provides a toll-free telephone number for pilots' use. If you dial 1-800-WX-BRIEF, you will automatically be connected to the FSS that serves the geographical area from which you are placing the call.

If you are a licensed pilot and wish to use your personal computer, you can access the FAA's weather briefing data by use of the *direct user access terminal (DUAT) system*. This service has been free to pilots since its inception. It uses another toll-free number to make the connection from a computer over a phone modem, but it is also usable by computers that have other media of communication. There is always a chance, given government belt-tightening, that some of these services may in the future involve a nominal charge. As this edition of this book is being written, DUAT services are still free to licensed pilots.

You can also access most of the data over the Internet. If you use your search engine to look for "aviation weather," you'll be greeted with more sites than you can imagine. Do some Web surfing, and bookmark the sites that you find to be the most easily usable.

Several private-sector companies offer weather briefing services by computer too, naturally for a fee. Some pilots prefer the commercial services, claiming that the output is more logically organized and easier to interpret than the government products. As you advance in your aviation career, you can try them and decide what's best for your needs.

Both the Aircraft Owners and Pilots Association (AOPA) and the Experimental Aircraft Association (EAA) have excellent Web sites that provide their members weather data either directly or via links to weather sites. Both of their Web home pages also link to their subweb sites for superb flight planning programs. A few hours spent with your computer will unleash a wealth of weather information and flight planning sources.

Home television can also be a source of weather data. Most cable systems carry The Weather Channel, which gives great real-time views of weather radar returns throughout the entire country. But this source of data provides only general weather pictures, outlooks, and trends. The information is not presented with an orientation to aviation needs. Although you should always get as much weather wisdom as possible from a multitude of sources, The Weather Channel and similar television products are never a substitute for a proper aviation weather briefing.

You can contact FSSs while you are in flight, using standard radio frequencies. If you need to update your briefing while airborne, want to report weather conditions that are different from what was forecast, or need any other FSS service, don't hesitate to use your radio and give them a call. Just be courteous, and don't use the radio, instead of the phone or computer for an initial, detailed briefing. Although the briefer at the FSS will accommodate you if you do that, it ties up the radio frequency for an extended period of time during which no one else can call. The same goes for filing your flight plan: If you depart from a remote airport where there is no payphone, or where your cell phone doesn't work, you can file over the radio. Otherwise, drop a coin in a payphone or use your cell phone and call the toll-free number. A VFR flight plan must be opened and then must also be closed by the pilot, and using the radio to call the FSS to perform those short tasks is a good example of the proper use of radio communications with FSSs.

Preflight Weather Briefings

The FARs require that you familiarize yourself with the weather forecast and conditions along your route of flight. It is required that you do so before you begin your flight. If you're going out for a local flight, around the area of the airport, a call to the FSS asking for the current conditions might suffice, satisfying both the legal requirement and the common-sense one. But if you're planning to leave the local area, you need to obtain a preflight briefing, either from an FSS or by using a proper computer service such as the DUAT service. Let's assume that we are planning a cross-country trip, away from the local airport.

Three preflight weather briefings are available through the FSS: standard, abbreviated, and outlook. Tell the specialist at the FSS which briefing you want, including some background information that is necessary for the specialist to conduct the briefing for your needs: aircraft type, route of flight, proposed departure time, and aircraft identification number or the pilot's name. While you are still a student pilot, tell the briefer so; you'll find that these people are very helpful, and most will go more slowly and anticipate your level of understanding if they know in advance that you are a student. All FSS contacts are recorded for everyone's protection in case a dispute arises later about whether the pilot ever received a briefing or what information he was given during that briefing. This information can be used for accident investigation purposes and in civil lawsuits that may arise as a result of an accident. The contents of the entire briefing are recorded.

You'll find your briefing to be much more productive if you don't interrupt the briefer with questions. Try to save them until the end, and then ask as many as you need to fully understand the briefing. Even though there is an established protocol for each of the types of briefings, some briefers are more complete than are others. Don't hesitate to ask and, if necessary, insist upon getting the information that you need.

Standard briefings

You should request a standard briefing for any planned flight when you have not received any previous briefing for this trip at this time. The specialist will automatically go through a predetermined list and provide the following information applicable to your proposed flight:

- *Adverse conditions.* This segment will include significant meteorological and aeronautical information that might cause you to alter your proposed flight plan. These items include hazardous weather, runway or airport closures, navigational aid outages, and the like.

- *VFR flight not recommended.* When a VFR flight is proposed (that is one of the things you should tell the briefer as a part of the opening comments that you make about the background information) and sky conditions or visibilities are present or forecast at the surface or aloft that, in the specialist's judgment, would make the successful outcome of the flight doubtful under VFR, the specialist will describe the conditions, the affected locations, and then say, "VFR flight is not recommended." This caution is advisory in nature because the pilot is the final authority for all aspects of the flight, including whether it should be commenced or continued.

- *Synopsis.* This is a brief statement that describes, in general terms, the type, location, and movement of weather systems or air masses that might affect your route of flight.

- *Current conditions.* In this section of the briefing, the briefer will give you the exact reports of the weather, current as of the most recent hourly report, at the airports of departure and arrival. In addition, you'll be told about the current weather at selected locations along your planned flight.

- *En route forecast.* You'll be told what the aviation weather forecast is at your destination airport. The specialist might also give you the forecast at your departure airport if it looks as though the departure airport weather might be a factor, as well as the forecasts at selected airports along your route.

- *Destination forecast.* If it is not given as part of the en route forecast, you'll be given the forecast at the destination airport.

- *Winds aloft.* Next the briefer will tell you the forecast for winds aloft. These are not current data but forecasts that tell you what to expect in terms of wind directions and velocities aloft. They are presented in 3,000-foot increments and also include the predicted temperatures at the various altitudes.

- *Notices to Airmen* (NOTAMs). These are reports of such things as runway closures, inoperative navigational aides, construction cranes operating near an airport, and similar information that you need to know, either along your route or at the airports of departure or destination.

- *ATC delays.* These are reports of IFR flight delays in the air traffic control system and are usually not important to the VFR pilot unless he is heading into a major airline airport.

- *Other information.* Normally the "other information" section of the standard briefing is optional on the part of the briefer, and it is given upon the pilot's request. Most briefers will tell you other important information without your requesting it, but don't assume that they will. Other information includes such items as activity along military training routes and in military operations areas (MOAs), approximate density altitudes at various airports, procedures for dealing with the U.S. Customs Service, and the like. In the days since September 11, 2001, and the tragic terrorist attacks that occurred that day, it has been necessary to close certain areas of the U.S. airspace. Other temporary flight restrictions (TFRs) have been imposed around major industrial and nuclear facilities, large gatherings of people for sporting events, and similar activities. Always ask the briefer if there are any NOTAMs or TFRs in existence for any place along or near your proposed route of flight.

Abbreviated briefings

You should request an abbreviated briefing only when you have already had a previous standard briefing for this proposed flight at the proposed time. The abbreviated briefing is used to supplement the data that you already have. When you talk to the briefer, be sure to tell her what information you do have and when you received it. If your data are totally obsolete, your abbreviated briefing may be converted to a new standard format briefing.

Outlook briefings

An outlook briefing is used when your proposed departure time is more than 6 hours from the time that you call the FSS. The outlook briefing is for planning purposes only, such as when you want to know whether a VFR flight is likely to be possible. A standard briefing should or must be obtained before takeoff. The closer in time that you get your standard briefing before your proposed departure time, the more reliable the information will be.

In-Flight Briefings

In-flight briefings should be used only when you can't get a briefing in person, over the telephone, or over official computer sources. Using the radio for an in-flight briefing ties up that radio frequency for an extended period of time and is discourteous to other pilots. A pilot may need the channel for a quick but important inquiry, and someone else "hogging" the frequency could prevent the dissemination of important information to another pilot. But, if you have to, use the radio because you don't ever want to conduct a cross-country flight with no briefing at all.

En Route Flight Advisory Services

This service, provided by the FAA through selected FSSs, is known as *Flight Watch*. It is designed to give pilots who are en route timely and meaningful updated weather advisories pertinent to the flight, route, altitude, and type of aircraft being flown.

Flight Watch is not intended to be used for obtaining complete weather briefings or for the opening or closing of flight plans. It mainly serves as a clearinghouse for weather conditions that have been reported by other pilots. As your trip progresses, if you encounter any significant weather, especially conditions either much better or worse than forecast, get on the radio and contact Flight Watch at the nearest FSS. Let them know what the conditions are that prompted your call. Pilot reports such as these are perhaps the most meaningful weather information that we can get. Forecasts are nice, current reported surface conditions are better, and knowing what another pilot actually encountered is best of all.

The Flight Watch services are provided by specially trained personnel at selected FSSs throughout the country. To contact one, set your transmitter frequency to 122.0 MHz. Begin your call by saying the name of the Flight Watch facility you're calling, followed by your aircraft type and identification, and then the name of the very high frequency omnidirectional radio (VOR) nearest to your position. For example, you would say: "Cleveland Flight Watch, Comanche 81 Lima Lima [the call sign for 81LL in phonetics] over Mansfield VOR."

In-Flight Weather Advisories

The National Weather Service issues three types of in-flight weather advisories that are designated as *convective SIGMETs, SIGMETs,* and *AIRMETs.*

The term *SIGMET* is derived from the words *significant meteorological.* When you hear an ATC facility or an FSS say that there is a SIGMET issued, pay close attention. You're about to hear something that has a significance to all aircraft, whether you are the pilot of a Cessna 150 or the captain of an airliner. A convective SIGMET is issued to warn all pilots of dangerous conditions caused by convection, such as tornadoes, lines of thunderstorms, thunderstorms embedded in other clouds, and areas with 40 percent or more thunderstorm coverage. All of this is bad stuff, and you don't want to stumble into any of it.

A SIGMET is issued for other very dangerous conditions, such as severe and extreme turbulence, severe icing, and widespread dust storms. These are dangers that would affect any aircraft, regardless of how sophisticated or well equipped it is.

AIRMETs warn of weather conditions that are potentially dangerous to light aircraft but don't pose a threat to larger, better-equipped airplanes such as airliners or corporate jets. An AIRMET is issued for moderate icing, moderate turbulence, sustained winds of 30 knots or more at the surface, widespread areas with ceilings below 1,000 feet or visibilities less than 3 miles, and extensive areas where mountains will be obscured by clouds or there are other restrictions to visibility.

Both SIGMETs and AIRMETs have a phonetic letter designator followed by a number—for instance, SIGMET Bravo 1. Succeeding advisories will retain the same alphabetic designator for as long as that particular weather condition exists, but the number changes as new advisories are sent out, to let you know how recent each report is. Alpha (for A) through November (for N) are used for SIGMETs, and the designators Oscar (for O) through Zulu (for Z) are attached to AIRMETs.

SIGMETs and AIRMETs are automatically announced as soon as they are issued. They are issued by radio from FSSs, and they are also distributed throughout the weather reporting system to all FSSs.

As you can see, the government has gone to considerable effort and expense to create a weather reporting system and to maintain it just to keep pilots informed of the conditions and to keep us out of trouble. To understand what you're being told by this system, you are required to learn enough about the basics of weather during your training so that this information is meaningful to you. Let's spend some time with those basics.

Air Pressure

As we stand upon the earth's surface, we are surrounded by an ocean of air around and above us. At sea level, that air weighs about $1^{1}/_{4}$ ounces per cubic foot, which means that it presses down and around us with a pressure of about 14.7 pounds per square inch. By international convention, it was decided that when the air pressure is such that it causes a column of mercury contained within a vacuum tube to rise 29.92 inches, we will call that *standard barometric pressure*. There is nothing really standard about this particular barometer reading; it's just an arbitrary point that was chosen as a starting place for measuring deviations in air pressure.

Our concern with air pressure is not limited to the fact that several of our most important flight instruments operate by sensing air pressure. For weather purposes, we need to understand that variations in air pressure are linked with and are harbingers of changes in the weather.

If the earth had a constant temperature over its entire surface, there wouldn't be any variations in air pressure, nor would there be any significant difference in the weather from the equator to the poles. But, of course, the temperature isn't the same everywhere. The sun heats the earth's surface unequally. Different kinds of terrain absorb different amounts of heat, even in the same season of the year.

For example, a certain portion of the surface, such as the paved areas of a city, will absorb much more heat than will the surrounding farm fields. The air above the city becomes warmer than the air around the city. As the air warms, it expands, and as it expands, it becomes lighter as a product of that expansion. Because this warmer air is now lighter than the cooler air around it, the warmer air rises. This rising column of air is called a *thermal,* or *convection, current.* A thermal will usually continue to rise until it reaches an altitude at which it cools to the point that whatever water vapor is in the air condenses and forms a cumulus cloud. These thermals are the rising currents that glider pilots search for because good thermals can sustain a glider in flight for hours.

Meanwhile, the rising and expanding thermal has created a small area of low pressure at its base, and the relatively cooler air of higher pressure surrounding the thermal wants to rush in and equalize the pressure. Presto, a wind is born. This same process, on a vastly bigger scale, creates the huge areas of low air pressure that move across the earth's surface, "making" our weather patterns.

Areas of high atmospheric pressure exist for just the opposite reason. Cool air is heavier and more dense, is often clear of extensive cloud cover, and is said to be stable. To a meteorologist, *stable air* is air in which cumulus clouds will not build up into thunderheads. Student pilots sometimes assume that bumpy air is "unstable," but the exact opposite is often true. For example, the cool air behind a cold front may be bumpy, as it usually is, but it is stable because it contains relatively little water vapor and it doesn't form thunderheads. This is why, as a flyer, you will normally associate highs with good weather and suspect lows of harboring or generating poor flying conditions.

When we speak of "warm" and "cool" air in this context, the terms aren't used in an absolute sense. Rather, they are relative. If the temperature at a given place is 90°F and that location is surrounded with 85°F air, the 85°F air is referred to as "cool."

In the Northern Hemisphere, the winds around a low-pressure area are counterclockwise, and a high has airflow rotating clockwise around its center. The air from a high is always flowing toward a low because the atmosphere is always trying to equalize the variations in pressure, but it never accomplishes it. This exchange of air from highs toward lows is deflected to one side by the earth's rotation from east to west. In the Southern Hemisphere, rotations around highs and lows are reversed from what we're used to north of the equator.

Fronts and Air Masses

There are two basic classifications of air masses, *tropical* and *polar.* These labels come from the parts of the world in which the particular air mass forms, which is either in a tropical region or in a colder area. When a particular air mass starts moving, it has to travel over a route that is predominantly over oceans or land. If it travels over open water before reaching us, it is further classified as *maritime,* and when its route takes the air mass over land, it is referred to as *continental*. Then, the last step in deciding upon the final nomenclature to attach to an air mass is to classify it according to its temperature, relative to the other air surrounding it. You might have already surmised that these last two classes are *cold* or *warm*. So the complete classification of an air mass might be "polar continental cold" or "tropical maritime warm."

The route that an air mass takes when it starts moving on its trek across the globe is important to a meteorologist because the route will define many of the future characteristics of that mass. The air mass that travels over water is going to pick up far more moisture than one that is journeying over land.

Once an air mass starts in motion over the surface of the earth, it will overtake or displace other air that is in its line of travel. The boundary line between the two masses is called a *front*. When one air mass is overtaking another, there is surprisingly little mixture of the two at the frontal boundary, and it will often take thousands of miles of travel on the part of an overtaking air mass before the front between the two dissipates.

A *cold front* is the transition and boundary area between a cooler air mass and warmer air that it is overtaking. Again, the term *cold* is relative and only implies that the invading air mass is cooler than the air being displaced.

When you view a cold front in cross section (FIG. 8-1), it appears to be wedge shaped at its leading edge because the heavier, cooler air overtakes the warmer air in its path by sinking under it. The warmer air is forced upward as it rises, the water contained in the warmer air condenses, and clouds form. The atmosphere is always colder, on a grand scale, as you go up in altitude because the sun heats the surface of the earth and the air is warmed from contact with the ground. Very little warming of the air occurs as the sun's rays pass through on their way toward the ground. Because the frontal zone of a cold front is fairly narrow, the warm air rises quickly as it is pushed up rapidly by the oncoming cold air. This causes the condensation of the water vapor in that warm air to also occur quickly, resulting in cumulus clouds that can rise very high,

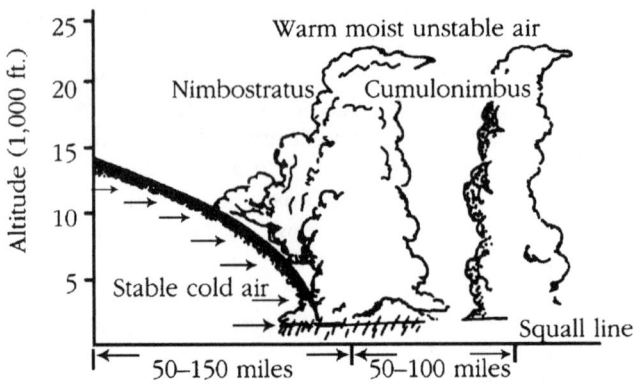

8-1 *A cold front usually travels about 300 to 400 miles per day in summer and about 500 miles per day in winter.*

even into the stratosphere, generating thunderstorms, sometimes of monumental proportions.

A cold front is usually a fast-moving phenomenon, and the cold air behind it is stable, heavy, and clean, generally resulting in good flight visibility. Because they move so fast, cold fronts normally come and go often within 24 hours. As a byproduct of their speed, the weather associated with cold fronts can be violent. Long and well-developed lines of thunderstorms, called *squall lines,* are a frequent occurrence along the boundary, or frontal zone. Most tornadoes that occur in the Midwest are another by-product of cold fronts. Generally, the greater the temperature differential between the oncoming cold air and the warm air being pushed up and out of the way, the more violent the weather in and near the frontal zone is likely to be.

Be especially careful of granddaddy thunderstorms accompanying cold fronts in the spring and early summer. In these seasons of the year, the polar air masses coming down from the Arctic are moving very fast. The Arctic region hasn't yet warmed, and the temperature of the Arctic air can be very cold relative to the air already in place over the Midwest, which has enjoyed warmer temperatures. These fast temperature differentials are so great that cold fronts in these times of the year have the potential to generate large thunderstorms and tornadoes. The storms alone, even without the associated tornadoes, can be lethal to any airplane in their paths, as well as also to people and structures on the ground. Some of the worst tornado outbreaks in U.S. history have occurred along springtime cold fronts.

The prime determining factors for the strength of the weather produced by a cold front are the speed of its movement across the surface, the temperature differential between the two air masses, and the moisture content of the warm air that is being forced upward as the invading cold air mass rushes in to displace it. For pilots, the saving grace with cold fronts is their speed. Because they generally do move so fast, the adverse effects that accompany them come and go quickly. If you have a cold front coming that dictates delaying a flight, you generally have to wait only a day for the front to be gone. Many pilots have landed at an airport during a long trip and sat in the FBO's office for a few hours, allowing the front to pass, and then resumed their cross-country flights.

A *warm front* is the transition area between an advancing mass of warm air and the cold air mass that the warm air is overtaking (FIG. 8-2). The leading edge of the advancing warm air rides up and over the cooler air. Warm fronts move more slowly than do cold fronts, and the weather changes that they produce are also different.

Because of their slower speed over the ground, the frontal zone of a warm front is much more spread out and less distinct than is the frontal zone of a cold front. Warm fronts also cover a much larger area. Warm fronts cause changes in the sky condition that consist of a gradual deterioration from the good flying

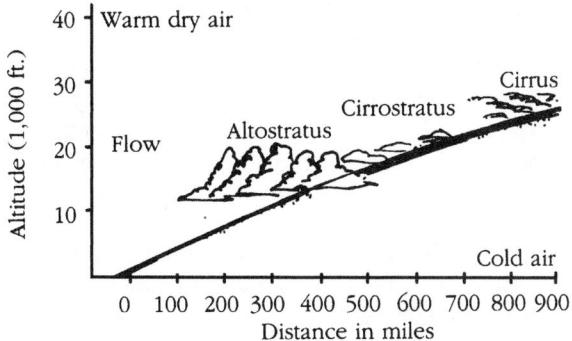

8-2 *Warm fronts are normally less violent than cold fronts and affect a much wider area. Improvement in the weather after they pass is much slower than it is after a cold front passes.*

weather in the cold air to the low clouds, poor visibility, and, usually, precipitation, all of which are contained within the oncoming warm air mass.

Warm air is inherently unstable and generally contains more moisture than does cold air. The poor aviation weather associated with a warm front can last for quite some time. Occasionally a warm front will really slow down and become a *stationary front*. A stationary front's presence is usually the cause of the days-long onset of misty, low-ceiling, and poor-visibility weather that is seen in many parts of the country, especially in the winter. But the weather that is associated with a warm front is seldom violent, and the air within it is seldom turbulent. Most instrument-rated pilots would far rather fly in a warm or stationary front than deal with the conditions found in a cold front.

But for the VFR pilot who is not rated to fly instruments, warm fronts can pose lethal risks. Because their effects cover large areas, sometimes hundreds of miles, if you fly into one, your only course of action is to retreat to the rear. Don't expect the weather in a warm or stationary front to improve any time soon because it won't. If you're on a cross-country trip and fail to get an accurate picture that would affect the route of the flight, and if you encounter a warm front, you may get to spend more than one night in a hotel along the way, waiting for the front to slowly work its way across the landscape. If the front becomes stationary, you might be riding an airliner home and then have to go back and get your airplane a few days later.

In contrast, a cold front moves fast, and the weather in it deteriorates and subsequently improves quickly. It is sometimes possible to successfully and safely fly VFR through a cold front. Sometimes the ceilings in a cold front are high enough to permit VFR flight through the frontal zone. But don't try it if the front is producing thunderstorms; if it is, they had better be widely scattered and not forming squall lines. If there aren't any more than widely scattered thunderstorms, and the ceiling is high, you can circumnavigate them. This decision is a difficult one to make, and the wise pilot always errs on the side of conservatism. I can't even tally the number of times that I've driven or taken an airliner all the way to my destination and back, thinking after I saw the weather firsthand that I could have flown the trip in a VFR airplane. But I completed each of those trips successfully while some who have chosen to fly in dubious weather are now statistics.

Dewpoints

There is always some water vapor in the air. When water vapor cools enough, that water condenses. Therefore, there is always a temperature at which the moisture that is present in the air will condense into visible water and become either clouds or fog. Fog isn't really different from a cloud; it's a cloud that has no separation between its bottom and the ground. In reality, fog is a cloud that goes right down to the ground. The temperature at which the condensation occurs is called the *dewpoint*. Depending upon how much water vapor there already is in an air mass, the air may have to cool only a very few degrees, sometimes as little as 1 or 2, before the water vapor condenses. Sometimes the amount of necessary cooling will be quite significant, such as 20° or more, before the water vapor will condense.

Pilots need to know the dewpoint of an air mass in which they're flying as well as the present surface temperature. When you know these two numbers, you can predict the likelihood that some form of visible water will pose a hazard to your flight. If the spread between the present temperature on the ground and the dewpoint (which is also measured at ground level) is less than about 4°F, look out. Rain, fog, low clouds, snow, or some kind of visible moisture or precipitation is likely if not immediately then in the near future.

Lapse Rates

Under normal conditions, the temperature of the atmosphere cools as you rise in altitude. The sun heats the surface of the earth, and that heat then radiates upward from the ground into the air. The normal decrease in air temperature with increasing altitude is about 3.5°F per 1,000 feet. This is known as the *normal lapse rate*. Remember this number; it will come in handy from time to time.

When the sun's heat and the radiation from the ground set up a thermal, the air within that ascending column of air cools at a different rate, which is about 5.5°F per 1,000 feet. The air within the thermal will continue to rise, and cool, until the air cools to its dewpoint. Then clouds will form at whatever altitude the air is when it reaches the dewpoint. This rate of cooling inside a thermal is called the *dry adiabatic lapse rate*. When the air in our thermal is rising, the dewpoint of that rising air is also declining along with the ambient temperature. The dewpoint in the column of air that makes up the thermal is decreasing at the rate of 1°F per 1,000 feet.

By performing some simple subtraction, you can see that the thermal is approaching the dewpoint at the rate of 4.5°F per 1,000 feet. Now that we have this number, we can easily determine the approximate height of the base of cumulus clouds. Take the ground temperature, subtract the dewpoint, and divide the result by 4.5. Then you'll have a fairly close approximation of the height, above the ground, of the cloud bases. For example, let's assume that the temperature at the airport is 87°F on the ground, and the dewpoint is 68°F. The difference between these two numbers is 19. When you divide 19 by 4.5, the result is 4.2. This tells us that the cloud bases will be about 4,200 feet above the ground.

This method of estimating cloud bases is valid only for cumulus clouds. There is a very good general rule that states that pilots who are not instrument rated should not fly above cloud layers even if the clouds are only of the scattered variety. A scattered layer of clouds can become a broken layer, and then become an overcast. Getting caught on top of an overcast for a pilot who doesn't have an instrument rating can be as much an emergency as is an engine failure, maybe even worse.

But there will be times when the cumulus clouds are very scattered and it may be safe for you to fly above their tops, as long as they aren't continuing to build vertically. When cumulus clouds are present, vertical thermals are too, and it's this vertical rising of the air within the thermals that produces what pilots call *low-level turbulence.* If the clouds are extremely few and very scattered and aren't building vertically, you can climb above the clouds and escape the *low-level turbulence* that exists below them. You'll generally find smooth air above the altitude at which the thermals reach their dewpoints. When you do elect to fly above such a widely scattered layer, be very alert for any thickening of the cloud cover. If more clouds start to appear, descend right then and get below their bases. Whatever you do, don't risk getting trapped on top of a solid layer of clouds.

Cloud Types

There are two primary types of clouds, called *cumulus* and *stratus,* that concern pilots. A third type of cloud, called *cirrus,* is not important to flyers of light airplanes. Cirrus clouds are frozen ice crystals, and they occur above 20,000 feet. Many subspecies of clouds result from the altitudes where the clouds form and from combinations of the primary kinds. As far as aviators are concerned, the classifications that are noted in the chart and discussion below are the easiest to understand because they are determined by the altitude of those clouds.

Cumulonimbus are cumulus clouds that are producing precipitation, usually rain. The word *nimbus* signifies rain, and when *nimbus* is used in connection with a class of cloud, it means that the cloud is producing rain, snow, sleet, or a mixture of precipitation. Cumulonimbus clouds are referred to as *Cbs* by the meteorologist and by other people as *thunderheads*. Cbs are formed from the ordinary and quite innocent little cumulus clouds when the air is unstable. In unstable air, the fluffy little cumulus clouds begin to build vertically, and their tops can rise well above 30,000 feet, from a relatively low base. Every thunderstorm you have ever seen had its genesis in a little puffball cumulus cloud.

The towering, castle-like cumulonimbus is full of turbulence generated by violent vertical winds within the massive cloud. It also likely contains lightning, hail, and drenching rain. These clouds are killers to all aircraft regardless of the size or type and whether they are in flight or on the ground. Fighter pilots, who fly the strongest airplanes, avoid them; lightplane pilots should take the cue and do the same. The ride through some storms will be unsurvivable, literally tearing the airplane apart.

In the early 1970s, I got caught in a thunderstorm. I was flying IFR, in a layer of clouds, talking to a controller as I was nearing the destination airport. The airplane had no radar, and the type of storm detector that senses lightning hadn't yet been invented. Because I was in the clouds, I didn't see what was coming. For a few seconds, the world got totally black, but the air was still smooth. Then, the hammers of hell let loose, and the twin-engine Piper Aztec was all over the sky. Only the fact that I had had aerobatic training probably saved the day because I was able to right the airplane from being nearly inverted. When I got out of the storm, I asked the controller if he had seen the storm on his radar (ATC radar, in those days, was much more able to "see" the precipitation associated with thunderstorms than it is today). He allowed as how he had seen the storm and told me that if I were to make the instrument approach to my destination, I would have to go through the edge of it. I promptly told him that there was no approach that I had to make that urgently and then I asked for radar vectors to another airport about 20 miles away. So much for relying on others to keep you out of thunderstorms. That evening, back at home, the newspaper reported that a tornado had hit about 5 miles from where I estimated I was when I penetrated the storm cloud.

A thunderhead is classified as a "low cloud" because the base of the cloudy area is low. You'll never be able to climb over a thunderstorm in a light airplane, or, for that matter, in most airliners. Even if you could get over the top, the hail spewing out of a thunderstorm could still get you. Never try to fly underneath a thunderstorm either because the violent vertical wings inside the cloud are accompanied by terrific updrafts and downdrafts from below. If you're caught in these vertical currents, you can't outclimb the downdrafts or dive through the updrafts without tearing the airplane apart—they're that strong.

Cumulus we've already discussed. Cumulus is the Latin word for *heap,* and that's a good description of the fair-weather cloud that is white and fluffy and forms at the top of a thermal. Glider pilots look for cumulus clouds as a primary marker of where they can find a thermal that will provide the upward current of air to keep a sailplane aloft, sometimes for hours.

Stratus is an even layer of clouds with a uniform base that is usually widespread. Fog that does not touch the ground is a good example of a stratus layer. Often, when there is one stratus layer that you can see, there are additional layers above it that you can't see from the ground. Often these multiple layers of stratus clouds will extend as high as 20,000 feet.

Nimbostratus is a low, dense, and dark stratus layer producing precipitation, which is usually in the form of steady rain, sleet, or snow. Its base is often ragged in appearance, and in most cases, a layer of altostratus, from which it has formed and settled, lies above the nimbostratus.

Stratocumulus is a layer of cumulus clouds that forms when the cumulus clouds are so numerous that they combine to form a solid layer. It forms in waves and rolls because the cumulus clouds are not uniform. Stratocumulus is low and potentially dangerous to the light airplane pilot because it presents a hazard of icing if the temperature in the clouds is near freezing. The vertical currents inherent in cumulus clouds are still there, with their associated turbu-

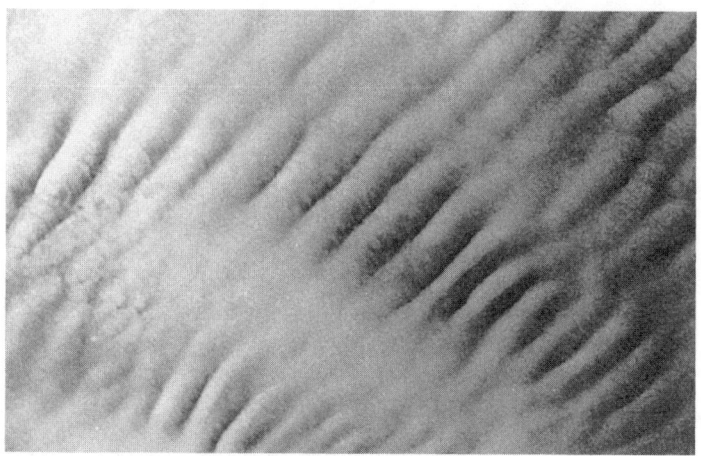

8-3 *Altocumulus clouds generally form between about 8,000 and 18,000 feet. These clouds often precede a progressively lower ceiling and some form of precipitation.*

lence. Usually stratocumulus doesn't produce steady rain, but mist and drizzle are possibilities.

Altocumulus is a layer of cumulus clouds that has formed at the medium altitudes and is somewhat like cumulus in appearance. However, the globules or ripples in altocumulus are more pronounced than they are in cirrostratus (FIG. 8-3). It is often called a *mackerel sky,* and its presence indicates brewing storm conditions.

Altostratus is a dense, grayish sheet, similar to cirrostratus, but it is heavier and occurs at the middle altitudes. It is ordinarily followed by rain, sleet, or snow.

Cirrocumulus is a small, high-altitude cumulus cloud with a fine-grain or ripple pattern. As with altocumulus, these clouds predict stormy weather to come (FIG. 8-4).

Cirrostratus is a layer that gives the sky a milky look. The thin, high haze is made up of ice crystals that often cause a ring to form around the sun or moon. These clouds usually indicate the approach of bad weather within the next 24 to 36 hours.

Cirrus is a general classification of all of the high-altitude clouds that are composed of ice crystals. Commonly called *mares' tails* or *feathers,* cirrus clouds are carried by very strong upper winds. They often originate from the anvil-shaped tops of distant thunderheads. When that happens, the high-altitude winds are so strong that the wind, which can easily exceed 100

8-4 *Cirrocumulus clouds form at about 20,000 feet and are composed of ice crystals or supercooled water droplets.*

mph in velocity, has actually ripped the top off of and away from a thunderstorm. Scattered cirrus are fair-weather clouds and indicate good weather for at least a day to come. When they get more dense and widespread, they become cirrostratus.

The Weather Map

The weather map can give you a tremendous amount of information after you have learned the basics of reading it. Few pilots are meteorologists, but there will be many times in your flying that you will be able to tell quite a bit about the weather from looking at the weather map, which is particularly useful when there is no professional meteorologist around to assist. You're not required to read a weather map of this sort to pass the knowledge test for a private pilot certificate, but like many other subjects, knowing more than the bare minimum to pass the test will serve you well.

The heavy, curvy lines from the typical surface weather map are lines connecting points of equal barometric pressure and are called *isobars*. Usually, they are drawn 4 millibars apart. A *millibar* is the unit of atmospheric pressure used by meteorologists instead of inches of mercury because the millibar is an international measurement. Standard sea-level pressure of

29.92 in Hg is equal to 1,013.2 millibars. Recall that wind is caused by differences in air pressure; the atmosphere is always trying to equalize its pressure. Isobars that are close together on the weather map indicate that the differences in air pressure are close together, which in turn means that the wind velocities will be stronger.

Around areas of low pressure, the wind rotates counter-clockwise in the Northern Hemisphere, and due to the friction of the wind's passing over the ground, the wind that blows inward crosses isobars at about a 30° angle, up to an altitude of 2,000 feet above ground level (AGL). Above that, the winds will shift to being more parallel to the isobars. Around high-pressure areas, the wind blows clockwise and outward at the same angles down low, and parallel to the isobars above 2,000 feet AGL.

A cold front is displayed on the map as a heavy line with a saw-toothed edge. The points of the saw teeth point in the direction toward which the front is moving. A cold front generally travels about 300 to 400 miles per day in summer and upward of 500 miles per day in the winter.

Warm fronts are depicted with semicircles along the side of the line. The semicircles point in the direction of travel of the front, just like the saw teeth do for a cold front.

Due to the general wind circulation patterns around the world, the United States has prevailing winds that blow from the west, toward the east. We refer to these as *westerly winds* because, when referring to wind direction, we label it as the direction from which the wind is coming. More often than not, especially in the summer, you can get a fairly good prediction of tomorrow's weather by noting what the weather is about 400 miles west of you today.

Each weather reporting station in the United States is shown on the weather map by means of a coded *station model*. FIG-URE 8-5 is an example of a typical station model. FIGURE 8-6 is a portion of a surface weather map that shows how these reporting stations' reports look on the map.

Mountain Effects

Mountains create conditions of both wind and weather that pilots trained in the flatlands are ill equipped to face. No pilot should fly in mountainous terrain without first undergoing both ground and flight training in the art and peculiarities of mountain flying.

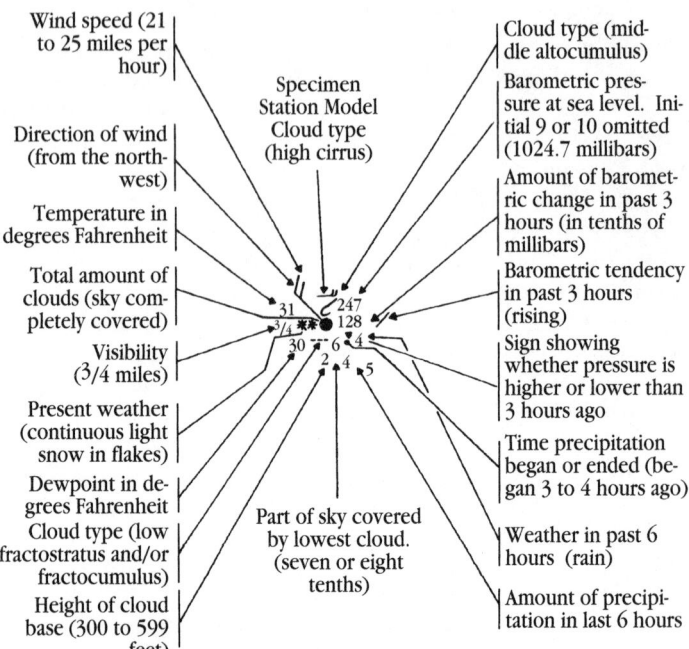

Wind speed (21 to 25 miles per hour)

Direction of wind (from the northwest)

Temperature in degrees Fahrenheit

Total amount of clouds (sky completely covered)

Visibility (3/4 miles)

Present weather (continuous light snow in flakes)

Dewpoint in degrees Fahrenheit

Cloud type (low fractostratus and/or fractocumulus)

Height of cloud base (300 to 599 feet)

Specimen Station Model Cloud type (high cirrus)

Part of sky covered by lowest cloud. (seven or eight tenths)

Cloud type (middle altocumulus)

Barometric pressure at sea level. Initial 9 or 10 omitted (1024.7 millibars)

Amount of barometric change in past 3 hours (in tenths of millibars)

Barometric tendency in past 3 hours (rising)

Sign showing whether pressure is higher or lower than 3 hours ago

Time precipitation began or ended (began 3 to 4 hours ago)

Weather in past 6 hours (rain)

Amount of precipitation in last 6 hours

8-5 *Weather reporting stations seldom report all of these data on a weather map.*

This is especially so when there is any appreciable wind blowing. On the windward, or upwind, side of a mountain, rapidly moving air dams up against the mountain because the mountain obstructs the normal airflow. This causes increased air pressure on the upwind side because the air slightly compresses as it is forced up against the side of the mountain. When you fly in this area of increased air pressure, your altimeter will sense, and display, an altitude *lower* than what would be correct.

As the wind blows up the side of the mountain, it creates an updraft. These updrafts can be very turbulent if it's a windy day. In an airplane like our Cessna 150, it's possible for the updraft to be so strong that you can't stay at a level altitude, even with the power at idle. Glider pilots, who are pros at what we call "flying the ridge," can intentionally get into this updraft and stay aloft from this "ridge lift" for hours. Sailplanes can fly for hundreds of miles, right along the face of a mountain ridge, when mountains make a chain formation such as the Appalachians do. Don't try this in an airplane, and don't try

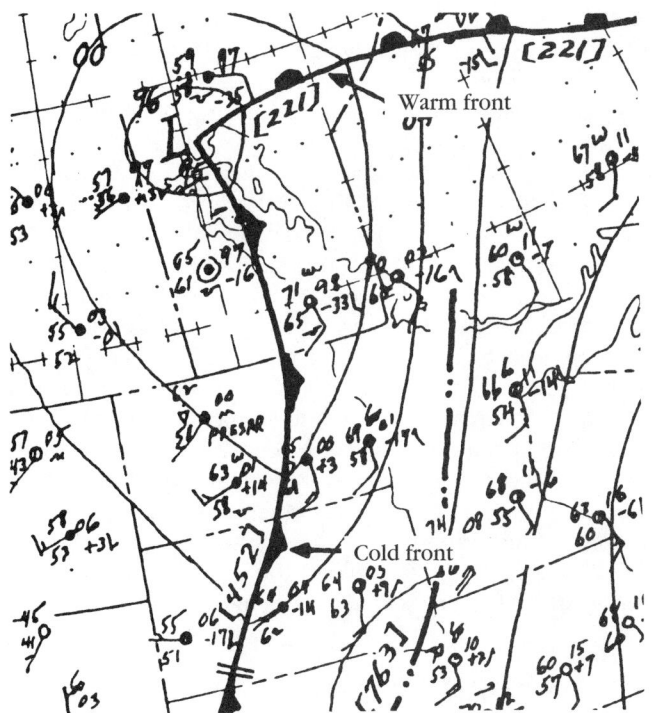

8-6 *This is a typical surface weather map showing data from several reporting stations.*

it in a glider for that matter until you are very experienced and get the proper instruction first.

On the downwind (leeward) side of a mountain, the air is spilling over the top and increasing in velocity. Recall from our study of aerodynamics that when air velocity increases, the pressure of that parcel of air decreases. So the increased velocity forms an area of low air pressure on the downwind side of the mountain. In this area, the airplane's altimeter will sense and show an indication that is *higher* than would be correct. This effect has killed more than one pilot who didn't know better and who flew into the terrain, thinking that the airplane was high enough to clear it.

As the air goes over the top of a mountain, it naturally creates a downdraft. These downdrafts can be lethal on windy days. Most light airplanes can't out climb the downdraft, particularly if the airplane is heavily loaded or the density altitude is high, which it usually is in mountainous terrain.

The best rule is not to fly in mountains if the wind is blowing hard. Even on a reasonably still day, be at least 2,000 feet above the highest peak or ridge in the area. Only the foolhardy try to fly in the mountains in marginal weather; the peaks and ridges are easily obscured by clouds or reduced visibility. Don't try to fly in the mountains in the winter in a light airplane. The chances are very high that the winds will be strong. If you were to be forced down, you'd probably not be found for months because the winter snows quickly blow in and cover all traces of people and airplanes within a very short time, far less time than it would take rescue crews to get to you.

For summer flying, plan your flights in the mountains to end no later than noon, perhaps even a little earlier. By restricting your flying to the mornings, when the temperatures are cooler, you won't suffer the ravages of high-density altitudes as much as you would later in the day. Also, the surface wind tends to increase in the late morning and continue until shortly before evening. With the early sunrise in the summer, if you get up and get going, you can obey this rule of thumb and still get several hours of flying in before it's time to park the airplane for the day.

Icing in Flight

When we talk about icing, we mean the ice that can form, in certain weather conditions, on the airframe of the airplane. It can adhere to the wings, tail, struts, landing gear, radio antennas, propeller, and anything else that sticks out into the wind. Icing is likely to be encountered any time that an airplane is flying through wet snow or rain when the outside air temperature is near freezing or slightly above 32°F. You'll also surely get severe icing if you fly in freezing rain. Ice can also be found in clouds when they are at temperatures near the freezing mark, but as a VFR private pilot, you should never be in clouds in the first place.

Rime ice resembles the flaky, milky stuff that gathers around the freezer unit of an inexpensive kitchen refrigerator. *Clear ice* is hard and translucent, like the surface of an ice skating rink. *Mixed icing* is a combination of rime and clear ice. All of the three types of ice are dangerous, but clear ice is the worst because it is denser, heavier, and more difficult to remove quickly.

Ice has several effects on an airplane, and none of them are pleasant. First, when ice forms on the wings, it alters their shape and deprives them of some of their ability to produce lift. When you are flying an airplane with ice on its wings, you are flying an unknown and constantly changing airfoil and are, therefore, truly an experimental test pilot. For sure, any ice on the wings increases the stalling speed, but nobody knows by how much.

Ice forming on the propeller causes it to lose efficiency in the same way, by changing its shape. You never know how much thrust the propeller can produce once it has accumulated any ice, until it quits generating enough to keep you flying. Ice on the blades of the propeller causes an imbalance between or among the blades. Propellers are carefully balanced because at their high rotational speeds, imbalance can create vibration, often very large amounts of vibration, depending upon the degree of imbalance. There have been cases of iced-up propellers causing enough vibration to literally tear an engine out of its mounts.

Ice is also very heavy. When it forms on the airframe, the wings must support that added weight. Now you have an airplane that quite easily is so heavy that it exceeds its maximum gross weight and must be kept in the air by wings that have already lost a part of their lift and by a propeller that isn't generating the proper amount of thrust. It's also quite probable that the ice will partially, or completely, block the engine's air intake; then the engine will be able to produce only partial power at best and will quit altogether at worst. None of this makes for a pretty scenario.

If you ever get into icing conditions, turn around and do so quickly, assuming that you've just left an area where there was no ice. Perhaps you can climb into colder air where the moisture is already frozen and therefore won't adhere to the airplane. That's the preferred tactic for a pilot who is instrument rated but not for the VFR pilot. You can't enter clouds without an instrument rating, and because there are surely clouds above you, producing the wet snow or rain, climbing isn't much of an option.

For the VFR pilot, the best bet is to safely descend into warmer air below while you are turning around. Best of all, always stay clear of ice and the conditions in which it is found. If the weather has any potential for icing—usually determined by a combination of cloud cover, ceiling, precipitation, and temperature—watch out. The FSS briefer should caution you about it because it will be the subject of either an AIRMET or a SIGMET, depending on the forecast severity. If you don't get such a warning, depending on the season of the year, ask the briefer about freezing levels and for any pilot reports of icing along your proposed route.

The Weather Decision

Now you should be able to easily identify the weather impediments to a safe flight. Remember that weather is the cause of more light airplane accidents than anything else. The weather problems to be aware of can be boiled down to three different hazards: reduced ceilings and visibility, winds and the resulting turbulence, and airframe icing. Avoid these dangers, and the weather won't get you. Separately or together in storms, these three conditions are the ones that threaten us if we fly in them. Every pilot must learn to accurately gauge the presence and extent of these dangers and understand the weather conditions and forces that produce them.

Most pilots have long depended upon the FSS network and its briefers to give complete weather briefings and help interpret the current and forecast conditions along the routes of planned cross-country flights. The weather briefing has always had its limitations, and these limitations may increase in the future. The FAA has steadily reduced the availability of live briefings, conducted face to face with an FSS specialist, by consolidating the FSS network into those few automated stations that we discussed earlier. Most of us can now talk to a briefer only by telephone.

In the future, if not really in the present, increased emphasis will be put on pilot self-briefing by DUAT or by contracting with one of the private weather information companies. Some day we may be left to our own devices to gather and interpret all weather data. You can do it, as many pilots have done for years. Obviously, experience is a valuable teacher; until you gain it, just make sure that your interpretations and the decisions guided by them are on the conservative side. It is easier to begin this educational process if you understand the weather reporting system, its inherent weaknesses, and the limitations of weather forecasting. First of all, there are situations that cannot, even today, be predicted with acceptable accuracy:

- The time that freezing rain will begin
- The location and even the occurrence of severe turbulence
- The location and occurrence of icing

- Ceilings of 100 feet or less before they occur

- Thunderstorms before they have visibly begun to form

- Fog

- Hurricane movement more than 24 hours in advance

In short, the worse the weather may become, the less accurate the forecast is likely to be. This underscores two important points: Pilots have to make decisions on the spot, and they have to be conservative in those decisions. If professional meteorologists cannot precisely predict where a thunderstorm will form, certainly a pilot can't be expected to. Being conservative means being safe (FIG. 8-7).

Here are some very general rules of thumb applicable to various weather situations that usually can be usefully forecast:

- A forecast of good flying weather (ceiling of 3,000 feet or more and visibilities of 5 miles or greater) is usually dependable for about 24 hours in advance.

- A forecast of poor flying weather (ceilings below 1,500 feet and visibility of less than 3 miles) is much less accurate 12 hours in advance, but it is very accurate for a 3- to 4-hour period in the future.

- Ceiling and visibility forecasts should be highly suspect beyond the first 2 to 3 hours of the forecast, especially if a significant change in either is predicted during the time span of that forecast.

8-7 *Again, your need to get somewhere should never influence your assessment of the weather.*

- Forecasts of poor flying conditions are most reliable when there is a distinct weather system involved, such as a low, a front, a trough, or the like. Be aware that there seems to be, from a pilot's perspective, a tendency among meteorologists to forecast these conditions on the optimistic side.

- The weather associated with fast-moving cold fronts, such as squall lines, severe thunderstorms, and tornadoes, is the most difficult to accurately foresee.

- Forecasts of surface visibilities are less reliable than predicted ceilings.

- The presence of snow in the forecast or in a station report makes any predictions about visibility pure guesswork.

You should take some useful guidelines from the above and apply the weather basics that you will learn in your training. Prepare for any cross-country flight by including the following in your analysis:

- Check the locations of areas of low pressure, fronts, and troughs. Cold fronts that are moving fast usually mean quickly developing violent weather, particularly if the air mass that they are displacing is warm and moist. They will be followed by quick clearing, with higher-than-normal surface winds and bumpy air. A slow-moving cold front can have much the same weather associated with it as does a warm front: wide frontal zones of clouds, poor visibility, precipitation, turbulence, and icing above the freezing level. Not all cold fronts are severe; the determining factors are usually the speed of movement of the front and the amount of moisture present.

- Check the moisture content of the air masses and their stability along your planned route of flight. The temperature-dewpoint spread can be used to estimate the amount of moisture, which is greater the closer the dewpoint is to the actual surface temperature. Unstable air allows thunderstorm development.

- When thunderstorms are present, request the altitudes of the bases and tops during your weather briefing. You'll never be able to fly on top of a thunderstorm, but knowing how high they are gives you a hint about how violent they may be. Thunderstorms will continue to build throughout the midday and into early evening. Never fly closer than 15 miles to a thunderstorm because the turbulence extends well beyond the visible thunderhead. Never fly underneath a thunderstorm, even if you can see the ground on the other side, because the vertical wind currents exist below the visible cloud as well as within it.

- The danger of structural icing exists in a moist air mass at temperatures within a few degrees either side of freezing, particularly within cumuliform clouds. Clear ice is most common in cumuliform clouds, and rime ice is usually found in stratiform clouds. But either type of ice can appear in any cloud. Carburetor ice can develop at temperatures as high as 75°F in moist air. Be aware of and watchful for symptoms of carb ice. In an airplane equipped with a fixed-pitch propeller, the noticeable symptom will be a gradual reduction of revolutions per minute. Correct the problem quickly by always applying full carburetor heat to clear the ice. Unless you have a carburetor air temperature gauge (which most trainers don't), don't use partial carburetor heat.

- Approach mountain ranges at an angle whenever possible, and make sure that you know the wind direction before getting close to them. If there are any clouds present, they will usually be on the downwind side. If there is any appreciable wind, be at least 2,000 feet above the ridge or peak before reaching it. Winds in excess of 50 knots at the top of the ridge or peak might create a *standing wave* over the downwind side of the mountain, and the turbulence from a standing wave might extend for more than a hundred miles downwind of the mountain. The presence of a flat but concave cloud, called a *lenticular cloud,* over or downwind of the mountain ridge or peak indicates the existence of standing waves. But this cloud won't form if the air mass is dry because it takes moisture to form clouds, even if there is a standing wave.

- Be aware of when windshear might be present. *Windshear* is the rapid change of velocity and direction of the wind within a very narrow altitude band.

Windshear can occur whenever there are high surface winds, high winds aloft at fairly low altitudes, thunderstorms in the vicinity, or a temperature inversion. A *temperature inversion* occurs when the air gets warmer at increasing altitudes, not colder as is normal. Inversions are usually caused by a warm air mass overtaking a cold air mass that does not retreat as it normally would. Sometimes the cold air gets trapped by geographical features, such as the walls of a valley.

- Most air traffic controllers feel that a clearance by ATC to change altitudes in flight, to approach and land, or to do anything at all means only that the airplane they are controlling won't conflict with other traffic under their jurisdiction. They see their job as having the sole responsibility to separate aircraft from each other. Controllers are often of the opinion that they are not responsible to any degree for determining the safety of what you want to do—that decision is up to the pilot in command. Often controllers are in a dark room, maybe hundreds of miles from your location, and they have no firsthand knowledge of the weather where you are flying. They have access to the same weather data as does the pilot, but often they can't judge what's going on as well as the pilot can who is there. The courts have frequently held controllers responsible, at least to some degree, for some accidents. But to think the way the courts do— arguing about who's at fault after an accident—is not nearly as productive as is preventing the accident in the first place.

The basic responsibility to determine all of the factors affecting the conduct and safety of each flight rests on the pilot in command. If you are ever given a clearance or a directive by a controller that, if executed, would put you in a precarious situation, don't do it. You have the regulatory right and sometimes the duty to request an amended clearance. You may be asked to explain your reasons, and if so, do it. Don't ever let someone else put you in a position of danger.

We've already said to always let controllers know that you are a student pilot during every call that you make to the controller at an ATC facility who is handling your flight. Even after you get your license, if you feel that you're getting into a pressure situation, let the controller know what your problem is. If you're approaching a large and busy airport for the first time, let the ATC know that you are unfamiliar with the area; otherwise, they may ask you to report passing over certain landmarks on the ground that you will not be able to identify. Often, especially at night, I'll tell a ground controller at a strange airport that I'm not familiar with the airport so that my taxi instructions will be more understandable. In my decades of flying, I can count on very few fingers the times that I have encountered a controller who was not polite, helpful, and courteous. A good many of them are also pilots, and all of them are there to smoothly and safety expedite the flow of air traffic. They take their job seriously, and most are very good at it.

9

VFR Navigation and Communications

In the United States, all aircraft fly under either VFR or IFR. Operating under IFR doesn't necessarily mean that the weather is poor; an IFR flight plan and flight can be conducted in very good weather as well as in weather that requires IFR. The choice depends primarily on the weather conditions, aircraft equipment, pilot qualifications, and pilot preference. As a student pilot or newly certificated private pilot, you'll be flying strictly under VFR until you gain sufficient training and flight experience to qualify for an instrument rating.

VFR Weather Minimums

VFR flight is permitted only when the weather conditions are at or above certain minimum ceiling and visibility values. We are going to assume, as we have for other portions of this book, that you are training to private pilot standards, rather than sport pilot requirements. The VFR weather minimums are different for a sport pilot than they are for a private pilot.

In addition to ceiling and visibility values, there are requirements for VFR flight that you must also maintain certain horizontal and vertical distances from any clouds. These minimums vary according to the various classes of airspace in which an aircraft might be operating, whether it's day or night, and the flight altitude of the aircraft. We'll go into the subject of the classes of airspace later in this chapter.

The most difficult part of determining whether you may legally fly under VFR is the determination of your distance from whatever clouds are present. In some instances, you're required to be at least 500 feet from a cloud; in others, the mandate might be 1,000 or 2,000 feet. Often it's nearly impossible to decide the distance that you truly are from a cloud or layer of clouds. The key here, as it is to all regulatory compliance, is to adopt a conservative approach. The keys to safety include that as well as the exercise of common sense. Because IFR traffic can fly right through the clouds, the idea for VFR pilots is to stay far enough away from the clouds so that if you see an IFR airplane pop out of a cloud, you have ample room to safely avoid a collision.

When the weather conditions are below the VFR minimums, you have no choice but to file an IFR flight plan, obtain an IFR clearance from the ATC, and fly under their control. But you cannot do that until you receive an instrument rating. For quite some time, every new pilot must adhere to the VFR rules.

Right-of-Way Rules

When you are operating under VFR, you won't be flying in the clouds or operating very often in airspace where the air traffic control system has the responsibility to keep airplanes apart. It will be solely your responsibility to "see and avoid" other aircraft. Rules have been established in FAR 91.113 to prevent midair collisions. Just as when you're driving a car, there must be a system of right-of-way rules and adherence to them, or chaos would quickly develop. You need to learn and remember these rules because the need to know them will come rapidly if you ever discover a potential conflict with another airplane. Then you won't have time to fish the regulations out of your flight bag and figure out who has the right-of-way. The rules are as follows:

FAR 91.113: Right-of-way rules; except water operations.

(a) *Inapplicability.* This section does not apply to the operation of an aircraft on water.

(b) *General.* When weather conditions permit, regardless of whether an operation is conducted under instrument flight rules or visual flight rules, vigilance shall be maintained by each person operating an aircraft so as to see and avoid other aircraft. When a rule of this section gives another aircraft the right-of-way, the pilot shall give way to that aircraft and may not pass over, under, or ahead of it unless well clear.

(c) *Distress.* An aircraft in distress has the right-of-way over all other air traffic.

(d) *Converging.* When aircraft of the same category are converging at approximately the same altitude (except head-on or nearly so), the aircraft to the other's right has the right-of-way. If the aircraft are of different categories—

> (1) A balloon has the right-of-way over any other category of aircraft;
> (2) A glider has the right-of-way over any airship, airplane, or rotorcraft; and
> (3) An airship has the right-of-way over an airplane or rotorcraft. However, an aircraft towing or refueling other aircraft has the right-of-way over all other engine-driven aircraft.

(e) *Approaching head-on.* When aircraft are approaching each other head-on, or nearly so, each pilot shall alter course to the right.

(f) *Overtaking.* Each aircraft that is being overtaken has the right-of-way, and each pilot of an overtaking aircraft shall alter course to the right and pass well clear.

(g) *Landing.* Aircraft, while on final approach to land or while landing, have the right-of-way over aircraft in flight or operating on the surface, except that they shall not take advantage of this rule to force an aircraft off the runway surface that has already landed and is attempting to make way for an aircraft on final approach. When two or more aircraft are approaching an airport for purpose of landing, the aircraft at the lower altitude has the right-of-way, but it shall not take advantage of this to cut in front of another aircraft that is on final approach or to overtake that aircraft.

As you can easily see, most of these rules are based on common sense and courtesy. From a practical point of view, never insist on your right-of-way if you have it in a particular situation. Always assume that you are the only pilot who sees the other aircraft and further that the pilot of any other aircraft does not see you. Whenever you are operating in the vicinity of military or airline traffic, it's especially important to assume that they don't see you. They're almost always operating under the IFR, regardless of how good the weather may be. Because of the speed differential between them and you, the high cockpit workloads that they have (especially during takeoff and landing), and the limited visibility from some large airplane cockpits, always operate under the assumption that other pilots cannot see you and be prepared to alter your course accordingly.

Navigation

Once you've learned how to physically handle an airplane and have a working knowledge of the regulations, flying your airplane cross country, on an accurate course, is a relatively simple matter (FIG. 9-1). There is a network of radio navigational stations that almost unfailingly lead you from anywhere to anywhere in the United States (and much of the rest of the world), and this, together with the satellite-based GPS navigation system, has made air navigation so painless and simple that the average private pilot routinely completes flights that were, only a few decades ago, largely reserved for professional aviators.

This doesn't mean that you only have to learn to operate aircraft radios and GPS receivers, all of which are lumped together in the term *avionics*. Aircraft electrical systems and radios fail, so you still have to know how to navigate on your own, by looking at your chart and the ground, the way it was done for a long time, before all of the electronic aids came into

9-1 *Cross-country flight is an expression of the freedom of flying. Just be sure that you thoroughly plan every flight.*

existence. The FAA has wisely seen fit to use the private pilot knowledge and flight tests as vehicles to ensure that you can adequately demonstrate your ability to plan, plot, and fly a course without resort to electronic navigational aids.

It's significant that the FAA considers the multi-billion-dollar electronic system as an *aid* to air navigation; it's there simply to make flying easier, more efficient, and somewhat safer. All of the electronic aids that you can cram into an instrument panel will never relieve you of your responsibilities to *plan* and *think*.

The term *contact navigation* refers to navigation using references on the ground to navigate from one place to another. It is not hard to do, and even with all of the electronic aids turned on, I still prefer to navigate by looking out the windows. The only things that you need for contact navigation are a ruler with a protractor attached, which is called a *plotter* (FIG. 9-2), the aeronautical chart for the area where you're flying, a pocket computer of either the circular slide rule or electronic type, the compass in your airplane, and a clock in the instrument panel or a watch on your wrist.

Aeronautical charts

The maps that aviators use to navigate are called *charts,* and they come in several different types to serve the needs of various kinds of operations and aircraft performance levels. The ones that are used by almost all light airplane pilots for VFR navigation are *sectional aeronautical charts.* They are published by the National Oceanic and Atmospheric Administration (NOAA), a part of the U.S. Department of Commerce.

Another chart format that can be used is the *world aeronautical chart,* commonly called a WAC. WACs are not used very often anymore because their scale is twice that of a sectional chart, and they do not have nearly as much surface detail as do sectionals. In the past, many high-performance airplanes used WACs, but today virtually all such airplanes operate their flights under IFR, so they use instrument charts. WACs may well be discontinued in the near future.

Sectional charts contain a truly amazing amount of information, and the reverse side of the face panel of the chart contains its legend. The legend can be daunting at first sight, but logic underlying the system of the symbols that are used will quickly be apparent to you once you study them (FIG. 9-3).

The sectional chart is drawn at a scale of 8 statute miles per inch, and the WAC is at 16 statute miles per inch. The sectional

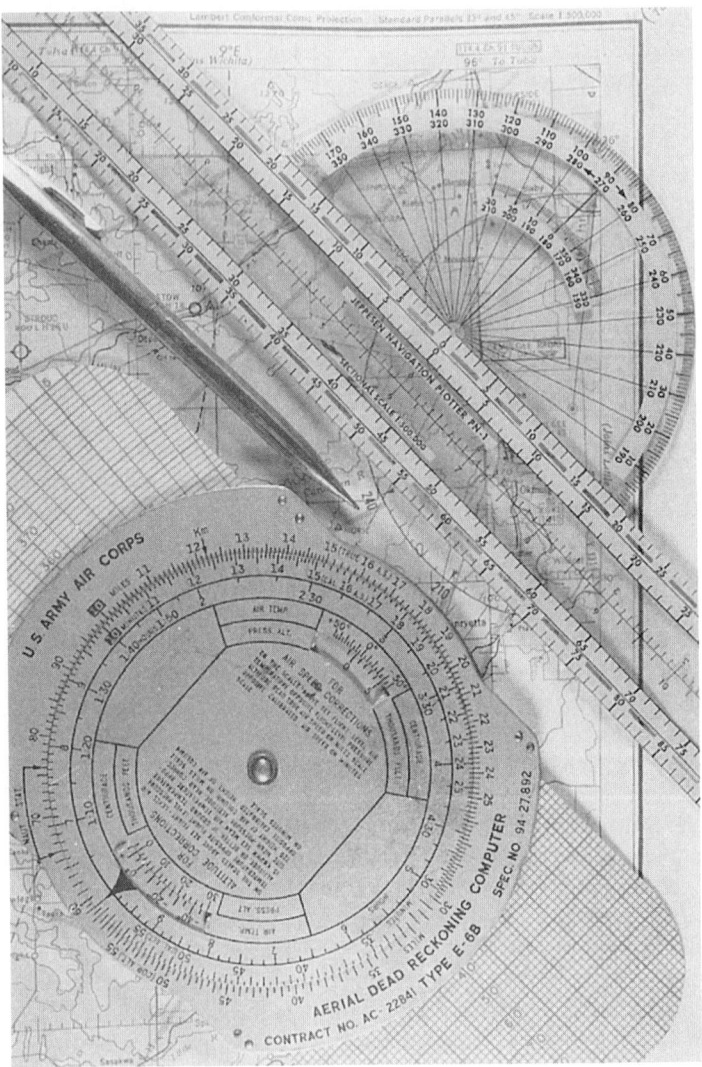

9-2 *Air navigation tools: a plotter and a circular slide rule computer. This type of computer is rapidly being supplanted by electronic pocket calculators that feature aviation functions.*

is much more detailed than is the WAC, and the WAC covers just about twice the geographical area as does a sectional. WACs can serve a valuable purpose for flight planning. The government does issue a wall planning chart, but it covers half of the United States on each side. The wall planning chart can

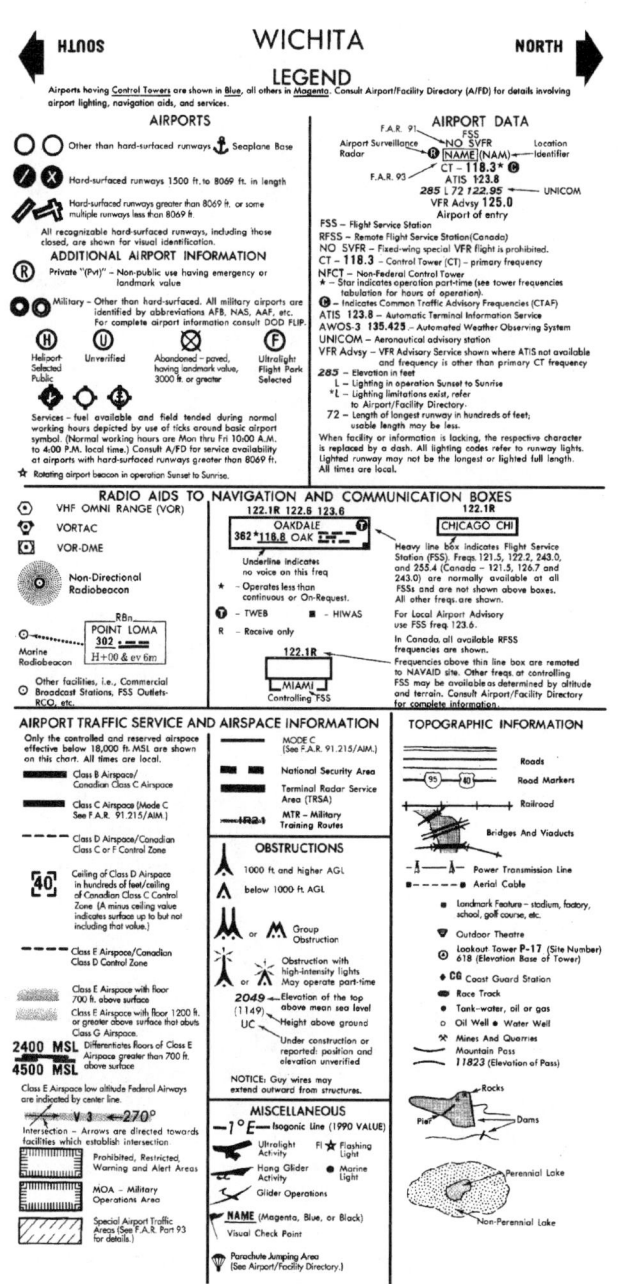

9-3 *A sectional chart has a legend for the information displayed on it.*

be used to get a general idea of how far things are apart, where radio navigational aids are located, and the like. But the WAC gives a much better view of the terrain and shows almost all of the airports. Because only a few light airplane flights are longer than 200 to 300 miles, WACs make great planning charts, but they aren't as useful for actual in-flight navigation as are the sectionals.

A sectional is the chart of choice for private pilots. Even if you go on in your training and obtain an instrument rating and then use IFR charts for en route navigation in the IFR system, you'll still need to have sectionals with you on every IFR flight. The IFR charts show almost no terrain features because the entire IFR system is set up to automatically give IFR airplanes the proper terrain clearance as they fly in that system. But an instrument pilot must rely on sectionals for all of the information displayed on them, much of which is not shown on IFR charts. Each sectional covers an area of about 150 by 285 miles, so it's not an overwhelming task to have the few charts onboard that you will need for a typical cross-country flight. There are 37 sections that cover all of the area within the 48 states, not including Hawaii and Alaska. Almost no one has them all because they are revised about every 6 months. Most pilots buy the 1 or 2 sectionals that cover their area of routine operations and then buy more for the few flights per year that go beyond that area.

The sectional chart displays ground elevations above sea level with different background colors ranging from green at sea level through successively darker shades of tan and brown as terrain height increases. As you learn to use the charts, you can get a good idea of the terrain elevation in any particular area just by noticing the background color of the chart.

Your flight instructor will help you learn the various symbols used on the sectional charts. Take a look at FIG. 9-3. At the very top there is the name of the chart, which is the name of a prominent city somewhere within its geographical coverage area, and then there are two arrows pointing in opposite directions. These arrows, labeled "north" and "south," allow you to unfold the chart to the side that displays the northern or southern half of the coverage area.

Right below the name of the chart is the section of the legend that contains all of the airport symbols, and that is on the left side of the panel. This system of airport symbols tells you a lot about an airport. It will tell you if the airport has fuel sales, the number of paved runways and the length of the longest one, and whether the runways are paved or of some other surface type. The symbol will also tell you whether the airport has a control tower and, if so, what the radio frequency is to contact the tower. You will also be able to see if the airport has ground lights for night operations. To the right of the airport symbol is a box of printed data that accompanies each symbol, and that gives even more detailed information about that airport. Below the airport symbols, the legend tells you how to identify the various radio aids to navigation and how to interpret the data shown about each one. Below that is the largest part of the legend, and it explains all the symbols for the ground features that are shown on the chart.

There is so much information on a sectional chart that no one can ever digest it all. When you need to know about a certain local area or route of flight, you'll study that portion in detail. All the areas of restricted airspace are also shown, as are the power lines, freeways, rivers, railroad tracks, and unusual terrain features. All of this is depicted to enable a pilot to know where she is and to guide her flight to its destination. Never fly with sectionals or any other charts that are out of date. The FARs require that we have both appropriate and current charts, even for a short cross-country flight. *Appropriate charts* means that the chart covers the area of your flight. *Current charts* means that the edition of the chart that you're using is the latest revision. Radio frequencies and airport identifiers get changed, new radio towers get built, and airports open and close.

Even when you're flying around the local area, you can't possibly memorize all of the radio communications and navigational frequencies that you might need to use. So carry a current chart, even if you don't plan to leave the airport traffic pattern. You might need to leave the traffic pattern because another airplane might get disabled on your airport's runway, and that would require you to go somewhere else to land and wait until your airport opens up again. There are many reasons that you might need to go to a different airport, and without a chart, you won't know its elevation or radio frequencies.

Your local FBO probably sells sectionals. If you're planning a flight in advance, get the chart as early as you can, as long as it will be current when the trip actually occurs. Because sectionals are revised about every 6 months, the date of the next revision is shown on the chart. That way, you can tell when the one you have will expire. Don't wait until the last minute to get a chart for a cross-country trip; the FBO may be out of stock. Many pilots buy their charts from catalog sources; you can choose the method that suits you best.

Meridians and parallels

You are probably familiar with the imaginary lines that have been drawn around the globe to determine position and direction. This system hasn't been changed for centuries, and it is still the basis for all modern concepts of where you are and how to get where you want to go. Navigation doesn't take a degree in mathematics, or I could have never learned how to do it. What it does require is an elementary understanding of how circles and spheres are divided into degrees of position around the circle or on the surface of a sphere.

The earth has been crisscrossed with imaginary lines of *latitude* and *longitude*. The horizontal lines that start at the equator and circle the earth between the equator and the North and South Poles are called *parallels* because they are parallel to each other; they never touch one another or converge. Parallels are used to express *latitude,* which is either north or south of the equator, and the distance from the equator. That's all you get from a parallel—one line that goes all the way around the globe and that is either north or south of the equator.

We obviously need to know more about our position than just how far north or south of the equator we are. To give us more data, the earth is further divided by vertical lines that run from the North Pole to the South Pole, and these are called *meridians*. Meridians offer the missing piece to the position puzzle. They all begin at the poles, run vertically across the equator, and then reconverge at the other pole. Because meridians all start at one pole and reconverge at the opposite pole, they are never parallel to each other.

Meridians tell us *longitude,* which is that missing piece of the problem if you try to determine where you are by using latitude alone. The meridian that runs through Greenwich, England, has been designated as the *prime,* or *zero, meridian*. This was decided by international agreement in the nineteenth century, when Britain ruled the waves and the worldwide navigation system was designated to serve marine navigation. Meridians give us east-west orientation on the surface of our sphere called *earth*. That, combined with the knowledge of our north-south line of position, gathered from knowing the parallel on which we're located, solves the puzzle. We can now express any position anywhere on our planet by using a simple combination of latitude and longitude because where a parallel crosses a meridian is a point of position. (Recall from your high school geometry that a point is created by the intersection of two lines. You never realized that you'd wait so long for that little ditty to become relevant to something that you'd really do.)

The prime meridian is the 0 meridian, and all meridians west of it, around the globe to the halfway point, are expressed as "west longitude." When you get exactly halfway around the world, you're on the 180th meridian. From the prime meridian eastbound, which is called *east longitude,* you go halfway around again to the 180th meridian. The 180th meridian is also know as the *international date line.*

Obtaining a Course

The *true course* (TC) is the direction, measured in degrees, in which your destination lies from your point of departure, in relation to the North Pole. From here on out, we are going to make the common-sense assumption that you're flying in the Northern Hemisphere. If you ever do fly south of the equator, all navigational references the reverse and are in reference to the South Pole.

Imagine yourself standing in the center of a large circle with your body facing due north. Your nose is then pointed at 0°, which can also be 360° because they are the same. Your right shoulder is pointed due east, and that's referred to as *090°*. Your posterior is looking due south, or 180°. Finally, your left shoulder is lined up to the west, or 270°. Remember that there are 360° in a circle.

In FIG. 9-4 we are measuring a true course, using the Dallas-Ft. Worth sectional. The first step in determining a true course is to use the ruler part of the plotter and lay the straightedge so that it bisects the airport symbols of both the departure and destination airports. Then take your pencil and actually draw a line on the chart between the two airports. Don't hesitate to draw on the chart; it's the only way to do it. Even if you fly frequently, you'll be getting a new chart about every 6 months, when the noticed revision comes out. In our example, we're planning a flight from Childress, Texas, to Mangum, Oklahoma. The airport symbol for Mangum is a little hard to see, but it's at the upper right edge of the figure.

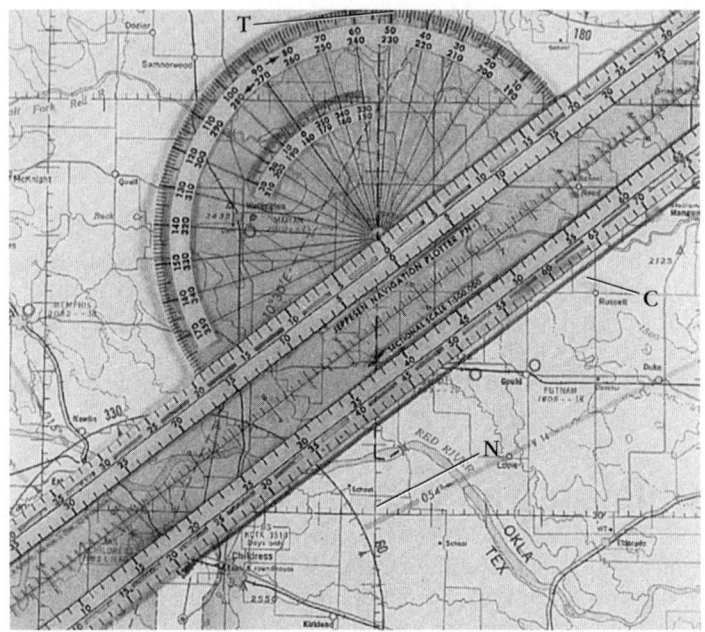

9-4 *Measuring a true course. Position the plotter with the protractor's center hole on the midmeridian N and the straightedge along the course line C. True course, 053°, is then read on the protractor's scale at the top.*

After drawing a course line between the two airports, you next have to determine the direction of the course line, referencing it from north. Find a meridian that is close to the halfway point along your route. That's easy in this case because this is a short trip, and there is only one on the chart between these two airports.

Then place your plotter's straightedge along the course line with the protractor's 0 hole on the point where it is directly over the meridian. Now read the direction of the course line at the outer edge of the circular part of the protractor, where the meridian emerges from the 0 hole up through the protractor. You see that the outer rim of the protractor is calibrated in degrees, with two sets of numbers, one set just below the other.

To measure your course line, you've got to use some common sense. From even the most cursory look at your course line, you see that when you are flying from Childress to Mangum, you are going northeast. Because northeast is somewhere between north (0 or 360°) and east (90°), you see that the direction of your course line is 053°. When we fly from Mangum back to Childress, the course will be 233°. Be careful that you have not accidentally measured the reciprocal of your actual course that you intend to fly. Always cross-check your work to see if the measurement that you've obtained makes sense.

Cruising altitudes

Before proceeding with further calculations, you need to determine your cruising altitude so that you can apply the winds aloft being forecast at or near that altitude to the rest of the navigational problem. The FARs dictate that, under VFR, if you want to cruise at more than 3,000 AGL, and below 18,000 feet MSL, you're limited to certain altitudes, based on your *magnetic course* (MC). Magnetic course is the TC corrected for magnetic variation, which is explained a bit later in this chapter.

If your MC is eastbound, anywhere from 0 to 179°, you must fly at an *odd* thousand-foot altitude *plus* 500 feet (3,500, 5,500, 7,500, and so on). If the MC is from 180° on around to 359°, or westbound, you are then required to fly at an *even* thousand-foot altitude *plus* 500 feet (4,500, 6,500, 8,500, and so on.).

Airplanes flying under IFR fly cruising altitudes based on the same system, but they don't add the 500 feet to either the odd or even thousand-foot altitudes. In this way, there is always 1,000 feet between VFR traffic that might approach each other head on and 500 feet between a VFR aircraft and an IFR aircraft that are converging somewhat head on. Obey this rule without fail and you'll go a long way toward preventing a midair collision.

There is a way to remember this rule that is, unfortunately, not very complimentary. An Air Force instructor once said that the memory device to use is to remember that "Only odd people fly east." Because I'm located in the Midwest and fly eastbound quite a bit, I've never forgotten which way the rule works.

The specific altitude that you will fly will be determined by several factors. These include the wind, terrain heights, obstructions along your course, airspace restrictions, cloud levels, distance of the trip, and freezing levels. Whenever possible, you will want to choose one of the permitted altitudes that gives you the best tailwind, or the least headwind. But because this is a relatively short trip, you'd burn quite a bit of excess fuel by climbing to the higher altitudes; we would be there only a short time before it would be time to start down again. Regardless, on the flight from Childress to Mangum, we are obligated to choose an odd-thousand altitude plus 500 feet.

Wind correction angles

You've already learned from the ground reference maneuvers discussed earlier that when an airplane is in flight, it is carried along in the same direction as the movement of the air mass that supports it. It will always fly *through* the air at its regular cruising speed, but at the same time, it will be carried *with* the air movement across the ground, just as a boat is carried with the current, independently of the speed of the boat through the water. Just as you must point the bow of a boat to one side of its intended destination to compensate for sideways drift caused by the current, so must you do the same with an airplane to compensate for drift caused by the wind.

In your preflight weather briefing, you obtained the forecast of the winds aloft. Because the forecast predicts the wind speed and direction at 3,000-foot intervals, you might have to do a little interpolation to arrive at the values applicable for your chosen cruising altitude.

To figure the wind correction angle, we'll draw a wind vector, which is an exercise in trigonometry made simple. In this day and age of electronic navigation, with pocket slide rule computers or electronic calculators, some instructors don't even teach wind vectors anymore. But this problem and its graphic solution are both very valuable in giving a student pilot a keen sense of what the wind is doing to the airplane and how that effect alters a flight's path over the ground. Doing wind vectors gives a "picture" that is worth a thousand words. It also imparts a "feel" to what the wind is doing to the airplane so that when the day comes that you need to alter course in midflight, to go to an alternate airport or divert around some weather, you can ad lib a wind correction angle that might be pretty close to what you'd figure if you had the time to accurately determine it. You might also have to calculate wind vectors if the batteries go dead in your electronic wonder calculator.

Let's go through the steps involved in drawing a wind vector:

1. Draw a vertical line on a blank piece of paper; this line will represent north-south. Mark the top of the line with an N. Place the 0 hole of the protractor part of your plotter on this line and then rotate the entire plotter until 053° appears on the outer edge, lined up with the N-S line. Make sure that as you rotate the plotter, you keep the 0 hole over the line. Then reproduce your course line by drawing another line, outward from the N-S line, with the straight edge of your plotter, as shown in FIG. 9-5. The length of this line is not important, but

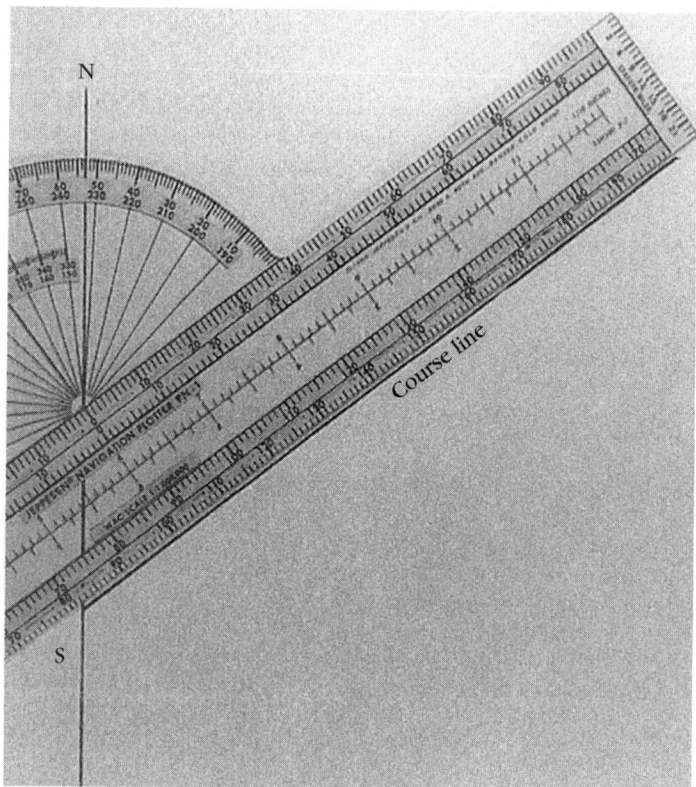

9-5 *The first step in drawing a wind vector. Reproduce the true course line. The vertical line represents the meridian.*

make it about 5 or 6 inches long. This line corresponds to your true course.

2. Now, let's enter the values for the wind. We need to know two things: the direction from which the wind is blowing and the speed of the wind. Assume that the wind aloft at your altitude is forecast to be from 330° at 30 knots. Line up the plotter with the 0 hole at the point where the course line intercepts the N-S line (our imaginary meridian). Use the point of your pencil, through the 0 hole, and put a dot there. Now move your plotter vertically up the paper, keeping the N-S line right under the 330° mark on the protractor, until the bottom straightedge intercepts the N-S line at the point that you just made with your pencil (which is also the point where the true course line intercepts the N-S line). Then draw a line to represent the wind

speed and direction. Draw this line along the bottom straight-edge, and, using the mileage scale on the straightedge, draw a line 30 miles long. If your paper is small, you can halve the wind speed if you want to keep the size of the diagram smaller, and if you do this, draw that line only 15 miles long. We've done this on FIG. 9-6 to compensate for the size of the page.

3. The final step is to intercept the course line with a line drawn from the end of the wind line that we drew in step 2. Make sure that you ascertain the very end of the 15-mile-long

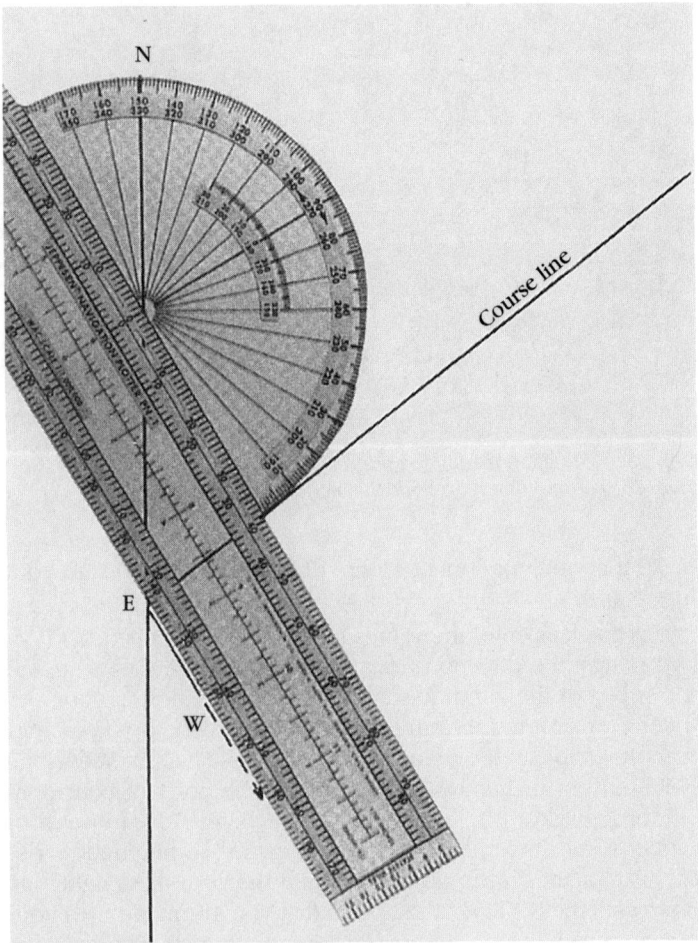

9-6 *The second step in drawing a wind vector. Draw a line representing the wind direction and speed.*

wind line that you drew. This measurement is important. This final line, from the end of the wind line to the course line, also has a definite length, and that is the cruising true airspeed of your airplane. Let's assume that our airplane will cruise at our chosen altitude at a speed of 115 knots. Because we halved the wind speed line, the airspeed line will only be 57 miles long, so that we keep the diagram in the same scale. So draw a line 57 miles long, again by using the scale at the bottom of the straight-edge by rotating the plotter as necessary until the airspeed line is 57 miles long. Remove the plotter from the paper for a moment.

The completed wind vector diagram appears in FIG. 9-7. Measure the angle at P with your protractor; that's the amount of angular correction necessary to compensate for this wind. It is called the *wind correction angle* (WCA). Magically, the length of the line from points E to P will be your ground speed when you measure the length of that line with the mileage scale of the straightedge of your plotter. When you measure the line E-P, the length is 54 miles. Because we halved all of the speed values, 54 times 2 equals 108; so your ground speed will be 108 knots. Measuring the angle at P, you discover that the WCA is 15°.

At this juncture, there is one note of caution that is in order. Some older airplanes have airspeed indicators that are calibrated in miles per hour, not knots. Wind speeds are always given in knots. So if you think in miles per hour for the true airspeed of your airplane, or if the airplane's manual speaks only in miles per hour, use your pocket computer to quickly convert those miles per hour into knots. In case you need to make the conversion by hand, without your computer, you can use the fairly accurate formula miles per hour divided by 1.15 equals knots to do so.

In our example, the wind vector diagram shows that the line E-W is from your left as you fly up the true course line (E-P) in the direction of 053°. Now we want to determine what our *true heading* is. We use the word *heading* to refer to the direction in which we'll point the nose of the airplane to compensate for the wind drift. The word *course* refers to our path over the ground. The rule for this correction is *subtract* for a wind from the left; *add* for a wind from the right. There really isn't a catch phrase to use to remember this rule other than to think of it as the fact that there are more right-handed people than there are left-handers, so right is more. If you are mathematically inclined, you'll remember the symbol <, pointing to the left indicates less than, while >, pointing to the right, means greater than. In this case, we need to subtract a WCA of 15° from our true course of 053°, which results in a true heading of 038°.

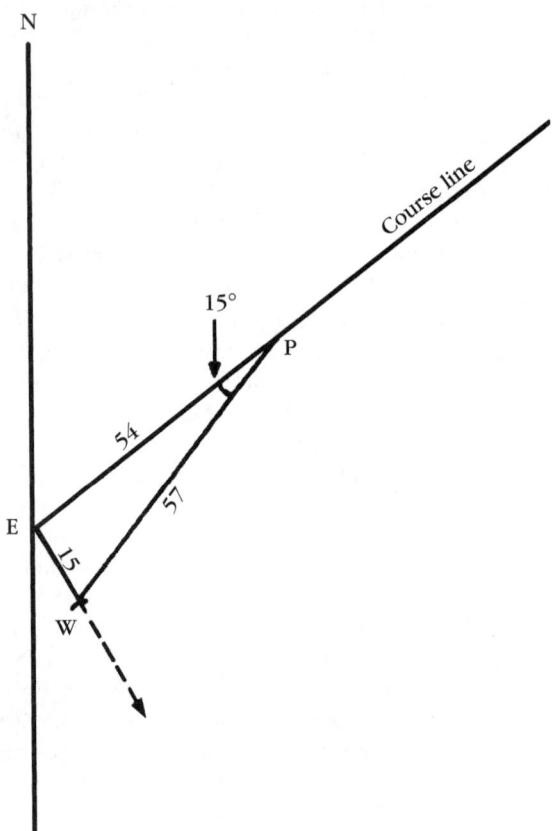

9-7 *The third and last step in drawing a wind vector. Draw a line connecting the end of the wind line W to the true course line EP. The length of this line is the airspeed at which you'll fly. Then, the angle at P is the wind correction angle, 15°. When measured, line EP reveals the ground speed.*

Variations and deviations

Don't go away just yet; there are a couple more simple corrections to make before you arrive at the number that will actually appear on your compass as the heading that you will fly.

The first of these corrections comes from information that is displayed on the aeronautical chart. It's called *variation*. Unfortunately, the magnetic north pole and the true, geographic North Pole are not in the same place. So the lines of magnetic force that radiate from the magnetic pole aren't the same as the meridians of longitude that we used to measure a course on our charts.

The variation, or difference between true north and magnetic north, changes as we go west and east of the line at which the two are the same. This line of 0 variation is located in the eastern United States. Here, since our navigational example is in the west, variation will be significant. The chart shows that the variation (the old-fashioned and more scientifically correct word is *declination*) along the route from Childress to Mangum is 8° east. These lines of variation are displayed on the chart by means of heavy, red lines running from the top of the chart to the bottom.

Here's your last navigation rule to remember: Add west variation, subtract east. The rhyme that works best to remember this one is, "West is best, east is least." Because the magnetic variation along our route is 8° east, we'll subtract it from the true heading of 038°, and arrive at our *magnetic heading* (MH) of 030°.

Finally, you need to correct for *deviation*. Deviation is the error in the compass itself. This error, which is inherent in the installation of any compass in any airplane, is caused by ferrous metal in the airplane, by the magnetic interference from the radios and other electronic devices in our airplane, and by the lack of precision inherent in all instruments. The ferrous metals in the engine, which sits right in front of the compass, inhibit compass accuracy.

Deviation figures are different for every airplane, even among airplanes of the same type. From time to time, especially when radios are either installed or removed, maintenance technicians determine the deviation applicable to each airplane, and they post the results on the *compass correction card,* which is required by the FARs to be placed very near the compass.

In our Cessna 150, the card is mounted in the same bracket that holds the compass. The card notes that when flying in a northeasterly direction, such as 030°, you must subtract 2° from the magnetic heading to arrive at the final figure, which is called the *compass heading.* So subtract 2°. The final result is 028°, the compass heading. This is the actual reading that you want to see on the magnetic compass in order to make a true course over the ground of 053°.

Here's a recap of all of the steps that are necessary to determine the compass heading:

Step 1	Start with	True course	053°
Step 2	Apply	WCA	−015°
	Result	True heading	038°
Step 3	Apply	Variation	−008°
	Result	Magnetic heading	030°
Step 4	Apply	Deviation	−002°
	Final result	Compass heading	028°

Remember the two rules: For variation, add west and subtract east (west is best, east is least). For wind, add right, subtract left.

You'll notice very quickly in your flight training that the magnetic compass oscillates in rough air and during a turn. After a turn is complete, it will take the compass a minute or so to stabilize. However, the DG doesn't bounce around at all and is rock steady in all normal flight regimes. But the DG cannot sense direction; it's just a dumb gyro that points wherever you've set it. You've already seen that we set the DG to match the reading of the compass before we take off, while everything is stable. In flight, you have to reset it about every 15 to 20 minutes because its precession will slowly drift from an accurate match with a compass heading. Always remember to check the DG against the compass and see if it needs to be reset. Even the newest of DGs will precess. Once you start flying cross-country flights, you will use the DG to accurately maintain the desired compass heading, and you will use the compass only as a cross-check and as a point of reference to set the DG.

Maintaining course by pilotage

Modern aerial navigation in light planes is a combination of three methods, *dead reckoning, pilotage,* and *electronic navigation.* We really don't use any of these methods in isolation unless we're flying under IFR.

The term *dead reckoning* has come into use as a misnomer for what is correctly called *deduced reckoning.* When we drew our wind vector diagram, we began the process of dead reckoning. This term comes from what the pilot is really doing, which is reckoning a heading to fly and the time that it will take to get from point A to point B as a deduction from known facts about the distance between the two points, the speed of the airplane, and the direction and speed of the wind. To be absolutely correct, it is *ded reckoning,* an abbreviation of the word *deduced* as *ded*. But that never looked right, so for decades pilots have used *dead reckoning*. Some remember the old saying from when it was the only form of long-distance navigation: "If you don't reckon right, you're dead." Dead reckoning, in its purest form, doesn't depend on looking at the ground and using checkpoints that the pilot can see to monitor the progress of the flight and the correctness of the heading.

Pilotage is the art of navigating by visual reference to points on the ground. As VFR private pilots, we certainly will navigate that way, and that is what this section of the chapter will cover. But we do a little dead reckoning in advance so that we have a good idea of what heading will get us to our destination, what our ground speed will be, and how long it ought to take to go from one ground reference point, called a *checkpoint,* to another.

You won't be—or, better point, should not be—using electronic navigation in a pure form unless and until you get an instrument rating and are flying in the clouds. Then you obviously don't have any ground references because you can't see them. No competent VFR pilot depends on radios alone to navigate because radios can fail without warning. You must always be prepared to complete your flight by pilotage and dead reckoning, without the benefit of any of the electronic aides to navigation.

Let's plan and fly a different cross-country trip to see how the three methods come together in everyday use. Start from Wichita, Kansas, and go to Tulsa, Oklahoma. First, draw the course line on your chart from the Wichita Mid-Continent Airport symbol to the Tulsa International Airport symbol (FIG. 9-8). Then take your plotter, place it on the meridian halfway between the two airports, and measure your true course. This will yield a true course of 140°.

Because you've learned how to properly plan a flight and have checked the weather first, you learned the winds aloft forecast during your briefing. You know the forecast wind directions and velocity for several of the altitudes at which it may be practical to fly this trip.

Let's assume that you choose to cruise on this VFR flight at 5,500 feet, where the wind is forecast to be from 270° at 25 knots. That's not squarely on your tail, but the wind will have a tailwind component, which will certainly help. Looking in the performance section of the airplane's POH, you figure that the airplane will cruise at 100 knots at that altitude, using a reasonably efficient power setting.

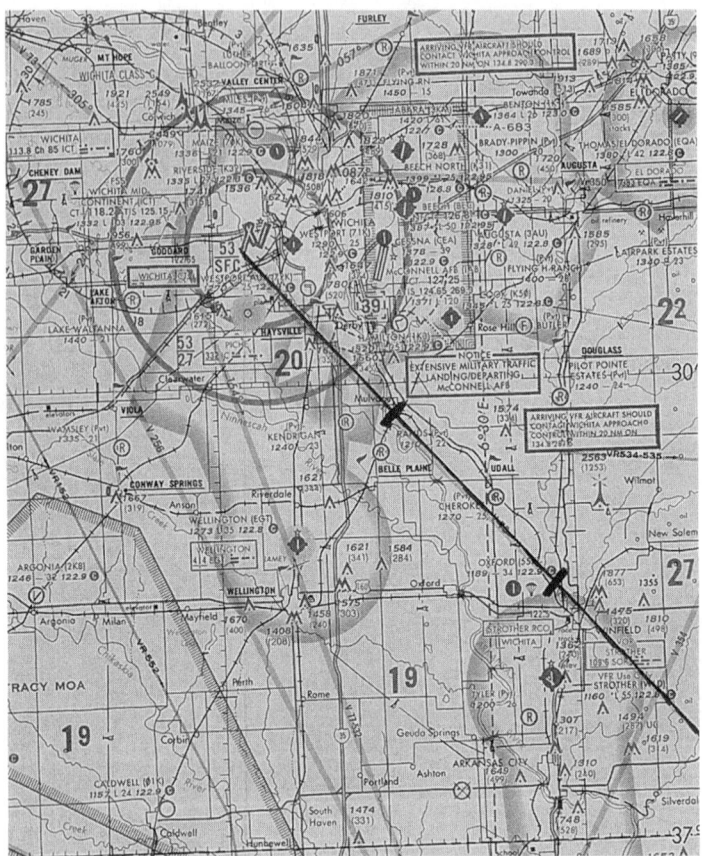

9-8 *Here's the first part of the Wichita-to-Tulsa course line on our chart. We've selected checkpoints that are 15 miles apart, indicated by the small hash marks perpendicular to the course line. (This chart is not for use in actual navigation.)*

Next, do your wind vector diagram. It should look like the one in FIG. 9-9. The diagram reveals that the wind correction angle, measured at P, is 12°. The wind today is from your right as you fly this course, so you add 12° to the TC to deduce a true heading of 152°. Your wind vector diagram also gives your ground speed when you measure the line from E to P. This comes out to be 115 knots, which means that the partial tailwind will be giving you a boost of 15 knots across the ground.

Now, looking at the sectional chart and finding the line of variation along the route, you see that the variation is 7° east in

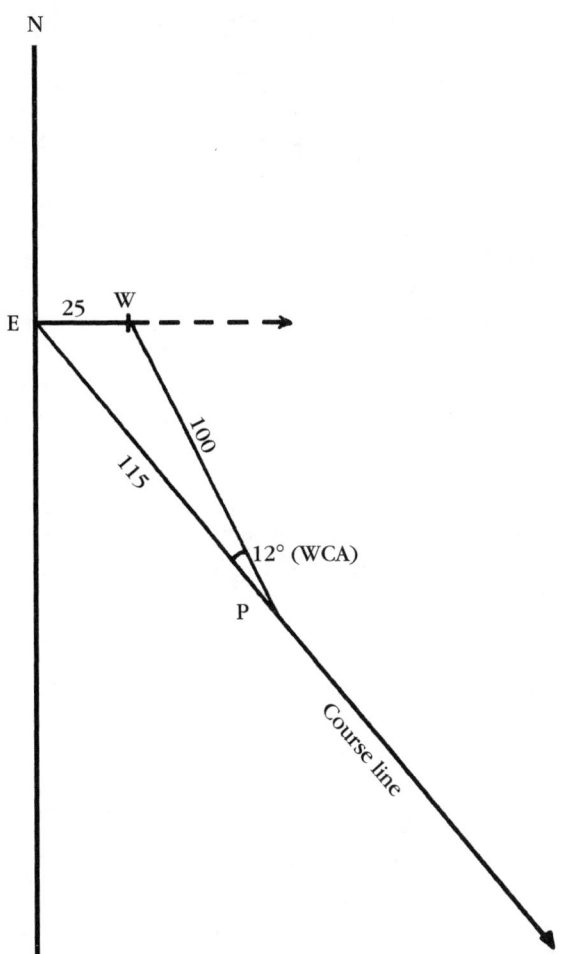

9-9 *The Wichita-to-Tulsa wind vector should look like this, drawn to full scale.*

this part of the country. Following the second rule of dead reckoning (add west, subtract east), subtract 7° from the true heading. This leaves you with a magnetic heading of 145°.

Finally, when you get in the cockpit, glance at the compass correction card and find that, in this quadrant of compass readings, you must steer a compass heading 2° greater than your magnetic heading. You then end up with a compass heading of 147°.

When you use your plotter to measure the course line that you drew on the sectional chart, you'll discover that it is 113 nautical miles from Wichita to Tulsa. Now you can figure your estimated time en route, either by arithmetic using a pencil and paper or more commonly and practically by using the pocket computer or electronic calculator. One of the finer points of dead reckoning is to realize that your true airspeed won't be the 100 knots that the POH shows, calculated over the entire length of the trip. You will have to spend some time climbing at a reduced speed before you reach your cruising altitude and get the airplane trimmed, the fuel mixture leaned, and start actually cruising at 100 knots. You could be very precise and use other tables in the POH to figure exactly how long the climb will take and what your speed will be while climbing. We do make these computations for instrument flying, but for VFR flying, we don't.

For all practical purposes, you can call your ground speed for the entire trip 100 knots, and that will compensate for the speed lost while climbing up to 5,500 feet. If the trip weren't so short, the detrimental effect of the climb would be less; it's a matter of experience before you can estimate it closely. At 100 knots, it'll take 68 minutes to fly this trip. To calculate this figure by hand, using pencil and paper isn't difficult. Just divide ground speed into the total distance and multiply the result by 60 to obtain the elapsed time in minutes.

Don't ever forget how to be precise. Planning a trip like the one we're discussing is easy, and flying it will be also, because there are many landmarks to serve as checkpoints and help us correct any minor errors in our dead reckoning. It is a wholly different matter if your flight is over a desert, a swamp, or a large body of water, or almost anywhere at night. Under those conditions, there won't be many checkpoints of much use, and those that there are will be far apart.

So let's talk about the need to establish checkpoints along your route that are easy to spot from the air. When using pilotage as a part of the total navigational picture, checkpoints are vital because they let you see if your compass heading is keeping you on course. Your calculations (dead reckoning) will never produce an error-free result for several reasons. The winds aloft forecasts are nothing more than forecasts. The actual winds will vary some from the forecast, although the forecast certainly gives you some idea of what to expect. The compass might have an error lesser or greater than the correction card shows. And finally, you just might possibly make a mistake in your reckoning. Without checkpoints, you won't be able to make the minor corrections you need to keep you on your course.

You want to space the checkpoints about 10 to 15 miles apart if possible. Closer than that and you'll overcorrect; farther apart and you can get pretty far off course before doing something about it. Now, go back to the wind diagram for a minute. The checkpoints will be used while you're at cruise speed, after the climb to altitude is completed, when your ground speed should be about 115 knots. A moment spent now with your computer tells you that, at 115 knots, you'll travel 15 nautical miles in about 8 minutes.

Take your aeronautical chart where you have drawn the course line on it, lay it out on a table or desk, and put your plotter along the route. Look for a landmark every 15 nautical miles or so, and at each one that you select, draw a little line at right angles to the course line. For example, the chart shows that if you are making good on your intended ground track, you should have crossed the small village of Mulvane. When you do cross Mulvane, a railroad bridge across a river should be just off of the right wing. Make Mulvane your first checkpoint.

About 18 minutes out of Wichita, you should be approaching the northwest edge of Winfield, Kansas. Make Winfield your second checkpoint because it is easy to identify; the chart shows that there is a racetrack and an outdoor theater northwest of town. The several highways and railroad tracks that converge at Winfield also help to identify it from the air. Continuing on the course, your next 15-nautical-mile checkpoint should be a prominent airport, Strother, about 5 miles ahead and to the right of your track.

Picking checkpoints is a matter of personal preference, and another pilot, flying the same trip, might pick different ones. Pick checkpoints that are easily discernible while flying. Be careful of landmarks like bridges or mines that don't have another feature nearby so that you are sure that you are seeing what you think you are. Little villages can all look alike from the air, so make sure that there is a way to differentiate the one you selected as a checkpoint. As long as you pick points that you can identify, your points are appropriately spaced, and they keep you on course, choose your checkpoints as you see fit.

Alternate airports

Every now and then, you may have to divert from your intended destination and go somewhere else. This problem can be thrust upon you because of deteriorating weather at the intended destination, a dwindling fuel supply, the closure of the airport where you intended to land because of some happening on the ground there, or for a host of other reasons. During your flight test for your license, the chances are very high that the examiner will ask you to demonstrate your ability to abandon your planned flight and proceed to an alternate airport.

Let's assume that the Wichita to Tulsa flight is your check ride and that the examiner suddenly tells you, 5 minutes after passing the third checkpoint, that the weather ahead makes it unwise for you to continue to Tulsa. Your first reaction might be, "Okay. Can we get back to Wichita?" But the examiner isn't about to make it that easy, so he says, "No. Wichita has just gone below VFR minimums."

Well, because you've been watching your checkpoints, and you know your ground speed, you have no trouble pinpointing your position on the chart. You should be about 8 or 9 miles beyond your last checkpoint. Quickly, but carefully, place your plotter straightedge along your course line and measure that distance. That should put you over the curved highway that runs east from Arkansas City. Yes, it's up ahead there, where it should be.

Now, since you know where you are, the next step is to check the chart for nearby airport symbols. The closest one shows by the R beside its symbol that it's a privately owned, restricted-use airport that should be used without prior permission only in an emergency. But because you flew right by it the first time without seeing it, it is probably a small sod strip that will be hard to find out here in the wide open Midwest. The next closest public-use airport is Strother, your last checkpoint. Strother is now about 5 miles behind you and to the right of your current location.

You wisely choose Strother, point it out on the chart for the examiner to see, and turn right, toward it. Simultaneously, you come back on the power to begin a normal descent. Even though you can't actually see the airport yet, you know exactly where it is relative to Arkansas City and Winfield. You look at the examiner and say, "We'll be there in about 4 minutes."

This example was fairly easy because there was an airport immediately at hand to use as an alternate. The same scenario could occur over sparsely populated or mountainous terrain where the nearest airport might be much farther away. In that case, the only thing to do is to quickly draw a new course line to the alternate that you select as the new destination. But you'll have to estimate your new heading because it's impractical, in most light airplane cockpits, to draw a wind vector diagram in flight. If you have your pocket computer handy, as you should, and if the winds aloft are significant, you can do the wind vector solution with the computer. Then carefully follow the new course line with your finger on the chart until everything settles down and you're sure that the new heading is taking you to the alternate airport. Doing this as the weather is going sour can be a daunting task.

That's why prudent and wise pilots always plan ahead of time for the possibility of needing to abandon the original plan and head to an alternate destination. If your originally planned flight is a long one, you might need to allow for more than one alternate, depending on where in the course of the trip the decision has to be made to go to the alternate. Before you finish your preflight planning, look over your route of flight. Pick out several airports along the way where you could land if needed. Because airports make wonderful checkpoints, picking them for this purpose also automatically gives you as many alternate fields as possible.

If deteriorating weather is the reason that you divert to an alternate field, the weather forecast was probably significantly in error; you would not have taken off if the prediction had been good VFR weather all along the route. When a forecast goes south, and they occasionally do, make sure that the alternate airport to which you're headed still has satisfactory weather conditions. Use your radio and call Flight Watch to get an update on the current weather and the forecast which, by then, will probably be an amended forecast. It isn't very smart to head for an alternate field, only to have the route blocked by weather at some point.

A vital part of flight planning is to ensure that you *always* have enough fuel to carry out not only your planned flight but also a diversion to appropriate alternates. A recipe for almost certain disaster is poor weather that necessitates diverting to an alternate airport, coupled with insufficient fuel to get there. That's why, when we look at the POH values given for the range of any light airplane, the mileage figure means little to a good pilot. The real range needed for a flight includes the distance to the planned destination plus the additional mileage to any alternate airports, plus a healthy reserve. The POH range numbers assume no wind condition because the authors at the factory can't possibly anticipate what headwind or tailwind their airplanes will face on any given flight. Take these range numbers with a grain of salt; their only real usefulness is in comparing the performance characteristics of one airplane to another.

Also, *never* trust fuel gauges in any airplane. They are there only as a matter of convenience and should never be counted on to be accurate. In fact, the certification regulations contained in the FARs require only that they be accurate when the tanks are empty. You know, from the POH, the amount of fuel per hour that your airplane will burn at any given altitude and power setting combination, assuming that you have properly leaned the mixture. The only way to tell how much fuel you have left is by looking at the clock. Always note your takeoff time, and unless your loading dictates otherwise, always depart, even for a short flight, with full fuel tanks.

Always have a reserve supply of fuel available in case your planning goes awry. Some pilots are comfortable with 45 minutes of extra fuel, on top of the fuel estimated for the planned trip and the alternate(s). That may be all right in faster airplanes, when 45 minutes of flying time means well over 100 miles of distance covered. But my personal rule, in slower airplanes like our Cessna 150, is to have 1 full hour of reserve fuel at all times as a minimum; and that is increased to $1\frac{1}{2}$ hours if my flight is over sparsely populated terrain or is at night.

The Cessna 150 carries $22\frac{1}{2}$ gallons of usable fuel. Almost every airplane has some fuel in its tanks that cannot physically get to the engine. Therefore, the important number for you to know is your airplane's useable fuel; total capacity is not nearly as important. Our 150 burns slightly less than 6 gallons per hour at normal cruise power settings and altitudes. This is roughly a $3\frac{3}{4}$-hour supply. If you keep 1 hour in reserve, you've got about $2\frac{3}{4}$ hours of cruising time, which gives you approximately a 275-mile range in a no-wind condition.

That's about as long as most people want to sit still in a small plane before a stop to stretch their legs. A stop every 2 to 3 hours is also helpful to get you a chance to get an update on the weather if the trip is a long one. As we said before, running out of gas is unthinkable, so make sure that it never happens to you.

Radio Aids to Navigation

In the 1930s, the first radio aids to navigation were low-frequency-range stations that emitted only four course legs from the station. The four courses were basically configured so that the "highways in the sky" were each at right angles to the other. This was great if you wanted only to go in one of four directions—north, south, east, or west—from the station or if you were inbound from one of these cardinal positions. This system didn't work well if you were anywhere else or wanted to go a different direction from the four courses that emanated from the station. Also, low-frequency radio signals are very susceptible to interference from bad weather, when you often need electronic navigation the most.

By the 1950s, the low-frequency system was replaced by *very high frequency* (VHF) *omnidirectional range stations,* also called *VOR stations.* Some people have referred to the VOR system as *omni,* but the correct term is *VOR,* and using the right nomenclature denotes a well-schooled pilot.

VOR equipment has gained worldwide acceptance, but it is now in its waning days. A subsequent portion of this chapter will examine the *global positioning system* (GPS), which will almost surely become the way that things are done in the future. But, for now, the VOR system is still used by most VFR pilots, and it is the one on which the entire federal airway system is based. VOR is also the system on which you'll be tested in the knowledge test that you have to pass before you can take the flight test for your private license.

The full name of the VOR suggests that it is omnidirectional. This means that the stations send out radio signals in all directions so that you can navigate directly to or from a station, from anywhere or to anywhere, as long as you are within reception range of the station. Because VORs transmit in the VHF band, the reception range is not very far. VHF signals go out from the station in what is known as *line of sight,* the same as do television and FM radio waves. The radio energy is transmitted from the station's antenna in a straight line, and it does not follow the curvature of the earth, nor does it reflect off of the upper layers of the atmosphere as do lower-frequency radio waves. That's why, on a good day or especially at night, you might pick up an AM radio station hundreds of miles away because it operates in the lower-frequency spectrum; but your TV reception is hardly ever any good beyond 60 to 75 miles from the transmitter antenna.

VOR signals can be received from a little farther out than you would think from drawing an analogy to a TV, but that is because we are receiving them in an aircraft that is flying above the ground, where the line of sight signals can still be received. It's the same principle that enables you to see farther from the top of a hill than you can on flat land. Still, most light airplane VOR receivers don't pick up a signal clearly enough for navigation much farther out from the station than about 100 miles, and it's far less than that if you're flying at the lower altitudes. So there are many VOR stations in the system to be able to provide adequate coverage throughout the country.

The VOR receiver in your airplane has three main components: a *course selector* or *omnibearing selector* (OBS), a *course deviation indicator* (CDI), and a TO-FROM indicator (FIG. 9-10).

Operating a VOR can seem to be intimidating at first, but it really is easy. With only a little practice, you'll get the hang of it very quickly. First, let's go into some more basics about how it works. The station transmits its signals out, away from the transmitter antenna. The actual station is large enough to be seen from the air as you pass over one. It is shaped like an inverted cone, large end down and pointed end up; all of them are painted white. The signals radiate from the station in the pattern of a

9-10 *A VOR receiver can lead you directly to your destination. Important parts of a receiver are the following: A, course selector knob; B, omnibearing selector; C, course deviation indicator; D, TO-FROM flag; and E, receiver tuner display. The tuner display for the communications side of the radio is shown as V.*

spoked wheel. The spokes of the wheel are called *radials*. Imagine yourself standing directly at the hub of the wheel facing north. The spoke that runs north, outward from the hub, is the 360°, or 0° radial. The one running from the hub outbound to your right is the 090° radial because it's going due east. The one running outbound from your left is going due west, so it is the 270° radial. Then, naturally, the one running outward from the hub, directly behind you, is going due south, so it is the 180° radial. From your nose all of the way around back to your nose again is 360°, and the VOR station emits 360 radials. This way, you can navigate on a radial outbound from the station in any direction you wish. You can also navigate inbound to a station from anywhere as long as you are within reception range.

Similar to highways on the ground that have either names or route numbers, we have a system for labeling VOR radials. They are labeled according to the magnetic course of the radial *outbound* from the station. So from your position at the center of the station, you would navigate in an easterly direction by following the 090° radial outbound from the station. If you were, at a different time, standing on the rim of the wheel, on the east side of it and wanted to go toward the station, you would need to go due west to get there. In that situation, you'd be flying inbound to the station but still tracking the 090° radial, but you would do it inbound to the station on a heading of 270° since you need to go west. In this latter example, the 090° has nothing to do with the direction you'll fly to get from the east side of the rim of the wheel to the center of the station; 090° is just the label of the radial that you'll follow. Now, let's get back to operating the system in an airplane.

The course selector, or OBS, is a circular dial that you rotate to set the direction that you want to track, either inbound toward the station or outbound away from it. You *don't* have to worry about the radial labels when setting the OBS. If you're east of the station and want to fly toward it, you know that you need to head 270° to head west. Just set the OBS to 270°.

The CDI is a vertical needle, usually hinged at the top, that swings either right or left to show your deviation from the course that you have set into the OBS.

The TO-FROM indicator is sometimes in a little window on the instrument face, and it is usually a little flip-flop device that either shows TO or FROM as its display. If it isn't steadily indicating either TO or FROM, you're beyond the reception range of the station that you're trying to use. When it does come to life, it is telling you whether the course that you have selected on the OBS will take you to or from the station from your present position.

There is one part of using the VOR system that is difficult for some people to initially conceptualize: The VOR system senses only your position *from* the station. The radio receiver in the panel of the airplane has no idea in which direction you're actually flying. All that it can do is tell you two things. First, it will tell you whether the course set into the OBS will take you toward or away from the station. Second, it will display the position of the airplane relative to that selected course. It does this with the CDI indications, which will tell you that you are exactly on the course when the CDI needle is either centered or off to the left or right of it as the needle is deflected.

Let's take an example and actually plan a flight using VOR as our system of electronic navigation. To make it even simpler, let's plan the same flight from Wichita to Tulsa that we did before, except that we will use VOR this time. Look at the chart and note that the Wichita VOR is about 5 miles northwest of Wichita Mid-Continent Airport. VOR stations are depicted on the chart by means of a blue dot inside of a hexagon and surrounded by a compass rose.

Actually, the Wichita VOR is a *VORTAC*, which is indicated by the three blue "legs" on the hexagon. Although the terms *VOR* and *VORTAC* are used interchangeably, a VORTAC also provides signals for *distance measuring equipment* (DME) and for tactical military navigation. You can purchase a DME receiver to go along with a VOR unit. The DME will then display the distance from your position to the station, and it will express that distance in nautical miles. Most DME units can also automatically calculate and display your ground speed and the time needed to fly to the station. The DME in your airplane sends out a signal that is received by the VORTAC station, and then it is retransmitted to your airplane. The DME unit in your panel notes the time that it took for the signal to make the roundtrip from the airplane, to the station and back, and calculates the distance involved. From successive similar calculations, it can then figure the ground speed and the time needed to fly to the station.

Along with the station symbol on the chart is a blue box that explains the station's radio frequency and its Morse code identifier. In this case, the blue box is at the bottom of the compass rows, and it says WICHITA, 113.8 CH 85 ICT, followed by the Morse code for ICT.

This information means that the VOR radio frequency is 113.8 MHz: you'll tune your VOR receiver to that frequency to receive that VOR. A military pilot would tune the tacan receiver in a military aircraft to channel 85 to use the station's tactical navigation capability. The identifier for this station, which is always composed of three letters, is ICT, followed by the Morse code for those three letters. Modern VOR receivers have digital tuners, just like modern AM or FM radios do. In former days, when we had to use a variable tuner, like the dial tuner on an old broadcast radio, you would have to listen carefully for the Morse code identifier to verify which station was actually tuned in. Although it's still a good practice to turn up the volume and confirm that you have the right station, few pilots bother with this anymore. Most just put 113.8 into the digital tuner and assume that they have ICT tuned. Always fly like a pro, and confirm the correct station by listening for the identifier. Frequencies do get changed periodically, and if you have an old chart (another no-no), you may have not tuned in the right station.

Now draw a course line from the Wichita VOR to the Tulsa VOR. It closely follows the course line you drew previously between the two airports. Near Tulsa, the new route is about 4 miles east of the track drawn for the flight that did not use radio aids for navigation (FIG. 9-11). The course line drawn between the two VOR stations emerges from the printed compass rose around the Wichita VOR at about 130°. Because the compass rose is already corrected for variation at the location of every station, 130° is the magnetic course to fly.

Before takeoff from Wichita, tune your VOR receiver to 113.8. Listen for the identifier and then dial 130° into the OBS. Right after takeoff, you'll be headed southeast but somewhat to the north of this course. Therefore, the CDI needle will be off center to the right. That indication is telling you that the selected course of 130° lies to the right of your present position. Your goal now is to intercept the 130° radial and then fly on it, outbound from the station. To make the interception, turn the airplane about 30° to the right of the selected course, to a heading of 160°. In a few moments, the CDI needle will start creeping toward the center. As it is centering, you are intercepting the 130° radial, so simply take out the intercept angle and turn back to a heading of 130°. That's all there is to it; you've just intercepted a VOR radial.

Now fly straight on a heading of 130°, and watch the CDI needle to see if there are any needed corrections. If it drifts to

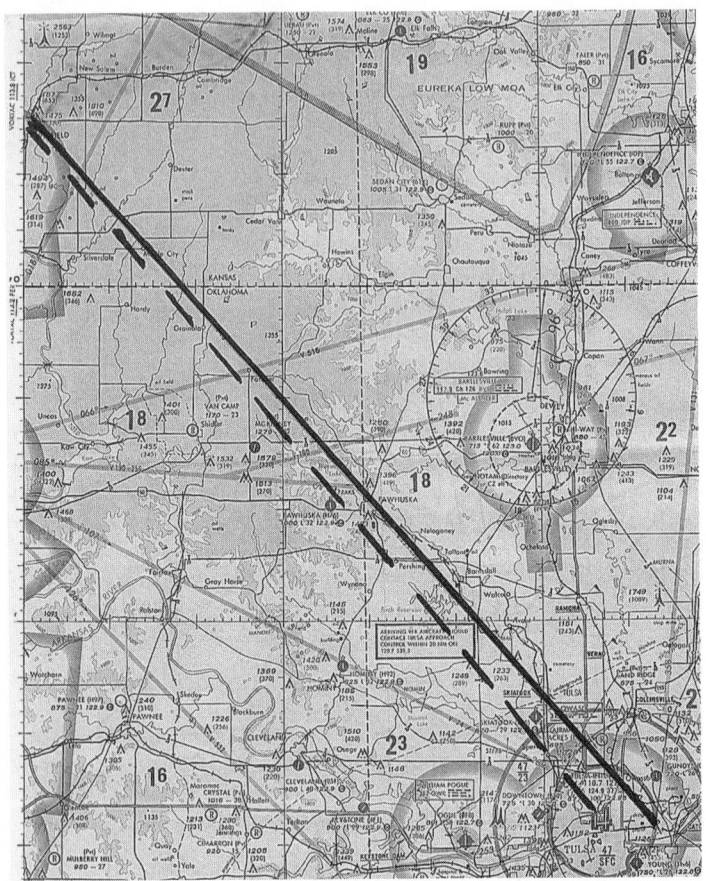

9-11 *The dashed line is the track you would fly using pilotage. The solid line is the track to the Tulsa VOR. VOR stations are not always located this close to your destination.*

the left, the radial is off to your left, and you will need to correct slightly to the left to intercept it again and track it. The same goes if the needle drifts to the right, except that you obviously need to correct to the right. As long as you keep the needle centered, you're tracking the 130° radial outbound from Wichita, heading straight for Tulsa. The TO-FROM window will be reading FROM because from your present position, flying along the 130° radial will take you outbound from Wichita.

If there is a crosswind present, you'll find that holding the heading of 130° on the DG or magnetic compass won't keep the needle centered because you'll be blown off course by the wind. Observe the needle, and you'll find that it might take a compass heading 5 to 10° different from the 130° to keep the needle centered. Guess what?

The VOR has just done your wind correction for you: The difference between your compass heading and 130° is the wind correction angle necessary to track 130° over the ground (discounting any deviation in the compass).

When tracking either toward or away from a station, as long as the TO-FROM indicator corresponds with your heading to or from that station, make course corrections toward the CDI needle to keep it centered. You should verify proper sensing by checking to see that the heading in which you're actually flying and the course dialed into the OBS are within 90° of each other. If you were a pro and you were tracking the course, you would take small cuts at the correction angle. If the needle in the CDI is off to the right, you don't want to just turn circles to the right because, if you do, you'll do nothing more than orbit over a small area, off course. What you want to do is turn slightly toward the needle. How much you turn and what degree of intercept angle that you establish will depend on how far the needle is directed from center, how close you are to the station, and how strong the wind is. Establish your correction angle and hold that new heading until you see what happens to the needle next. If it starts coming back to the center, you're intercepting the course and you have to remove only some of the correction angle as the needle centers, so that you do not go through the course.

If the needle doesn't move at all after you've turned toward it, you're probably just paralleling the course, and you need a little bit more cut into the course to intercept it. If, after making your initial attempt to intercept, the needle continues to deflect away from center, you will need even more correction angle to stop the deviation and get back on course.

Because the radials of a VOR go out from the station like the spokes of a wheel, those radials are very close together near the station and very far apart when you are so far from the station that you're at the limit of reception range. In close, the needle gets very sensitive, and the correction angles need to be quite small. The results of a correction angle applied when you are only 10 miles from the station are a lot more dramatic than they are when you are 40 or 50 miles away.

As your flight progresses and when you are halfway to Tulsa, look again at the chart and you'll see that the frequency for the

Tulsa VOR is 114.4 MHz. So switch the receiver to 114.4, and listen for the Morse code identifier to confirm that you've tuned in the right station. The TO-FROM indicator flops over to TO, and you're now tracking inbound to the Tulsa VOR. If you're on course, the needle will stay centered.

In practice, there is no need to fly all the way to the Tulsa VOR itself. The chart shows that the station is about 4 or 5 miles due east of the Tulsa International Airport, so you call Tulsa Approach Control when you get within 20 miles of the airport. The controller will probably give you a suggested heading or two as she sees your position and ground track on her radar scope. She will then suggest headings that will both steer you toward the airport and put you into the flow of traffic coming into this busy, airline airport.

VOR equipment can do other things besides allowing you to fly from one station to the next. Assume that you are unsure of your position after you've been doing a lot of practice maneuvers and haven't been paying attention, as you should have been, to exactly where you are. Most pilots never get *lost*; they are only unsure of their positions from time to time. If you fall for that prevarication, you're a good prospect for a bridge salesman. In any event, you can use your VOR receiver to pinpoint your location in short order. Tune to a nearby station, and just twist the OBS slowly until the needle centers and the TO-FROM indicator shows FROM. Note what radial the OBS says, and draw a line on your chart from the station that you tuned, outbound from the station, along that radial. You are somewhere along this radial line.

Then pick another VOR station on the chart that is located well off to one side of the first *line of position* that you just drew. Make sure that the second station is close enough to be within reception range at your altitude; if it is not, climb to a higher altitude to increase your reception range. Repeat the process of determining which radial you are on from this second station. Draw that line of position on your chart, and where the two lines intercept is where you are.

Automatic Directional Finders

Another radio navigation receiver is the *automatic directional finder* (ADF). The ADF doesn't actually find any directions, but it does enable the pilot to use it to home directly in on virtually any low-frequency transmitter. *Nondirectional beacons* (NDBs) send out a signal that the airplane's ADF can receive.

The station is called "nondirectional" because it does not send out any kind of discrete or directional signal as does the VOR. The signal from the NDB is uniform throughout its compass rose. The ADF receiver in the airplane is composed of two parts: receiver and display head. Sometimes the display head is mounted in the same box as the receiver, but they are usually separate. This display head is circular and shows the points of the compass around it, usually in increments of 10 or 20°. A needle pivots in the center of the display and rotates to point to a direction: 360°, 090°, 180°, and the like.

When the receiver is tuned to a station, the ADF needle points to where the station is located in relation to the nose of the airplane. So if the needle says 360°, the station is directly in front of your nose. If it displays 270°, the station is abeam the left wing, and so on around the circle. Advanced maneuvering and trigonometry calculations are required to determine a distance from an ADF station, and almost no one does this anymore; it's not even on the knowledge test for an airline transport pilot certificate these days.

At first blush, it might seem easy to just fly directly to an NDB by putting the station on your nose. But the NDB doesn't send out directional signals that automatically compensate for wind drift as the VOR radials do. So when you home into an NDB station, you have to learn how to determine and then apply your own wind correction. Most private pilot courses don't even include instruction on the use of an ADF, leaving that subject until a pilot advances to training for the instrument rating.

The beauty of the ADF is that it will tune in on and show the direction to any low-frequency station, including not only aeronautical NDBs but also marine radio beacons and all commercial AM radio stations as well. Also, because the low-frequency radio is not line of sight, as is the VHF band in which VORs operate, the ADF's range is sometimes hundreds of miles, limited only by the power of the transmitter and the present atmospheric conditions.

The bad side of ADF is that low-frequency radio transmissions are susceptible to interference from many sources. When there is any thunderstorm activity anywhere near your flight path, the ADF might go nuts, and the needle might swing wildly because those thunderstorms emit tremendous amounts of electromagnetic energy in the form of lightning. The main reason that ADF technology has stayed around as long as it has in the United States is that the transmitters and receivers are relatively inexpensive, as radio aids to navigation go. The NDBs around the country exist primarily to allow smaller airports to have at least a rudimentary instrument approach for IFR traffic flying into them. An IFR approach is necessary for an airport to handle IFR flights if the weather is below VFR minimums.

In some parts of the world, particularly in South America and northwestern Canada, large and powerful NDBs are the foundation of the airway systems in use. The VOR stations have to be relatively close together to make up an airway, and in these remote parts of the world, it's just too difficult and expensive to install and maintain a sufficient number of VOR stations to make up an airway.

The Global Positioning System

GPS has taken the general aviation industry by storm, and it has quickly become the most popular form of electronic navigation. The FAA has even proposed a loose timetable to begin eliminating VOR stations and to switch the entire system over to a GPS-based navigation system. Originally this was set to occur around 2004, but the timetable has been pushed back some. The FAA's timetables for many improvements over the years have been very optimistic, and this one has been also. But regardless of exactly when it will happen, GPS is certainly the navigation device of the present and, even more so, for the future.

GPS is based on a network of 24 earth satellites. Each satellite transmits a radio signal that is received and processed by a GPS receiver, whether that receiver is mounted in the panel of an airplane, in a pilot's lap, on a boat, in a car, or held in a hiker's hand out in the woods. The entire idea began as a military navigation system that would free military aircraft from any dependence upon ground-based transmitters.

In times of armed conflict, transmitters on the ground are vulnerable and are certainly attractive targets for an enemy to eliminate. In these days when the United States has interests around the world and possibly undertakes military action related to those interests, our combat aircraft, ships, tanks, and even foot soldiers often operate in remote areas where there is no ground-based radio navigation system at all. Even though military aircraft are often equipped with inertial navigation systems that do not depend on any outside references to operate, they are not the total or best answer.

So the military developed GPS to serve its needs well into the foreseeable future. GPS can also be used by modern, light-weight receivers now being made for a multitude of civilian applications, including aviation. In the military application, GPS is fantastically accurate, allowing a fighter to put a bomb right in the front door of a building. For civilian use, the system is desensitized somewhat, but it is clearly more sensitive and accurate than anything else we've previously had.

GPS operates by triangulating the signals received from the satellites. Because electronic data that the receiver processes are coming from a source in space, several benefits follow. First, GPS is truly global. It works everywhere, from Antarctica to New York City, from the middle of the Pacific, or in the center of Kansas. It is dependent on nothing on the ground. GPS can also determine an aircraft's altitude because it measures its distance from the satellite. We now have the best backup method for determining altitude, totally independent of the airplane's pressure altimeter and pitot/static system.

While in flight, the GPS unit is not particularly difficult to use. But because it can display so much data, you will have to spend some time practicing with yours to become completely at ease with this new system. When you tell the unit to find its present position, in a few seconds you'll know exactly where you are to within a few meters' tolerance. It can be quickly programmed to take you from that position to anywhere on the globe that you want to go, and it will compute the most efficient routing to get there.

While you are en route, the GPS receiver will display a lot of data: your track over the ground, your ground speed, and the time to go until you get where you've told it to take you. The first aviation units depended on a pilot's inputting the latitude and longitude coordinates of destinations, points of departure, and any points along the way that the pilot wanted to be identified. Now almost all of the GPS receivers on the market, even those designed to be portable and held in your hand or mounted to the control wheel with a small bracket, come with a database. This database generally includes every airport in the United States, all of the VORs, all NDBs, and about everything else you'd ever want to find. Just let the unit have a few seconds to access the satellite signals, figure its present position, and it's ready to go. In a flash you can input the identifier of the place you want to go, and the GPS receiver will tell you the heading to get there, how far it is, and how long it will take you to get there.

Many of the units now on the market also have a moving-map display, which displays a little airplane symbol as the cursor on a screen. You then watch the symbol move as you fly along. The database on these moving-map units often includes major landmarks such as highways, towns, bodies of water, airports, and other things of a purely aeronautical nature. Some are so full of data that you can call up the scale of the ground display and use it to have a pizza delivered.

The moving-map units, which are slightly more expensive, are designed to be mounted in the airplane's panel. Their database memory is updateable so that the unit can display the current radio frequencies of nearby airports, FSSs, and ATC facilities. Almost all of them, panel mounted or handheld, have a feature to quickly call up the nearest airports, in case you need to land in an emergency. If you have one of the updateable units, you generally just order the data card from the manufacturer every so often, slip it into a slot in the GPS set, and presto, everything you would ever want to know is a push button away, and the information is current. You can order the card or cards that cover the geographical areas in which you fly, from the central United States, to the Caribbean, to South America, and even foreign continents outside of our hemisphere.

Since the 1950s, aviation radios have been made in a combination called *navcom,* which simply means that a communications radio and navigation receiver are both physically contained within the same black box. This enables a pilot to navigate on the VOR side of the instrument while being able to use the communications side independently to talk to someone. Since their inception, navcoms have been combined communications and VOR radios. Now manufacturers are offering navcoms that put together, in one box, the typical communications radio with a GPS receiver, at a cost not much higher than before.

GPS will more than likely completely replace the VOR system in the near future. The VOR transmitters are aging, and they are becoming increasingly costly to either maintain or replace. Hordes of FAA technicians are required to constantly fix and check them. The FAA must buy the sites upon which VOR stations are put and then spend millions to keep them running. Now a satellite system is in place, paid for by the military, and which the military will continue to maintain. Civilians, and not only aviators, can get in on the act without all of the costs of supporting the VOR network.

When this replacement comes, we'll have an uncanny and amazing ability to navigate at will across the country. The IFR system will be freed from fixed airways, making direct routing between airports the way to go, saving the time and expense of flying between VOR stations as the present airways zig-zag across the country. GPS will additionally allow virtually any airport with acceptable terrain and obstacle clearance properties to have an IFR approach, all free from ground-based radio equipment. You can get in on most of these advantages right now. For about $500, you can buy a handheld unit that has so much capability that as a private pilot, you may never tap into it all. Buck Rogers has arrived.

Airspace Classifications

Progress has always had its price, and sometimes we don't all agree on what progress is. Up until the late 1920s, pilots flew where, when, and how they felt like it, in whatever weather they were willing to brave and in whatever machine they trusted to leave terra firma. Then, as flying became more popular and accepted, the federal government decided to begin regulating it. First came the licensing of pilots, then the certification of airplanes, and after all of that, the regulation of the airlines.

Early in their existence, the airline companies realized that if something weren't done soon to prevent it, someday two airplanes might come together in the air with the predictable disastrous result. So the airlines themselves got together and created the air traffic control system, which had jurisdiction over only the flights of the various companies that voluntarily cooperated in it.

Everyone else flew at will, but because the totality of aviation was still minuscule, little went wrong. As airline traffic grew, the airlines eventually turned over their air traffic controllers and their system to the government, which has operated the ATC ever since.

To make a system work that kept airplanes, particularly those flying IFR in the clouds, from running into each other, the government devised the notion that the airspace ought to be broken up into different blocks, where different rules and procedures would be in force. VFR pilots can identify the various blocks, or classifications of airspace in which they fly, by looking at the same aeronautical charts they use for planning and plotting a flight.

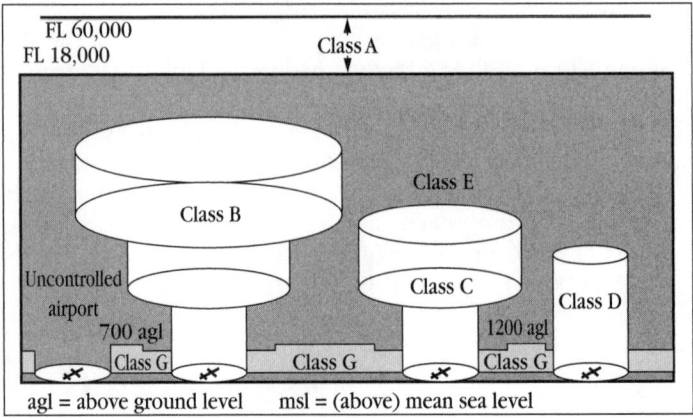

9-12 *Airspace classifications in the United States.*

In 1993, the entire American system of airspace classification was altered to comply with the classifications used internationally. If you have older texts, or worse yet, older aeronautical charts published before this massive change took place, relegate them to your souvenir pile. The new system is easier to understand than what we previously had to learn. The descriptive names of the different classes of airspace are gone, replaced now with letter designations of A, B, C, D, E, and G. There is no F in the United States. Let's get into the system, and summarize the various classes. First, take a good look at FIG. 9-12.

Class A is that airspace between 18,000 and 60,000 feet (FL180 through FL600). This is where the big guys fly: airliners, turboprops, business jets, and occasionally turbocharged piston engine airplanes. Everything operating in Class A airspace must be under IFR, and there are certain aircraft equipment requirements for flying up there. As a light plane pilot, this class of airspace, and its operational rules, are of academic interest at most.

Class B airspace is the area around many large city airports where most of the air traffic is made up of airliners. Class B is positively controlled by the ATC at all times, and you cannot enter it without a clearance from the controller. Many small airplanes operate in Class B airspace either going completely through from one side to the other, going to a satellite airport still within the circle of coverage of the Class B airspace, or when taking off from or landing at the major airport at the center of the area. The requirements for operating in Class B airspace include a two-way radio, a transponder, and a device called an *altitude encoder,* which displays the airplane's altitude right on the controller's radar screen.

Access to Class B by a student pilot is highly restricted, but it is wide open to all pilots who hold a private certificate or higher, as long as their aircraft have the necessary and required equipment. With more Boeings and other heavies to watch for than they sometimes have the time or personnel for, the controllers just can't have any student pilot in there, solo, mixing it up and potentially requiring special handling.

Class C airspace is that area surrounding busier airports that are not quite as large or don't have enough traffic to justify the restrictions inherent in a Class B designation. Class C also requires a two-way radio, a transponder, and an altitude encoder.

The idea of Class C is to identify all traffic within it and to let the controller know what's going on without the aircraft actually being controlled. The ATC controllers must be contacted by every aircraft prior to entry into the Class C, and entry can be denied if controller workload or any other reason justifies keeping traffic out. When this happens, it's usually for just a few minutes, until a particular burst of traffic is handled, and then a Class C is opened again for new arrivals. Although there is a regulatory difference between Classes B and C, in practice, operations within the two are very similar. In Class B, you must have a clearance to enter. In Class C, you have to only communicate with the controller prior to entering. Student pilots have the same rights as everyone else to fly in Class C, and in fact, quite a few large flight schools are located at airports within Class C airspace.

Both Class B and Class C airspace have a vertical limit. In most cases, this is around 8,000 feet or so, but it varies according to the primary airport's elevation above sea level and local ATC requirements. So it is possible to overfly Class B and C airspace, but it is not very practical to do so in most light airplanes.

Class D airspace surrounds an airport that has a control tower and one that primarily serves general aviation traffic. Unless prior arrangements are made with the ATC, you have to have a two-way radio to be able to talk to the tower in order to enter Class D. You're not presently required to have a transponder or altitude encoder unless the airport lies within a 30-mile radius of a Class B airport.

Class D airspace is usually a cylinder-shaped space, typically about 5 miles in radius from the airport and it extends up to 2,500 feet above it. It is legal and quite practical to fly over Class D airspace during a cross-country flight. Class D airspace exists for airports that are busy enough to merit a tower to control the local traffic that is taxiing, taking off, approaching to land, and landing. However, the control towers at these airports generally have no reason to limit overflight as long as the overflying aircraft is higher than 2,500 feet above the ground level. Check the elevation of the airport on the chart if you want to overfly a Class D—you've got to be more than 2,500 feet AGL, not 2,500 on the altimeter, which would be the altitude above mean sea level.

Class E airspace is virtually all of the other airspace. Class E starts at either 700 or 1,200 feet AGL, depending on the local requirements of the abutting airspace. In Class E, the minimum requirement for day VFR flight is visibility of 3 statute miles, except when you are above 10,000 feet MSL, at which the minimum goes to 5 statute miles. In Class E airspace, you have to stay away from clouds and the requirements are that you must be at least 500 feet below, 1,000 above and 2,000 horizontally from any cloud. Above 10,000 MSL, the cloud clearance requirements increase to a minimum of 1,000 below, 1,000 above and 1 statute mile horizontally from a cloud. While you are flying in Class E airspace, you are not required to be talking to any controller and you seldom will be when flying VFR. Of course, all of that changes when you become instrument rated and start flying IFR. Most of your cross-country flights between airports will occur, at least partially, in Class E airspace.

Class G airspace is not often traversed by fixed-wing airplanes because most of it goes up only to either 700 or 1,200 AGL. This volume of airspace is about as free as it gets. The VFR visibility requirement is only 1 statute mile as a minimum, and traffic in Class G airspace is only required to stay clear of clouds, with no minimum distances involved. Above 1,200 feet, when you get into Class E airspace, you already know the cloud separation minimums that apply. Class G airspace is fairly sparsely used, and the traffic that does use it is primarily helicopters.

Unfortunately, many private pilots probably forget about the airspace classifications after passing their knowledge and flight tests, and some just avoid Classes B and C. There are even a few who won't operate into Class D, where there are control towers, thinking that communication with ATC is a hassle to be avoided. Communicating with controllers is not difficult nor is it intimidating after the first few times. Too many private pilots go too far out of their way to avoid that small imposition and, in so doing, waste thousands of gallons of fuel and hours of flight time each year.

You'll have to know the airspace rules to pass both the knowledge and practical tests. It's just not that hard to retain and use that knowledge. If you do, your trips will be more efficient and the services that the system provides, primarily in aircraft separation, will also enhance your flying safety.

There are other types of airspace that still carry descriptive names: *special-use airspace, prohibited areas, restricted areas,* and *military operations areas* (MOAs). These will be covered in detail in your ground school or home study course, but they are actually pretty simple to explain and understand.

Prohibited areas are just that; you can't fly there, period. They rarely exist, and where they do, they are around some place where it would be very dangerous to fly, like a gunnery range, or they surround very sensitive government facilities such as the White House, Camp David, and the Capitol.

Restricted areas are areas of airspace to which pilots are denied access at certain times and at certain altitudes. These are often military aviation test sites, military parachuting areas, part-time gunnery ranges, and the like. Danger lurks within the restricted area when the hazardous activity warning is active. When the restricted area is "cold," which means at times other than when active, and you are outside of the restricted altitudes, there is no restriction to flight operations.

Since the tragic events of September 11, 2001, the government has also imposed *temporary flight restrictions* (TFRs) from time to time to enhance national security. All pilots must get a briefing from the nearest FSS, before making even local flights, to see if any TFRs exist in the planned route of flight. It is up to all of us who fly to obey the rules and to particularly avoid any TFRs or other restricted or prohibited areas. For decades, pilots in the United States have enjoyed the most freedom of any civilized nation, both within flight operations and as citizens in general. If we are to maintain and retain our ability to freely roam around the skies, we have to be extremely diligent in staying away from permanently and temporarily restricted areas.

MOAs are not restricted areas, and you may fly through them if you wish. These areas exist where there is intense military flight activity. Fighter pilots training in air-to-air combat or low-level, high-speed operations, and similar military maneuvers, and other military pilots can't be vigilant for a Cessna or Piper popping up in their canopies. These military airplanes are often operating at near supersonic speeds. Because so much military flying is concentrated today at the lower altitudes, don't think that it's safer to try to sneak through an MOA at low altitude—often that's where the MOA traffic is most intense. Be extremely alert and watchful if you traverse an MOA; stay on your toes, and keep your head on a swivel. Avoidance is probably the better and safer option.

Air-to-Ground Communications

Before you start talking over the radio, you need to learn the phonetic alphabet used in aviation radio communications. Using this alphabet assures clarity in communications and avoids misunderstandings. A phonetic alphabet word is used whenever a letter normally stands for the letter itself such as it would in the identification number of your airplane. For instance, if the airplane registration number is N4517C, you would say, "Cessna 4-5-1-7 Charlie," not "45-17 see." All airplanes of U.S. registration have a number that begins with the letter N. In practice, the N is omitted, and it's assumed that you're flying an airplane of U.S. registry. One number, 9, is pronounced as "niner" over the radio; all the others are said normally. The international phonetic alphabet is easily learned with practice or regular use.

A	Alpha	J	Juliet	S	Sierra
B	Bravo	K	Kilo	T	Tango
C	Charlie	L	Lima	U	Uniform
D	Delta	M	Mike	V	Victor
E	Echo	N	November	W	Whiskey
F	Foxtrot	O	Oscar	X	X-ray
G	Golf	P	Papa	Y	Yankee
H	Hotel	Q	Quebec	Z	Zulu
I	India	R	Romeo		

Tower Talk

Now that you've progressed this far through this book, you are familiar with most of the terminology that is used during radio communications with air traffic control facilities (FIG. 9-13). As

9-13 *The tower of a controlled airport handles aircraft movements on the ground at the airport and in the air in the vicinity of the airport. Be sure to visit a control tower before you complete your training.*

a private pilot, you will primarily talk to three parts of the ATC system: ground control, control towers, and approach-departure control facilities. The *air route traffic control centers* (ARTCCs) normally deal with en route IFR traffic. Occasionally you might have reason to call an ARTCC, but not very often until you get your instrument rating. The FSS network is not a part of the control function of the ATC centers, but naturally, you'll deal with and talk to FSSs quite a bit. Let's use an example of some typical talk back and forth between some controllers to see how it works in practice.

For the flight that we planned from Wichita to Tulsa, the first controller with whom we'll talk is Wichita ground control. After starting the engine but *before* moving the airplane, we'll call on 121.7 MHz, one of the standard ground control frequencies, and the conversation will go like this:

Us "Wichita Ground Cessna 4-5-1-7 Charlie, at Yingling hangar, ready to taxi, VFR to Tulsa, student pilot."

Whenever you first initiate communication with a controller for the first time, remember that there are four Ws to state:

- Whom you are talking to (Wichita ground control)
- Who you are (Cessna 4-5-1-7 Charlie)
- Where you are (Yingling hangar)
- What you want to do (ready for taxi, going VFR to Tulsa)

This is also a good time to let the controller know that you are a student pilot by ending your first transmission with the words "student pilot." You'll be surprised how that will simplify things for you in the beginning.

Remember the four Ws, and that is all there is to starting the conversation. The response from the controller will have important information and instructions:

Ground control "Cessna 1-7 Charlie, taxi to runway 3-5. Wind, 3-6-0 degrees at 7. Altimeter 2-niner-niner-7. Hold short of the runway."

First, the controller referred to us by the last three numbers or letters of the airplane's registration number; from here on out, with *that controller only,* we may also abbreviate the number the same way. She told us to taxi to runway 35; runways are always numbered by the first two digits of the runway's magnetic direction, so runway 35 points toward 350°, which is almost due north. The wind is blowing from 360°, which is out of the north, at 7 knots. Our takeoff will have virtually a straight headwind, only 10° off of the nose of the airplane. The barometric pressure, and therefore the altimeter setting, is 29.97 in Hg.

Last, she told us to hold short of the runway, which means that we are to taxi up to it but not go on the runway. She might have had other instructions. For example, she might have told us to hold at various points on the airport until cleared to proceed. That frequently happens if a taxi route will take you across other taxiways or runway intersections. Sometimes a controller might tell you to give way to another taxiing airplane. If the controller recognizes your call sign as an airplane based on the field, you might not be given the frequency for the control tower, as our controller didn't. If there is any doubt, don't ever hesitate to ask for it.

Whenever you don't understand any of ATC's instructions, use the phrase "say again" to request a repeat. This is a common occurrence because radios are hard to hear, another aircraft might have transmitted at the same time, blocking the controller's transmission, or maybe you just didn't catch it. Again, don't be bashful; even the pros often use "say again."

When you fully understand the controller's comments, your response is straightforward:

Us "Roger, 1-7 Charlie."

"Roger" is used today to indicate that you heard and understood what you're supposed to do. You might hear a pilot say "wilco" instead, which is an abbreviation for "will comply." That's old military terminology, and it is obsolete and incorrect in civilian aviation.

We'll taxi to the runway. If you don't know how to get there, ask for a "progressive taxi," which means that you need directions to the runway. Don't hesitate to ask because the controller has no way to know if you know the airport's taxiway layout. If you don't ask, she'll assume that you know where to go and how to get there. When you've arrived at the runway, you are *not permitted* to get onto the runway itself yet. First, do all of your pretakeoff engine and cockpit checks that we did in our first flight and that your instructor will teach you, using the airplane's checklist. When the checklist is complete, we're ready for takeoff.

Switch the communications radio to the frequency for the control tower, which is 118.2 MHz at Wichita. Listen for a few seconds before transmitting to make sure that you won't block out the controller or another pilot. Then press the mike key and say:

Us "Wichita tower, Cessna 4-5-1-7 Charlie, at runway 3-5, ready for takeoff." (Remember the four Ws.)
Tower "Cessna 1-7 Charlie, cleared for takeoff."

That is all there is to it. Now we're cleared to taxi onto the runway and take off. Unless the controller tells you to do something different, he'll assume that you'll do a normal takeoff, exit the traffic pattern normally, and then proceed on your course to Tulsa. Because Wichita is in Class C airspace, he will probably tell us to contact Wichita departure so that we can be separated from other traffic within the Class C area by a radar controller.

We will call the departure controller when the tower tells us to switch to departure. We'll tell that controller who we are, that we've just taken off, and that we're going VFR to Tulsa. We will be advised of any traffic that the departure controller sees on the radar scope that might pose a hazard to us. Even though we're talking to a radar controller, we still have the responsibility to look out of the cockpit for other traffic.

Remember to always listen on each new frequency for a few seconds before transmitting; there is only one frequency available to all of the people who want to talk to a particular controller, and it can be a busy party line. Don't block a transmission already in progress. Hold the microphone so that it almost touches your upper lip but doesn't quite. If you're wearing a headset, which most pilots do these days, adjust the mike boom on it so that the mike rests very near your lips. Also, don't yell into the mike; it will pick up your voice properly at a normal speaking volume.

By and large, controllers are nice folks, and many of them are pilots themselves. They do a tremendously complex job very competently. They don't have time for idle chatter, but never hesitate to ask for an elaboration if you don't understand any instructions. That's why it's a good idea to identify yourself as a student pilot on each initial call-up to a new facility. Then the controller can take more time with you from the outset and perhaps avoid either confusion on your part or the need to repeat instructions. The goal of both the pilot and the controller is to communicate effectively and clearly so that everyone understands, in as few words as are needed and with as little frequency time tied up as is practical. This goal will be met if you let ATC know that you are student pilot.

At some point in your training, you should personally visit a control tower before you take your private pilot flight test. With the increased security since September 11, 2001, many control towers now require that you make an advance appointment for a visit. When you do visit, you will find the controllers welcome such opportunities for pilots to see their side of the fence. Telephone the tower office and schedule your visit. Don't be insulted if the controller begs off of a visit at that time if your suggested time happens to be a busy period in the workload, as they might not be able to be interrupted. Nighttime is usually a good time to visit most towers, when fewer airplanes are in the area and the controllers can spend some personal time with you, explaining and showing you how the tower works and what is done by the various people in it.

Back to our flight. Notice that Tulsa is also in Class C airspace, and that means that we must contact and establish communications with Tulsa approach control before entering the Class C itself. So monitor your flight progress, and about 5 to 10 miles before reaching the boundary of the Class C, make a call-up as follows:

Us "Tulsa approach, Cessna 4-5-1-7 Charlie, 25 north, landing Tulsa."

Again, you followed the four Ws of radio communication by addressing Tulsa approach control, telling the controller who you are, where you are, and what you want to do.

The approach controller will then acknowledge us, probably telling us the runway to expect to land on at Tulsa. He may start giving us headings to fly and altitudes to maintain. His job is to sequence arrivals in the Class C airspace so that each airplane gets into the proper traffic pattern or gets established on the proper approach to the runway(s) in use and avoids excess maneuvering when close to the airport. In addition, he'll give us traffic advisories of other aircraft that he sees on the radar scope that might present a hazard to us if they weren't pointed out, and if we didn't see them. Don't forget that we're always responsible to look for and avoid other traffic—don't depend on the controller to do it for you. When you're given a traffic advisory, tell the controller whether you see the other airplane; when you do see the other airplane and report the sighting, the controller transfers the total responsibility to remain clear of that traffic to you alone.

Within the last few miles of our flight, the approach controller will tell us when to contact Tulsa tower and the frequency to use. Again, we'll use the four Ws to call the tower, telling the controller who we are, where we are, and what we want to do, which is to land.

After the tower clears us to land, we'll land on the runway that we're told to use. As we roll out after landing, the tower controller will tell us where to turn off of the runway and then to contact ground control, and she will further give us the frequency. Following those instructions, we'll roll out after landing and turn off of the runway.

Only after we're completely clear of the runway and on a taxiway will we slow to a stop and contact ground control. If you're at a strange airport, you might not know precisely where you want to go at the airport. If you want to go to a parking place, tell the controller that you want to taxi to "transient parking." If the airport serves both airline and general aviation users, say that you want to go to "general aviation transient parking." If you do know the name of the FBO where you want to park, use that name as the last W—where you want to go.

And don't be bashful about requesting a progressive taxi; you don't want to taxi along the wrong routes or end up at the wrong place. Worse yet, you don't want to taxi onto a runway or conflict with other airplanes' taxiing. Especially at night, an airport can resemble a meaningless sea of blue, white, red, and green lights on the ground. The controller would always much rather help you with a progressive taxi than to have you either aimlessly wandering around, or committing one of the worst sins a pilot can commit, which is making an incursion onto a runway.

Light Signals

What happens if the radio fails while you're talking to a controller at a towered airport? Every control tower still has a signaling device called a *light gun*. In the early days of aviation, aircraft were routinely controlled at tower airports with the use of the light gun signals shown in the accompanying table. These guns emit a very bright and highly directional beam of light. By the end of the 1950s, all aircraft using towered fields were required to have a two-way radio, and light gun signals faded from the scene as the normal way of a tower's communicating with pilots under its control. But because every radio has the potential to quit at the most inopportune of moments, the entire air traffic control system has alternate means built into it to deal with this possibility (maybe an eventuality). I've had radios fail and have used light gun signals to finish the job on many occasions.

Airplanes that can fly at night have position lights on their wingtips and tails. The tail light is white, and the lights on the wingtips are red and green. Because color is so important to be able to identify where another airplane is at night, and which side or end of it you are seeing, a part of your physical exam will include a test of your color vision. Very few women have any color blindness, but a surprisingly large percentage of men do suffer at least some impairment in their ability to distinguish colors.

Recently the color vision requirements were changed by the FAA to include only the ability to see and differentiate among aviation red, green, and white colors. Many doctors still use a different color test that was previously required. The old test consisted of a small book with pages of pastel-colored dots. Those of us with normal color vision can discern circles and triangles amid the maze of dots, whereas the color deficient can see only the maze of pastel dots without the "hidden" figures on the page. If you receive this test when taking your physical exam and fail it, ask the doctor to follow the new regulations and administer the test that calls to determine your ability to see only the bright red, green, and white colors used

Light gun signals

Color and type of signal	Meaning		
	Movement of vehicles, equipment, and personnel	Aircraft on the ground	Aircraft in flight
Steady green	Cleared to cross, proceed, or go	Cleared for takeoff	Cleared to land
Flashing green	Not applicable	Cleared for taxi	Return for landing (to be followed by steady green at the proper time)
Steady red	STOP	STOP	Give way to other aircraft and continue circling
Flashing red	Clear the taxiway/runway	Taxi clear of the runway in use	Airport unsafe, do not land
Flashing white	Return to starting point of airport	Return to starting point of airport	Not applicable
Alternating red and green	Exercise extreme caution	Exercise extreme caution	Exercise extreme caution

in aviation. Most applicants who fail the pastel dot test breeze through the examination for aviation red, green, and white. If you can see normal traffic lights and you can discern between the red, green, and amber portions of them, you should have no problem passing this part of a properly administered flight physical.

Common Traffic Advisory Frequencies

A *common traffic advisory frequency* (CTAF) is a radio communications frequency that pilots can use at nontowered airports to communicate with other traffic in the vicinity of the airport, to talk to someone on the ground—usually the FBO's office—or to broadcast their position and attentions when either taking off or approaching the airport to land. The FAA publishes the *Airport/Facilities Directory,* which gives quite a bit of information about each public airport and what is available at that airport in terms of runways and services. The directory also shows the CTAF for each airport. If you don't have an issue of the directory with you, or if you failed to use one before takeoff to see what the CTAF is at your airport of intended destination, don't worry about it. The frequencies are shown on your sectional chart as a part of the data block right beside the airport symbols.

There are technically two types of nontowered airports: those with no tower at all and those that have a part-time tower. At airports that have no tower at all, we used to call the CTAF the *unicom.* You will find that in aviation, just as in many other areas of endeavor, old habits die hard. Many pilots still refer to CTAF as "unicom," and they will even use that word in their call-ups, by beginning with the name of the airport, saying, "Delaware Unicom, Pacer 3-9-5-8 Pop." The best use of CTAF is to communicate your position and intentions to other aircraft that may be in the vicinity of the nontowered airport. Most often, the CTAF frequency will be either 122.7 or 122.8 MHz.

As you approach such a field with the intent of landing there, when you are about 5 miles away, look up the appropriate CTAF frequency on the chart and make a call. It should go something like this: "Delaware traffic, Pacer 3-9-5-8 Pop, 5 south, landing advisory, please." If someone is manning the FBO's CTAF radio, that person will respond, telling you, in general, what runway is actively in use and, if known, the winds and what other traffic is in the area. Don't be at all surprised if you don't get any reply because many FBOs don't have a person constantly at the radio. Sometimes you will get a response from another airplane in the traffic pattern or taxiing on the airport surface.

When you get close to the pattern, announce your position over the CTAF frequency, and include a statement that you will be entering downwind and say which runway you intend to use. If the wind isn't very strong or if you've flown a distance such that the wind may have changed from its direction at your departure airport, don't hesitate to fly a rectangular pattern at single-runway airports to observe the wind sock and traffic tee before you commit to a runway. If the airport has multiple runways, you can stay at least 500 feet above the pattern altitude, fly over the airport, decide which runway is favored by the wind, and then go out from the pattern, descend the pattern altitude, and enter a downwind leg for the runway that you want to use.

Be aware that almost all midair collisions occur very close to airports. Keep your head on a swivel and your eyes peeled for other traffic at all times. Don't assume that other pilots will be as careful or as discerning as you are. I've been on the final approach more than once only to see another airplane on the final approach for the opposite direction of the same runway, headed right at me. Some instructors teach their students to make an announcement, over the CTAF, as they are flying on each of the three legs of the landing pattern. That's fine, and it helps everyone keep all of the other airplanes' positions in mind, especially if the pattern is busy. Use good judgment about whether to broadcast this much. If you fly in a metropolitan area, where several airports within reception range may be using the same CTAF, too much chatter clogs the airwaves, sometimes so much that effective communication is reduced.

When you are departing from a nontower airport, use the CTAF to announce when you're getting on the runway for takeoff and say what your departure direction will be, along with the runway identification from which you're departing. Don't depend on this call to take the place of a careful visual scan of the pattern before you get onto the runway. Never depend on other pilots to have their radios on, to understand what you've said, or to heed the fact that you are in the air also or are about to be. Many pilots fly into nontower airports without turning on their radios, or they keep the volume so low that they don't hear many transmissions. The best collision avoidance device available is still the two eyes in your head.

Before you make any radio transmission on the CTAF, whether approaching or leaving the airport, always listen for a few seconds before you transmit. If you do so while someone else is doing likewise, no one gets through. The same advice goes for any time that you transmit over the radio, whether it be to a controller or on the CTAF.

Although the CTAF is designed to be used by aircraft to broadcast their positions and intentions on and around the airport, it can serve a few other needs too. Again, don't crowd a busy frequency with transmissions that are not traffic related. The CTAF is not a substitute for a cell phone. But if the traffic is very light and the CTAF isn't chattering away, it's permissible to use that frequency to contact the airport to inquire about such things as the services available, to ask the FBO to call a taxicab for you, to see if a passenger has yet arrived, or other such informal things. Just use your good judgment about the type and number of calls that you make that are not traffic related.

At some airports, the CTAF is connected to a device that automatically turns the runway lights on at night, increases their intensity, or both. Look in the airport directory to see how many clicks of the transmit switch it takes to accomplish that with the runway lights. I am one of those pilots who likes to have the lights up full bright both for a runway at night and in my office. However, there are others who prefer lights to be a little dimmer. When the CTAF controls the runway lighting, as it does at many small airports where the FBO is not open at night, you can turn the lights on, and with the proper knowledge of how many clicks of the transmit switch are required, you can also set the intensity of those lights right where you like it, from your seat in the cockpit.

Since the early 1980s, when the FAA was beset with a strike of the air traffic controllers, which led to most of them being fired, many of the smaller towered fields have been reduced to part-time towers. These are general aviation airports, usually classed as reliever airports in larger metropolitan areas. They can by quite busy during the day, but the traffic falls off so much at night that there is no real justification to have controllers in the tower 24 hours a day. Quite often the hours of operation at part-time towers will be from 7:00 A.M. until 11:00 P.M., local time. That way, the tower is operational for 16 hours per day, which makes up two work shifts for the controllers, and it is closed 8 hours, which would otherwise be the third shift of the 24-hour day. That way, an entire work shift is eliminated, with the attendant cost savings for the FAA. When you fly from or into an airport with a part-time tower during the hours that the tower is closed, the tower radio frequency becomes a CTAF. Use it the same way as you would at a non-towered airport, but don't try to talk to anyone on the ground to get a cab or inquire about anything else.

Multicom Frequency

Multicom is the label attached to air-to-air communications between aircraft. For private aircraft, the frequency is 122.75 MHz. You can use multicom to talk to another airplane while both of you are airborne. In these days of cell phones, widespread use of mobile radios, and other forms of portable communications devices, all too many pilots think that multicom is a wide-open chat site. It isn't. The proper use of multicom is to coordinate group flights of airplanes traveling together and for other legitimate needs for air-to-air communication. We mentioned cell phones a few times, but their use in airplanes while in flight is absolutely forbidden. Their range becomes so wide at high altitudes that using a cell phone in flight would clutter the cell frequency spectrum for a tremendous distance.

10

The Examinations

Obtaining your private pilot's license will be a rather informal proposition, just as your flight training was. At some point while learning to fly the airplane, you either attended a ground school, studied text materials in your home, or purchased one of the ground school courses now available on videotape or DVD. Regardless of how you did it, you have thoroughly absorbed the subjects that we've covered in this book—and some others too. You now have at least 40 to 60 hours of flight time in your logbook and quite possibly more. You've done most of your flying 1 hour at a time, except for your cross-country flights, because the learning curve for flying drops off severely after much more than an hour for the typical lesson.

Like most other physical tasks, you've learned to fly mostly by doing. One of my early instructors said that his primary job was to keep a student alive and well while the student taught himself to fly. That is oversimplifying it quite a bit because a good instructor shows you how to do what needs to be done, but in the final analysis, you will have to teach yourself most of the art of flying.

Most students will hit a point, usually after 6 or 7 hours of dual instruction, when it seems to them that they can't do anything right. You didn't get discouraged when you came to this point because your instructor made you realize that this was a positive sign that you had learned enough to start being critical of your own performance. Your instructor also explained that the learning curve has flat spots and plateaus in it, when progress seems to slow down for a short time. One day after practicing a few touch-and-go landings, your instructor told you to taxi over to the ramp, and when you reached the ramp, he asked you to get your student pilot certificate out of your purse or wallet. Then you were signed off for solo flight, and you immediately made a few takeoffs and landings alone. This event occurred without warning or ceremony.

That wonderful day of your first solo flight will be burned in your memory for the rest of your life. Every pilot I know remembers every small detail of that short flight, which is usually just two or three trips around the traffic pattern, on a beautiful day without much wind. After all of the sweat, time, and expense, you've done it. After your first solo, there will probably be some sort of ritual, which varies from one flight school to the next. At some locales, especially if you're a male, you might have a large chunk of your shirt cut out and the instructor will take a large marker and write your name, the date, the airplane's registration number, and "first solo" on the scrap of cloth that used to be a part of your wardrobe. The instructor will then ceremoniously hang it on the office wall for all to see.

You'll be able to tell when the time for solo is getting close. The FARs require that you pass a presolo written exam, which is administered by your flight instructor. Most instructors don't give a student the presolo written exam until the time for solo flight is getting close. This exam is not long or difficult, and it is actually developed by the instructor. The wise student doesn't wear expensive shirts after that, until the great day of the first solo has come and gone. You might even be smart to have another shirt in your car to wear home. Some flight schools think that this rite has become passé and omit it. When I taught my father-in-law to fly, when he was nearly 60 years old, I didn't cut his shirt. I just made him buy dinner that night for his daughter and her new husband. However the occasion is celebrated, you'll never forget your first solo.

In a rather delightful way, your first solo may be a bit anticlimactic as it is happening. You've been flying the airplane for weeks, maybe months, while the instructor sat there apparently admiring the scenery and occasionally dispensing some wisdom in a thoughtful, pointed, and perhaps even a curt manner. The first time alone wasn't that much different than a dozen other flights that you'd recently made, except for two things. Because you trained in the Cessna 150, which has side-by-side seating, you were aware of the instructor's absence immediately. Then, without that extra weight, the little trainer seemed more eager to take off, and it climbed much more sprightly than you had experienced before.

After your first solo, you took more instruction in cross-country, night, and instrument flying, plus a few more hours polishing up on the maneuvers required for the flight test. Interspersed were several hours of solo practice in the local area and those great solo cross-country flights when you were always worried about getting lost. Somehow you made it back to your airport every time.

When you reached at least 40 hours in your logbook, and probably much more, your instructor felt that you were ready to join the ranks of licensed pilots. Before you actually got your private pilot's certificate, you had to go through some testing.

Knowledge Test

Before the computer age caught up with flight training, candidates for the various pilot certificates and for some ratings were required to pass a written test. There are a few ratings that don't require a separate written test; a flight test suffices. These written tests were multiple-choice exams that used separate answer sheets that were sent to FAA headquarters in Oklahoma City for grading. Back when the answer sheets were used, the student would receive her grade by mail within a couple of weeks of taking the test. It took a score of 70 percent to pass the test. Now these tests are administered using a computerized format.

Because the test is no longer truly a written exam, its name was recently changed to *knowledge test*. The concept hasn't been altered, only the name and means of taking the test. You will use a computer screen to read the questions and the possible answers, which are still multiple choice. When the exam is finished, you will know right then whether you've passed; there is no more waiting for your grade to be mailed to you.

The knowledge test is taken at the offices of contractors who have arranged with the FAA to administer the various exams. Some of these places are at FBOs or flight schools, and others are located at colleges, private schools, or other learning centers. Your local FAA office, which is known as the Flight Standards District Office (FSDO), can give you a list of the places where you can take the test in your area. You will be asked to pay the contractor a nominal fee when you sit for the exam.

Before you can actually take the test, your instructor will have to sign a form that says that you have been given the appropriate instruction to prepare you for the test and that you are considered ready to pass it. So you'll spend some time with your instructor getting ready for the knowledge test. You'll be quizzed as much as necessary until the instructor is convinced that you know what it takes to pass.

The test has no trick questions, but it is constructed like most multiple-choice tests are. There are four possible choices of an answer for each question. Because you will have studied the material carefully, you'll easily recognize one or two of the choices as clearly erroneous; but then the others will be much closer, and only one of them is correct. The key to passing this test, beyond the obvious need to understand the subject matter, is to carefully read each question and be certain that you understand it before you try to answer. Some people find it more efficient and simpler to go through the entire test, answering those questions that are the easiest, and then take the time to ponder the questions that take the most thought or require calculations, such as those queries in the flight planning areas.

Because all the questions have an equal weight in the points attached to them and because the test does have a time limit (which is usually more than ample), I like that approach to test taking in a multiple-choice exam. I don't want to get hung up early in the test on the more difficult or time-consuming questions, using up time and energy, when I might then become concerned or tired or find that I am running low on time with many of the questions yet to go. Work through the test in whichever way is easier for you, either the way we've just discussed or taking each question in the order in which it is presented on the test. If you do go out of the order and try to hit the easier ones first, be very careful that when you go back to the other questions, you do not miss some of them.

Bring your pocket computer with you, either the circular slide rule type or the electronic variety. If you use the electronic calculator, be sure that you have extra batteries with you. The main reason that I like the old-fashioned circular slide rules is that I don't have to worry about batteries.

The test will give you all of the excerpts from the mythical airplane's POH, the weather information, and all of the other data upon which the questions are based. No notes or study materials are permitted in the test area. If you relax and come prepared to pass, you'll have no problem.

Practical Test

What we used to call the "flight test" is now called a *practical test*. This is the in-flight examination, actually conducted in your training airplane. The person who administers it is usually a designated examiner. On rare occasions, FAA inspectors give a private pilot practical test, but their time is generally reserved for testing applicants for flight instructor certificates and airline transport pilot licenses. The FAA employees also give the tests that are routinely required for commercial operators running air taxi flights and those for pilots seeking type ratings to fly heavy aircraft and jets. A *designated examiner* is an active flight instructor who has been found specially qualified by reason of experience and skill to have the weighty responsibilities of determining whether applicants for pilot certificates can demonstrate the required skills to be licensed to fly.

Some nervousness is normal on any flight test, so there isn't much point in telling you not to be nervous at all. Do remember that the designated examiner is a fellow pilot who also went through the same stages of training and licensure but who then went on to become a commercial pilot and a flight instructor and was further chosen and was additionally tested by the FAA in order to become an examiner. So your examiner has been through multiple flight tests (FIG. 10-1). Examiners have no quotas of applicants to fail. The purpose of the practical test to ensure that you can perform, in flight, up to the published required standards in the FAA's *Practical Test Standards* (PTS). Your instructor will have told you to purchase a copy of this small booklet so you know not only what areas of flight will be covered during the practical test but also what the acceptable levels of performance are.

The examiner is no more critical than is a good flight instructor. You've satisfied your instructor—she signed the recommendation form that has to be presented to the examiner before the test begins—so you should have no trouble with the practical test. As a flight instructor myself, I use a very simple standard for recommending a student for a flight test: beyond the PTS requirements, would I let a nonpilot member of my family fly with this person? If the answer is yes, I sign the recommendation form; if not, we go back for some more dual instruction.

The first part of the practical test is usually planning a cross-country flight for which the examiner tells you the route that he wants to fly. But this exercise won't be mythical. You'll at least get started on it once you take off. The examiner wants to see

10-1 *Don't worry about the flight test. To lessen your nervousness, keep in mind that the examiner is a fellow pilot who wants to see you do well.*

if you plan all aspects of the flight correctly, and because weight and balance are part of the planning, ask him for his weight if he doesn't volunteer the number. You can't do a weight and balance problem if you don't know your exact cabin load.

Once your flight planning is completed, the examiner will start the oral portion of the test. In this phase, prior to ever flying with you, he's looking to see what you know about flight planning, weather, regulations, operating procedures, aircraft performance, and the like. These are subjects that can't be adequately covered in a few short questions and answers while airborne, so expect to spend about an hour, maybe even more, getting quizzed on the ground.

Throughout the exam, both during the oral portion and while aloft, the examiner is not permitted, by FAA regulation, to give you instruction. Sometimes an examiner will offer you some insight, but don't expect her to tell you how to do something right. This is your show, not hers. Don't ever try to snow an examiner; if you don't know the answer to a question, admit it. That is likely to happen, especially during the oral phase. Just tell her how you would get the answer to the question before flying and what sources of information you would consult to find out. No one knows everything, but the wise know where to look to find an answer. You're not expected to be perfect, and one wrong answer or instance of ignorance doesn't mean that you will fail, unless it's so basic as to show that you are too ignorant to go on. Examiners have heard all of the artful dodges before, and they are much more respectful of honesty in judgment than anything else that you can imagine.

After the oral phase is completed, it'll shortly be time to go flying. Before you do, be sure that you perform a good preflight inspection of the airplane, even if the examiner doesn't affirmatively ask you to do so. The examiner will undoubtedly watch your preflight, even if you are unaware that you are being observed. Do the preflight the way you were taught, and use the manufacturer's checklist. If you had to fly to another airport, away from your home base to meet the examiner, do a full preflight just as you would for the first flight of the day in this airplane. Don't ever eliminate or shorten a preflight inspection because you just flew this airplane to this airport a short while ago. The examiner will be able to see you do only one preflight, and that is the one that will be graded.

When you enter the cockpit with the examiner at your side, you should act as if you are already licensed, and this other person is a passenger. Use the checklist at every stage of the flight, from before starting the engine to shutting it down after landing and taxiing to your parking spot. Pilots aren't supposed to memorize checklists—that's why they are printed for our use. Good judgment is probably the most important thing that you can impress upon the examiner, and good pilots always use their checklists.

After takeoff, the test will usually begin by flying at least a few miles of the planned cross-country trip. Here the examiner is looking to see if your altitude is appropriate for the course being flown, if you can establish yourself on that course, and if you can identify at least the first checkpoint or two. You're also being observed to see if you know how to use the radios and other avionics in the airplane and to determine if you are basically competent at cross-country flying. Once you demonstrate that you are, don't be surprised if the examiner asks you to assume that the weather has just gone down below VFR minimums at your intended destination and that you need to proceed to your alternate field. This shows how you deal with an unexpected situation.

When the cross-country phase is completed, your next testing will cover basic airwork. At this stage, you'll be asked to demonstrate slow flight, stalls, steep turns, and probably some of the ground reference maneuvers. At some point, probably while you are engrossed in some maneuver, a hand will appear from the right seat, and it will bring the power back to idle as you are hearing an announcement that the engine just gave up its labors for the day. You will then show the examiner how to set up for a forced landing. You won't, of course, actually land in some farm field, but the exercise will go on until the examiner is satisfied that you know how to perform an actual emergency forced landing.

The next part of the test will probably involve some takeoffs and landings. You may be asked to land at an unfamiliar airport so that you can show how you would handle the challenge of determining which runway to use and how well you can fit into the traffic flow at a strange place. This might even be a towered airport so that your radio communication skills can be tested at the same time. During this phase, you will also be asked to do some crosswind takeoffs and landings and demonstrate short field and soft field techniques.

At some time during the test, you'll put on the instrument hood that restricts your outside vision, and you will fly the airplane solely by reference to the flight instruments. The examiner will put the airplane into some unusual attitudes and then ask you to recover to normal flight, while you're wearing the hood.

Before you get all worked up over what is required during the practical test, and fret endlessly, remember that you've done each and every maneuver and you have encountered every situation with your flight instructor. If you do fail the test the first time, which is highly unlikely, it isn't a black mark against you, but it certainly is one against your instructor. Instructors must renew their licenses every 2 years. If a particular instructor has a higher-than-normal failure rate for his students on flight tests, that instructor will come under some extra scrutiny by the FAA at renewal time. Therefore, your instructor won't recommend you for the practical test until you are ready. Because you've already shown the instructor that you can fly, you'll finish your practical test in the examiner's office as you watch the typing of your newest and proudest possession—your pilot's license.

Glossary

ADF Automatic direction finder.

aerodynamics The forces, such as resistance, pressure, velocity, and other forces, involved in the movement of air or gases around a moving body, or the branch of dynamics and physics dealing with these forces.

AGL Above ground level.

ailerons The primary control surfaces located at the trailing edges of the outer wing panels that, when moved up or down, cause the airplane in flight to bank.

AIM *Aeronautical Information Manual.* An FAA periodical providing basic flight information and air traffic control procedures.

airfoil Any surface designed to create lift, either positive or negative, when moving through the air at a given speed. Examples include wings, control surfaces, propellers, and helicopter blades.

airspace When used in aviation the term means the navigable sky, for all practical purposes, between ground level and 60,000 feet.

airspeed The speed at which an aircraft is moving with relation to the air around it. It may be expressed as indicated airspeed, calibrated airspeed, and true airspeed.

airspeed indicator A flight instrument with a cockpit readout that, in terms of knots or mph, shows the difference between pitot pressure and static pressure. The reading obtained from the airspeed indicator is indicated airspeed.

alternator An electrical device that is driven by the engine and supplies current to the battery and to all on-board electrical equipment except the ignition system.

altimeter A flight instrument capable of displaying the height above sea level (or any other predetermined level), activated by an aneroid barometer measuring atmospheric pressure at the given altitude.

altimeter setting The barometric pressure reading in the small window provided for that purpose on the face of the altimeter.

angle of attack The angle at which the chord line of the wing or any other airfoil meets the relative wind. Angle of attack determines the amount of lift developed at a given airspeed.

approach Airplane maneuver performed to prepare for landing.

approach control The ATC facility monitoring and directing traffic approaching an airport where such a facility is in operation.

artificial horizon A gyro instrument showing the attitude of the aircraft with reference to pitch and roll as compared to the horizon.

ATC Air traffic control.

atmospheric pressure The weight of the air surrounding the earth. Standard atmospheric pressure is expressed as 29.92 inches of mercury, or 1013.2 millibars.

avionics A catch-all phrase for communication, navigation, and related instrumentation in an aircraft. A contraction of "aviation electronics."

back pressure Aft force on the control wheel.

base leg A part of the airport traffic pattern. A flight path at a right angle to the runway, after the downwind leg and before the final approach.

calibrated airspeed Indicated airspeed corrected for instrument and installation errors.

carburetor heat A heating unit located near the carburetor throat and controlled in the cockpit. It is used to melt carburetor ice.

carburetor ice Ice forming in the carburetor throat due to excessive moisture in the air.

compass, gyro *See* directional gyro.

compass, magnetic A compass that, during straight and level flight, automatically aligns itself with magnetic north.

constant-speed propeller A controllable-pitch propeller that maintains a constant rpm by automatically changing the blade angle in relation to engine output.

course The direction of flight of an aircraft across the ground.

course deviation indicator The needle, bar, or other indicator that displays the position of an aircraft relative to a radial or bearing from or to a VOR.

cross-country flight A flight with a landing made at a point other than the initial airport of takeoff, usually farther than 25 nautical miles.

dead reckoning   A method of navigation by which an aircraft's course and time between two given points is estimated by taking into consideration course, speed, and wind components calculated with a wind triangle. The phrase comes from the term "deduced reckoning."

density altitude   Pressure altitude corrected for prevailing temperature conditions.

dewpoint   The temperature to which air must cool without change in pressure or vapor content, in order for condensation to take place.

DG   Directional gyro.

directional gyro   A gyroscopic flight instrument that, when set to conform with the magnetic compass, will continue to indicate the aircraft heading for some time, regardless of turns or pitch changes. It tends to develop heading errors and must be adjusted intermittently.

downwind   In the direction that the wind is blowing.

downwind leg   The flight path parallel to the runway in the direction opposite to landing. It is part of the standard airport traffic pattern.

drag   The force created by friction of the air on objects in motion. It must be overcome by thrust in order to achieve flight parallel to the relative wind. Two types of drag are induced drag and parasite drag. Induced drag is created through the process of creating lift. Parasite drag is all drag from surfaces that do not contribute to lift. It increases with an increase in airspeed.

E6-B   A circular slide rule computer used to compute a variety of aviation mathematics problems.

elevator   The primary control surface (attached to the horizontal stabilizer) that can be moved up or down to control the pitch of the aircraft. It is a speed control as much as an altitude control.

FAA   Federal Aviation Administration.

FAR   Federal Aviation Regulation.

FBO   Fixed-base operator.

final approach   The final portion of an airport traffic pattern during which the descending aircraft is aligned with the runway centerline.

fixed-base operator   A person or organization providing aviation services at an airport: flight instruction, fuel, maintenance, and perhaps more.

fixed-pitch propeller A propeller with blades at a predetermined angle that cannot be changed or adjusted.

FL Flight level; FL180 stands for 18,000 feet.

flaps Auxiliary control surfaces that are usually located at the trailing edges of the inner wing panels between the fuselage and the ailerons. Flaps can be extended and/or turned down to increase the wing camber and/or surface, creating additional lift and drag.

flare A smooth leveling of the aircraft during which the nose is raised at the end of the landing glide and just prior to touchdown.

flight service station An FAA facility that provides weather briefings and other services to general aviation pilots, in person or via telephone or radio.

fpm Feet per minute (rate of climb or descent).

FSS Flight service station.

generator A device identical in construction to an electrical motor that, when driven by the engine, generates electrical current and continuously recharges the battery.

global positioning system A system of air navigation in which a receiver mounted in the aircraft receives signals from satellites in orbit, which enable the receiver to electronically calculate the aircraft's position, course to a selected destination, altitude, time en route, and ground speed.

GPS Global positioning system.

ground control An ATC service at controlled airports that is responsible for the safe and efficient movement of aircraft and airport vehicles on the ground.

ground effect Additional lift that takes effect when the aircraft is close to the ground. It is the result of air being compressed between the wings and the ground. Low-wing aircraft are more susceptible to the effect than high-wing aircraft.

ground speed The speed with which an aircraft moves relative to the surface of the earth.

heading The direction in which the aircraft flies through the air, not with reference to the ground. In other words, the direction in which the nose of the aircraft is pointing.

Hg Mercury, as in 30.12" Hg (inches of mercury).

horizontal stabilizer The fixed horizontal portion of the tail section to which the elevator is attached.

HP Horsepower.

IAS Indicated airspeed.

IFR   Instrument flight rules due to weather conditions that are less than the minimum VFR requirements.

inches of mercury   Units of measurement of atmospheric pressure used to indicate the height in inches to which a column of mercury will rise in a glass tube in response to the weight of the atmosphere exerting pressure on a bowl of mercury at the base of the tube.

indicated airspeed   The airspeed that is shown by the airspeed indicator. It is nearly always less than true airspeed, but usually not much different from calibrated airspeed.

induced drag   *See* drag.

kHz   Kilohertz or kilocycles.

knots   Nautical miles per hour.

kts   Knots.

lift   The generally upward force created by the difference of pressure between the upper and lower surfaces of an airfoil in motion. In level flight, lift is balanced by the force of gravity.

magnetic course   The course of an aircraft referenced to magnetic north.

magnetic heading   The heading of an aircraft referenced to magnetic north.

magnetic north   The location, some distance from the geographic north pole, where the earth's magnetic lines converge.

magneto   A self-contained generator that supplies electrical current to the spark plugs in the ignition system.

manifold   An arrangement of tubing (on an aircraft engine) with one orifice on one end and several on the other.

manifold pressure   The pressure of the fuel-air mixture in the intake manifold.

MC   Magnetic course.

MH   Magnetic heading.

MHz   Megahertz or megacycles.

millibar   A unit of atmospheric pressure. *See* atmospheric pressure.

mixture   The mixture of fuel and air necessary for combustion in reciprocating engines.

mph   Statute miles per hour.

MSL   Mean sea level.

nautical mile   A unit of linear measure equal to 6,076.1 feet.

needle and ball   An instrument that shows the rate of turn of the aircraft and displays whether the aircraft is in a skid or a slip. An older version of the turn-and-slip indicator and turn coordinator.

nm   Nautical mile(s).

parasite drag   *See* drag.

pattern   Airport landing pattern: takeoff, crosswind, downwind, base, and final.

pilot in command   The pilot responsible for the operation and safety of an aircraft during flight time.

pilotage   Navigation by reference to visible landmarks. Used usually in conjunction with sectional charts on which all meaningful landmarks are shown.

pitch   The attitude of the aircraft with reference to a horizontal axis at right angles to the fuselage. In other words, nose-down or nose-up.

pitot-static system   A device that compares impact pressure with static or atmospheric pressure and presents the result in the cockpit by means of the airspeed indicator, the altimeter, and the vertical speed indicator.

pitot tube   A protrusion, usually from the wing, with a small orifice exposed to the airstream and designed to measure the pressure with which an aircraft meets the air. Also called a "pitot head."

precession   The tendency of a directional gyro to gradually become unreliable due to friction.

propeller   Two or more airfoil-shaped blades designed to convert the turning force of the engine into thrust.

psi   Pressure in terms of pounds per square inch.

relative wind   The movement of air relative to the movement of an airfoil. It is parallel to and in the opposite direction of the flight path of an airplane.

rpm   Revolutions per minute.

rudder   The primary control surface attached to the vertical stabilizer, movement of which causes the tail of the aircraft to swing either left or right. The rudder controls yaw.

runup   A pretakeoff check of the performance of the engine and, in aircraft equipped with constant-speed props, the operation of the propeller.

sectional chart   An aeronautical chart of a section of the United States at a scale of 1:500,000, which is approximately 7 nautical miles per inch.

service ceiling   The maximum altitude above sea level that an aircraft can climb to and then maintain horizontal flight under standard atmospheric conditions.

skid   Lateral movement of an airplane toward the outside of a turn. The skid is caused by incorrect use of the rudder.

slip The tendency of an aircraft to lose altitude by slipping toward the center of a turn. The slip is caused by incorrect use of the rudder.

spin A maneuver in which the airplane, after stalling, descends nearly vertically, nose-low, with the tail revolving around the vertical axis of the descent.

stall The inability of an airplane to continue flight due to an excessive angle of attack. The airplane will either drop its nose and thus reduce the angle of attack and regain flying speed or, if forced to retain the excessive angle of attack, the airplane might fall into a spin.

stall speed The speed, at a given angle of attack, at which airflow separation begins and the stall occurs. Aircraft can stall at virtually any speed if an acceptable angle of attack is exceeded.

stall-spin The combination of a stall followed by a spin, a major cause of fatal accidents.

stall warning A buzzer, a light, or both that indicates to a pilot that the aircraft is about to stall.

static vent A hole, usually located in the side of the fuselage, that provides air at atmospheric pressure to operate the pitot-static system.

statute mile A unit of measure equivalent to 5,280 feet.

stick Control wheel or yoke.

TAS True airspeed.

taxi To move an aircraft on the ground under its own power.

torque The normal tendency of an aircraft to rotate to the left in reaction to the right-hand rotation of the propeller. Torque varies with changes in power.

tower Control tower at a controlled airport.

trim tab A small airfoil attached to a control surface—usually the elevator and occasionally the rudder—that can be adjusted to cause changes in the position of the control surface under varying flight conditions.

true airspeed The actual speed at which an aircraft is moving in relation to undisturbed air. True airspeed is calibrated airspeed adjusted for actual air density and altitude.

true course Course referenced to true north.

true heading Heading referenced to true north.

true north Geographic (not magnetic) north. The direction to the northern end of the earth's axis.

turn-and-slip indicator *See* needle and ball.

unicom Aeronautical advisory station for communication with aircraft. Unicoms are usually staffed by FBO employees or airport personnel and provide pilots with such information as the active runway, wind direction and velocity, and other conditions of importance to pilots. Unicoms are not authorized to give takeoff or landing clearances, or in any way control traffic, except when relaying word from ATC, in which case any such transmission must be preceded by "ATC clears."

unusual attitude Any attitude of an aircraft in terms of pitch or roll or both that is beyond the normal operating attitude. Recovery from unusual attitudes by reference to instruments is an important part of instrument training.

vertical speed indicator An instrument in the pitot-static system that indicates the rate of climb or descent in terms of feet per minute. It is usually calibrated in units of either 100 or 1,000 fpm.

vertical stabilizer A fixed vertical airfoil on the empennage to which the rudder is attached.

VFR Visual flight rules or weather conditions equal to or better than minimum visual flight rule requirements.

VHF Very high frequency; electromagnetic frequencies between 30 and 300 MHz.

VOR Very high frequency omnidirectional radio; a ground-based VHF navigation aid.

VSI Vertical speed indicator.

WCA Wind correction angle.

wind shear An abrupt change in wind direction or velocity.

yaw The movement of an aircraft to either side, turning around its vertical axis, without banking.

yoke Control wheel; stick.

Index

About the Author

Jerry A. Eichenberger has written three other books for McGraw-Hill: *General Aviation Law,* now in its Second Edition; *Handling In-Flight Emergencies,* now in its Second Edition; and *Cross-Country Flying.* He has also written more than 200 magazine articles dealing with aviation law and aviation safety. His work is featured regularly in several monthly publications that serve the general aviation and commuter airline industries.

Mr. Eichenberger is a licensed commercial pilot, rated for single- and multiengine airplanes, helicopters, and gliders. He holds an airplane instrument rating, and is also a certificated flight instructor, rated for airplanes, single- and multiengine, and instrument instruction. He has logged over 5,000 flying hours.

He is a practicing attorney who devotes his legal time to the area of aviation law, representing manufacturers, maintenance facilities, flight schools, airlines, FBOs, airports, and individual pilots and aircraft owners. Mr. Eichenberger lives and practices in the Columbus, Ohio, area, where he remains an active general aviation pilot and flight instructor. He has owned a total of eight aircraft over the years since he learned to fly in 1965, and currently owns a totally restored classic Piper PA-22/20 Pacer.